170

THE CHALLENGE
OF SOVIET EDUCATION

Books by George S. Counts

THE CHALLENGE OF SOVIET EDUCATION

GEORGE S. COUNTS, *Professor emeritus*
Teachers College, Columbia University
assisted by NUCIA LODGE

McGRAW-HILL BOOK COMPANY, INC.
New York   Toronto   London

*To the Great Russian people and the many other peoples
of the Soviet Union, with the hope that in the course
of time they may take their destiny into their own hands,
achieve the blessings of political liberty, and join the
family of free nations*

PREFACE

The present volume is an ambitious undertaking. It constitutes an attempt to give in brief compass a comprehensive account of Soviet education—one of the great and inescapable realities of the contemporary epoch, and one which free peoples can ignore only at their peril. Because of limitations of space much has been omitted. Some institutions, such as the kindergartens, schools for working youth, and schools for peasant youth, are scarcely mentioned. I have sought to present in broad outline the basic features of Soviet education rather than confine the account to a more detailed treatment of a few of its special aspects. As a matter of fact, unless one grasps the broad sweep and controlling purposes of the effort on the part of the Bolsheviks to transform the peoples of the Soviet Union through the institutions and processes of education, one can scarcely comprehend intelligently any particular segment of the program.

I have long contemplated the preparation of such an account of Soviet education. In 1936 I made my third extended visit to the Soviet Union with this in mind. But since Soviet education at the time appeared to be passing through a period of vast and profound change, I decided to await the stabilization of both the system of practices and the guiding philosophy. This happened during the following years under the rule of Stalin. Now, with the denunciation of the great dictator at the Twentieth Congress of the Communist Party of the Soviet Union in February, 1956, the situation may be once more in flux.

What the new political orientation will mean for Soviet education in the coming years, no one can say with assurance at the present time. With the opening of the new school year in September some changes were discernible. The textbooks in history covering the Stalin era were revised in accordance with the new line of the Party. Also, the severity of the school regimen was somewhat moderated through the abolition of certain examinations in the middle school, the elimination of tuition fees in the upper grades and higher institutions, the relaxation of the emphasis on the mastery of abstract knowledge, and the movement toward universal education up to the seventeenth year of age. Such changes, however, can hardly be regarded as substantial or fundamental. The evidence at hand would seem to support the thesis that the basic features of Soviet education reported in the present volume will endure as long as Stalin's pupils, represented by Khrushchev and Bulganin, hold the reins of power in the Soviet Union. Before any basic transformation can occur, Bolshevism in its central doctrines, purposes, and practices will have to be repudiated. This would mean nothing less than the repudiation of Lenin and Leninism. Only a revolution could bring such consequences in the proximate future. And the Central Committee of the Party in a powerful and unequivocal resolution in July rejected this possibility. The methods of Soviet education have changed in the past, are changing today, and will doubtless change in the future, but its guiding spirit and overarching purposes seem to withstand remarkably the ravages of time.

II

For the completion of this work I am indebted to many persons. First of all, I would like to express my indebtedness to President William F. Russell of Teachers College, who supported me for more than a quarter of a century in my interest in Soviet education. And his successor in 1955, President Hollis L. Caswell, provided me with some funds and office space to enable me after my retirement to complete the study. For additional funds to conduct my researches I turned to a number of agencies, but without success. As a last resort I called upon some of my old friends in the labor movement who are far better informed on the nature of Communism than the ordinary educated citizen or even most university professors. The response was immediate and generous. I consequently desire to express my gratitude to David Dubinsky, president of the International Ladies' Garment Workers' Union, Alex Rose, president of the Hatters, Cap, and Millinery Workers International Union, and Harry Uviller, Impartial Chairman of the Garment Industry. Without their assistance the study could not have been completed.

My colleagues and students at Teachers College since 1927 have been an enduring source of stimulation and helpful criticism. Among them I would make special mention of William H. Kilpatrick and John L. Childs, with whom I have worked closely in professional and public affairs for over two decades. From Dr. Childs I received a number of valuable suggestions in the preparation of this book. Among my former students I would mention William H. E. Johnson, of the University of Pittsburgh, who is one of our foremost authorities on Soviet education. Then there is my long-time research assistant, Nucia Lodge, whose work is reflected on every page. Also there is my wife, Lois B. Counts, who supported my researches through the years.

For suggestions, leads, and assistance in the development of insights and gathering of materials I am indebted to W. W. Kulski of Syracuse; Michael T. Florinsky of Columbia; Nicholas DeWitt, Merle J. Fainsod, and Michael Karpovich of Harvard; Leonard Schapiro of the London School of Economics; C. A. Smith of Cambridge University; J. G. T. Sheringham of the British Broadcasting System; and Leon J. Barat of the Institute for the Study of the U.S.S.R. in Munich. I am especially grateful to Professor Karpovich for his assistance in unraveling certain mysteries regarding the fabulous character of Peter Tkachev and his relation to the evolution of the basic doctrines of Bolshevism. Among my creditors also are such long-time students of the Russian revolution and the Soviet regime as Raphael Abramovich, David J. Dallin, René Fulop-Miller, Max Nomad, David Shub, and Bertram D. Wolfe. Mr. Dallin was particularly helpful. For access to unpublished materials prepared by former Soviet citizens I wish to thank Philip E. Mosely, director, and Robert Slusser, associate director, of the Research Program on the U.S.S.R. in New York. For the unfailing cooperation of Mr. Slusser I am especially grateful. In the same category I would like to place Lev F. Magerovsky, curator of the Archive of Russian and East European History and Culture. Most helpful too was Joseph Zack Kornfeder, one-time student in the famous Lenin School of Moscow. Finally, I am indebted to William Benton for placing at my disposal a collection of Soviet history textbooks which he brought from the Soviet Union in the autumn of 1955.

I want to thank Nicholas DeWitt and the National Science Foundation for permission to quote passages from the most authoritative work to date on an important aspect of Soviet education—*Soviet Professional Manpower*. For the same courtesy I want to thank Charles Scribner's Sons and the anonymous author of *The Dark Side of the Moon*, one of the most revealing reports on the Soviet forced-labor camps. For the privilege of making free use of materials from two of my earlier books, *The Soviet Challenge to America* (1931) and *The Country of the Blind: The Soviet System of Mind Control* (1949), I am grateful to the John Day Company, Inc., and Houghton Mifflin Company respectively.

III

The reader who wishes to pursue further the study of Soviet *school* education may find the following carefully selected works in English as helpful as I have found them:

S. N. Harper, *Civic Training in Soviet Russia*, Chicago, 1929.

Albert P. Pinkevich, *The New Education in the Soviet Republic*, John Day, 1929.

M. Ilin, *New Russia's Primer*, Houghton Mifflin, 1931.

Thomas Woody, *New Minds: New Men?*, Macmillan, 1932.

William Clark Trow (ed.), *Character Education in Soviet Russia*, Ann Arbor, Mich., 1934.

Eric Ashby, *Scientist in Russia*, Penguin, 1947.

Maurice J. Shore, *Soviet Education*, Philosophical Library, 1947.

B. P. Yesipov and N. K. Goncharov, *"I Want to Be Like Stalin,"* John Day, 1947.

William H. E. Johnson, *Russia's Educational Heritage*, Rutgers, 1950.

Ruth Carol Widmayer, *The Communist Party and the Soviet Schools—1917–1937*, doctoral study, Harvard, 1952.

Nicholas DeWitt, *Soviet Professional Manpower*, National Science Foundation, 1955.

Fredrika M. Tandler, *The Workers' Faculty (Rabfac) System in the U.S.S.R.*, doctoral study, Columbia, 1955.

George Kline (ed.), *Studies in Soviet Education*, Columbia, 1956.

GEORGE S. COUNTS

CONTENTS

There are at the present time two great nations in the world, which started from different points, but seem to tend towards the same end. I allude to the Russians and the Americans. Both of them have grown up unnoticed; and whilst the attention of mankind was directed elsewhere, they have suddenly placed themselves in the front rank among the nations, and the world learned of their existence and their greatness at almost the same time.

All other nations seem to have nearly reached their natural limits, and they have only to maintain their power; but these are still in the act of growth. All the others have stopped, or continue to advance with extreme difficulty; these alone are proceeding with ease and celerity along a path to which no limit can be perceived. The American struggles against the obstacles which nature opposes to him; the adversaries of the Russian are men. The former combats the wilderness and savage life; the latter, civilization with all its arms. The conquests of the American are therefore gained by the ploughshare; those of the Russian by the sword. The Anglo-American relies upon personal interest to accomplish his ends, and gives free scope to the unguided strength and common sense of the people; the Russian centres all the authority of society in a single arm. The principal instrument of the former is freedom; of the latter, servitude. Their starting-points are different, and their courses are not the same; yet each of them seems marked out by the will of Heaven to sway the destinies of half the globe.

ALEXIS DE TOCQUEVILLE, 1835

1

SOVIET EDUCATION
AND SOVIET POWER

In the early years of the present century eight so-called "great powers" ruled the world. One of these states, Austria-Hungary, disintegrated toward the end of World War I. A glance at the international landscape today shows that World War II brought truly cataclysmic changes in the relative strength of nations. The fact has been noted with pardonable pride by Soviet spokesmen since 1945. In a powerful address in September, 1947, before the assembled leaders of the Communist parties of Europe, Andrei Zhdanov, generally recognized at the time as the probable successor of Stalin, observed that Germany, Italy, and Japan had "disappeared as a result of military defeat," that France had "lost her former significance as a great power," and that Britain had "showed herself to be weak in both military and political relations." Only two great powers remained—the United States of America and the Union of Soviet Socialist Republics. Thus, the remarkable prophecy of Alexis de Tocqueville in 1835, printed at the beginning of this volume, was fulfilled. Each of these powers appears to be in a position "to sway the destinies of half the globe." And the two states, in history, government, and social philosophy, are as far apart today as they were in the days of Andrew Jackson and Nicholas I.

The rise of the Soviet state since that fateful day in November, 1917, when the Party of Bolsheviks, numbering less than a quarter-million members, seized power by force of arms is perhaps the outstanding political fact of the first half of the twentieth century. Conceded practically no chance of survival during the first days, weeks, months, and even years of its existence, the Bolshevik dictatorship swiftly liquidated its enemies and established its absolute rule over practically the entire territory of the old Russian empire. It then proceeded to the radical reconstruction

1

of all social institutions, created a novel form of political despotism, built a collectivist economy in city and country, moved rapidly along the road of industrialization, and developed a vast network of educational and cultural agencies. At the same time it directed its energies outward through the Communist International, propagated its ideas in all lands, and shook the foundations of many societies. With the assistance of the Western democracies, an assistance which goes unrecognized for the most part in the Soviet Union today, the Bolshevik state survived the ordeal of four years of war, pushed back the Nazi armies from the gates of Stalingrad, and presented itself to the world as the "savior of civilization from Hitlerite barbarism."

Taking advantage of the prestige gained in the struggle, the political blindness of the Western Allies, the position of Soviet armed forces at the close of the war, the growth of national Communist parties in Europe and Asia, and the tide of unrest flowing with great strength in various parts of the world, the Soviet state took possession of all lands, except Finland, formerly held by the tsars, pushed forward its official boundaries east and west, established its effective rule over six countries of Eastern Europe, advanced its actual frontier beyond the Elbe, and demanded a voice in the settlement of the affairs of the Middle East and North Africa. Also, through political subversion and economic, technical, and military intervention it extended its sway over the Chinese people and the lands of North Korea and North Indochina. In all history no religious movement ever advanced so far and so swiftly. Little wonder that a frown or a smile in Moscow, a journey of an American congressman to the Soviet Union, or a visit of a delegation of Soviet "farmers" to Iowa is reported excitedly in the press of the free world. And the idea is sedulously propagated by Communist agents everywhere that, in the words of Molotov, "all roads today lead to Communism." Without question the Soviet Union stands in a position of great and growing power in the contemporary world. At the same time, in the summer of 1956, the free nations of the earth seem to be falling apart without leadership or a common faith.

The fact is that the Soviet Union has moved very rapidly along the path of industrialization, and particularly since the launching of the First Five-Year Plan in the autumn of 1928. It should of course be recalled that in 1917 Russia was only two generations from feudalism, the serfs having been freed officially in 1861. A few measures of industrial growth should convey some idea of this advance. Coal production, which amounted to 29,100,000 tons in 1913, rose to 35,000,000 in 1928, and to 264,000,000 in 1950. Corresponding data for steel are 4,200,000, 3,900,000, and 24,000,000; and for oil 9,200,000, 11,600,000, and 37,000,000. And the electrical industry, which was in its early infancy in 1913 produced 82,-000,000,000 kilowatthours of electricity in 1950. While these figures remain far below the achievements of American industry, the rate of growth is impressive. Moreover, according to the Sixth Five-Year Plan, the figure for coal in 1960 will reach 593,000,000 tons, for steel, 68,300,000 tons, for oil 135,000,000 tons, and for electricity 320,000,000,000 kilowatthours.[1] To be sure, the advances in the realms of agriculture and consumers' goods have lagged far behind and the population generally has been held close to the margin of subsistence. Yet the high level of science and technology achieved in certain areas is revealed in the unexpected Soviet successes in the production of atomic and hydrogen bombs, the perfection of airplanes, the mastery of electronics, and the improvement of weapons of warfare generally. That some of these advances have been gained through espionage and the drafting of German scientists is well known. This fact, however, should not lead to any underestimation of Soviet achievements. In terms of skills, knowledges, and understandings, the people of Russia have moved into the industrial age. The nations of the free world can gain no strength by imitating the ostrich and burying their heads in the sand. American scientists of the first order of competence, after inspecting Russian laboratories in May, 1956, reported that the "Soviet Union had achieved a lead in high energy research physics that the United States probably could not overcome within the next ten years." One scientist predicted that the "Soviet Union would lead the world in pure nuclear research within the next decade." [2]

The swift scientific and technological advance of the Soviet Union is dramatically revealed by the current policy of granting technical assistance to underdeveloped countries outside the Communist orbit. In the autumn of 1955, according to James Reston, programs of technical assistance were "either under way or under negotiation in India, Afghanistan, Yugoslavia, Burma, Indonesia, Jordan, Ceylon, Ecuador and Pakistan." And aid to many other countries was being considered. The Soviet Ambassador to Cairo was quoted as saying that his government was prepared to "offer industrial and agricultural equipment to all Arab and Asian countries that wanted it." He then added, "We will send economic missions, scientific missions, agricultural missions, meteorological missions and any other kind of mission you can imagine that will help these countries." [3] That this statement contains an element of boastful exaggeration is obvious. It is also obvious that the actual and proposed assistance are taken out of the low standards of living of the Soviet people and are extended for the purpose of strengthening Communist penetration into the countries involved. Nevertheless, the reader should recall that in its own program of industrialization under the First and Second Five-Year Plans, less than a generation ago, the Soviet government was compelled to seek assistance in the form of machines, engineers, technicians, and even skilled workers from Germany, France, Britain, America, and other industrial nations. How far events have moved since 1928 is indicated by Marguerite Higgins in a newspaper story in the *New York Herald Tribune* in March, 1956. "For the first time in history," she writes, "the State Department is faced with an American company's request to permit Soviet engineers to come to this country to teach Americans to operate machinery, the design of which is also to be imported from the Soviet Union." [4] In June, 1956, Foreign Minister Shepilov was reported to have offered Egypt a loan of $1,120,000,000 for the construction of the Aswan Dam.

That all of these material advances of the Soviet state might have been achieved under a regime of freedom and constitutional government is possible. Indeed, this is the fundamental thesis of Nicholas S. Timasheff in his fascinating and challenging book, *The Great Retreat*, published in 1946. After pointing to the rapid progress in many fields during the decades before the Bolshevik seizure of power and after projecting the curves of growth down to 1940, he concludes as follows: "In regard to many important phases of sociocultural life, twenty-five years after the Communist Revolution Russia was approximately where she would have been if no revolution would have occurred." [5] The evidence presented in support of this thesis is highly persuasive. Yet the fact remains that it is a despotic Russia rather than a democratic Russia that confronts the world today. And it is this state that we must strive to understand. Moreover, the "retreat" with respect to the outward thrust of Bolshevism is much less apparent in 1956 than it was in 1946. Indeed, during the intervening years that thrust has moved with great strength, and in the post-Stalin era of "collective leadership" it has assumed new forms and a new vigor.

The growth of Soviet power would have been impossible in the absence of the phenomenal development of Soviet education. In fact, apart from the dictatorship itself, the program of organized education launched, molded, and expanded by the Communist Party is the key to the understanding of this mighty colossus. More than any other great state in history, it has marshaled all the forces of *organized* education to achieve its purposes and advance toward its distant apocalyptic goals. Its only rivals in the contemporary epoch were Germany under the Nazis and Imperial Japan under the military caste. But these regimes did not survive long enough to perfect their educational programs. It is of course obvious that every human society maintains itself through the generations by means of organized and unorganized processes of learning and education. If at any point these processes were to be interrupted for an extended period, the group would lose its heritage and perish. But in the case of the Soviet Union we are speaking of education in its organized forms. From the moment the Bolsheviks consolidated their rule over the Russian empire they have employed the full force of education not to maintain the *status quo,* but to change the course of history and the nature of man. Here is one of the ineluctable facts of the contemporary world.

One of the first impressions gained by an informed visitor to Russia or by a student of Russian cultural affairs is that education is extremely broad in conception and practice. As a matter of fact, it embraces the entire cultural apparatus, all of the agencies involved in the molding and the informing of the minds of both young and old. It includes the school system from nursery school and kindergarten to university and scientific institute, as well as a wide range of schools designed to give occupational training at different levels. In fact, it includes several systems of schools which will be described in detail in coming chapters. But it also includes for all practical purposes the press in its many forms and manifestations— the newspaper, the periodical, the book, the library, the bookstore, and even the lowly calendar. It includes the newer media of mass communication such as the radio and television. It includes all agencies of amusement and entertainment—the theater, the moving picture, the circus, the playground, the club, the museum, and the public park. It includes the works of literature, music, graphic art, science, scholarship, and philosophy. It includes the political and cultural aspects of all organizations and particularly the organizations for children and youth. It even includes the processes of oral persuasion which through the activities of a disciplined Party membership of seven or eight millions are carefully organized and carried to the most distant villages and the far borders of the Union.

Communist spokesmen whether inside or outside the Soviet Union, never tire of praising in the most extravagant terms the Soviet system of education, even when some basic policy is changed or even reversed. It is the "most advanced in the world"; it expresses the most fully developed "ideological convictions"; it rests on "scientific foundations"; it assures the "harmonious development of the intellectual, moral, aesthetic, and physical powers" of the individual; and it is committed without reservation to the great cause of "peace, democracy, and the liberation of peoples everywhere"—to the "cause of Communism." It is guided in all of its operations by the oft-quoted dictum of the "Great Stalin," a dictum which probably will not be repudiated by his successors: "People must be grown carefully and tenderly, just as a gardener grows a favorite fruit tree." A recent edition of the officially approved textbook on the theory and practice of Soviet education for the training of secondary school teachers closes with these words: "The system of people's education in the Soviet Union has no equal in the entire world." And Khrushchev in his opening address at the Twentieth Congress of the Party on February 14, 1956, declared amid applause that "not one capitalist country has such a quantity of schools, technicums, higher educational establishments, scientific research institutes, experimental stations and laboratories, theaters, clubs, libraries, and other institutions of cultural enlightenment, as the Soviet Union." [6]

That this total system of institutions has many positive achievements to its credit cannot be denied. Within a single generation it has reduced the rate of illiteracy from 60 or 65 to perhaps 5 or 10 per cent. It has played a basic role in the preparation of the millions of skilled workers, technicians, and specialists of all types and grades involved in the conversion of a technically backward country into a modern industrial state. It has made an indispensable contribution to the training and the equipping of the mightiest armed force on the earth today. It has transmitted the rudiments of scientific knowledge to a vast population not far removed from serfdom. It has been instrumental in raising hundreds of thousands from the lowest depths to positions of power and responsibility in the state. It has given to successive generations of youth a sense of mission in the world. It has endeavored, probably with a measure of success, to imprint on the minds of the people inhabiting one-sixth of the land surface of the globe the basic doctrines, outlooks, values, and loyalties of Marxism-Leninism. It has done all these things, as well as many others which will be reported in the present volume. The Soviet educational system is a formidable factor in the present struggle between two worlds—in that "most ferocious struggle," in the words of Konstantin Simonov, a leading Soviet playwright, "between two systems, between two world outlooks, between two conceptions of the future of mankind [which] has been, is being, and will be waged in the world." [7] The great shift in Soviet tactics in this world struggle following the death of Stalin was made possible by spectacular advances in the training of specialists of all kinds.

The growth of this system is truly impressive. The development of a vast network of educational agencies and institutions which embraces the entire country from Leningrad to Vladivostok and from Samarkand to Novaya Zemlya is a physical achievement of the first order of magnitude. The number of pupils and students of all ages attending schools and classes of all grades and types provides one measure of the achievement. In 1914 the figure stood at approximately eight and one-half millions. By 1955, according to Soviet statistics, it had reached the enormous proportions of approximately sixty millions. The point can be taken for granted, of course, that this figure is no understatement of the situation. Undoubtedly it includes every individual who by any stretch of the imagination could be classified as pupil or student. He might merely be taking a correspondence course, attending an evening class, or listening to a series of lectures. But after making full allowance for exaggeration, the skeptic must moderate his skepticism. A common boast today is that one person in every four of the entire population is going to school. And the data on newspapers, books, libraries, museums, theaters, radio stations, and other cultural agencies show comparable increases.*

This record of achievement suggests that the business of organized education is regarded far more seriously in the Soviet Union than it is in the United States, or perhaps in any free society. The highest authorities in the Soviet state give close and constant attention to the program of the schools and other educational agencies. Lenin and Stalin, and the members of the Central Committee of the Communist Party, have always regarded education as an indispensable instrument or weapon for the achievement of their purposes both at home and abroad. This conviction of the importance of education is expressed also in the emphasis which it receives in the press and other agencies of communication, as well as in the widespread practice of glorifying the work and the person of the teacher. Also, whatever the situation may have been in the 1920s, an unceasing effort is made to develop in the young a sense of the seriousness of their work in school which goes well beyond anything known in the whole history of American education. Practically every form of motivation is employed to this end. Rarely if ever have the members of an entire younger generation of any people been subjected to an equally severe regimen in the institutions of organized education. They are told over and over again that "a person educated in the Soviet school must stand much higher in the scale of intellectual education than a person who has gone through a bourgeois school." Whatever the results may be, this statement certainly expresses the intent of the Soviet leadership and probably applies with even greater force in the domain of "education in Communist morality."

An interesting index of the Soviet concern over education may be witnessed at the anniversary celebration of the Bolshevik revolution on November 7—the most important date on the Soviet calendar. For this event the Central Committee always prepares a long list of slogans to direct attention to the most important tasks confronting the country. Invariably several of these slogans are directed toward the work of the schools. The following are taken from the list for 1955:

> Teachers! Raise the quality of the instruction and education of children! Cultivate in children the spirit of love and devotion to the Soviet Motherland, of friendship among peoples! Prepare fully developed, cultured, and industrious citizens of socialist society, active builders of Communism!
>
> Young men and young women, our glorious Soviet youth! Participate more actively in economic and cultural construction, in the entire socio-political life of the country! Stubbornly master the achievements of progressive science and technology, master the knowledge of industrial and agricultural

---

* See Appendix, page 809, for the most reliable data available.

production! Be steadfast and brave in the struggle for victory of the great cause of Communism in our land!

School children! Stubbornly and persistently master knowledge! Be industrious and disciplined, strive for success in your studies! [8]

A more effective measure, perhaps, of the importance which any society attaches to education is its willingness to provide material support. By this measure the Soviet performance must be given a very high rating, though certainly not as high as the Communist spokesmen claim. According to the latter, the expenditures on education amount to more than 10 per cent of the total national income, while the corresponding figure for the United States is less than 3 per cent. This comparison has been widely publicized in America and throughout the world. However, before accepting the Communist claim, we should note that the meaning of the word "education" is not the same in the two countries. The word unquestionably, as already suggested, embraces much more in the Soviet Union than it does in America. If it is limited to the work of the schools, an analysis of the details of the Soviet state budget for 1955 shows the Soviet expenditure to be only about five and one-half or six per cent of the national income.[9] Yet, the point must be conceded that, in view of the relatively low productivity of the economy and the generally low standard of living of the people, the Soviet state probably supports schools at least as generously as any other state in history.

The vast potentials of the Soviet program of education constitute one of the major realities in the contemporary world—as important, perhaps, as the strength of the Soviet armed forces. The reactions in America, however, are somewhat ambivalent. On the one hand, during the past two years alarm has been expressed again and again over the fact that the Soviet Union is training more engineers than we are. Indeed, it has become almost commonplace for a speaker on higher education to call attention to this condition in the course of his address. All sorts of proposals have been and are being made to expand the program of training in engineering and to attract talented youth to the profession. And as these lines are being written the press reports a statement by Representative Wright Patman to the effect that "Soviet Russia will graduate thirty-two times as many technicians as the United States next year." [10] To students of Soviet education this aspect of the Soviet program has long been recognized. Indeed, ever since the launching of the First Five-Year Plan in 1928 for the industrialization of the country, unprecedented emphasis has been placed on technical, engineering, and scientific education. It should be recalled that the slogan of that "Plan of Great Works" read as follows: "We must strive in the shortest possible historical period to overtake and surpass the most advanced capitalistic countries and thus insure the victory of socialism in its historic competition with the system of capitalism." This was interpreted by a member of the All-Union State Planning Commission to mean "that by 1943, in the event of the peaceful development of the country, we shall surpass the level of production achieved in the United States of America in 1929 and shall overtake, if we do not significantly surpass, the current level of technical equipment of industry in that country." [11]

On the other hand, many have viewed with complacency the development of Soviet education. Nurtured on the tradition that despotisms fear schools because "they want to keep the people in ignorance," they have interpreted the expansion of the Soviet system of schools as certifying the essentially democratic tendency of the regime and ensuring the ultimate triumph of political freedom. In an address at Columbia University on June 1, 1955, Allen W. Dulles seemed to defend this position in the following words:

> . . . mass education in the Soviet Union may well become a threat to their own Communist system of government. . . . In introducing mass education the troubled Soviet leaders have loosed forces dangerous to themselves. It will be very difficult henceforth to close off their people from access to the realities of the outside world." [12]

In a concluding chapter we shall return to the question: What is the meaning of Soviet education to the cause of human freedom in Russia and the world? But it seems probable that no valid and trustworthy answer will be possible before the passing of many years.

The repudiation of Stalin at the Twentieth Congress in February, 1956, is undoubtedly subjecting Soviet education to a most severe test. For a quarter of a century succeeding generations of Soviet children and youth have been taught with all the power of a monolithic system of indoctrination that Stalin was all-wise and all-good, that every one of his utterances and actions was an expression of sublime genius. At the same time they have been told to follow with implicit faith the teachings of Marx, Engels, and Lenin and to accept without qualification the line laid down by the Central Committee of the Party on all questions of doctrine and policy. Will the Soviet people accept this great reversal as they have accepted other reversals in the past, such as the New Economic Policy of 1921 or the Stalin-Hitler Pact of 1939? The first indications suggest that the all-embracing physical, ideological, and moral controls of the Party will carry the Soviet ship of state safely through the storm. That this can be done, without a Stalinist purge, however, is by no means certain.

2

THE ROOTS OF
SOVIET EDUCATION

The roots of Soviet education reach far back into the past of Western man. They reach back to the invention of the school as a special institution devoted exclusively to the process of education. When and where this happened is lost in the mists of history. But it probably occurred some five thousand years ago in the valley of the Nile for the training of the novitiates of a priestly caste in the skills of reading and writing and in the mastery of a precious body of esoteric knowledge deemed essential to the welfare and survival of the group. Those roots may also be traced back to the initiation ceremonies and apprenticeship practices of primitive peoples.

The heritage of Plato is clearly evident in the Soviet Union. In fact, the present author on his first visit to Russia in 1927 was reminded again and again of the *Republic*, in which the power of rule rested in the hands of a small caste of "philosophers." And the evolution of the Soviet system of education has moved in the direction of Plato's ideas. It will be recalled that the ancient philosopher in his classical work drew the outlines of an ideal society in which the citizens were divided into three classes: the philosophers, who governed the state; the warriors, who defended it; and the farmers and craftsmen, who produced and distributed its material wealth. For the selection and training of the members of each of these classes a special system of educational institutions was provided. In the Soviet Union today there are at least three systems of schools: the system of people's schools, the system of military schools, and the system of Party schools. It requires little imagination to see the parallel with the *Republic*.

The major source of Soviet educational institutions, however, was modern Europe and America. The indebtedness here is as great as it is in

10

the realm of industrialization. Although Peter the Great built the capital city of his empire on the shores of the Baltic and thus "opened a window" on Europe at the beginning of the eighteenth century, Russia continued to lag behind the Western nations in practically all spheres of economic, political, and cultural development. Consequently, when the revolution came in 1917, Russia, in terms of its educational institutions and practices, was living in the late eighteenth or early nineteenth century of the Western world. Imperial Russia, to be sure, possessed some excellent universities and secondary schools and boasted a brilliant intellectual class, but the great masses of the people were illiterate and unschooled. A comprehensive program of popular education, which had become a characteristic feature of all advanced Western states, was still to be established. The Bolsheviks consequently had to turn in considerable measure to the vast heritage of educational institutions, practices, and conceptions evolved in Europe and America. The situation in the realm of industrial technology and machine production was fundamentally the same. If the revolution had occurred a century earlier, the development of education, as well as the organization of the economy, would have taken a very different course. It is interesting to note that in its external features and patterns the Soviet system of people's schools resembles closely the systems established in the United States and Germany.

Yet, in its purpose and spirit Soviet education is distinctive. What are the historical sources of its special qualities? It has been customary to answer this question in terms of the doctrines of Karl Marx, the practices of the old Russian autocracy, and the liberal and humanistic ideas developed after the liberation of the serfs in 1861 during the latter part of the nineteenth and the early part of the twentieth century. All three of these sources must be taken into account, for each has left its imprint on the form and spirit of Soviet education. But there is a fourth source which has been generally overlooked and which in the author's opinion is the most important of all: a certain revolutionary conception which stems from the thought, writings, and activities of such men as Peter Zaichnevsky (1842–1896), Peter N. Tkachev (1844–1886), and Sergei Nechaiev (1847–1883). The first three sources will be treated briefly, the fourth at greater length.

II

The Bolsheviks seized power under the banners of Marxism. Lenin regarded himself as a 100 per cent Marxist and an ardent defender of Marxian orthodoxy against all revisionists. In truth, however, he was a far more radical revisionist than any of the great European socialist leaders against whom he inveighed so bitterly and savagely: Eduard

Bernstein, Jean Jaurès, Henry Mayers Hyndman, and Karl Kautsky. For when put to the test in the summer and autumn of 1917, he repudiated in action a most basic, perhaps the most basic, law of historical materialism: "No social order ever perishes before all the productive forces for which there is room in it have developed." According to this "law," the transition from capitalism to socialism would take place only after the system of capitalism had made its full contribution to the development of the productive forces of the economy and had thus become a barrier to further economic progress. Obviously, Russia in 1917, if compared with Germany, Britain, or the United States, was in the early stages of capitalism. And there was more room for the growth of productive forces there than almost anywhere else in the Western world.

Marx gave relatively little attention to the development of the theory and practice of education under socialism. This neglect was probably due for the most part to the fact that the absorbing concern of his life lay elsewhere—in the achievement of the socialist revolution itself. It was probably due also in some measure to his conception of the social and historical process. According to this view, the entire social, political, moral, and ideological superstructure of society is an expression of the "prevailing mode of production and exchange." The Central Committee of the Communist Party of the Soviet Union puts the matter even more bluntly and dogmatically: "The material life of society is an objective reality existing independently of the will of men, while the spiritual life of society is a reflection of this objective reality, a reflection of being." The Central Committee then proceeds to quote the famous statement by Marx: "It is not the consciousness of men that determines their being, but, on the contrary, their social being that determines their consciousness." [1] Holding such beliefs, Marx could logically leave the question of education to the future.

Marx, however, did bequeath some educational ideas to the Bolsheviks which have played an important role in the history of Soviet education. On the negative side was his view of education under capitalism. Since the ruling classes in all societies wish to maintain the *status quo* and thus protect their privileges, capitalists look upon the education of the masses as likely to breed unrest and therefore dangerous. Yet, with the advance of technology and the complication of the modes of production, a minimum of education is necessary to make the laborer efficient. It follows that emphasis must be placed in the process of education on the cultivation in the workers of attitudes of obedience and docility toward their masters. Such is the picture of education in capitalist countries, and particularly in America, which is painted in the Soviet Union today. The following statement by Engels is contemporary Communist orthodoxy: "Since the bourgeoisie vouchsafes them [the workers] only so much of life as is absolutely necessary, we need not wonder that it bestows upon them only so much education as lies in the interest of the bourgeoisie." [2]

On the positive side, Marx placed great stress on the role of labor in the educative process. Since he regarded human labor as the source of all value and since he made the working class the builder of socialism, this position is easy to understand. In certain provisions in the Factory Acts of mid-nineteenth-century England which called for the alternation of work in school and work in factory Marx saw the "germs of the education of the future," in which "education and physical culture" would be combined with "manual labour," and "manual labour" with "education and physical culture." [3] This idea enjoyed great vogue in Soviet education in the 1920s. The combined primary and secondary school was called the "unified labor school," and "socially useful labor" was given a central role in the process of education. With the reforms of the early thirties this emphasis practically disappeared along with many other practices of the preceding decade.

The combination of "work with the mind" and "work with the hand" is perhaps the most fundamental conception in the Marxian theory of education. On one occasion Marx made the idea concrete in a program for children nine to seventeen years of age. From nine to twelve the child should work with his hands in the factory two hours a day; from thirteen to fifteen, four hours, and from sixteen to eighteen, six hours. The work in school would include intellectual education, physical education through gymnastics and military exercises, and technical education. By technical education he meant an education which would acquaint "the child with the basic principles of all processes of production" and also give him the "habits of dealing with the most simple instruments of all production." [4] Out of this formulation emerged the idea of "polytechnical education" which acquired great authority and prestige in the Soviet complete middle school in the late twenties. In fact for a brief period that school was called the "polytechnical school." But this idea was submerged in the early thirties, only to come back with considerable strength at the Nineteenth Congress of the Party in the autumn of 1952. The conception has lived through the years of Soviet power in the slogan "union of theory and practice."

Marx elaborated his educational ideas further in 1871. On May 30 of that year, two days after the fall of the Paris Commune, he read a paper in which he spoke approvingly of the educational reforms introduced by the Communards during their brief triumph of seventy-two days. These revolutionists, according to Marx, proposed to establish a system of education completely open to all the people, controlled by the citizens of each locality, freed from the fetters of class, government, and church, committed to the ideal of intellectual freedom, devoted to the full development of the talents and powers of each individual, dedicated to the fostering of the "eternal principles of justice and liberty," and guided in its instruction by that ancient precept which is the "basis of all true equality: 'He who does not work must not eat.'" [5] Except for the spirit of individual and political freedom which permeates this program, the educational reforms of the Paris Commune were generally adopted, at least in words, by the Bolsheviks when they proceeded at the time of the revolution to build their own system of education.

III

A traveler in the Soviet Union in the 1920s was constantly reminded of the cultural and technical backwardness of the country. He was reminded both by the facts of life and by the remarks and questions of Soviet citizens and even children. It was commonplace to hear someone say, by way of apology for some condition, "Of course, our country is very backward." Lenin himself set the pattern in his "Farewell Letter to Swiss Workers" in April, 1917, on the eve of his departure for Russia following the March Revolution. "Russia," he said, "is a peasant country, one of the most backward in Europe." [6] Indeed, he regarded his native land as so backward that the socialist revolution would not survive if it failed to spread to the more advanced countries. In 1918, after the seizure of power, he wrote: "History has taught you a lesson. It is a lesson, because it is the absolute truth that without a German revolution we are doomed. . . . At all events, under all conceivable vicissitudes, if the German revolution does not come, we are doomed." [7]

Children were taught in the schools that, except for the words and deeds of rebels and revolutionists reaching back through the centuries and more particularly to the revolt of Stenka Razin in the valley of the Volga in the years from 1667 to 1671, the past of Russia was a story of unrelieved poverty, ignorance, brutality, cruelty, oppression, and exploitation. Indeed, history really seemed to begin with the October Revolution of 1917. The thought of many a visitor to the "First Workers' Republic in History" went back to the time when the French revolutionists substituted the Goddess of Reason for the Christian God, fashioned a new calendar, and established the year of the revolution as the bench mark for the recording of time. In referring to important events in Russia it was always either *do revolutsii* (before the revolution) or *posle revolutsii* (after the revolution).

The fact, of course, is that the Bolsheviks inherited from the tsars a considerable body of educational practices, institutions, and ideas. It would appear that the interest in schools in old Russia dates from the conversion of Prince Vladimir of Kiev to Orthodox Christianity in 988 or 989. Under the the auspices of the Church and with priests as teachers a few schools were opened. At the beginning of the seventeenth century Boris Godunov attached great importance to learning, provided "a very good" education for his son, and sent Russian young men to European countries to be trained as "teachers for schools which he planned." A century later Peter the Great manifested deep interest in education, founded technical and special schools, launched an academy of sciences, and conceived a plan for a university on the German model. Catherine the Great appointed a special committee to prepare a plan for the "establishment of public schools" open to all classes. And so, down through the nineteenth century, even during the reigns of Nicholas I and Alexander III, much attention was given to the problem of education, even though achievements lagged far behind schemes, conceptions, and visions. Following the revolution of 1905 and the establishment of the Duma, plans were formulated for the "gradual enforcement of compulsory school attendance for all children aged eight to eleven." While genuine progress toward this goal was made in the succeeding years, the development was retarded by World War I. Consequently, when the Bolsheviks came to power in 1917, the goal still lay far in the future.[8]

A few figures from the Soviet statistical yearbook for 1936 will give a fairly adequate picture of the scope of the educational program in the last days of the empire. In 1914–1915 there were 106,400 schools of all kinds serving the purposes of *general* education and enrolling 7,800,600 pupils. Of the total number of schools 1,800 were classified as secondary in the European sense and enrolled 564,600 pupils.[9] At the same time there were 91 higher educational institutions with 124,700 students, 233 technical schools with 48,000 students, and 2,644 lower vocational schools with 219,000 students.[10] In 1913 the publication of books involved 28,132 titles and 113,400,000 copies. For newspapers and journals the corresponding figures were 859 and 2,729,000.[11] Also prerevolutionary Russia had 222 cottage reading rooms, 12,600 libraries, and 224 theaters.[12] While these data clearly reveal a condition of cultural backwardness in a country of approximately 180 millions, they also show that Russia was by no means a land without educational institutions. And it should be said that much of the work, particularly in the secondary and higher schools, was of superior academic quality. German influence was everywhere in evidence.

From the standpoint of impact on the developemnt of Soviet education, the spirit, ideals, and purposes of education under the tsars are more important than forms, institutions, and numbers. One of the most striking features of this heritage was the presence in every generation since the days of Catherine the Great and Alexander I of a small group of intellectuals of unsurpassed idealism and devotion to the welfare of the people who saw in education the road to national salvation. In the reign of

Nicholas I, perhaps the most tyrannical of the tsars after Ivan the Terrible, one of the educational leaders of the time wrote: "In Russia we need but three things—education, education, and education." And the more en-lightened tsars, at least during some periods of their reigns, tended to share this view. It was in the years and decades following the liberation of the serfs in 1861, however, that faith in and enthusiasm for education came into full flower. This faith survived down to the Bolshevik revolu-tion and left its obvious imprint on Soviet education in the 1920s. But this story will be told in part in a later section of the present chapter. Our concern here is with the legacy from the autocracy.

The autocrats of Russia all viewed education with mixed feelings. On the one hand, they recognized that without a modern system of schools their country would lag behind the great states of the West. They also felt keenly the label of backwardness and uncouthness attached to Russia by Western critics and commentators. On the other hand, they tended to fear schools, and particularly universities, as seedbeds of unrest, heresy, and revolution. Consequently, as they moved inexorably toward the development of educational institutions, they generally sought to prevent the importation of dangerous ideas from the West and to cultivate in the younger generation unquestioned loyalty to the regime.

The most celebrated exposition of the purposes of education under the tsars was made in 1832 by Count S. S. Uvarov in a report to Nicholas I. A year later he was appointed Minister of Education. In order to counter-act the influence of subversive ideas from the West, he proposed a system of education based on "the truly-Russian conservative principles of Ortho-doxy, autocracy, and nationality, our last anchor of salvation and the best guarantees of Russia's strength and greatness." [13] The meanings of "Ortho-doxy" and "autocracy" are clear. But the same cannot be said for "nation-ality." In fact, the Russian word *narodnost* has no precise equivalent in the English language. Florinsky suggests "official patriotism" or "official nationalism." However translated, the words of Uvarov were often recalled a century later, when under the rule of Stalin three sacred conceptions appeared: Marxism-Leninism-Stalinism, the Communist Party, and love of the Motherland. There is, however, a difference. Whereas Nicholas I sought to maintain the existing order of things, the Bolsheviks professed devotion to the building of something radically new—a "Communist so-ciety."

The struggle between the autocracy and the schools, and particularly the universities, became a characteristic feature of the Russian state. In 1840 Uvarov, alarmed by "the desire for education which was everywhere growing," contended that "this extraordinary aspiration toward the higher subjects of study should not be suffered to disturb in any way the existing class system, by awakening in youthful minds the impulse to acquire

unnecessary knowledge, which cannot be applied in practice." According
to the father of Russian historiography, S. M. Soloviev, "with the reign of
Nicholas education ceased to be a virtue—in the eyes of the government
it was a crime." The most diverse methods and devices were employed at
this time, as well as before and after, to control the content of instruction.
Natural science, social science, and philosophy were often regarded as
dangerous. Foreign professors and Russians who had studied abroad were
viewed with suspicion. The extension of higher educational opportunities
to women and to youth from the lower classes was opposed, but eventually without success. As late as 1887 the Minister of Education instructed
the gymnasia to refuse admission to "children of coachmen, lackeys, cooks,
washerwomen, small tradesmen, and the like." In the 1920s the Bolsheviks
applied the same principle, but in reverse. Another practice of the autocracy which the Soviets perfected was that of spying on both students
and professors in the search for dangerous thoughts and subversive characters.

This struggle between the political authority and the university led in
the course of time to student disturbances and even strikes. The early
1850s were marked by many such "incidents," as they were called. In
1861, as a protest against the curtailment of their liberties, students at
St. Petersburg petitioned the curator for a redress of grievances. The
curator refused to accept the petition and had two of the students
arrested. When the students marched in a body to the office of the governor general, they were attacked by the mounted police, whipped un-
sparingly, trampled upon, and pursued ruthlessly. Disorders occurred
frequently during the remaining decades of the nineteenth and on into
the twentieth century. Little wonder that the student was looked upon
with suspicion by the authorities and regarded as a possible revolutionist
or an enemy of the state. However, the fact that both students and professors, on occasion, raised their voices against the imperial authority
suggests that the autocracy of the Romanovs was somewhat less autocratic
than the autocracy of the Bolsheviks. Students neither protest nor strike
in the Soviet Union.[14] The demonstration of students at the University of
Tiflis against the repudiation of Stalin in February, 1956, is the one known
exception.

Another educational practice under the tsars which has meaning today
concerns the non-Russian nationalities. After the "liberation from the
Tartar yoke" toward the end of the fifteenth century the Great Russians
moved out in all directions and eventually took possession of "one-sixth
of the land surface of the globe." During this process they conquered and
established their rule over many peoples. Today they constitute little
more than one-half of the population of the Soviet Union. In the interests
of building a strong empire and extending the sway of the Orthodox

Church, the Russian autocracy generally pursued the policy of Russification. This meant conversion to Orthodoxy and adoption of the Russian
language. Schools and all cultural agencies were generally directed toward
this goal. Russian was made the language of instruction and communication wherever and whenever possible. On coming to power, the Bolsheviks
reversed this policy and proclaimed the right of each nationality to conduct instruction in the schools in its own language. What happened to
this new policy will be told later in the present volume.

Censorship of the press in all its forms was an indispensable arm of
the autocracy. Though its severity varied with the times and the persons
of the tsars, it remained down to February, 1917, a characteristic feature
of Russian society. Its spirit is revealed in an official communication issued
on May 14, 1818, which runs as follows: "All questions pertaining to
government policies may be discussed only in accordance with the wishes
of the authorities, who know better what information should be given to
the public; private persons must not write on political topics, either for
or against."[15] During times of social or political unrest in the empire itself
or in Europe, the authorities were especially watchful and severe. Yet,
M. N. Katkov, journalist and publicist with Pan-Slavic tendencies, wrote
at the end of 1886 that "the press in Russia, and perhaps in Russia alone,
is placed in a position approaching complete independence. We know of
no organ of the foreign press that could be called independent in the
true meaning of the term." His argument was that in the "so-called constitutional states" the press was, "not an expression of public conscience,"
but a tool of party interests. Since political parties were not permitted to
exist in Russia, the press could be independent.[16] All this sounds very
familiar to the student of the Soviet "society without classes" and therefore without political parties. The reader should know, however, that
censorship under the tsars was far more lenient and inefficient than it is
under the Bolsheviks. In old Russia revolutionary newspapers, journals,
books, and proclamations were printed and distributed in spite of the
official prohibitions and the vigilance of the police. Even revolutionists
in prison were able to put their thoughts in writing and pass them through
the guards to their associates.

IV

The word "autocracy" does not embrace by any means all that was
Russia before the October Revolution. The tsars themselves, as we have
noted, were not all made in the same image; and a particular tsar presented different faces to the world at different times. The relatively
benevolent despotism of Alexander I and Alexander II may be contrasted
with the brutal tyrannies of Nicholas I. Alexander I, moreover, beginning

his reign as a comparatively liberal monarch, turned toward reaction in his later years. And Catherine II, who at one time cultivated the acquaintance of Voltaire, Diderot, and other foreign philosophers, repudiated her friendship with Alexander Radishchev and imposed on him the death penalty for having written a book recommending constitutional government and a free press for Russia. Though the sentence was commuted to exile in Siberia, the great philosopher committed suicide after serving his term.

Within the limitations to freedom set by the autocracy, the liberal ideas of the West found their way into Russia, and talented Russians went abroad to study, think, and write. During the first half of the nineteenth century, even during the reign of Nicholas I, there emerged in Russia a group of distinguished writers and thinkers who were profoundly moved by the backwardness of their country, became interested in the disciplines of history, philosophy, social thought, and natural science, and, while not teachers or educators in the formal sense, turned their minds to educational ideas and reforms. Among them were Vissarion G. Belinsky (1811–1849), Alexander Hertzen (1812–1870), Nikolai G. Chernyshevsky (1828–1889), and Nikolai A. Dobroliubov (1836–1861). These men also planted the seeds of social revolution and conceived socialism or communism as the ideal society for mankind. Regarding their educational thought, it must suffice to quote a passage from Belinsky. Believing in formal education for all children, he suggested that its basic purpose should be the inculcation of "respect for the name of man, . . . without any reference to him as an individual or to his nationality, religion or rank, or even to his personal dignity; in a word, unbounded love and unbounded respect for mankind even as represented by the least of its members." [17]

These seeds bore fruit after the death of Nicholas I in 1855 and the ascension to the throne of Alexander II. Under a more liberal regime Russia entered the period of the "Great Reforms," or the "Age of Enlightenment." In 1861 came the liberation of the serfs, though as free peasants their condition was not greatly improved. In 1864 elective county councils, or zemstvos, and six years later town councils, were created. Though these councils were largely controlled in actuality by the more privileged classes in town and country, they constituted a radical departure from custom and an important step on the road to political democracy. And they played a most significant role in the extension of educational opportunities to the people.

In the field of education new ideas emerged, hope blossomed, and all sorts of plans and schemes sprouted in the land. The question of compulsory primary education under state control became a subject of discussion, although some of the liberal-minded, knowing from experience the repressive predilections of governmental intervention in the realm of affairs of the mind, preferred to place their trust in popular enthusiasm, cooperative enterprise, and individual initiative. A galaxy of able, devoted, and idealistic men and women, recruited from the privileged and educated classes, threw themselves into the cause of the education of the people with the zeal of missionaries of a new faith. They turned to this cause as others of their generation turned to the use of terror and the advocacy of violent revolution. Many of the educational inventions of this movement were appropriated by the Bolsheviks a generation or more later and adapted to their quite different purposes.

Perhaps the most distinguished of these educational leaders, with the possible exception of Leo Tolstoy whose major claim to fame derives from another sphere of achievement, was Konstantin D. Ushinsky (1824–1870), one of the truly great educators of Europe in the nineteenth century. He has been called, even by a leading Soviet educator, "the founder of the Russian primary school and pedagogical training for teachers" in Russia. He held a number of important educational posts under both Nicholas I and Alexander II. From one of these posts he resigned in defense of intellectual freedom; from others he was dismissed because of his liberal ideas. He spent five years in Europe as a semi-exile. He drew his inspiration from Bacon, Locke, Mill, Spencer, Kant, and Descartes rather than from Feuerbach, Marx, and Bakunin. He lectured widely and wrote much on the subject of education.[18] Other outstanding figures in this group were N. I. Pirogov (1810–1881), V. I. Vodovozov (1825–1886), V. Ya. Stoyunin (1826–1888), N. F. Bunakov (1837–1904), V. P. Ostrogorsky (1840–1902), D. I. Pisarev (1841–1868), P. I. Makushin (1844–1926), and S. T. Shatsky (1878–1934). The basic ideas of this galaxy of educators and the movement which they led down to the October Revolution will be briefly summarized.

These men and their followers were moved primarily by a deep love of country. They were patriotic without being chauvinistic. They followed closely social, cultural, and educational developments in other countries. But, as Stoyunin said, they were passionately opposed "to blind imitation of foreign models." [19] They were convinced that Russian educational ideas and practices should have deep roots in and grow out of the Russian soil. For this reason Ushinsky placed great emphasis on the mastery of the native language. Here are his poetic words:

> The language is the spirit of a people, his motherland . . . it translates into sound the landscape of the fatherland—the air, the climate, the fields, the mountains, the valleys, the forests, and the rivers. . . . Generations of people come and go, but the experience of each generation remains in the language as a legacy to the heirs. . . . By mastering the native tongue, the child masters not words only, but also an infinite variety of concepts, views, feelings, and artistic images.[20]

In spite of the tremendous efforts of the Bolsheviks to "change the character of the Russian people," it is possible that the continuity of the language will prove an insurmountable obstacle to their designs.

Implicit in love of country was love of the people. Indeed, here was one of the mainsprings of the movement. These educators, like the apostles of revolution, were deeply moved by the condition of poverty, ignorance, and oppression under which the great masses of the people lived and suffered. But they regarded the slow processes of education as the means for the improvement of the quality of life and society. And they expressed a sublime faith in the people and their potentialities. The more extreme of the revolutionists, as we shall see later, while professing love of the people and concern for their welfare, cherished little faith in their powers of mind and heart. At any rate, they did not believe that the people could or should play an active role in the building of the ideal society. This was the responsibility of the tiny minority of professional revolutionists.

Faith in the people and in popular education was founded on a belief in the essential goodness of man, or at least in the capacity of man to acquire goodness—"the selfless love of honesty and truth" and devotion to the "universally human moral qualities," including "love of mankind" and "the placing of the general above personal welfare." But in order that this potential goodness may develop, the individual human being, regardless of race, nation, or class, must be regarded as a creature of worth and dignity. This conception of man called for a kind of education profoundly different from that which had been provided in the past.

The first object of education should be, not the training of specialists in engineering, medicine, military science, or some other vocation, but rather the full and rounded development of the individual as *man*. This meant great emphasis on the formation of character. Ushinsky expressed the thought in these words: "Serve the idea of truth and goodness, the idea of civilization, the idea of state and people, even if it should cost you the greatest efforts and sacrifices, even if it should bring upon you grief, poverty, and disgrace, even if it should cost you your very life." [21] But this end cannot be achieved without the fullest development of men's rational faculties. Consequently, throughout the history of the movement much stress was placed on enlightenment and the liberation of the human mind. Pirogov said: "We must bring science to the people with all the means at our disposal." [22] Makushin argued that "the road to the freedom and welfare of the people lies in enlightenment." According to Tolstoy, "only a freely developed personality armed with information and scientific knowledge can change life." His ideal of a "critically thinking personality" [23] was generally shared.

The conduct of the school and all educational agencies and processes should always be marked by love of man and love of the child. "Only our love of man," wrote Stoyunin, can rescue a people "sunk in the darkness of ignorance and oppressive poverty. Severity and punishment will not avail. . . . Love and more love of man alone will tell us to do what must be done to save man. And such is its power that whatever it tells us to do will not remain as mere words but will be transformed into deeds." [24]

In the school this led to emphasis on respect for the personality of the child, freedom of expression, and abolition of the punishments characteristic of the traditional school. It even led to the abolition of marks and examinations and the organization of instruction around the needs of the learner. These Russian educators of the third quarter of the nineteenth century even contended that the school should be a place where children would be happy. All of this sounds very much like the "child-centered school" of twentieth-century America. At the same time great emphasis was placed on labor as the "source of man's dignity and morality and happiness," and also on the development of habits of work in the young.

These educational leaders also believed that the school should be intellectually free for both instructor and learner. Here they revolted against the ancient tradition of harassment of teacher and pupil established by the autocracy. The teacher in the government school was called "the man in a box," because he was a mere functionary of the state and was forced to follow detailed programs prepared by the ministry of education or some higher authority. As a consequence, there developed in the movement emphasis on local activity, private initiative, and popular involvement in the realm of educational affairs. "Beware," admonished Stoyunin, "lest there should creep into the pedagogical purposes of the school some political designs or ideas to which programs and morals would be forced to conform." [25] Interestingly enough, this admonition applied not only to governmental prescriptions but also to efforts of the revolutionists to penetrate the school and direct it into the service of their purposes. Although the educational leaders generally shared the ideals of the revolutionary movements, they rejected the revolutionary tactics which were saturated with violations of the human personality. As a teacher, moreover, the revolutionist tended to subordinate the interests of education to the revolutionary cause.

Teaching was regarded as a great and noble calling, requiring special qualities of mind and heart. And the teacher was regarded as a person who had dedicated his life to the greatest of causes. He was also regarded as the key to the entire educative process. "The personality of the teacher," said Ushinsky, "means everything in education." Moreover, there are no unimportant posts in education. Even if he is working in an impoverished and unpretentious school, he "must realize the tremendous social significance of his work." If adequately prepared, he must know that he is "a living member of a great organism which is toiling for the perfection of mankind, which is striving for truth and justice." He must know too that his cause, though modest at first sight, is "one of the greatest causes of history—a cause on which kingdoms and generations rest." [26] He therefore should be completely devoted to his calling, and should also love it. "A teacher who loves his calling only," wrote Tolstoy, "will be a good teacher." And "a teacher who loves his pupils will be better than one who has read all the books but loves neither his calling nor his pupils." Then he added that a teacher "who combines love of his calling and love of his pupils will be a perfect teacher." [27] It was the duty of the teacher to transmit to the young this selfless concern for the welfare of others and of society. Such was the ideal of the extraordinary educational movement which contributed so much to the enlightenment of the Russian people following the liberation of the serfs.

Driven by unsurpassed zeal for enlightening and raising the cultural level of the people, a growing company of men and women created a vast range of institutions to serve their purposes. They naturally gave much attention from the beginning to the establishment of primary schools to teach reading, writing, and elementary subjects. Interest in secondary schools emerged toward the end of the nineteenth century. One of the most effective inventions was the Sunday school, so called simply because it was open on Sunday when the people had some hours of leisure. Much attention was given to the publication and distribution of books at a price of one and one-half kopecks—less than one penny. Libraries, reading centers, and bookstores followed naturally. Museums were founded to promote interest and knowledge in the various sciences. These men and women also launched kindergartens and crèches, children's clubs and colonies. They even organized schools in jails and prisons. They created factory schools, higher peasant schools, people's universities, literary circles, evening and Sunday classes for adults, and evening and Sunday lectures and readings. They established people's and children's theaters, people's homes and cultural centers, people's recreation circles, village choirs, village parks and playgrounds. And all these agencies were developed free from state and Church control by means of local enterprise, popular cooperation, and private initiative. They were open to all persons, irrespective of sex, religion, nationality, or social position, and their activities were conducted in the native tongue. The movement began among a people almost entirely illiterate. With the assistance of diverse governmental educational reforms it bequeathed to the Bolsheviks in 1917 a population with a literacy rate of 35 or 40 per cent. Olga Kaidanova, who became identified with the movement in the 1880s and lived on into the postrevolutionary period, thus summarizes its aims, ideas, and spirit:

. . . a unified school, universal education free and accessible to all at all
levels, freedom of private initiative in matters of people's education, expansion of the curriculum of the primary school, coeducation, wide use of out-
of-school educational agencies and processes, closer identification of school
with life, vitalization of methods of teaching by means of handwork, excursions, and laboratories, equipment of schools with collections and exhibits
prepared by the pupils, study of the local community, democratization of
preschool education, and people's universities.[28]

Many an American visitor to the Soviet Union in the 1920s was impressed by the great variety of educational and cultural institutions. He
naturally assumed that they were the creation of the Bolshevik power,
and he was commonly permitted and even encouraged to believe this to
be true. As a matter of historical fact, the Bolsheviks inherited a rich and
varied legacy from the past which had been largely the inspired creation
of private initiative and personal idealism. They did, of course, take over
the institutions, but they converted them into agencies for strengthening
the Soviet state and the achievement of their goals. And it cannot be
doubted that something of the liberal and humanist spirit of this remarkable movement survives down to this day in the minds of the Russian
people. Perhaps this is what the Bolsheviks mean by the "survival of
vestiges of capitalism in the consciousness of men."

V

A fourth source of Soviet education is found in a certain revolutionary
tradition which developed in the middle of the nineteenth century—the
tradition of revolutionary absolutism or revolutionary Machiavellism—
the tradition of revolution by a tightly organized and disciplined minority
of intellectuals committed to a utopian vision of the ideal society. This
source has been almost completely ignored in discussions of Soviet education. Yet it is probably more important than the other three combined.
In fact, it seems to be the key to an understanding of Soviet education.
On coming to power the Bolsheviks found themselves in almost precisely
the position envisaged by their predecessors two generations earlier. The
logic of that position with regard to education was irrefragable.

The most basic conception in this tradition is the conception of a
revolutionary organization on the pattern of the French Jacobins, the
Italian Carbonari, or the "Society of the Families" of Auguste Blanqui.
The conception apparently first took practical form in Russia in the first
quarter of the nineteenth century. Its architect was Paul Pestel (1762–
1826), an aristocrat by birth and a soldier by profession. As one of the
leaders of the unsuccessful revolutionary attempt of December, 1825, he
was arrested and executed. But he left a legacy which was destined to

live and flourish in the coming decades and generations. Though an apostle of constitutional government, he believed in the violent overthrow of the autocracy, the seizure of power by a militant minority, and the establishment of a temporary dictatorship. Also he conceived a revolutionary association modeled on the structure of an army with three levels of membership—at the top the fully initiated, in the middle the partly initiated, and at the bottom the wholly uninitiated, the common soldiers of the revolution committed to unquestioned obedience. Standing on the fringes of the association, without power or obligation, were sympathizers or, in the language of a later day, "fellow travelers." Its membership was to be secret and its mode of operation conspiratorial.

That such a conception would emerge in a land long marked by tyranny and oppression is easily understood. But by the middle of the nineteenth century, possibly due to the influence of Auguste Blanqui and the French anarchists, a fateful idea was added to the original conception—the idea that the revolutionary society was necessary, not only to overthrow the old order, but also to build the new. The noted Russian anarchist, Michael Bakunin (1814–1876), contemporary and adversary of Karl Marx (1818–1883), elaborated and propagated the doctrine of an all-destroying revolution guided and directed by a secret central committee whose members would be unknown to the revolutionary organization as a whole and whose absolute tsar would be Bakunin himself.[29] But it was the work of three young men in their twenties already mentioned that brought together the ideas current at the mid-century and forged a powerful and persuasive doctrine of the role of the revolutionary minority both before and after the revolution—Peter G. Zaichnevsky, Peter N. Tkachev, and Sergei Nechaiev. Each of these men, and particularly Tkachev, made an important contribution to the shaping of the revolutionary theory out of which the Bolshevik patterns of education emerged. Each of them also spent years in prison and exile. Their work will be discussed in relation to the goals, the morals, and the strategy and tactics of the revolutionary movement.

In the autumn of 1861, the year of the liberation of the serfs, the leaders of a group of young revolutionists in Moscow were arrested and sent to prison. Composed largely of Moscow students, this group published illegal books with its own printing press, published revolutionary leaflets addressed to the peasants, the soldiers, and the army officers, infiltrated Sunday schools for the dissemination of their ideas, and made revolutionary speeches calling on the people to seize arms and overthrow the autocracy. The leader of this group was Zaichnevsky, a highly talented youth of only twenty years. While in prison he continued his activities and succeeded in creating a new organization called "The Russian Central Revolutionary Committee." In May, 1862, this committee published

one of the most famous revolutionary appeals of the period to Russian
youth under the name of *Molodaia Rossiia* ("Young Russia"). Here were
set down revolutionary goals which were destined to leave their clear
imprint on Bolshevism. Tkachev, though only eighteen, was an active
member of the committee.

The appeal called for the overthrow of "the present despotic government" and the formation of a "federated Russian republic." It proposed
the socialization of the land under the control of the *mir* and the socialization of factories and stores with managers elected by the people. It
advocated a system of public education for all children, "provision by
society of maintenance grants to the end of the period of instruction,"
and social insurance for "the ailing and the aged." It attacked savagely
the institutions of marriage, family, and church. It demanded, on the one
hand, the "complete emancipation of woman and equality of political
and civic rights with man," and, on the other, the "liquidation of marriage
as a highly immoral condition" and of the family as an obstacle to "the
development of man" and a barrier to the "liquidation of inheritance."
Monasteries and convents had to go, on the grounds that they were "sinks
of iniquity," inhabited by "vagrants, parasites, and idlers" committed to
lives of "drunkenness and dissipation." It followed that "their properties,
as well as the properties of all churches, must be confiscated by the
state." [30]

The moral position of this extreme revolutionary tendency was formulated by Sergei Nechaiev in the *Catechism of a Revolutionist*.[31] Here
undoubtedly is one of the most extraordinary documents in the whole
history of the human struggle. The *Catechism* endeavors to answer all
questions regarding the "revolutionist's attitude toward himself," his
"relations with his comrades in the cause," and his "relations with society." The most fundamental moral conception of the *Catechism,* and
one that pervades the entire document, is stated without equivocation in
Article IV. The revolutionist, according to this instruction, "despises and
hates the present-day code of morals with all its motivations and manifestations. To him whatever aids the revolution is ethical; all that which
hinders it is unethical and criminal." He is advised to be "merciless
toward the state and toward the entire system of privileged educated
classes." He must snuff out "all tender, softening sentiments of kinship,
friendship, love, gratitude and even honor itself" and be guided in all
he does and at all times by the "one cold passion of the revolutionary
cause." Likewise he must never be moved by sentiments of "personal
hatred and revenge" or of "infatuation and exaltation." He must not even
go to the rescue of a comrade in danger unless such action advances the
"revolutionary cause." In his relations with society he may have to pretend
"to be something entirely different from what he is." Through deception

and fraud, he must make use of "brutes in high positions," "liberals of various shades," "doctrinaires" in revolution, and even "empty-headed, stupid, soulless" women. Between truth and falsehood there exists no valid moral distinction. Indeed, truth itself is whatsoever serves the revolutionary cause. Little wonder that this body of ideas was called by other revolutionists at the time "revolutionary Machiavellism." Lenin and the Bolsheviks, however, have espoused and practiced this brand of morality in both domestic and foreign relations.

From the standpoint of the sources of Soviet education the most significant of the three young revolutionists of the third quarter of the nineteenth century was Peter Tkachev—a man whom Michael Karpovich, the historian, has called a "forerunner of Lenin." [32] Perhaps the central idea in Tkachev's conception of revolution in Russia was the principle of "jumps," or, as a physicist today might say, the principle of "indeterminacy." This was strictly an un-Marxian or anti-Marxian idea. Indeed, it was much closer to fascism with its glorification of will. He contended that the course of history is not predestined, that all societies are not compelled by the laws of history to pass through the same stages of development and follow the same road into the future. It is possible, he argued, that Russia, because of special conditions, might "jump" from feudalism into socialism without passing through the stage of capitalism. In an exchange of letters with Friedrich Engels he defended this position on the grounds that the Russian state at the time was feeble and decadent and consequently might be easily overthrown by a resolute and disciplined minority eager to take power in the name of the people. On the other hand, if reforms were introduced and a bourgeois order established, the system would be strengthened and the revolution "postponed, perhaps forever." By reason of her backwardness Russia might be the first country to achieve socialism. Engels charged Tkachev with "hanging in the air."

In the very nature of the case, this achievement would not be possible by the method of reform, of gradualism, education, enlightenment, and liberal toleration. Tkachev poured scorn on the advocates of such methods. "The so-called road of peaceful reform, of peaceful progress," he said, "is one of the most fantastic utopias ever invented by mankind for the purpose of quieting its conscience and lulling its mind to sleep." [33] The appeal of 1862, with which Tkachev was associated, called for a "bloody and merciless revolution"—a revolution which "we do not fear, even though we know that a river of blood will be shed and that innocent victims will perhaps perish. . . . We will not even be frightened if in the overthrow of the contemporary order it will be necessary to shed three times as much blood as was shed by the Jacobins of 1790." [34] In a society divided into two irreconcilable classes, with one exploiting the other without mercy, violence is the only sane course of action.

The revolution, however, could not be achieved by a spontaneous uprising of the people. Tkachev did not share the idealistic, optimistic, and romantic view of the peasant which was common to many revolutionists of the period. "Who," wrote Tkachev, "does not know that a Russian, having resolved to do something, never begins by doing it at once; he first begins to get ready, and he gets ready so long that in the process he forgets what it is that he set out to do." [35] And in another passage he had this to say about the Russian character: "The average man is generally a man without passions. This is especially true of the Russian average man, that is, the Russian people. Centuries of slavery, centuries of oppression have taught him to be patient and silently obedient, have developed in him slavish instincts." [36] The people therefore must be aroused to action by a resolute and determined revolutionary minority. And the struggle itself "can be waged successfully only through centralization, strict discipline, speed, resolution, and unity in action." [37] This is pure Bolshevism.

After the overthrow of the despotism, when the revolution passes from its destructive to its constructive phase, there is even greater need for a "tight organization" of "all sincere revolutionists devoted to their cause"— "a disciplined and hierarchical organization which subjects personal initiative to a general leadership, which gives unity and direction to the activities of all members." [38] In a word it must establish a dictatorship and direct the people in their own interests—interests which they themselves are unable to comprehend. The dictatorship must provide immediately for an elective National Assembly. But the elections must be so conducted that no enemies of the new regime will enter into the assembly. Indeed, all enemies must be destroyed.

The great task of the revolution was to build on the ruins of autocratic and backward Russia an ideal society founded on the principles of brotherhood and equality. This required, first of all, the destruction of "all those institutions which engender inequality, hostility, envy, and competition in the life of the people" and the laying of "the foundations of institutions which engender the opposite qualities in the life of the people." There would follow then the second and long-time task of the revolution, "to reeducate man and change his very nature." [39] For it must be obvious that after the victorious *coup d'état* the people would remain substantially as they had been before; they would still be remote in habit and disposition, in knowledge and loyalty, in mind and heart from the utopian dream of the revolutionary minority. This meant that a tremendous educational task would lie ahead. It meant also that the people could not reeducate themselves in the ways and the spirit of socialism or communism.

All of this Tkachev saw very clearly. And being a realist, he met the issue boldly. The reeducation of the people, the transformation of human nature, was a responsibility of the revolutionary organization. If left to itself the majority "would probably revert to the old ways." The task of education therefore must be entrusted to "people who understand" this great problem and "sincerely strive to solve it, that is, to people who are intellectually and morally developed, that is, to the minority. By virtue of its high intellectual development this minority always has and always must exercise intellectual and moral power over the majority." [40] This is a duty which no true revolutionist could repudiate. Thus Tkachev and his associates, by proposing to "jump" over the capitalistic stage of economic and social development, sought to achieve through the processes of a rigorously controlled education what Marx assumed would be achieved through the processes of historical development. And the Bolsheviks in 1917 found themselves in a situation not radically different from that contemplated by the supporters of *Molodaia Rossiia* in the 1860s. The more one studies the course of Soviet education, the more one is impressed by the parallel.

There is yet another parallel in the realm of thought and character which may be drawn between Tkachev and the Bolsheviks. In the words of the former's sister, "It would have been hard to find a milder, a gentler, a more peace-loving man in his private life. Knowing him intimately, it was hard to believe that this same man could be the merciless critic . . . who dealt so harshly with writers and artists. Even harder was it to expect from him those fierce political theories which he expounded." It seems that when he returned from a prison sentence in the Kronshtadt fortress his faith in the power of education was somewhat shaken. He suggested that "the rejuvenation of Russia would require the extermination of all persons over the age of twenty-five years." Although he later "abandoned this man-killing plan," he continued to maintain that "the general good . . . made necessary the sacrifice of individuals" and that the "majority was always passive, incapable of either understanding or defending its interests." This meant to him that a "conscious, revolutionary, inspired minority had to create the new and better way of life and force the majority to accept the new order." [41] This sketch reminds the student of Soviet affairs of Felix Dzerzhinsky, first head of the dread Cheka, the Bolshevik political police, who, according to legend, was so gentle and so horrified by bloodshed that he could not kill a fly.

VI

One might think that Jacobinism, the doctrine of the seizure of power by a revolutionary elite, would be wholly contrary to the teachings of Karl Marx. Yet the fact is that Lenin, though a professed Marxist, recognized the affinity of Bolshevism with the thought of Tkachev, Zaichnev-

sky, and even Nechaiev. Around the year 1904, when Lenin was in the
process of formulating the basic ideas of Bolshevism, he "read over most
of the old revolutionary literature." According to V. D. Bonch-Bruyevich,
an old Bolshevik and associate of Lenin, the latter said at this time that
Tkachev "was unquestionably closer to our point of view than the
others." [42] He attributed "very great significance to Tkachev whom he
urged everybody to read and study." [43] He also spoke of Nechaiev as
"this titan of revolution, possessing such will power, such enthusiasm." He
said further that this man was "endowed with exceptional organizational
talent, was able to establish everywhere habits of conspiratorial work,
knew how to express his thoughts in such overpowering forms that they
were remembered for a life-time. . . . Nechaiev must be published in
his entirety." [44] It seems too that Lenin came under the influence of the
thought of Zaichnevsky and *Molodaia Rossiia* when he was twenty-one
years of age. Thirteen years later, responding to the charge of Jacobinism
made against himself and his followers, he answered in the spirit of
Zaichnevsky: "Without a Jacobin violence the dictatorship of the proletariat is a word completely void of any meaning." [45]

Following the establishment of the Soviet state, the Institute for the
Study of the History of the Party was founded and the works of these
early revolutionists were collected, published, and discussed. There was
also founded, as an organ of the Institute, a journal called *Proletarskaia
Revolutsia*. In this journal there appeared in 1927 an article entitled
"*Russkiie Yakobintsy*" written by an old Bolshevik, S. Mitskevich. After
reviewing the central ideas of Zaichnevsky and Tkachev and comparing
them with the ideas of the Bolsheviks, he concludes that with the death of
Zaichnevsky in 1896, "Russian Jacobinism died," only "to be resurrected
in a new guise, in the guise of Russian Marxism . . . in Bolshevism." He
then observes that many members of the circle of Zaichnevsky became
Bolsheviks. And "it was the Bolsheviks who proved to be the successors
of the Jacobins for they were able to create a centralized, firmly disciplined party, tightly linked with the working masses." Zaichnevsky and
Tkachev, to be sure, were utopians because they spoke in the name of the
"people" instead of that of the "proletariat." Yet it must be conceded
that in the sixties and seventies the proletariat scarcely existed in Russia.
Consequently, "it is high time that we recall our glorious forerunners."

It should be said in conclusion that for the most part the great Russian
revolutionists of the last half of the nineteenth century generally repudiated the strategy and tactics of Zaichnevsky, Tkachev, and Nechaiev.
The case of Peter Lavrov (1823–1900) may be regarded as illustrative.
In 1874 he appealed to "Russian Social Revolutionary Youth" to reject
without qualification the idea of a self-constituted dictatorship as the instrument for building a new order of life. "History proves and psychology

confirms," he said, "that unlimited power or dictatorship corrupts the very best men, and that even persons of genius, thinking to benefit the people by means of decrees, are unable to do so." And then he added: "Every dictatorship must surround itself with coercive power and blindly obedient tools." He concluded with the maxim: "Falsehood cannot be the means for the dissemination of truth, nor the authoritarian rule of a person the means for the realization of justice." [46] To this attack Tkachev replied by saying that history simply does not prove that "power corrupts man." In fact, there is much evidence to the contrary. Thus, "power did not change by as much as one iota" the moral character, the ideals, and the aspirations of the great leaders of the French Revolution. The history of education under Bolshevism should throw some light on this question.

One final word. In the thought of Tkachev we may see the essential spirit of Soviet education—the employment of all educational institutions and processes for the building of an ideal society and the transformation of human nature under the ever watchful and ruthless direction of a "morally and intellectually developed" revolutionary minority—the Central Committee of the Communist Party of the Soviet Union. While there are conflicting elements in the educational heritage of the Soviet Union, Bolshevism has been driven by its own inner logic to adopt the conception of the role of education expounded in the writings of Peter Tkachev. How long it will take to change the character of the Soviet people in conformity with the demands of Communism is a question which cannot be answered at this time. But the data presented in the present volume suggest that the Bolsheviks may be well on their way toward the goal.

3

THE GOALS OF
SOVIET EDUCATION

The goals of Soviet education are to be found in the Bolshevik conception of history, the nature of the social structure, the controlling purposes of the Party, the cultural heritage from old Russia, and the shifting tides of change among the nations.

There is in orthodox Marxist doctrine a fairly clear conception of the succession of social systems. According to this body of thought, mankind has built and lived under four such systems. The first, communist in essence and preceding the emergence of the institution of private property, was the characteristic and usual form of primitive tribal society. The second was the slaveholding state of antiquity; the third, the manorial or feudal order of the Middle Ages; and the fourth, the system of private capitalism of the advanced countries of the modern period. Each of these systems was superior to its predecessor in its ability to release productive energies and raise the productivity of human labor. Even slavery represented an advance over tribal communism because it cultivated in man labor discipline and steady habits of work. Private capitalism carried mankind a long step forward and during its early stages was a progressive force in history. Its ultimate fate, however, was certain, because of its class character: it would be superseded by a greatly superior system, the system of socialism which would in time evolve without violence into the final and perfect form of human society—a society marked by brotherhood, equality, and abundance where each would work according to his ability and receive according to his needs—communism. This transition from capitalism to socialism would take place, not as a result of human thought, will, and idealism, but in accordance with the laws of history and social development. But socialism would follow capitalism only after the latter had made its full contribution to the growth of the productive energies of the economy.

32

In her economic development Russia lagged far behind the advanced countries of the West. At the time of the Bolshevik seizure of power in 1917, therefore, Russian capitalism must have been in its early and consequently progressive phase. A glance at the "class structure of the population" in 1913, as reported in Soviet statistics, constitutes the best of documentation on this point. It appears that only 16.7 per cent of the population could be classified as workers. But this category included, not only industrial workers, the true proletariat of the Marxian analysis, but also agricultural workers and service workers, "white collar" workers in industry, transport, construction, social-cultural institutions, and the government apparatus. The corresponding figure for the United States in 1940, a highly developed capitalist society, was over 80 per cent. The genuine proletariat at the time of the Bolshevik revolution must have been well under 10 per cent of the population. On the other hand, the peasantry constituted almost 80 per cent.[1] We have noted in the first chapter the low level of industrial production in 1913. And this vast country, approximately three times the size of continental United States, possessed only 35,129 miles of railroads and 30,500 miles of telegraph and telephone lines.[2]

The general cultural level of the people, except for a very small educated class, was correspondingly low in comparison with the West. Not only was gross illiteracy the prevailing condition of the masses, the level of technical and scientific knowledge was also in the preindustrial age. In 1929 the author saw wooden plows in use in the more backward regions, and the most primitive methods of harvesting and threshing grain. He visited "deaf villages" and talked to "dark people"—villages and people completely isolated from the great world outside. The tasks of the revolution were further complicated by the factors of cultural and national diversity. While the Great Russians constituted approximately one-half of the total population, there were at least 180 other "nations, nationalities, and tribes" which had been conquered by the Russians from the early sixteenth century. Some of the peoples living along the western border from Finland to Poland and even the Ukraine were more advanced culturally than the Russians. On the other hand, in the northern reaches of this land from the White Sea to the Bering Straits primitive tribes were still living in the preliterate stage of human culture. The country was also backward in the realm of political affairs. Except for the zemstvos and town councils formed after the liberation of the serfs, and the Duma conceded by Nicholas II at the time of the revolution of 1905, they had had almost no experience in self-government and political freedom. The election of delegates to the Constituent Assembly on November 25, 1917, was the only election approaching the practice of the democracies in the whole history of Russia, either before or after the revolution of 1917. Following the overthrow, or rather the collapse, of

the autocracy in March of that year, the peoples of Russia seemed
to be on the road to the establishment of a constitutional system. The
prospect was violently destroyed by Lenin and his Bolsheviks in November.

II

On coming to power the Bolsheviks inherited this legacy of cultural,
economic, and political backwardness. Yet they were committed to the
building of the ideal commonwealth of their professed Marxian doctrines—a classless society marked by universal brotherhood and equality,
founded on the most advanced technology, and capable of bringing
abundance to all. It would be a society in which the "great promises" of
international revolutionary socialism would be fulfilled: the promise of
the abolition of the exploitation of man by man; the promise of the abolition of the exploitation of one people by another; the promise of the
abolition of the exploitation of woman by man; and the promise of the
abolition of war. These grand commitments demanded an historical
"jump" far greater than the jump into agrarian communism contemplated
by Tkachev almost two generations before. It demanded a jump from
the eighteenth or early nineteenth into the twenty-first century. But the
word "jump" would seem to be scarcely adequate for the characterization of the feat to be performed. The term "flight" would appear to be
more appropriate. Lenin and his associates proposed to fly within a single
generation from backward Russia into utopia and carry the country and
its people with them. It is little wonder that at the time the great majority
of spectators in other lands prophesied a speedy demise of the Soviet
state. After thirty-nine years, though the Bolshevik plane has not reached
the shores of utopia, it has flown a long distance from its starting place.
That Karl Marx, however, would recognize the "First Workers' Republic
in History" as the promised land of socialism would seem quite unlikely.

Though Lenin envisaged utopia, in a sense he was no utopian. He
certainly regarded himself as a realist of the first order and thus distinguished himself from Tkachev and from all who disagreed with him.
He recognized clearly the major obstacles to be surmounted in the fulfillment of his vision, even though he may have greatly underestimated
their strength. He placed his faith in the tightly organized and strongly
disciplined revolutionary association of Russian tradition with power of
decision and direction in the hands of a central committee of professional
revolutionists dedicated to the cause. Such was the Bolshevik wing of
the All-Russian Social Democratic Labor Party which he formed at the
Second Congress of the Party in London in 1903 and which he led to
victory in November, 1917. In 1918 this organization assumed the name
of the All-Union Communist Party of Bolsheviks. In the manner of

Zaichnevsky, Nechaiev, and Tkachev, Lenin regarded his party as the indispensable weapon, not only for the overthrow of the old order, but also for the building of the new.

On seizing power, Lenin proclaimed a "dictatorship of the proletariat," an expression to be found in the writings of Marx. But he gave to the words a special Bolshevik meaning. Marx had foreseen the industrial proletariat at the time of the socialist revolution constituting a majority or a near majority of the total population. His dictatorship, therefore, could only mean the employment of the power of the state by the majority against the small dispossessed class of capitalists. And it was in such terms that Lenin interpreted Marx in his famous brochure entitled *The Teachings of Karl Marx* published in 1914. At the time of the Bolshevik triumph, as we have seen, the Russian proletariat amounted to less than 10 per cent of the total population. Lenin's "dictatorship of the proletariat," however, was not in actuality a dictatorship of even this small fraction of the population, but rather a "dictatorship of the Party" in the name of the industrial workers and poor peasants. He had always been scornful of the ability of the masses to conduct a revolution and establish a system of socialism. In his opinion the most to be expected of even the industrial workers, when proceeding on their own initiative and understanding, was the development of "trade unionism" or "Gomperism"—a development which would foster contentment and postpone his revolution. Without the Party, "the vanguard of the proletariat," the proletariat itself would be helpless. In a pamphlet completed at the time of the seizure of power he stated frankly that, if the Tsar could rule Russia with his 130,000 aristocrats and landlords, the Bolsheviks should be able to do the same with their 240,000 members.

All this means that the founder of Bolshevism, in spite of some words to the contrary in his earlier years, had no faith in or respect for democratic processes and values. In April, 1918, he wrote: "There is absolutely no contradiction in principle between the Soviet (that is, socialist) democracy and the assumption of dictatorial powers by particular individuals." [3] In October of the following year he sent a revealing message to "Italian, French, and German Communists." "Only scoundrels and half-wits," he said, "can think that the proletariat must first win a majority of votes in elections conducted under *bourgeois oppression,* under the *oppression of hired slaves,* and only then seek to win power. This is the height of stupidity and hypocrisy." [4] Regarding the meaning of dictatorship he— to paraphrase the words of the *Communist Manifesto*—"disdained to conceal his views." In the autumn of 1920 he said that "dictatorship . . . means unlimited power resting on force and not on law." [5] The morality of the Party is derived from the ethics of battle under which the enemy must be destroyed at all costs. "We say," wrote Lenin, "that our morality is subjected entirely to the interests of the class struggle of the proletariat. Our morality is derived from the interests of the class struggle of the proletariat." More specifically, "we say that morality is that which serves to destroy the old exploiting society and to unite all toilers around the proletariat which is creating the new Communist society." [6] In the name of this cause one must be prepared "to resort to all kinds of tricks and ruses, to employ illegal measures, secretiveness, and concealment of truth." [7] Even a war, if it "is waged with the object of strengthening and extending socialism, is legitimate and 'holy.' "[8] In all this may be seen the moral precepts of the *Catechism of a Revolutionist,* and more particularly of Article IV: "To him (the revolutionist) whatever aids the triumph of the revolution is ethical; all that which hinders it is unethical and criminal." And these precepts were applied with equal force before and after the seizure of power. They apply today in the Soviet Union and in the entire Communist world. They are Leninism.

The flight to the utopia of socialism and communism would be long and difficult, requiring heavy sacrifices on the part of the people and the ability to sustain a steady course through the vicissitudes of history. Clearly the direction of the flight could not be placed in the hands of the people, because they themselves would have to be transformed before they could enter the Garden of Eden of the future. And they lacked both the moral and intellectual qualities necessary to the performance of the arduous task of creation and construction. Only the Party, commanded by its Central Committee, could be expected to discharge such responsibilities. This tiny body of men and women who had devoted their lives to the study of revolution, who had mastered the laws of transition from capitalism to socialism, who had been tested in the fires of the revolutionary struggle, and who knew the road to the future—they, and they alone, could be entrusted to pilot the revolutionary state safely and surely to its destination. The loyalty of these men and women, of course, could not be doubted, although during the first generation after the revolution practically all of the foremost Party leaders of 1917 who did not die of natural causes were liquidated by the victors in the internal struggle over policy and power.

III

The key to an understanding of the nature of Bolshevism, the course of the Soviet state, and the development of Soviet education is found in the Communist Party of the Soviet Union. Created by Lenin out of the Russian tradition of revolutionary absolutism, it stands today as one of the great political realities of the world—a social invention of far-reaching consequence which has taken root in all countries. From the very beginning of Soviet power it has been responsible for the making of all important decisions involved in the transformation of the old order and the building of the new. Although the founder of Bolshevism would probably have repudiated the harsher features of the dictatorship framed by his successor, the seeds of Stalinism are to be found in the teachings and practices of Leninism. Indeed, they may be found in the following statement made by Lenin during the fateful struggle for power in the summer of 1917: "By educating the party of workers, Marxism educates the vanguard of the proletariat, capable of grasping power and *leading the entire people* to socialism, of directing and organizing the new order, of being the teacher, guide, and leader of all the toiling and exploited masses in the cause of the building of their social life without the bourgeoisie and against the bourgeoisie." [9] This "party of workers," this "vanguard of the proletariat," is the Communist Party.

Kommunist (formerly *Bol'shevik*), the theoretical and political organ of the Central Committee of the Party, puts the matter even more bluntly today. A leading article in the issue of September, 1955, entitled "The Leninist Plan for the Building of Communism in the USSR," states without equivocation: "The unity and might of the Communist Party constitute the decisive condition of the stability of the socialist state and of the successful discharge of its internal and external functions. The Party is the guiding and directing force of the dictatorship of the proletariat, the leader and teacher of the Soviet people." [10] Another authoritative organ of the Party proclaims the basic principle in its most extreme form: "Not one important question of policy or organization is decided in our country without a Party directive." [11] The crucial role of the Party was spelled out to the last letter in a public lecture delivered on October 31, 1947, by P. N. Pospelov, editor of *Pravda* at the time and now Secretary of the Central Committee of the Party. In pamphlet form the lecture is entitled *The Party of Lenin and Stalin—The Leading and Directing Force of Soviet Society.* The Soviet press is filled with exhortations to the people "to rally around the Party and its Central Committee in the building of Communism." The Soviet government is essentially an instrument through which the Party achieves its purposes.

The basic fact to be kept in mind is that the Communist Party of the Soviet Union is not a political party at all in the sense in which the term is employed in free societies. As we have noted earlier, and as we shall have occasion to emphasize later, in both organization and function it is a kind of political army designed to rule the Soviet Union, build a Communist order, and direct the course of a world-wide movement to overthrow the system of "capitalism" everywhere. The military character of the organization was recognized explicitly and truly by Stalin in his report to the Plenum of the Central Committee on March 3, 1937. In discussing the organizational structure of the Party he observed that it contained "3,000 to 4,000 leaders of higher rank" composing the "corps of generals," "30,000 to 40,000 leaders of middle rank" composing the "corps of officers," and "100,000 to 150,000 of lower rank" who might be called "noncommissioned officers." At the time the total membership of the Party, including candidates, was approximately 2,000,000. At the top of the pyramid was the Central Committee of about 125 members, which constituted the Party high command, and at the base approximately 1,800,000 ordinary members of the Party—the common soldiers of the revolution.[12]

Following the violent overthrow of the provisional government and the dispersal of the Constituent Assembly, the Party proceeded in all haste to the consolidation of its rule. Overriding several associated revolutionary factions, it took firmly into its hands all the instruments and symbols of power and authority. It seized the organs of government, disfranchised the "former people," outlawed all rival organizations, · established a monopoly of legality in the realm of political activity, and fashioned a revolutionary state unreservedly committed, in the strict Marxian sense, to the service of the new ruling class. It converted the laws and the courts into instruments of a dictatorship which always acts in the name of the "toiling masses." It created the Red Army "for the protection of the revolution" against both internal and external enemies. And it ensured the loyalty of this army by means of an all-pervasive system of political commissars and Party activists operating in the spirit of "revolutionary vigilance." For the purpose of liquidating opponents and crushing dissent within the territory of its rule, it created the Cheka, the "unsheathed sword of the revolution," a political police reminiscent of the Okhrana of the tsars whose lineage reached back to the Oprichniki of Ivan the Terrible in the sixteenth century. The function of this organization, moreover, was not only to destroy avowed enemies of the regime but also to spread terror throughout the ranks of those social classes which, according to Leninist dogma, were hostile toward socialism. The policy was stated quite unambiguously by M. Latsis, one of the chieftains of the Cheka. "We are not waging war against particular individuals," he advised his lieutenants. "We are exterminating the bourgeoisie as a class. Don't look for evidence to prove that the accused acted by *deed* or *word* against the Soviet power. The first question you should ask him is: To what class he belongs, what is his origin, his training, and his occupation? This should determine the fate of the accused. Herein lies the meaning and the 'essence of the Red Terror.'"[13]

One is reminded of these words from *Molodaia Rossiia* in 1862: "Remember that whoever is not with us is against us, that whoever is against us is our enemy, and that an enemy must be exterminated by all possible means." One is also reminded of the prophecy that "a river of blood will be shed." How many persons were actually exterminated during the first years of the revolution is unknown and probably will remain unknown until the Bolshevik archives are opened to the world. But we do know that, though the Cheka changed its name first to the GPU, then to the OGPU, and later to the NKVD, the MVD, and the MGB, it survives down to this day as the KGB—probably the most numerous and powerful political police in all history. Under the watchful direction of the Party it permeates every important institution and organization of Soviet society.

The extermination of enemies and the silencing of critics, however, constitute only the negative aspect of the "Leninist plan for the building of Communism in the Soviet Union." During the first year and a half of the Bolshevik regime, the Party moved swiftly toward the radical transformation of the economy in the direction of socialism. In a series of decrees, beginning with a decree creating factory committees of workers to participate in the management of industries, practically the entire economy outside agriculture and the handicrafts was socialized. Banking, foreign commerce, domestic trade, transportation and communication, and industrial production were converted into state monopolies and brought under the general direction of the Supreme Council of the National Economy. All land was declared nationalized, and the peasants were encouraged to confiscate and divide the holdings of the landlords. In the realm of distribution, a highly complicated, bureaucratic, and coercive system was established. It is not surprising, therefore, that under the pressures of revolution, civil war, and intervention, of ignorance and self-interest, the entire economic system was on the verge of collapse by 1921. Thus ended the so-called period of War or Military Communism. There collapsed also the romantic notion that the mere socialization of the means of production would lead swiftly and inevitably to a great release of productive energy on the part of the worker. At any rate, in March, 1921, the Party retreated somewhat in the direction of capitalistic practices and motivations under the so-called New Economic Policy. But with the launching of the First Five-Year Plan in the autumn of 1928 the Party moved over to the offensive with great power. This "plan of great works," as it was called, was conceived in terms of the complete socialization of industry, trade, and finance, the collectivization of agriculture, and the industrialization of the economy. By 1936, according to the "Great Stalinist Constitution" adopted in December of that year, the Soviet Union had become "a socialist state of workers and peasants" whose guiding principle is: "From each according to his ability, to each according to his work." There still remained the goal of building Communism and the fulfillment of the ancient vision of a society in which the guiding principle would be: "From each according to his ability, to each according to his needs." The current Soviet dogma proclaims that this happy condition is just around the corner. The Party will not have achieved its purpose, and therefore cannot relinquish its tight control over the course of Soviet society, until this condition is realized and firmly established.

The fact should be emphasized that in the swift transformation of the Soviet economy the Party was guided, not by the expressed will of the people at any time, but by its own long-term objectives. In fact, certain phases of the transformation encountered determined and desperate popular resistance. In the case of the forced collectivization of agriculture during the First Five-Year Plan and under the slogan of "the liquidation of the kulaks [the more well-to-do peasants] as a class," Soviet agriculture was all but wrecked. Rather than enter the collective farms, millions of peasants refused to plant their crops and slaughtered their animals. The result was the worst famine in Russian history in 1931 and 1932 and the loss of approximately one-half of the country's livestock. It has been estimated that millions of peasants died of starvation and perhaps four or five million more were deported to labor camps in Siberia and the Far North. And agriculture remains to this day the weakest sector of the Soviet economy. In the realm of industrial production the record is truly impressive. By 1936 the Soviet Union claimed to have moved from fifth to second place among the nations. But this spectacular advance and a similar advance in the years following World War II were not marked by a corresponding improvement in the living standards of the people. The emphasis throughout was placed on the development of the heavy and strategic industries. The production of consumers' goods was neglected and the masses of the people were held near the margin of subsistence. History records no more striking instance of the triumph of political over economic power. Though quite contrary to the teachings of Marx which the Bolsheviks propagate throughout the world, the achievement undoubtedly constitutes a powerful appeal to ambitious individuals and minorities in the technically underdeveloped countries of the world. Khrushchev at the Twentieth Congress in February, 1956, reaffirmed this basic principle of Stalinism.

This suggests a second major positive task which the Bolsheviks assumed on coming to power. Their precursors in the Russian revolutionary tradition, men like Zaichnevsky and Tkachev, developed their conceptions and programs in terms of Russia. Lenin and his followers down to the present moment have worn the mantle of international revolutionary socialism. They see the present epoch as the epoch of the world revolution in the Marxian sense, a revolution which will ultimately spread from Russia to all countries and carry their system of society, ideology, and morals throughout the world. Following the seizure of power in

Russia they endeavored to capture the Second or Socialist International, but, failing in this, they launched in March, 1919, the Third or Communist International. Although this organization was avowedly dissolved in May, 1943, the Communist movement in all countries, with the exception of Yugoslavia and possibly of China, remains under the direction of Moscow; and the swift advance of Communism beyond Soviet borders since 1939 is without precedent in the history of political and religious faiths. The First Five-Year Plan was launched under the slogan of "building socialism in one country," but the Bolsheviks have never given any sign that they have abandoned their apocalyptic vision of world triumph. Certainly, Khrushchev gave no such sign at the Twentieth Congress.

Marxian and Communist literature, since the publication of the *Communist Manifesto* in 1848, has given uninterrupted expression to this vision. One of the clearest statements of the Bolshevik version of the ultimate triumph of Communism was made by Stalin in an address on "The International Situation" at the Fourteenth Conference of the Russian Communist Party in 1925, before he had become a "megalomaniac." The essence of the statement follows:

> Lenin said that after the victory of the proletariat in our country a new epoch began, the epoch of the world revolution, an epoch marked by conflicts and wars, by attacks and counter-attacks, by victories and defeats, an epoch leading to the victory of the proletariat in the principal countries of capitalism. . . . The epoch of the world revolution is a new stage of the revolution, a whole strategic period embracing many years, and perhaps even decades. In the course of this period there may be and there must be ebbs and flows in the revolutionary tide.

Conceding that "the world revolutionary movement was then [1925] in an ebb of the revolutionary tide," he was certain that this ebb "will be followed by a flow which may end in the victory of the proletariat." But conceding again that "it may not end in victory" and that "it may be followed by a new ebb," he is also certain that the new ebb "in turn will be followed by a new flow in the revolutionary tide." [14]

It is of course understood that when Stalin used the word "proletariat" he meant the "vanguard of the proletariat"—the Communist Party. This interpretation has been made explicit over and over again in the writings of Lenin and in the official language of Bolshevism. Moreover, it is given the overtones of Great Russian nationalism and even messianism in an important article appearing in the September 15, 1948, issue of *Bol'shevik* which contains these lines:

> The assertion that every country travels toward socialism along its own and entirely original path, and that there are as many paths as there are countries is incorrect. To speak thus is to deny the international significance

of the experience of Bolshevism. The general laws of transition from capitalism to socialism, revealed by Marx and Engels, tested, applied, and developed by Lenin and Stalin on the basis of the experience of the Bolshevik Party and the Soviet state, are obligatory for all countries. . . . The great historic experience of the Bolshevik Party is a guide for the action of Communists and toilers of all countries.[15]

In the Joint Soviet-Yugoslav Declaration signed by Bulganin and Tito in Belgrade on June 22, 1955, this doctrine was apparently softened somewhat. Among other things, the declaration stated that "questions of internal organization . . . are solely the concern of the individual countries."[16] And at the Twentieth Congress of the Party Khrushchev endorsed, wittingly or unwittingly, the position taken by Marx in 1872 that in some countries "the workers may hope to secure their ends by peaceful means." Yet, more than two years after Stalin's death, the October, 1955, issue of *Kommunist* declared that "the Leninist theory of the socialist revolution is the most important component of the Marxist-Leninist science." This theory, "formed in a ferocious struggle against Russian and international opportunism, and tested by the experience of three Russian revolutions, by the experience of Communist construction in the USSR, and by the revolutionary transformation in the countries of peoples' democracy in Europe and Asia, has become the international banner of Communist and workers' parties in all lands." This theory "serves as a mighty weapon in the revolutionary transformation of the world which is now being successfully achieved in the camp of socialism and democracy and toward which all contemporary mankind is irresistibly moving."[17] Only the more gullible leaders of the free world will assume in the absence of deeds that the struggle will now and in the future take on the character of a peaceful and friendly competition. The fact should not be forgotten that the Central Committee, as it repudiates Stalin, places Lenin and all his works on a still higher pedestal. The "cult of personality" survives.

A third major task assumed by the Bolsheviks was the propagation of an all-embracing philosophy which has come to be called "Marxism-Leninism" or the "science of the sciences." This philosophy, originally formulated by Marx and Engels and later elaborated, adapted, and altered by Lenin, was deliberately forged as an intellectual weapon for the undermining and the overthrow of the social system of capitalism. It embraces an outlook on the universe, a theory of the nature of man, an interpretation of history, a conception of the state, an analysis of capitalist society, a method of revolutionary action, and a view of the destiny of man. This entire body of doctrine has assumed the authority of religion with its three or four (?) great prophets and its corpus of sacred scripture. The most fundamental philosophical position, from which all else is presumed to flow, is that of dialectical materialism—the outlook on the universe.

The Bolsheviks reject the ancient dualism of mind and body, of spirit and matter, of God and nature. They also reject every system of thought that seeks to explain the realm of nature in terms of the creative activity of some outside spiritual force or power, whether it be personal deity or abstract idea. To them matter is the foundation and source of all existence, and the external world rather than the data of individual consciousness is the fundamental reality. They hold that all phenomena are manifestations of one basic substance in process and that both life and mind are but functions of certain delicate and complex forms of matter. The difference between the loftiest and the lowliest orders of existence is to be traced to differences in the organization of matter: there is but one sphere of being. There is no God, no supernatural realm, no world of pure spirit. In the words of Engels, "Matter is not a product of mind, but mind itself is only the highest product of matter."

The practical significance of this philosophical position is clear. Since the early Marxists and their Bolshevik successors were committed to the "forcible overthrow of all existing social conditions," and since religion with its supernatural conceptions and sanctions is both a central component and a powerful support of the traditional social system, religious outlooks and institutions had to be destroyed. Such a view was particularly applicable to old Russia where the head of the state was also the head of the Church, where the word "holy" was traditionally coupled with name of country, and where the people were described as "God-seeking people." Following Marx, as well as Tkachev and other Russian revolutionists, Lenin called religion "the opium of the people . . . a kind of spiritual brandy in which the slaves of capital drown their human form and their claims to any worthy human life." [18] In another oft-quoted passage Lenin described religion as "one of the forms of spiritual oppression, lying everywhere on the masses of the people." To the poor and exploited worker "religion teaches passivity and patience in earthly life, consoling him with the hope of heavenly reward." To Lenin religion was a body of superstitions cunningly devised by the exploiters to hold the exploited in perpetual bondage.

On coming to power, therefore, the Bolsheviks proceeded to attack religion in all of its manifestations, whether Orthodox, Roman Catholic, Protestant, Islamic, Judaic, or some other. They withdrew state aid from the Church, nationalized Church property, disfranchised clergymen of all denominations, eliminated religious teaching in the schools, and prohibited by law the giving of religious instruction to children under eighteen in groups of more than three. In the struggle that ensued between the revolutionary state and the Church, priests and bishops felt the full weight of the Red Terror, art treasures of the Church were requisitioned for secular purposes, and cultural relations between the clergy and the people were severely circumscribed. Under direct or indirect pressure from the state many churches, monasteries, synagogues, and mosques were closed and converted into clubs, schools, nurseries, libraries, and even antireligious museums. On the other side, all the agencies of education and propaganda were directed toward the inculcation of a "scientific-atheistic" outlook. And a special organization, the Society of the Godless, was launched for the purpose of providing leadership in the country-wide antireligious campaign.[19] Although the emphasis has shifted and the methods have changed from time to time, the Bolsheviks on the whole have followed a consistent course down to the present time. That course is indicated, somewhat equivocally, by Article 124 of the 1936 constitution which reads as follows: "In order to ensure to citizens freedom of conscience, the church in the USSR is separated from the state, and the school from the church. Freedom of religious worship and freedom of antireligious propaganda are recognized for all citizens." The point to be noted here is that freedom of *religious* propaganda is not guaranteed by the constitution.

IV

The great goals and controlling purposes of Soviet education are implicit in the foregoing central tasks of the revolution and in the Leninist plan for the building of Communism in backward Russia. Yet the undertaking itself is so stupendous that it almost passes the understanding of anyone who thinks out of the educational practices and conceptions of any other society in history. The early Bolshevik leaders certainly did not grasp fully the sweep, the complexities, and the difficulties of the enterprise on which they had embarked. They proposed by an act of will on the part of a closely organized and disciplined body of professional revolutionists to direct the course of social development and make a gigantic leap into the future. After destroying their enemies and silencing all opposition they could issue decrees and devise plans and programs for the building of the new society. But after the decision of the physical struggle the people for the most part remained unchanged, possessing the same qualities of hand, mind, and heart as before. But these people had to be prepared to participate in the building of Communism and eventually to live in and support a Communist order. Here was the all-embracing educational task, even as Tkachev and his friends had foreseen in the sixties and seventies of the preceding century.

In 1927 Albert P. Pinkevich, a leading Soviet educator, told the writer that the over-all task of Soviet education was to "change the character of the Russian people." At the time this seemed to be nonsense, because "everyone knows" that the influence of organized education can never match the influence of the unorganized processes of family, community, industry, and life. Today, after the passing of a generation, such a judgment requires critical reexamination. Certainly the Bolsheviks, like their predecessors in the Russian tradition of revolution by a small organized and militant minority, have placed unsurpassed faith in the power of education, though not in an education dedicated primarily to the general enlightenment of the people. Their faith has rested rather on the conception of an education closely controlled by themselves and directed toward the fashioning of man in their own preconceived image. Russian revolutionists always talked in romantic tones about "the people of the future," people who would grow more or less spontaneously after the destruction of the existing oppressive and tyrannical order. And so, since the 1920s, the Bolsheviks have talked endlessly about the "new man" and the "new people," and in these later years about "the New Soviet Man." But this new human creature is emerging, not spontaneously, but rather out of a rigorous and comprehensive process of nurture, tuition, and mind control.

In the making of the New Soviet Man the first task of education is the eradication from the consciousness of the people of all traces of capitalist, neutralist, and anti-Bolshevik mentality. This applies particularly to attitudes toward labor, property, religion, individualism, social class, and the Party. On the positive side, education must dedicate itself to the development of the Communist mentality in these realms. And this means unqualified indoctrination in the teachings of Marx, Engels, and Lenin regarding the nature of the universe, the laws of social development, the transition from capitalism to socialism, the Great October Revolution, the policies of the Communist Party, the oppression of labor in capitalist countries, the freedom and plenty of the Soviet peoples, and the ultimate triumph of Communism in the world. The point is well made in the following quotation: "The Soviet school does not prepare merely educated people. Resting on the facts and deductions of progressive science, it must instill in the consciousness of the younger generation the ideology of Communism, mold pupils in the Marxist-Leninist world outlook, and nurture them in the spirit of Soviet patriotism and Bolshevik ideals." [20]

This mandate requires unremitting emphasis on what is called "Communist morality." And one of the most basic moral traits of the New Soviet Man is loyalty to the Party and its Central Committee—a loyalty so deep and unswerving that the individual will follow the Party line even when it reverses itself completely and declares something to be true today that was declared false yesterday, or vice versa. The development of such loyalty is undoubtedly one of the most difficult and crucial tasks of Soviet education. How well it has been achieved is a question that can scarcely be answered with confidence at the present time. Yet the stability and perdurance of the system require that, when the Party issues a decree in the name of the people, they actually believe their interests are being protected and advanced. The true Bolshevik can entertain no doubts in this realm. The repudiation of Stalin is almost the ultimate test of the program of education in Communist morality.

A coordinate task of education in the making of the New Soviet Man lies in the realm of the general cultural level of the people. The fact must be kept clearly in mind that the Bolsheviks committed themselves to the building of a modern industrial state on the foundations of the severe cultural backwardness of old Russia. Lenin was keenly aware of the dilemma. At the Third All-Russian Congress of the Young Communist League he emphasized the necessity of acquiring "knowledge of the culture created in the entire development of mankind" and stated that "one can become a Communist only by enriching one's mind with knowledge of all these riches which mankind has developed." [21] This knowledge, of course, must always be placed in the frame of Marxism-Leninism. Very special attention is devoted to that part of the human heitage which embraces practical knowledge, technology, science, and mathematics— the fruits of man's effort to understand and control the forces of nature. The magnitude of the task confronting Soviet education was described graphically by Stalin at a Workers' Conference in February, 1931. "The history of old Russia consisted, incidentally," he said, "in her being continually beaten for her backwardness." He then supplied the documentation: "She was beaten by the Mongol khans. She was beaten by the Turkish beys. She was beaten by the Swedish feudal lords. She was beaten by the Polish-Lithuanian nobles. She was beaten by the Anglo-French capitalists. She was beaten by the Japanese barons." And she was beaten "because of her backwardness: because of her military backwardness, because of her cultural backwardness, because of her political backwardness, because of her industrial backwardness, because of her agricultural backwardness." Stalin warned his listeners that "we are lagging 50–100 years behind the advanced countries," that "we must run this distance in ten years," and that "we will do this, or we will be crushed." He supported his position with the famous statement from Lenin: "We either overtake and surpass the advanced capitalist countries, or we perish." [22] Such was one of the great tasks assigned to Soviet educational institutions.

The use of education in the process of transforming a society and a people makes the whole educational undertaking a matter of deepest concern to the Party. Without it the achievement of the avowed purposes of the revolution would be impossible. In fact, it makes of education an indispensable political weapon. Applying their version of the historical materialism of Marx and Engels and influenced by the entire cultural heritage from old Russia, the Bolsheviks subscribed unreservedly to the dogma that thoughout history organized education has been the handmaiden of politics, that the very idea of the school standing outside of politics is, in the words of Lenin, "a lie and an hypocrisy," that since the dissolution of primitive tribal society education has always been the servant of the ruling class, that this was the condition in the slaveholding states of antiquity and in the feudal order of the Middle Ages, and that it is the condition in contemporary capitalist society everywhere, regardless of differences in political forms and ideologies. The true Bolshevik scoffs at the very idea of "freedom in education" in any "bourgeois" state. Applying this dogma on coming to power, the Bolsheviks moved to convert all educational agencies into an instrument wholly and militantly committed to their cause.

The way in which education is conceived in the Soviet Union was outlined with utter clarity by Lenin in a passage which is more widely quoted today than when he was alive. "In the field of people's education," he wrote, "the Communist Party sets itself the aim of concluding the task begun by the October Revolution of 1917 of converting the school from a weapon for the class domination of the bourgeoisie into a weapon for the destruction of this domination, as well as for the complete destruction of the division of society into classes. The school must become a weapon of the dictatorship of the proletariat." It must become "not only the conductor of the principles of Communism in general, but also the conductor of the ideological, organizational, and educational influence of the proletariat on the proletarian and semi-proletarian strata of the toiling masses for the purpose of preparing a generation capable of finally establishing Communism." [23] Stalin, as was his habit, put the matter even more bluntly in a conversation with H. G. Wells in July, 1934. "Education is a weapon," he said, "whose effect depends on who holds it in his hands and who is struck with it." [24] This means that the teacher is regarded as a soldier in the great battle for the ultimate victory of Communism at home and abroad. In fact, Andrei Zhdanov told the assembled literary writers on August 21, 1946, that "all of our ideological workers are standing today in the advanced line of fire." [25] For any one of these workers, including the teacher, to refuse to use his weapon, whether it be voice, pen, or textbook, is to betray the Soviet Motherland. He has no more right to freedom of action or conscience than a soldier on the battlefield. To be sure, the degree with which this principle is applied has varied from time to time. Strangely enough, the "ideological worker" enjoyed more freedom during the early years of Bolshevik rule than he has enjoyed in any subsequent period.

In order that the educational program might operate with maximum effectiveness in the making of the New Soviet Man, it was necessary to protect the people, both young and old, from all competing, hostile, or alien influences. The development of an appropriate system of controls proceeded more or less gradually from the revolution down to the end of the 1930s. At the very beginning the great object was to isolate or silence all who held anti-Bolshevik views or cherished memories from the past. Efforts were undertaken to weaken the family and break the hold of parents on their children. Yet, in those first years before Stalin had overcome all his rivals, differences in ideas and policies among the recognized Bolshevik leaders were matters of public knowledge and comment. But, in the course of time, a fairly ideal system was established. In the realm of contact with the outside world Stalin and his associates established a pattern for preventing the importation of dangerous ideas surpassing in scope and efficiency that of Nicholas I. No Soviet citizen is permitted to travel abroad without being subjected to the most thorough inquisition and preparation, and then only as a member of a group in which he will find himself under close surveillance. And visitors to the Soviet Union from foreign lands find their movements carefully restricted by Soviet law and managed by the Soviet bureau of travel, Intourist. The same principle applies to the realm of person-to-person communication and in the sphere of newspapers, periodicals, books, and radio. And in 1932 the Soviet state adopted the system of internal passports for the purpose of controlling the movements of Soviet citizens within the country—a system regarded by Russian revolutionists, including Lenin, as one of the most oppressive features of the imperial regime. Six years later "labor books" were introduced for all industrial, cooperative, and government employees. The "labor book" is a device for providing a continuous and permanent record of the employment of each individual worker, with particular reference to his merits and demerits. Without it he cannot get a job. Under such a regime it is possible to propagate two myths—one about the Soviet Union itself and the other about the "countries of capitalism." The nature of these myths will be revealed in later chapters. Whether the post-Stalin era will see any fundamental and lasting changes in the system of controls remains to be demonstrated. Only the first feeble steps have been taken in this direction.

In the plan for the development of the New Soviet Man, for the development of the "people of the future," the question of rewards and punishments has not been overlooked. In fact, the most careful attention has been given to the matter of motivation in all of its aspects. The individual who violates the Party line or a directive of the Central Committee, whether he be a factory worker, a primary teacher, a manager of industry, a great scientist, a world-famous musical composer, or even a powerful Party leader, is almost certain to receive public censure. It may be merely a notice in a local paper, or it may be, if the individual is of sufficient stature or influence, dishonorable mention in a decree of the Central Committee. Every Soviet citizen knows that in the latter case, behind the decree stands the absolute power of the Soviet state. And the individual attacked knows that he can save himself only by the ordeal of public confession of his errors. But even after confessing his guilt, he knows that he may be demoted and shorn of his honors, that he must then begin the arduous climb back to status and acceptance by deeds which demonstrate that he has taken the criticism to heart and become a "new man." For those who fail at any point along this road the gates to the forced-labor camp loom in the distance, gates which in the course of the years have swallowed millions and millions of Soviet dissenters and alleged dissenters, among whom he is almost certain to have acquaintances, friends, or relatives. They know that they are being watched day and night by the sleepless eyes of the political and security police numbering hundreds of thousands of members. It is a matter of small wonder, therefore, that on all important questions of ideology and politics there is practically complete public unanimity throughout the Soviet Union.

But there are rewards as well as punishments in this far-flung system of mind control. For the individual of talent and industry who conforms with unabashed enthusiasm the doors to an earthly paradise lie open. Public praise is given as freely and extravagantly as public censure. Anyone receiving the approval of the Party authorities will be showered with applause from every part of the cultural apparatus. He will be presented to the people as the perfect example of the New Soviet Man, as a living demonstration of the superiority of "socialism" over "capitalism," as a true representative of "all progressive mankind." Accounts of his "grandiose achievements" will appear in the press and over the radio. His picture will grace the pages of *Pravda* and may even be immortalized in the common calendar.

The darling of the Party may be "elected" to the Supreme Soviet and thus be accorded both high recognition and generous remuneration, without being expected to bear the heavy responsibility of framing the laws. He may be promoted to some important post in his profession and receive material emoluments which equal the financial rewards of the most favored ones in a "class society" and which were scarcely contemplated in the philosophy of Marx or Lenin. Finally, he may be awarded one of the highly coveted "prizes," or even the "Order of Lenin" or the "Order of Suvorov." Incidentally, the Soviet Union has evolved the most comprehensive system of honorifics to be found in any society of history. There is a gradation of awards of honor, with tangible perquisites, in practically every sphere of approved activity, from coal mining to political leadership, from teaching to mastery of the curriculum, from factory work to military achievement, from inventing a gadget to composing an opera, from managing a railroad to making a scientific discovery, from breeding cattle to bearing children. And material compensation is "scientifically" adjusted to the productivity of the worker in practically every branch of the Soviet economy. It must not be forgotten that under the rule of the Bolshevik dictatorship and in consonance with the Party line, rewards, as well as punishments, are supposed to fit the deed.

There is yet another positive side to the Soviet system for fashioning the New Soviet Man which should not be overlooked. The Bolsheviks, as we have noted, appropriated the apocalyptic vision of the future of mankind developed by the Marxian socialists in the nineteenth century. The appeal of this vision is expressed in the following words of August Bebel, stalwart leader of German socialism:

> And if, in the course of this great battle for the emancipation of the human race, we should fall, those now in the rear will step forward; and we shall fall with the consciousness of having done our duty as human beings, and with the conviction that the goal will be reached, however the powers hostile to humanity may struggle or strain in resistance. Ours is the world despite all.

Everything undertaken in the Soviet Union is justified by the Bolshevik version of this apocalypse—a vision of the swift coming of a domestic and world order which will surpass immeasurably in plenty, justice, fraternity, and beauty all that has gone before in human history—a vision of the coming of Communism under the consecrated leadership and direction of Russia and the Bolshevik Party. It is this apocalyptic vision that rationalizes the privations, the suppressions, and the cruelties of the regime and inspires the devotion of millions in the Soviet Union and throughout the world.

Within the framework of this comprehensive and complicated system of social controls and incentives, the positive educational task of making the New Soviet Man is carried on. And in order that the desired end be achieved, it is obviously necessary that all of the agencies and processes of education be coordinated and directed by a single authority. And that authority can only be the small body of professional revolutionists, the Central Committee of the Communist Party. Regardless of the forms of administration, which recognize the organs of the Soviet government and the political divisions and subdivisions of the country, actual control of this vast system of educational institutions rests in all crucial matters squarely in the hands of this committee. Neither the citizens nor the ordinary Party members take part in the process of decision making, unless they are invited to do so. Teachers and educators as such, moreover, are essentially technicians who translate into practice the general and specific directives formulated by the Party leadership. This does not mean that they may not on occasion influence that leadership. But when they do, they must take care lest they overstep the shifting boundaries imposed by the monolithic nature of the Soviet state. The history of Soviet education is strewn with the wrecked lives of teachers and distinguished educators who for one reason or another found themselves convicted or suspected of espousing "counterrevolutionary" doctrines or of failing to follow with visible enthusiasm changes in the Party line. A well-known professor may have his doctor's degree revoked because the position taken in his dissertation years before is declared mistaken by the Central Committee. It is not surprising, therefore, that the author of a textbook in educational psychology or modern history may confine his citations of authority to the writings of Marx, Engels, Lenin, and—Stalin or some Khrushchev. The justification of this control is found in the assertion made in the official textbook on the theory and practice of education that the Party is composed of "our best people." Perhaps the inference may be drawn that the members of the Central Committee are the "very best of our best people." And so we are back to the dictum of Tkachev that the people who are "intellectually and morally developed" should "have intellectual and moral power over the majority."

All this is regarded today as an integral part of the "Leninist plan for the building of Communism in the USSR." This plan embraces, along with "political, military, and economic" features, the organization of a cultural revolution—a revolution "directed toward the repression of the ideological resistance of the capitalists and toward the socialist reeducation of society." [26] The basic elements of this plan, designed to reach all categories of the population, will be reported in the chapters to follow. Special attention will be devoted to the general, political, and moral education of the younger generation, the transformation of the intellectual class, the training of specialists, the political education of the people, the reeducation of the offender, the political education of the soldier, and the education of the political elite. The Central Committee has neither overlooked nor neglected any important segment of the population. All must march together as a "friendly united family toward the radiant summits of Communism."

THE GENERAL EDUCATION
OF THE YOUNGER GENERATION

The education of the younger generation must be a matter of deep concern to any movement that aspires to possess the future. This is true for the simple reason that the younger generation of today will be the older generation of tomorrow. Consequently, the leaders of a successful revolution must give close attention to the rearing of children and youth in the ideas and values, the purposes and loyalties, of the new order. The more radical the revolution, the more necessary the task of education becomes. And the Bolshevik revolution, as we know, was very radical indeed, contemplating the transformation of both man and society.

But there is another and more fundamental reason for concentrating on the education of the young. The old are already formed, and to change them is difficult, if not impossible. A. V. Lunacharsky, the first Commissar of Education of the Russian Republic, was wont to emphasize this point. Paraphrasing and expanding an old Russian proverb, he put the case in these words: "We can mold a child of 5–6 years into anything we wish; at the age of 8–9 we have to bend him; at the age of 16–17 we must break him; and thereafter, one may well say, 'only the grave can correct a hunchback.'" [1] But while the Bolsheviks may have shared these sentiments, they refused to march down the road suggested by Tkachev in one of his wilder moments and proceed to exterminate all persons of both sexes over twenty-five years of age. In fact, they directed enormous energies and resources to the education and the reeducation of the older generation. This must be said, even though they did not hesitate to employ the most extreme measures of coercion against great numbers, even up to and including physical liquidation.

At the same time, steps were taken to weaken the hold of parents and elders on children and youth. Deep in Marxian ideology is the doctrine that the family is a "bourgeois" institution, conservative and even reactionary in its influence. In the early years of Soviet power and down to the middle thirties, marriage was merely a matter of registration at the matrimonial bureau. Some of the more "progressive" young people even regarded this as "bourgeois" and gave evidence of their emancipation from the past by simply living together as man and wife without ceremony of any kind. A marriage contract could be dissolved by either party through a simple declaration before the bureau, and the divorced person might be notified of the fact by postcard. While this weakening of the marriage bond was officially justified in terms of the principle of equality of the sexes and the liberation of woman from slavery, it undoubtedly lent support to the theory that children should be regarded as wards of the state and educated from the earliest years in nurseries, crèches, and kindergartens. Also the revolutionary authorities gave great attention to the organization of activities outside the home for children and youth. Certainly a systematic and wide-reaching effort was made to capture their loyalties. In the summer of 1929 the author approached a group of twelve-year-old children playing on a street in Moscow and put to them the question: "Should children obey their parents?" Regarding the question as entirely proper, the children discussed it among themselves and arrived at the conclusion that they should obey if the parents were right, but certainly not if they were wrong. And in the Soviet Union it is the Party that decides what is right and what is wrong.

II

As early as 1903 the Russian Social Democratic Labor Party, of which the Bolsheviks constituted one of the two leading factions, outlined a comprehensive program for the education of the young. In May, 1917, Lenin formulated and published a new program. But it was the program adopted at the Eighth Congress of the Russian Communist Party in March, 1919, that laid the foundation of the Soviet system of people's education. This program outlined the controlling purposes and the general structure of the system.

The role of education in the Bolshevik state is made entirely explicit. The Party proposes to "convert the school from a weapon of the class domination of the bourgeoisie into a weapon for the complete liquidation of the division of society into classes, into a weapon for the Communist rebirth of society." During the "period of preparing the conditions essential to the complete realization of Communism" the school devotes itself to the "education of a generation capable of finally establishing Communism." The first task is the "introduction of free, compulsory general and polytechnical . . . education for all children of both sexes up to the

age of seventeen." By "polytechnical" education is meant the acquainting
of the young "in both theory and practice with all of the chief branches
of production." The program also calls for the "creation of pre-school
institutions, nurseries, kindergartens, hearths, etc., for the purpose of
improving social nurture and emancipating women." The school is to be
called the "unified labor school" and is to be marked by "instruction in
the native tongue, coeducation of the two sexes, and unconditioned secular control, that is, free from every kind of religious influence." It is to
be a school which maintains "intimate relations between instruction and
socially productive labor" and "prepares fully developed members of a
Communist society." And "food, clothing, shoes, and instructional materials are to be furnished to all pupils at the expense of the state." This
ambitious program obviously calls for "the preparation of a new staff of
teachers imbued with the ideas of Communism."

The program provides further for the development of educational institutions for older people. There is to be a "broad development of vocational and professional training linked with general polytechnical knowledge for persons over seventeen years of age." Access to the higher
schools is to be extended to "all who wish to learn, and first of all to
workers"; opportunities to teach in these schools are to be open to "all
those capable of teaching"; "all artificial barriers between the fresh scholarly forces and the established faculty" are to be "eliminated"; and by
means of "material provision for students proletarians and peasants will
be given opportunity in actuality to take advantage of the higher school."
The program also calls for the "most generous government assistance for
the self-education and self-development of workers and peasants" through
the "creation of a network of institutions for out-of-school education:
libraries, schools for adults, people's homes and universities, courses, lectures, studios, moving pictures, etc." All "toilers" are to be given access
to those "art treasures which were created by the exploitation of their
labor and which heretofore have been at the exclusive disposal of the
exploiters." The statement closes with a call for the "development of the
widest propaganda of Communist ideas through the utilization of the
apparatus and the resources of state power." [2]

This entire pronouncement is clearly derived from the Marxian ideology
and the Marxian conception of education. The repeated reference to
"polytechnical" education and to the linking of instruction with productive labor obviously come from this source. At the same time, in the
comprehensive effort to reach the people, one may see in it the influence
of the great educational "awakening" of the second half of the nineteenth
century. Also one need not look far to see the stamp of Peter Tkachev
and the circle of *Molodaia Rossiia*. But, be all this as it may, the program
announced in 1919 gives in broad outline the characteristic features of

Soviet education which, with changing emphasis, method, and content, have prevailed down to the present. Here may be found the general structure of the system of people's schools, the vast scope of the total educational undertaking, and the conception of education as a political weapon. Here too are the patterns of monolithic control by the Party and the direction of all the agencies and processes of education toward the building of a "Communist society." To be sure, as we shall note later, some of the more utopian goals, such as material provision for all pupils, have been abandoned, and others, such as organizing instruction around productive labor, have been modified or repudiated. Moreover, although the Stalin epoch was marked by a strengthening of the harsher features of the program and although it makes no mention of the Party schools, the military schools, and institutions for training foreign Communist leaders, it remains an authentic Soviet document.

Central in this program is the system of *people's* schools which in general structure follows the traditional pattern of the Western world. Perhaps one might add that it combines certain features of the American and the German system. Imperial Russia had always been profoundly influenced by the latter. From the former the Bolsheviks took the "educational ladder" and made it universal through the assumption of state control of practically all educational institutions. At the base of the ladder, as provided in the program of 1919, are the nursery school, the crèche, and the kindergarten which, however, have never served more than a small fraction of the children of appropriate age. Above these preschool institutions is the basic agency for providing the general education of the younger generation—the complete middle school. Beginning its career as a nine-year school, it evolved into a ten-year school in the early thirties, enrolling children from seven to seventeen years of age. This institution is composed of three units—a four-year primary school, a three-year junior secondary school, and a three-year senior secondary school. In some rural communities the primary school probably still stands alone, though not according to official pronouncements. In some other communities the primary school and the junior secondary school are combined to form the incomplete middle school. In the larger communities the ten-year or complete middle school is the prevailing pattern. Above this institution, in conformity with German practice, are the higher schools with programs embracing from four to six years and with provision for graduate work leading to the doctorate of science. Altogether there are almost 900 higher schools of all types, of which 33 are classified as universities and the remainder as technical or scientific institutes. The Soviet system includes no college of liberal arts and all the faculties in the higher schools, including the universities, prepare students for professional careers. Branching out from this central stem of the Soviet system of people's schools at different levels is a great variety of schools for training Soviet youth for occupations of lower and middle qualification.

In its original conception the system of people's schools was to be guided by four basic principles. First of all was the principle of classlessness. The school was to be a mighty weapon in building a society without social classes. Everything in the curriculum which suggested differences in status was to be eliminated. The second principle was that of equality of the sexes. Not only would boys and girls attend the same schools; they would also receive precisely the same instruction. No influences were to be tolerated in the schools which would suggest that the two sexes would follow different careers in adult life. Equality of races and nationalities constituted the third principle. Differential treatment of the Great Russians, the Ukrainians, the Jews, the Kazakhs, or any other national group was to be abolished. There were to be no superior peoples, languages, or cultures in the Soviet school. In order to ensure the realization of this ideal, each nationality was to have instruction organized in its own language and culture. The fourth principle had to do with the world outlook. On the negative side, religious influence in all of its forms was to be thoroughly eradicated from the school. On the positive side, a materialistic-atheistic-scientific view of the universe and human history would be sedulously cultivated in the members of the younger generation. The conduct of a school dedicated to these purposes would not, of course, be left to local authorities. Although each of the six Union Republics initially composing the Soviet Union was supposed to have complete autonomy in the organization and administration of education, the development of programs and policies within each republic was highly centralized in the People's Commissariat of Education. And the All-Union Communist Party controlled the several commissariats. Consequently, in view of the widely publicized principle of republican and national autonomy, the visitor to the Soviet Union in the 1920s was often surprised by the general uniformity from republic to republic of educational ideas and practices.

One further word should be said about the general administration and control of education in the Soviet Union in the early years of the revolution. Before the general administrative reorganization which was launched in the summer of 1930, practically all the agencies and processes for the education and reeducation of both young and old were administered by the Commissariat of Education in each of the Union Republics through the following seven great departments: Social Education, Professional (Vocational) Education, Political Education, Art, Literature and Publishing, Science, and Organization and Planning. For the most part, only the first two departments were responsible for administering the system of people's schools. In the next decade the pattern of administration was greatly changed for the purpose of increasing the authority of the central government in Moscow and of bringing educational institutions into a more organic relation with the program of construction developed by the State Planning Commission. Some of these institutions were transferred to other commissariats—Union and republican. However, that this reorganization involved any fundamental change in the Soviet conception of the scope of the educational enterprise cannot be assumed. In fact, during subsequent years the Party strengthened its control over all the agencies and processes of education.

III

The basic institution for the general education of the younger generation is the complete middle school—the ten-year school which enrolls children from seven to seventeen years of age and which, according to the official Soviet plan, will by 1960 enroll all children of appropriate age. With a single program of instruction, that is, with practically no elective subjects or curricula even in its senior division embracing the eighth, ninth, and tenth grades, this school is the major agency on which the Soviet leaders are placing first responsibility for molding the mind of the New Soviet Man. Its basic purpose is to give to all members of the younger generation a common body of skills, knowledges, ideas, values, and loyalties. In its methods of instruction, its program of studies, and its prescribed activities may be seen the picture of the future as envisaged by the Bolsheviks. The work of this institution may prove to be far more prophetic of the course of the Soviet state than the success of Soviet higher schools in training technicians and engineers. As a matter of fact, the political significance of the education of the Soviet specialist is probably found in the character of this ambitious program for shaping the character of children and youth. It is for this reason that three chapters in the present volume will be devoted to the program of the complete middle school. The first will deal with general education, the second with political, and the third with moral. Naturally, the reader should know that under the Soviet system everything is controlled that can be controlled and that the line laid down so carefully and systematically in the school is followed and reinforced by other institutions and processes.

The category of "general education," as employed in these pages, is arbitrarily conceived in terms of the mastery of the cultural heritage of skills and knowledges. It is of course obvious that no sharp line can be drawn in any society between this aspect of education and either "moral" or "political" education. Least of all is this possible in the Soviet Union, where everything is viewed from the standpoint of its bearing on "*politika,*" that is, the policies of the Party. To quote Lenin again on this point is quite unnecessary. It is stated repeatedly in the official Soviet pedagogies. And the powerful decrees on ideology issued by the Central Committee of the Party, beginning on August 14, 1946, condemned without reservation all members of the intellectual class who had chosen the path of ideological neutrality or apoliticality. In those days "art for art's sake," "laughter for laughter's sake," and even "love for love's sake" were declared to be bourgeois. Unquestionably the entire program of the middle school has been, is, and doubtless will be saturated with moral and political ideas, values, and loyalties. We must never forget the basic Bolshevik maxim that education is a "political weapon." Nevertheless, the writer is convinced that understanding of the scope and power of Soviet education can best be advanced by providing separate treatment of each of these three aspects of the program.

The task of giving a trustworthy account of the work of the middle school, or of any other sector of Soviet education, is complicated by the dynamism of the institution, or rather of Party policies and programs. On the quantitative side the changes are truly impressive. In 1913 the total number of pupils in institutions corresponding to the middle school was about 8 millions. By 1928 this figure had increased to 12 millions, and by 1940 to 35 millions. The writer knows of no school in history that ever achieved a comparable record of growth. After 1940, because of the war, the number gradually declined to 30 millions in 1955.

On the side of quality or substance, in spite of certain enduring features already mentioned, the changes which have taken place since the Bolshevik seizure of power are equally profound. So great have been the changes in the realm of curriculum content, moral emphases, methods of teaching, concepts of discipline, and pupil-teacher relationships that the observer would be justified in concluding that a revolution or counterrevolution had taken place. Indeed, certain of the ideas and practices of today would have been regarded as counterrevolutionary in the early years of the Soviet regime. If some Rip van Winkle, on quaffing the favorite drink of the Russians in place of the schnapps of the ghosts of Henry Hudson and his companions, had fallen into a deep sleep in 1927 after visiting a Soviet school, had slept for twenty or even ten years, and then on waking had returned to the same school, he would have been quite as bewildered as Washington Irving's hero was on discovering that his wife was dead, his cronies gone, the American Republic launched, and himself forgotten. Except for the Russian language, the glorification of the Great October Revolution, the commitment to a materialistic world view, the luxuriant whiskers of Marx and the neatly trimmed beard of Lenin, the enduring physical structure of building and equipment, and perhaps the red scarves of the Young Pioneers, he would have found himself moving amid very strange surroundings indeed. Although both the curriculum and the methods of instruction were profoundly altered, political rather than pedagogical considerations seem to have been primarily responsible for the transformation. Because of the dictatorial role of the Party in Soviet affairs, one may say in a very special sense that the more things change, the more they remain the same.

The history of Soviet education in general, and of the middle school in particular, may be divided into three periods. The first was the brief period of War Communism which ended in 1921 with the launching of the New Economic Policy. This was a period of relative chaos, hardship, and uncertainty, when the Bolsheviks were struggling for sheer survival against both internal and external enemies—a period of civil war, foreign intervention, and paralysis of productive energies in industry and agriculture culminating in the disastrous famine in the valley of the Volga. Yet, for those who accepted Bolshevik rule and were interested in education, it was a period marked by inspired discussions of basic educational and cultural problems facing the revolutionary order. Not a few educators of idealistic temper responded to the perspectives and promises of the pronouncements of the Party much as an earlier generation had responded to the liberation of the serfs in 1861. The writer recalls a conversation with a thirty-year-old educator in Kharkov in 1929. He asked this young man what he was doing in the terrible winter of 1921 when thousands were dying of starvation and diseases of malnutrition. The reply astonished the inquirer. With sparkling eyes he said he looked back on those months as the most exciting time of his life. It seems that he was a student at the Second University of Moscow, where all were living on shortened rations of both food and fuel. Yet students and faculty alike debated day and night a question of supreme concern at the time—the question of whether the new Russia should cultivate pure science or science related to life! The champions of the second position, with the assistance of the Party, prevailed in the debate.

Although a complete account of the development of the middle school would have to include the period of War Communism, attention here will be confined to the two major periods in the history of Soviet education. The first embraces roughly the ten years following 1921; the second, the years from 1931 to 1953. Whether another period opened with the death of Stalin in March, 1953, or the denunciation of Stalin in February, 1956, is a question which cannot be answered with assurance at this time. Although some changes have come, the available evidence suggests that the basic conceptions established in the 1930s will not be abandoned or greatly modified in the immediate future. What happens will doubtless be determined by the outcome of the struggle over the succession at the top of the Bolshevik power structure which in all probability is going on in the Soviet Union. The student of Soviet affairs is justified in regarding the present pattern of "collective leadership" as a temporary response to the passing of the "Great Leader and Teacher," the "Truth and Clear Conscience of the People," the "Heart and Eyes of the People," the "Coryphaeus of Science," the "Way of the Ages"—"Comrade Stalin." Yet no one can be certain.

IV

Soviet educators have called the period from 1921 to 1931 the "experimental" period in the history of Soviet education. It might also be called the "romantic" period. And the student of Soviet politics might with good reason call it the period of the capture of the school, the pupil, and the teacher by the Party. At any rate, during these years the mastery of knowledge was clearly subordinated to the political education of the younger generation. The Party did not give the close attention to details of school management that characterized the later period. To be sure, it endorsed certain broad conceptions of education, such as the "unified labor school" and "polytechnical education," to which it gave the Marxian label. But this left broad areas in which educators and teachers could conduct discussions, engage in experimentation, and espouse divergent approaches to educational tasks and objectives. Moreover, the Soviet educator took pride in his knowledge of the educational ideas and practices of capitalist countries. There was abundant evidence in the 1920s of the persisting influence of the liberal and humanist movement of the two preceding generations.

Several of the leading educators of the period had actually worked in this movement. N. K. Krupskaia, wife and widow of Lenin, and head of the important department of political education of the Commissariat of Education, had taught in the Sunday schools before the revolution. Invariably she impressed all who came to know her as a person of deep human sympathies. Albert Pinkevich, whose books on the theory and practice of education were widely used in teacher-training institutions, had been principal of a secondary school for boys in St. Petersburg which was renowned for its progressive methods—progressive in the Western meaning of the word. And then there was S. T. Shatsky, a remarkable personality who had been influenced by Jane Addams and John Dewey and who after the revolution was appointed head of the First Experimental Station in People's Education in Moscow. All these persons, and many others, had experienced harsh treatment at the hands of the Russian autocracy. Little wonder that they interpreted the revolution as a sort of key to the gates of an educational paradise. In his memoirs Shatsky contrasted the old school which he had attended as a boy with the new school of the Soviet regime. The former was marked by harsh discipline, mastery of subject matter, and preparation for adult life; the latter, by regard for the child as a human being and the organization of instruction around his current interests.[3] And Paul Blonsky, father of Soviet pedology and author of *The Unified Labor School* published in 1919, was a devout advocate of freedom for the child. An admirer of Rousseau, he suggested that Robinson Crusoe on the desert island provided a sound method for the education of the younger generation. He condemned as "prejudices of the old school" the recitation, the teaching plan, the separate subjects, the gradation of classes, the system of marks, the lack of faith in the child, and the passion for book learning.

In the light of developments in the 1930s, to be reported later, it is important to note that in this period a Soviet educator might express his own ideas and take exception to pronouncements by the state authorities. The case of Pinkevich may serve as an illustration. In his preface to the American edition of his *Outlines of Pedagogy*, which went through several editions in the Russian language, he addresses the following words to the English reader:

> I wish to make it perfectly clear . . . that the system expounded in the present book is not the generally accepted system, nor is it the official system. Although the basic principles upon which Soviet educators are striving to build a system of Marxian pedagogy are everywhere the same, there may be wide differences in details and in the handling of individual questions. Moreover, the development of a uniform theory of education is neither possible nor desirable. In the present case it is sufficient to note that my position on fundamental issues is *typical* of the great majority of Soviet educators.[4]

In discussing the Programs of the Primary School prepared by the State Scientific Council of the Commissariat of Education, Pinkevich says that, while they "contain extremely valuable material," they are subject to the "fundamental criticism" of violating the "principle of objective teaching." After giving an example, he argues that there is "danger of the blind acceptance on faith of the dogmatic statements of the instructor" and that in "our opinion the entire program is threatened with dogmatization."[5] He disappeared in the purges of 1937.

In this period there was widespread interest in the development of education in other lands. A writer in the field of pedagogy would invariably present the theories of leading educators in Europe and America, and do so in a friendly spirit and with a considerable measure of objectivity. Thus Pinkevich could say that he found the works of American educators "a rich source of materials" and "the most valuable source"[6] from beyond the borders of the Soviet Union. Also, after reviewing the ideas of leading Western educators, he speaks of "the great American philosopher, John Dewey," and ranks him "among the bourgeois forerunners of the true labor school."[7] And Blonsky, perhaps the most erudite Soviet scholar in the whole field of education, followed very closely the work of E. L. Thorndike, Charles H. Judd, and others. Incidentally, his subject of pedology was declared a pseudo science by the Central Committee of the Party in 1936. The subject was forthwith abolished and Blonsky disappeared. A. V. Lunacharsky, a friend of Lenin and the first Commissar of Education in the Russian Republic, was something of a cosmopolitan, a man of broad cultural interests, a connoisseur and patron of the arts who intervened with Lenin at the time of the revolution to save from destruction the art treasures of old Russia. In 1928, four years after the death of Lenin, he was removed from office. A visitor to the Soviet Union in the 1920s was generally impressed by the eagerness of Soviet teachers and educators to learn about educational practices in other lands. As a rule, however, they would state explicitly that the techniques, and not the purposes, of education in capitalist countries would be of value to them.

The school which these people and their collaborators built under the directives issued by the Party was called the "unified labor school." It was "unified" because it was organized at three levels as a single school, with provision for the unimpeded progress of the child from the first grade to the ninth or tenth. It was called "labor" because in Marxian theory human labor is the source of all value and the laboring class is the builder of the new society. Thus labor is endowed with that mystical quality in a Communist order which marks the role of the proletariat in the history of the present epoch. By labor even a member of the despised bourgeoisie may redeem himself and become whole. And so the education of the young must be linked with labor as theory must be linked with practice, words with deeds. Here, the Soviet leaders contended, was the greatest and most fruitful invention in the whole history of education, but an invention which could be put to use only under the rule of the proletariat.

This school was an activity school, a school in which children learned by doing. In contrasting their school with the school of the past, the Soviet educators were fond of saying that their school was a "school that does" rather than a "school that talks." But the word "activity" in the Soviet context was given a meaning which distinguished it radically from that prevailing in the so-called progressive schools of the West. It carried a moral and social content. As one enthusiast said, "The question of 'the socially useful activities of the school' must be regarded at the present moment as the most important question of Soviet pedagogy, because it constitutes the sharpest and brightest trait which distinguishes the Soviet school, not only from the tsarist school, but also from every other contemporary school." The Soviet school must be as "bright and unique" as the "Soviet Union which gave it birth." And this basic characteristic is not found in the "complex method, self-government, or the social work of the teacher. Relatively speaking, all of these are trivialities." The

Soviet school, "being created in the epoch of the stupendous sweep of a program for building the country, *must itself participate in the building of life.*" [8] In a word, education must be a central factor in the direct transformation of both man and society.

The authority for this approach to the problem of education was Lenin himself. In an address at the Third Congress of the League of Young Communists in 1920 he stated that "one of the greatest evils and calamities which we have inherited from the old capitalist society is the complete gap between the book and practical life." Then he warned the assembled Young Communists that "without labor, and without struggle, book knowledge about Communism obtained from Communist brochures and other writings is absolutely worthless for it would continue the old gap between theory and practice." [9] This obviously meant that the school could not rear a generation of real Communists through books and words. And so in the same address Lenin advised as follows: "The generation which is now 15 years old and which in 10–20 years will live in a Communist society *must so conceive the aims of learning that every day in every village, in every city the young should actually perform some task of social labor, be it ever so small, be it ever so simple.*" [10] So was born the dominant conception of Soviet pedagogy of the 1920s, the idea of *socially useful labor,* of labor performed by pupils and school useful to the community. Through labor the work of the school would be integrated with life and made meaningful.

But there were other and more compelling considerations. The more fundamental of these considerations were outlined briefly in the New Programs for the Unified Labor School issued by the State Scientific Council in 1923. The programs, according to the Council, not only "provide new materials" and "presuppose new methods" for the work of the school; they also "place at the basis of the whole educative process an entirely new direction of the child's will, a direction which is contemporary and revolutionary-proletarian" in character. Children of workers and peasants "go to school, not to advance themselves above their station, to rise above their class and enter the higher class of the intelligentsia, as was customary in the old pre-revolutionary school, but to enter the foremost organized ranks of their own class, to become worthy aids and comrades of the organized revolutionary proletarian and peasant." The first task of the school is to "help children find socially valuable work suited to their strength and enable them to participate effectively in such work." [11] The controlling purpose of these proposals is "to liquidate the division of society into classes" and to "make all forms of socially useful human labor equally important." Every kind of such labor "must be given a lawful and dignified place" in the program of the Soviet school. [12]

During the 1920s the idea of socially useful labor spread far and wide through the Soviet Union. The practice developed more or less spontaneously and in accordance with conceptions emerging in particular schools and localities. Practically every educator of standing evolved his own theoretical position on the question and sought to bring order out of chaos through some system of classification. At least one Union-wide questionnaire study was made and numerous conferences were held. Pinkevich proposed that socially useful work be organized under ten categories: "(1) economic activities; (2) socio-political work; (3) public enlightenment; (4) health protection; (5) communal welfare; (6) communication; (7) cooperation; (8) regional work; (9) conservation of natural resources; (10) individual aid to the population." [13] He then made concrete suggestions for relating the work of the pupils and the school to each type of activity. A couple of illustrations must suffice. The children and teachers agitate for "rational cultivation of land," they make "reports, public addresses, etc.," they engage in "sorting of grain, destruction of weeds, disinfecting of grain with formaldehyde, etc." All of this was supposed to constitute an integral part of the curriculum of the school. Another Soviet educator suggested how the extermination of the bedbug, one of the common scourges of old Russia, might be utilized as a form of socially useful labor. First, the pupils study the "biology of the bedbug"; second, they "discover by laboratory experiments the most radical means for exterminating them"; third, they "find the funds necessary to purchase the supplies"; and fourth, they "organize the extermination in cottages." [14] Literally hundreds of such projects were undertaken by the Soviet school during this period. The launching of the First Five-Year Plan toward the end of 1928 had a tremendous immediate impact on this basic feature of Soviet education. The whole program of instruction was reorganized and directed toward the promotion of the plan. Every pupil, every teacher, every school was expected to assume responsibility for the fulfillment of this "Program of Great Works." When in the summer and autumn of 1929 the author asked school children in many parts of the Union what was their first obligation, the answer came almost invariably: "We must help make the plan successful."

The point should be emphasized that socially useful labor was not merely a method of teaching. Nor was it a substitute for the traditional curriculum. As a matter of fact, it was both method and curriculum. In the opinion of Soviet educators it added content and gave vitality to the entire program of instruction. The school continued to teach the native tongue, natural science, social studies, and mathematics, but it did all these things in relation to contemporary life and the tasks of Soviet society as determined by the Bolshevik dictatorship. Socially useful labor gave a new dimension to the curriculum and profoundly altered its structure. The mastery of academic subjects as such was relegated to a subordinate position. Some Soviet educators contended that subjects should be abolished and that the child should acquire necessary skills and knowledges as a by-product of the pursuit of socially desirable ends. This led to the development of interest in the "method of projects" and convinced many American visitors that the Bolsheviks had adopted the philosophy and program of "progressive education." The Soviet educators also were attracted to the "Dalton plan" and the "laboratory method," not only for the natural sciences, but also for other subjects. One of the most enthusiastic advocates of socially useful labor was V. N. Shul'gin, director of the Institute of School Methods in Moscow. Taking seriously the Marxian prophecy that the state would "wither away" after the establishment of socialism and confident that socialism was not far away, he developed and expounded the doctrine of the "withering away of the school." He saw the child of the future acquiring his education by participating in the life of society, each of whose institutions would perform its appropriate educational function. The child would grow up, "not in a school, not in a kindergarten, not in a retort of a chemical laboratory," but in the "factory, the mill, the agricultural economy, the class struggle." And he would be taught, "not by a teacher in a box, in a knit cap," but "by the entire order of things." [15] Also, "industry will be placed at the service of education. It will be organized for educational purposes, as will be the street." [16] According to a report received by the writer in Moscow in 1936, Shul'gin himself was at that time "withering away" on an engineering project in the region of the North Caucasus. And he was not serving as an engineer.

In the course of time Soviet educators developed a method of their own, known as the "complex method." According to Pinkevich, this meant:

> . . . the study in the school of some problem, theme, or complex manifestation which from the standpoint of our educational aims is significant. A consistent introduction of this form of concentration results in the replacement of the usual curriculum by a number of problems or manifestations which are united by one general idea and are organized according to a certain system. Naturally, these themes or complexes cannot be confined within the boundaries set by the conventional subjects; on the contrary, they must embrace absolutely all fields of knowledge.[17]

On the basis of the "complex" a distinctive curriculum for the Soviet school from the first grade to the ninth, inclusive, was evolved. The State Scientific Council developed a comprehensive program with appropriate complexes for each year of study. Suggestions were made for the organization and development of instruction in relation to the three great realities recognized by Soviet pedagogy at the time: nature, labor, and society, with labor at the center.

Toward the end of the period the basic Marxian conception of polytechnical education emerged and the unified labor school became the polytechnical school. In August, 1930, there was convened in Moscow the First All-Russian Congress on Polytechnical Education. The congress was opened by Krupskaia and a representative of the Central Committee of the Party. Twenty-seven papers were presented and almost every conceivable aspect of the subject was developed. The uninitiated might assume that a polytechnical school is one in which several technical specialties are taught. The Soviet conception was something quite different. According to that conception polytechnical education is the authentic form of general education *à la* Marx. In a word it means an education organized around the basic productive forces of industrial society—electrical energy, machine production, chemical production, and agricultural production. The conduct of the process of instruction involves work in school shops and on land plots, study of the underlying sciences, experience in a factory and on a farm, and study of labor management and economic planning. The object seems to be the development of an individual familiar with and experienced in the scientific foundations and the practical operations of the main branches of industrial economy in a socialist state.[18] The vogue of polytechnical education, however, was quickly submerged by the decrees on education of the Central Committee of the Party in the early thirties, only to emerge again at the Nineteenth Congress of the Party in the autumn of 1952.

The position of the pupil in the school, the relation of the pupil to the teacher, and the departure from the subject-centered curriculum in the 1920s also inspired many foreign observers to conclude that the Bolsheviks had adopted the ideas and practices of "progressive education." The curriculum seemed to be made on the spot, the textbook was a secondary aid to instruction, examinations were scorned, and school marks abolished by decree; homework in the traditional sense was not expected, corporal punishment was forbidden by law, and the children seemed to be running things. Pupils, teachers, and all school workers constituted a single collective for the management of the institution. The children not only operated a system of self-government for the conduct of their affairs but they also had committees on sanitation, on the curriculum, on methods of teaching, and the like. The collective might decide to close the school, if something more important should come along, as often happened. Anything involving the welfare of the state or the construction of socialism should obviously take precedence over the routine work of the school. Socially useful labor in the community always had its attractions for the children. Hunting and fishing, however, did not fall in this category. One other observation is relevant here. Not infrequently teachers seemed to fear their pupils, not because of what they might do, but rather because of what they might say and to whom they might say it.

Another characteristic feature of the middle school during this period, which was completely liquidated in the 1930s, was socialistic competition. In accordance with the anti-individualistic doctrines of the Bolsheviks, a great deal of emphasis was placed on group work, group projects, and group undertakings of all kinds. Socialistic competition constituted an attempt to take advantage of this situation and utilize a form of motivation which was social in character. During the period of the First Five-Year Plan this Soviet device spread like wildfire throughout the Soviet Union and in all kinds of establishments. In its organized form socialistic competition assumes the guise of a written and duly signed contract between two enterprises or groups to fulfill certain specifically enumerated conditions. The parties to the agreement may be two factories, two mines, two collective farms, two cultural agencies, a factory and a library, a bank and a theater, or any other combination of enterprises. Inevitably the school became involved. A particular school might compete with a factory or with another school, one grade or class with another, one group of children with another. The laurels, of course, would go to the group and not to the individual. As a consequence, some children might be rewarded or punished regardless of their own contributions. In the subsequent period the individual child is held strictly accountable for his work.

A concluding word should be said about the freedom accorded the pupil in the unified labor school. This freedom, which so impressed many foreign visitors, had its political as well as its pedagogical sources. It seems quite unlikely that the tough-minded, unsentimental, and fanatical men and women who overthrew the provisional government, routed the Constituent Assembly, and established a dictatorship by armed force were prepared to follow the interests of children and place the fate of the revolution in the hands of the young. The probability is that they were moved by quite different considerations. When the Bolsheviks seized power they found themselves ruling a vast and diverse population which neither understood nor shared their purposes. Indeed, among the educated classes they encountered widespread and bitter hostility. And this hostility was present in the teaching profession. Teachers struck against the new government in several cities, including Petrograd and Moscow, and the All-Russian Teachers' Union openly opposed the Bolsheviks. The latter resolved both to win the young and to rear a generation of teachers loyal to them and their cause. Since the school was absolutely essential to the achievement of their goals, they could not liquidate the teacher as they might liquidate a parasitic or expendable class. They had to capture both the school and the teacher.

The process of capture assumed diverse forms. But the creation and utilization of the Society of Young Pioneers and the League of Young Communists, Bolshevik organizations of children and youth to be described in detail later, constituted perhaps their most effective response to the situation. Under the watchful eye and the directing hand of the Party these institutions became both instruments and weapons for the seizure of the schools and the subduing of the teachers. They were the eyes and ears, and even the voice, of the Party. Moreover, they were the active element whose work in pupil committees attracted the notice of foreign travelers. "Self-government," wrote Pinkevich, "played the role of a 'militant organ of struggle' against the old school and the old teacher who neither understood nor wished to understand the aims of the new school." [19] And in an officially approved Pedagogy, edited by I. A. Kairov and published twenty years later, we find an almost identical statement: "One should note the large positive role which children's self-government played in the school during the first years of the revolution in the struggle with the old reactionary traditions of the school, with its inflexible habits and the conservative temper of a certain part of the body of teachers. Revolutionary youth, standing on the side of Soviet power, played a large role in demolishing the old and creating the new Soviet school." [20] Indeed, a "flying brigade" of Young Communists might enter a classroom or lecture hall at any time for the purpose of finding out whether the teacher or instructor was propagating the "truth"—the truth of the toiling masses of the world.

V

With the launching of the great program for the industrialization of the country in the autumn of 1928 and the complete triumph of Stalin over his rivals by the early thirties, the so-called "experimental period" came to a close. The educational practices of that period had been at least measurably successful in the propagation of Bolshevik doctrines among children and youth. Many of the old teachers had been either reconciled with the revolution or eliminated from the profession by natural or political causes. As early as June 12, 1925, the Soviet of People's Commissars of the RSFSR "notices a considerable improvement in the ideas and attitudes of the body of teachers toward the new regime," and "a parallel improvement of the same order generally among scientists." [21] Also a new generation of teachers, reared in large part under Soviet institutions and presumably loyal to the regime, was emerging. At the same time, the program of construction carried through in the early years with the assistance of foreign engineers, technicians, and even skilled workers, called for the swift mastery of science and technology. As a consequence, novel and exacting demands were made on the schools. They were asked to participate actively in the conversion of a technically and culturally backward country into a modern industrial state. In 1936, when the author inquired of teachers and children in both European Russia and Siberia regarding the first duty of the pupil, the response was everywhere the same—"the mastery of knowledge." The immediate fulfillment of the Five-Year Plan was left to the older generation. The pupil's first responsibility was to study language, mathematics, and science. Added to all this was the profound shift in the whole orientation and configuration of Soviet life and institutions associated with the rise of Stalin and Stalinism. In the process of adjustment to the new conditions many of the practices and doctrines of the earlier period were modified, abandoned, or reversed. But only in a limited sense were the issues pedagogical in nature. At bottom, like everything else in the Soviet Union, including the content of the calendar and the humor of the circus, they were essentially political issues—political issues of critical concern to the dictatorship.

The demands of the program of construction and the slogan of overtaking and surpassing the most advanced capitalist countries merit an additional word. As the Soviet leaders struggled to achieve the goals of the First Five-Year Plan, they became painfully aware of the general backwardness of Russia. This they had all said many times; indeed, Soviet literature had been filled with this lament all through the period of the battle to consolidate Bolshevik rule. But only as they undertook the heavy tasks of industrial construction did they realize fully the truth of the oft-repeated indictment of the past. They found to their sorrow that the rank and file of Soviet citizens did indeed lag far behind the peoples of the West in the most elementary mastery of the skills, knowledges, and understandings required in the building of an industrial economy—skills, knowledges, and understandings which the child in America acquires more or less incidentally in the process of growing up amid complicated tools, machines, motors, and electricity. The unified labor school, with its emphasis on socially useful work, freedom from discipline, unorganized curricula, political indoctrination, and diverse romantic notions about education stemming from Marx and Lenin, simply was not sufficient to the task. As a consequence, practically the entire regimen of the middle school was swiftly transformed by decrees issued either directly or indirectly by the Central Committee of the Party. These decrees were directed, not only to broad educational policies, but also to the details of instruction and school management. As a consequence, a new Soviet school emerged which was profoundly different from the school of the 1920s—a school which resembled in many respects the school of old

Russia and would have been labeled counterrevolutionary in the earlier period, but one which in fact expresses the basic philosophy of Bolshevism far more faithfully than its predecessor.

The first of these important decrees, issued on September 5, 1931, called for the simple mastery of knowledge. According to the Central Committee, "the basic defect of our school at the present moment" is the "fact that school instruction fails to give a sufficient body of general knowledge" and thus fails to "prepare for the technicums and higher schools fully literate people with a good command of the basic sciences (physics, chemistry, mathematics, native language, geography and others)." While continuing to stress the principle of "polytechnical education," the decree condemns the traditional practice in these sharp words: "Every attempt to separate the polytechnization of the school from a systematic and firm mastery of the sciences, and of physics, chemistry, and mathematics in particular . . . constitutes the most flagrant perversion of the ideas of the polytechnical school." The teaching of these subjects "must be conducted by means of strictly established schedules." In order to emphasize the importance and urgency of the need for a fundamental reorganization of the entire program of instruction, the Central Committee asked the commissariats of education in the Union Republics "to organize immediately a scientific-Marxian revision of the program, making certain that it contains a strictly defined body of systematic knowledge (native language, mathematics, physics, chemistry, geography, history)." The date for the introduction of the "new revised programs" was set for January 1, 1932. In the meantime, all necessary practical measures were to be taken to instruct the teachers and prepare directives for launching the new programs without delay. To expedite the reforms, "all members of the Party engaged in the work of people's education" were instructed "to master the new procedures in the shortest possible time." Thus was restored the curriculum of separate subjects—subjects with clearly defined content to be mastered by the pupil.[22] And this curriculum was to be uniform for practically all children from the first grade to the tenth.

The decree of September 5, 1931, ordered corresponding changes in the field of methods of instruction. While recognizing the value of some of the new methods of teaching "in the development of initiative and the preparation of active participants in socialist construction," it demanded the launching of a "decisive warfare against irresponsible projectorizing and the introduction on a mass scale of methods untested in practice." This error assumed its most glaring form in the "adoption of the so-called 'project method.' Stemming directly from the anti-Leninist theory of the 'withering away of the school,' the attempts to place the 'project method' at the basis of the entire school actually led to the destruction of the school."[23] It is interesting to note, incidentally, that

Krupskaia had been particularly enthusiastic about this method. The Central Committee warned the entire teaching profession against both "extreme left tendencies" and "attempts to go back to the bourgeois school." However, the response to this initial decree was quite unsatisfactory. Consequently, on August 25, 1932, the Central Committee issued another decree, which ordered the "liquidation of the perversions of laboratory-brigade methods" and then proceeded to a positive definition of the appropriate method for the Soviet school: "The chief form of the organization of instruction in the primary and secondary school must be the recitation with a given group of pupils following a strict schedule of studies. Under the leadership of the teacher this form must include group, brigade, and individual work of each pupil," and "the teacher must present the subject he is teaching systematically and consistently." [24]

Implicit in the emphasis on the mastery of knowledge and the revival of the recitation is a fundamental change in the relations between teacher and pupil. The decree of September 5, 1931, called upon the commissariats of education to strengthen "individual authority in the management of the school" and to "increase the responsibility of the teaching body in their work by promoting and encouraging loyal and well-trained teachers." At the same time, "the work of children's self-government in the school" was to be "directed chiefly toward the improvement of the quality of learning and the strengthening of school discipline." [25] The decree may be understood also as marking the emergence of a body of teachers presumably loyal to the regime.

The Society of Young Pioneers was almost immediately involved in these reforms. On April 21, 1932, the Central Committee issued a decree which laid down the new line for these youngsters. "The weakest link in Pioneer work," it declared, "is that up to this time the tremendous activity of children is not directed in sufficient measure toward their most important task which consists in the struggle for quality of work in the school, for the mastery of the 'foundations of science,' for the strengthening of discipline among children and particularly in the school." Without this, "the successful preparation of the growing generation to become builders of Communist society is unthinkable." The Young Pioneers are told further that "a conscious, responsible, accurate, and exact performance by each pupil of his school responsibilities, his assignments in social-practical work, and the rules of the internal school regimen should become 'a matter of his honor.'" [26] In the spring of 1944 the central organ of the Young Communist League condemned the practice of criticizing teachers, of taking pupils away from class during school hours, and of failing to assist teachers in improving discipline and order in the school. [27]

The demand of the Central Committee that the mastery of a definite body of knowledge should be the basic purpose of the middle school led speedily to the reversal of a fairly well established Soviet tradition regarding the role of the textbook in the educative process. Many of the foremost leaders of Soviet education, including Krupskaia, Shatsky, and Blonsky, were fond of saying that "life must be the textbook." This position was officially proclaimed by the Russian Commissariat of Education in the following words contained in a circular letter dated August, 1918: "Textbooks in general should be thrown out of the school." As late as May, 1930, an all-Russian conference of educators "definitely repudiates the principle of the stabilization of textbooks." In the same year the Plenum of the Central Committee of the Professional Union of Educational Workers declared that the standardization of textbooks is "incorrect and politically injurious." But on February 12, 1933, the Central Committee of the Party pronounced this attitude toward the textbook "incorrect" and "intolerable." It then proceeded to instruct the Commissariat of Education to prepare "stable textbooks" in the "native language, mathematics, geography, physics, chemistry, biology, etc." And the date of publication was set for "July 15, 1933, in order that they may be ready for the opening of the academic year—September 1, 1933"! In the sense of the Committee, a "stable textbook" is one "designed for use over a period of many years" and "approved after a preliminary scrupulous examination by the Collegium of the Commissariat of Education." In such a textbook, as Stalin once said, "every word and every definition must be weighed." And such a textbook must be prepared for "each subject" taught in the school.[28]

The next step to ensure the mastery of knowledge was the development of a rigorous system of marks, examinations, promotion, and awards. On September 3, 1935, the Central Committee issued a decree reviving the prerevolutionary five-point marking scale: "1—very poor, 2—poor, 3—satisfactory, 4—good, and 5—excellent." All commissariats of education were instructed to cooperate with the Central Committee to establish "norms for the evaluation of the work of pupils" which would be "compulsory for all the schools of the USSR." Thereafter promotion from one grade to another was to carry a "certificate with an enumeration of marks" received in all subjects and in conduct. Pupils passing "the final and transfer examinations" were to be awarded "honor scrolls," and on graduation from the secondary school, "diplomas—with marks in all subjects." Graduates from the secondary school receiving the "mark of 'excellent' in the basic subjects and a mark of not less than 'good' in other subjects" were to "have the right to enter the higher schools without entrance examinations."[29] A decree of the Soviet of Ministers of the U.S.S.R. of June 21, 1944, called for special examinations at the end of the fourth, seventh, and tenth grades, to be given by groups of teachers selected for the purpose. The decree also established the system of gold and silver medals to be awarded on the completion of the tenth grade for "excellent scholarship and exemplary conduct." [30] Thus the Soviet system of honorifics was extended to pupils in the middle school. On December 30, 1946, the Russian Ministry of Education approved a set of instructions designed to establish a comprehensive system of promotion and final examinations for all schools and for all grades above the third. According to this order, pupils in the first three grades receiving an annual mark below 3 in either the Russian language or arithmetic must repeat the course the following year, unless through special dispensation granted by the authorities he fulfills certain special assignments during the summer vacation. In the upper grades "pupils with marks lower than 3 in one or two of the basic subjects" are generally expected to remain in the grade a second year.[31] In the spring of 1956, on the grounds of safeguarding the health of children, instructions for softening the rigors of the system of examinations were issued.

This tremendous emphasis on marks, as contrasted with the practice of the 1920s, greatly impressed the writer in the autumn and winter of 1936. In a rather intensive study of School No. 25 in Moscow he noted that the pictures of all pupils who had received excellent marks in all subjects the preceding quarter were prominently displayed on the bulletin board. He also attended a meeting of the Young Pioneers of the school devoted to the election of officers. The children nominated took places on the rostrum of the assembly room. Each was then required to give an account of himself and was questioned from the floor by other members of the organization. One of the first questions addressed to the candidate was "What are your school marks?" If in reply he admitted to anything below "good," he was greeted with boos and catcalls. The clear implication was that every officer of the Society of Young Pioneers should stand high in the realm of scholarship and set a worthy example for all children.

This transformation of the purposes, the curriculum, and methods of the school was accompanied by an expression of widespread concern regarding the behavior of pupils. From the early thirties the Soviet press contained numerous references to "hooliganism" on the part of children and youth in schools and public places. The general lack of discipline on the part of the young was deplored and a widespread campaign to correct these evils was launched. Even Stalin gave the matter his attention, and the famous cavalry leader, General Budenny, almost a legendary figure, went into the school in 1935 to impress on children the necessity of loving and respecting their teachers and elders. The pupil was told over and over again that his first duty was to study and learn. No longer was he to assume responsibility for running the school, correcting his parents, managing the affairs of the community, or even assisting directly in the great program of construction. He was subjected increasingly to strict supervision in school, at home, and on the street. Moreover, he was held accountable for his successes and failures as an individual. In 1943 "socialistic competition" in the schools was abolished. The doctrine that "there are no poor pupils, only poor teachers" was repudiated. Also the school assumed some responsibility for regulating the out-of-school life of pupils. Attendance at movies, the theater, and other places of amusement was placed under the control of the teachers. On July 12, 1943, the government ordered the stopping of "the sale of tickets for evening performances to children under sixteen in all theaters (except children's theaters), concert halls, and circuses." [32] Homework was made an integral and important part of the process of education. And if entertainment conflicted with the mastery of knowledge, that is, if his school marks were low, the pupil was advised to stay home and study.

This total situation led the Party to consider the question of a code of conduct for children and youth. In a decree on September 3, 1935, the Central Committee declared that, in spite of a "number of decrees" on the subject, "the commissariats of education have not yet issued rules of conduct for pupils in the school and outside the school, nor have they prepared a standard set of school regulations which would establish a firm order in the school and serve as a guide to the administration of the school, the teachers, the school organizations, and the pupils." [33] Although some moves were made in the direction indicated by the decree, it was not until August 2, 1943, that the issue was resolved with authority and power. On that day the Soviet of People's Commissars of the RSFSR promulgated the following code of "Rules for School Children."

It is the duty of every school child:
1. To strive with tenacity and perseverance to master knowledge, in order to become an educated and cultured citizen and to serve most fully the Soviet Motherland.
2. To be diligent in study and punctual in attendance, never being late to classes.
3. To obey without question the orders of school director and teachers.
4. To bring to school all necessary books and writing materials, to have everything ready before the arrival of the teacher.
5. To appear at school washed, combed, and neatly dressed.
6. To keep his desk in the classroom clean and orderly.
7. To enter the classroom and take his seat immediately after the ringing of the bell, to enter or leave the classroom during the lesson period only with the permission of the teacher.
8. To sit erect during the lesson period, not leaning on the elbows or slouching in the seat; to attend closely to the explanations of the teacher and the responses of the pupils, not talking or engaging in mischief.
9. To rise as the teacher or the director enters or leaves the classroom.

10. To rise and stand erect while reciting; to sit down only on permission of the teacher; to raise the hand when desiring to answer or ask a question.
11. To make accurate notes of the teacher's assignment for the next lesson, to show these notes to parents, and to do all homework without assistance.
12. To be respectful to the school director and the teachers, to greet them on the street with a polite bow, boys removing their hats.
13. To be polite to his elders, to conduct himself modestly and properly in school, on the street, and in public places.
14. To abstain from using bad language, from smoking and gambling.
15. To take good care of school property, to guard well his own possessions and those of his comrades.
16. To be courteous and considerate toward little children, toward the aged, the weak, and the sick, to give them the seat on the trolley or the right of way on the street, to help them in every way.
17. To obey his parents and assist in the care of little brothers and sisters.
18. To maintain cleanliness in the home by keeping his own clothes, shoes, and bed in order.
19. To carry always his pupil's card, guarding it carefully, not passing it to other children, but presenting it on request of the director or the teacher of the school.
20. To prize the honor of his school and his class as his very own.

For violation of these rules the pupil is subject to punishment, even to expulsion from school.[34]

In the preparation of teachers much emphasis is placed on these rules. According to Kairov, they "must be a strict law, obeyed unwaveringly by every pupil." Teachers, parents, and all others in authority "must follow a single line in this respect and thus create an order that would make violation of the 'rules' an intolerable exception, running directly contrary to firmly established traditions and habits." The code of rules should be regarded as a "state document, universal for all schools." It is important also to "establish in every school the time of the arrival of pupils at school, the time of the ringing of the bell for the beginning and the ending of each recitation, the time of each recess and of lunch for each class, the time for departure from school and for out-of-school occupations." In a word, a "twenty-four-hour regimen" should be established for all pupils.[35]

Rule No. 19 merits a word of comment. The "pupil card" may be understood as the introduction into the period of childhood of the internal passport of adult society. It is undoubtedly a very effective device for strengthening the supervision of the younger generation. Of similar import is the pupil's uniform, an innovation promised for 1937 but not achieved until 1954–1955. Both the card and the uniform are presumably regarded as "marks of honor" under the Soviet social system.

These reforms brought profound changes in the role and functions of the Young Pioneers and Young Communists. The new orientation is clearly revealed in a decree issued by the Twelfth Plenum of the League of Young Communists on April 30, 1944. In the words of the decree, "the task of the Komsomol (Young Communist) organizations in the school is to assist the teacher." And in order to perform this task, the decree states "that teachers can be present at all Komsomol meetings of pupils and participate in their work and that in recruiting members into the Komsomol it is necessary to take into account the opinions of the teachers." It further states "that the director of the school has the right to stop the execution of a wrong decision on the part of the school Komsomol organization and to propose to the regional Komsomol organ the question of vetoing the decision." [36] Kairov summarizes the matter in these words: "Komsomol organizations must assist the director of the school and the teachers in raising to a high level the quality of instruction, in raising the authority of the teacher, in strengthening discipline among the pupils, and in achieving strict observation of the 'Rules for School Children.'" [37] The same authority characterizes the Pioneer as a "good student," a "hard worker," and an "example for all children."[38]

The stern regimen of the ten-year school as outlined in the preceding pages was developed for the purpose of ensuring the mastery by the great body of pupils of a carefully prescribed curriculum of subject matter, certainly far more severe in design than the curriculum of the twelve-year American school. The general content and major emphases of this curriculum are revealed in the "teaching plan" opposite, prepared by the Ministry of Education of the Russian Republic for the school year 1954–1955.

There are six features of this program of study which merit special attention. In the first place, all children follow the same curriculum from the first grade to the tenth, except for differentiation between the sexes in the realm of military-physical preparation and opportunity to choose among foreign languages, if two or more are offered in the same school. In the second place, all ten-year schools throughout the Soviet Union teach the same subjects in the same grades, except the non-Russian schools in which the Russian language is taught as an additional subject from the third to the tenth grade inclusive. In the third place, the school year is long, ranging from 213 days in the first three grades to 230 in the tenth, and the school week embraces six days. In the fourth place, the curriculum emphasizes the native language, mathematics, and physical science. Moreover, according to the plan, the Soviet pupil is carried much further in mathematics and science than the American pupil. Though not stated in the table, mathematics includes trigonometry, as well as astronomy. And the study of physics and chemistry begins in the sixth and seventh grades respectively. Both science and mathematics are classified

No. of Subjects	SUBJECTS	Number of class hours per week										Total hours	
		I	II	III	IV	V	VI	VII	VIII	IX	X	week	year
1	Russian language and literature	13	13	13	9	9	8	6	5	4	4	84	2,772
2	Mathematics	6	6	6	6	6	6	6	6	6	6	60	1,980
3	History	—	—	—	2	2	2	2	4	4	4	20	660
4	Constitution of USSR	—	—	—	—	—	—	—	—	—	1	1	33
5	Geography	—	—	—	2	3	2	2	2	3	—	14	462
6	Biology	—	—	—	2	2	2	3	2	1	—	12	396
7	Physics	—	—	—	—	—	2	3	3	4	4	16	528
8	Astronomy	—	—	—	—	—	—	—	—	—	1	1	33
9	Chemistry	—	—	—	—	—	—	2	2	3	4	11	363
10	Psychology	—	—	—	—	—	—	—	—	—	1	1	33
11	Foreign Language	—	—	—	—	4	4	3	3	3	3	20	660
12	Physical culture	2	2	2	2	2	2	2	2	2	2	20	660
13	Drawing	1	1	1	1	1	1	—	—	—	—	6	198
14	Drafting	—	—	—	—	—	—	1	1	1	1	4	132
15	Singing	1	1	1	1	1	1	—	—	—	—	6	198
16	Labor	1	1	1	1	2	2	2	—	—	—	10	330
17	Practical work in agricultural economy, machine operation, and electro-technique	—	—	—	—	—	—	—	3	2	2	7	231
	Excursions												293
	Total	24	24	24	26	32	32	32	32	33	33	293	9,962

Remark. The number of class weeks in a year, not including the time devoted to examinations, is 34; of them 33 weeks are reserved to the study of class subjects and one week to excursions.[39]

as "important subjects." In the fifth place, the study of foreign languages, usually English, German, and French, is taken very seriously. Instruction begins in the fifth grade. In the sixth place, systematic physical education is provided in all grades from the first to the tenth for the purpose of "cultivating such qualities in the younger generation as bravery, persistence and will." The reader should not forget those gold and silver medals shining and beckoning in the distance which open freely the doors to the higher schools.

In the administration of this curriculum little is left to chance. In addition to the officially approved "stable textbook," mentioned above, the highest educational authority of the state prepares detailed "instructional programs" which are designed to fix further both content and method, achieve integration of the various subjects, establish sequences from the first grade to the tenth, and relate words and theory to practice and life. These programs, according to Yesipov and Goncharov, are "compulsory state documents." Every teacher and every school director "bear responsibility for their fulfillment." "Arbitrary changes," even the "interchange of hour" between two subjects, "are inadmissible." Such "compulsory uniformity of programs for all schools is one of the most important conditions . . . for the improvement of the work of the school." [40] And Kairov puts the matter even more succinctly. "The instructional program," he writes, "cannot be arbitrarily changed either by the director of the school or by the directors of the local organs of people's education, and far less by individual teachers. The fulfillment of the instructional program is obligatory for the school." [41]

On June 17, 1946, the Ministry of Education of the RSFSR approved a code of "Rules of Internal Order" for teachers and other workers in the ten-year school. Under this code the teacher is obligated:

a. To work honestly and conscientiously.
b. To maintain discipline of labor and to follow strictly the teaching regimen and the rules of internal order: to fulfill the instructions of the administration quickly and precisely.
c. To appear at work on time; to follow, without any violations, the established length of the day; to utilize the entire working time in productive work, without engaging in any personal affairs or conversations or distracting others from their work.
d. To fulfill assignments satisfactorily and on time, to maintain high quality of teaching, and improve continuously their own qualifications.
e. To guard socialist property: school equipment, teaching aids, etc.
f. To maintain the rules of sanitation and fire prevention.

The rules also include many details regarding preparation for each lesson, keeping of daily records, enforcement of the "Rules for School Children," visitation of homes of pupils, organization of out-of-school work, and conduct of class meetings of parents and pupils.

The "Rules of Internal Order" also prescribe punishments for violations. For "violation of labor discipline," such as being late to work, leaving school before the closing hour, taking too much time for lunch, or closing a class period contrary to schedule, the punishment may take the form of: "(a) a remark, (b) a reprimand, (c) a strict reprimand." Such punishments are imposed directly by the administration. For more serious violations, such as "willfully leaving the work of the school," "shirking one's duty," "theft of school property," and "hooliganism," the guilty party is arraigned before the court. Apparently in order to encourage compliance, the pronouncement from the ministry closes with the words: "These Rules of Internal Labor Order are obligatory for all workers of the school and must be prominently displayed in the teachers' room of every school." [42] A positive source of encouragement is doubtless found in "the repeated mass award to Soviet Teachers of orders and medals." [43]

Ultimate responsibility for the conduct of the ten-year school, like everything else in the Soviet Union, rests on the Central Committee of the Party. At the same time, the Central Committee achieves its purposes through the organs of the Soviet government from the Supreme Soviet down to local soviets. In the case of the middle school the Ministry of Education in each of the Union Republics is administratively responsible through the school director whom it appoints. And he, according to the "Rules of Internal Order," is "immediately responsible for the entire work of the school." In the words of the official textbook, "the administration of the school must be built on the foundation of one-man management and full personal responsibility by the director for the entire institution, for the work as a whole and for its several parts." The director in turn "exacts personal responsibility of each separate worker for the business entrusted to him." He must check the "execution of assignments—the execution of all the directives of the state, the execution of the orders of immediate superiors for a given task, the execution by each worker of the plans of his work and duties." He must "check the work of each teacher, visiting classes, becoming acquainted with the record and the condition of knowledge of the pupils." In case of deficiencies, he "must undertake immediately measures for their correction." [44] Obviously the middle school is thoroughly organized and administered to serve the directives of the Party.

VI

The course of the evolution of the Soviet middle school presented in the foregoing pages is marked by profound changes and reversals. In this respect it resembles the course of any other Soviet institution. This is merely to say that the middle school has followed faithfully the Party line through all its zigs and zags as formulated by the Central Committee. And such changes and reversals may be expected in the coming years. The repudiation of Stalin will doubtless be accompanied in the Stalin manner by unexpected developments in the field of education. It may be fitting, therefore, to report briefly two recent important shifts in the program of the middle school. The first concerns the question of co-education, and the second the revival of the Marxian conception of poly-technical education.

One of the proudest boasts of the Bolsheviks during the first twenty-five years of Soviet power was that they had applied the principle of co-education throughout the system of people's schools in its purest form. Not only did boys and girls attend the same schools; they pursued precisely the same course of instruction and looked forward to precisely the same careers in adult life. This was done in accordance with the doctrine of the equality of the sexes and of the emancipation of woman from the slavery of bourgeois society. Suddenly, on July 23, 1943, the Soviet of People's Commissars issued a decree entitled "On the Introduction of Separate Instruction of Boys and Girls." [45] Although the decision applied only to the ten-year school in the larger population centers, it created something of a shock to Communists and fellow travelers in other countries, and probably to millions of citizens of the Soviet Union. The basic reason for the action was the "necessity of differentiating the military-physical preparation of the youth of the two sexes." It was also supported by the findings of Soviet pedagogical science regarding the different rates of maturation of boys and girls. The immediate public reactions to the "wise policy" announced by the state were universally favorable.

In the summer of 1954 coeducation was restored by a decree of the Council of Ministers, but with a striking difference. For some months the Party and the government had actually encouraged public discussion of the question. In reporting the episode in August, the Minister of Education of the RSFSR remarked that "speakers at the meetings pointed out with great satisfaction that the Party and the Government had given parents the opportunity of expressing their opinions on a question which was of much importance to them, affecting, as it did, the education of their children." Such a statement reveals a great deal about the formulation of educational policy in the Soviet Union. It should be noted further that the people voted neither for nor against the introduction or the abolition of segregated schools.

In the autumn of 1952, after a lapse of approximately twenty years, the polytechnical principle for the organization of the program of the middle school was brought back with authority. The action was taken by the Nineteenth Congress of the Party while Stalin was still alive. The educational officials were asked to prepare new programs to give expression to the changed line. The object of the reorganization was to give to all pupils "solid, systematic knowledge of the foundations of science and at the same time acquaint them with the foundations of contemporary industrial and agricultural practices." The reforms of the early thirties conducted under the aegis of the "mastery of knowledge" were criticized on the grounds that they had led to formalism and the separation of theory and practice—the bête noire of Lenin. This does not mean a return to the patterns of the 1920s. It means rather a concern for laying the foundations in the middle school for the preparation of specialists in the lower and middle technical institutions. The discussions of the question place particular attention on the strengthening of the weakest sector of the Soviet economy—agriculture. It is expected that every school will be equipped with shops, practical laboratories, and garden plots. Systematic visitation to productive enterprises will be an integral part of the curriculum. There is no suggestion, however, that the level of academic scholarship will be lowered. At the same time, without becoming a comprehensive high school on the American pattern, the middle school will broaden its purposes. It will certainly be less a preparatory school for the higher educational institutions than it has been in the immediate past. This return to polytechnization is doubtless due in part to the decision to abolish tuition fees in the upper three grades and to extend universal education through the seventeenth year during the period of the Sixth Five-Year Plan.[46]

5

THE POLITICAL EDUCATION
OF THE YOUNGER GENERATION

In the Soviet Union everything is viewed from the standpoint of *politika,* that is, the policies and purposes of the Communist Party. The entire program of the middle school, outlined in the preceding chapter, is shaped by the immediate and long-term interests of the Party as formulated by the Central Committee. This generalization applies no less to the methods of instruction than to the content of the curriculum, no less to the teaching of aesthetics than to premilitary training, no less to instruction in mathematics than to instruction in history. Every subject in the program of studies is regarded as a means to the building of a Communist society and the creation of the "new man." The same holds true for the vast number of nonschool agencies and organized processes for the molding of the mind. Likewise for the circus and the theater, and for art, music, literature, and science. It should of course be stated that the intensity of concern has varied from time to time in response to both internal and external conditions. It should be stated too that in the first years of Soviet power the direction by the Party was not as all-embracing as it became in the Stalin era. At the very beginning, as we have already seen, the apostles of individual freedom and popular control enjoyed a measure of tolerance.

Paul Blonsky belonged to this group. One may read his *Unified Labor School* from beginning to end and find nothing that would suggest the severe political course which Soviet education was destined to travel during the coming years. This volume, written in the first year of Bolshevik rule and published on January 20, 1919, was the first comprehensive statement of Soviet educational principles following the revolution. It was widely read by teachers and teachers in training, and the present author once considered its translation into the English language. Except for its

82

glorification of human labor, it would seem to belong to an entirely different world and age, as no doubt it does. The closing brief section of the volume is fittingly captioned, "The people, as the creator of the school." Blonsky begins with a question: "Will the new labor school be created quickly?" His answer is that "it will be created not one second before the broad popular masses participate in its construction," and it "will be created not only for the people but also by the people." It should be noted that he does not say that it will be created by the Party, by the "vanguard of the proletariat," or by the proletariat, but by the "broad popular masses." Can the people do this, Blonsky asks again, and then gives his answer: "It is clear that they cannot create a bureaucratic or a monastic-scholastic school. But it is clear that the labor school is just the kind of school they can create because it is a copy of their life in its yearning and consciousness, and which nobody, except the people, can create." [1] This sounds very much like *vox populi, vox Dei*. Yet Blonsky survived and worked in Soviet education until 1936!

Blonsky, however, had some authoritative support for his position at the time he wrote his book. On May 6, 1917, just six months before the seizure of power, the Bolshevik wing of the Russian Social Democratic Labor Party adopted a program which proclaimed the following principles for the control and administration of education: "The transfer of the business of education into the hands of the democratic organs of local self-government; the removal of the central government from every kind of interference in the determination of school programs and in the selection of teaching personnel; the choice of teachers directly by the people themselves and the right of the people to dismiss objectionable teachers." [2] The application of these principles would lead obviously to a program for the political education of the younger generation radically hostile to the logic of the Bolshevik conception of the revolution. Consequently they were never applied.

The true Bolshevik position was not revealed until after the overthrow of the provisional government and the establishment of the dictatorship. On August 28, 1918, presumably at the very time Blonsky was writing his book, Lenin outlined the revised position with utter clarity. Speaking at the First All-Russian Congress on Education, he made a statement regarding the relation of education to politics which reflected the Marxian doctrine of the class struggle in its harshest form. "The more cultured was the bourgeois state," he said, "the more subtly it lied in asserting that the school can remain outside of politics and serve society as a whole." In such a state, he declared, "the school was in fact converted wholly into a weapon of the class domination of the bourgeoisie; it was saturated with the cast of the bourgeois spirit: its aim was to provide capitalists with servile grovelers and efficient workers." Therefore, "we say that our task in the field of education is also a struggle for the overthrow of the bourgeoisie; we openly declare that the school outside of life, outside of politics is a lie and an hypocrisy." [3]

We see here the Marxian conception of the state in every society marked by social classes—of a state which serves faithfully through all its organs the interests of the ruling and exploiting class, untempered by considerations of either mercy, compassion, or general welfare. Lenin embraced this conception and on gaining power applied it in reverse. Education was to become a "mighty weapon," not only to complete the overthrow of the bourgeoisie, but also to build Communist society. It would be a weapon, however, wielded not *by* the people but *for* the people *by* the Party and the dictatorship. These words of Lenin have been repeated endlessly in Soviet pedagogical literature down to this day in all expositions of the relations between education and society. We see in the Soviet Union the most complete and systematic fulfillment of the Marxian conception of the state in the realm of education. We may see also the full application of the dogma of Peter Tkachev that after the completion of the revolution in its physical phase, the "morally and intellectually developed" minority should assume without wavering the education of the people and the transformation of human nature itself. The first task of the Bolsheviks was the political education of the younger generation— a task that is still far from accomplished. And until this task is completed, the Soviet state cannot be expected to relax its control over political education.

II

Political education in the Soviet Union is broadly conceived. It not only means training for citizenship in a dictatorial regime; it involves equally the negative task of the eradication of the "vestiges of capitalism in the consciousness of people." It also involves the positive, uncritical, and enthusiastic acceptance of the practices and doctrines of Communism as they have been developed and projected in the Soviet Union. It means too the unquestioned adoption of the view of the universe known as dialectical materialism and the view of history known as historical materialism. And more important for the rest of the world, perhaps, it means the acceptance of two great myths about "we and they," about the Soviet Union and the so-called people's democracies, on the one side, and all other countries, and particularly the United States of America, on the other. It means further a great body of habits, attitudes, loyalties, and traits of character whose treatment will be reserved somewhat arbitrarily for the succeeding chapter on moral education. The fact is of course recognized that no sharp line can be drawn between morals and politics, or between morals and any other form of human interest or activity. The point should also be made that this brief account of the political education of the younger generation will have to be confined to the major features of the record. And it will be well to keep in mind the primary fact that the basic aim of Soviet education throughout the period of Bolshevik rule has been the conversion of boys and girls and youth into valiant "builders and warriors of Communism."

During the 1920s the program of the complete middle school from the first grade subordinated the "mastery of knowledge," as this was conceived in the next decade, to the political education of the young. This emphasis is easily understood in the light of the conditions prevailing at the time. Even after military victory was won and organized opposition destroyed, the revolutionary forces knew that they were surrounded by alien and hostile elements which were by no means reconciled to the new regime. In 1921 the Bolsheviks were compelled to retreat from their advanced positions and launch the New Economic Policy. A more or less silent struggle was going on in those years in every village, town, and city in the land. That the Soviet power would endure was far from certain. In this situation the school was employed as an indispensable weapon in the capture of the young. If the Bolsheviks were to fail here, everything would be lost.

The entire regimen of the school was organized with the political goal in mind, even though many teachers and educators, nurtured on contrary traditions, probably did not fully realize precisely what was happening. Inspired by the conception of freedom of the child, they accepted the new dispensation in the school for pedagogical reasons. But that very freedom had its political purposes. It served to break the hold of tradition on the young, not only in the school itself, but also in the child-parent relationship and in the wider realm of the community. The past, except for the history of the revolutionary struggle and the backwardness and oppression of the Russian autocracy, was to be forgotten. The youth were told over and over again that they were engaged in the building of a new life, in the building of that Communist society about which the "best people in all ages had dreamed." In the words of the authors of *The School Commune* of Narkompros, "Contemporary life must be understood as a struggle which was started at the broken breach—a struggle which will grow and become more bitter until victory rests with the revolution." [4] According to Pinkevich, a distinguishing trait of the Soviet school "is its aim to prepare a shift of warriors for the revolution, to train the builders of a new society, to produce capable organizers and firm revolutionaries." [5] The freedom of the child consequently was a freedom which was carefully directed by the revolutionary forces.

The concept of socially useful labor, with its Marxian lineage, also bore an indelible political imprint. Pinkevich stressed "the tremendous social and political role of labor" in Soviet education. "To us," he wrote, "this labor does not mean 'labor processes,' nor 'self-service,' nor 'school work-shops,' but the central axis of the entire school. As long as labor is looked upon as something utilitarian or valuable from the point of view of motor training we shall not have a school which merits the name of socialist or communist." The great object of participation in socially useful labor is to make the pupil "feel himself a member of and a worker in a laboring society" and thus take "the first step toward an understanding of the in-terests of the proletariat and of the mutual struggle for the revolution." [6] For pedagogical reasons socially useful labor was advocated as a means of relating theory with practice, of integrating subject matter with life. But it served equally the political purpose of molding attitudes and changing life in the direction of Communism. Every effort was made to persuade children and youth that through their activities they were par-ticipating directly in fulfilling the great human purposes of the revolution. It should be said that many of the activities which were labeled "socially useful labor" were strictly political in the narrower sense of the term. Children and youth were expected to encourage their elders to vote on election day, to organize celebrations of important events in the history of the revolution, to engage actually in the class struggle, and to propagate in numerous ways the policies of the Party. The importance of the class-struggle motif in this sector of Soviet education was developed quite un-ambiguously in a small volume published in 1929 which expounds the theoretical and practical foundations of socially useful work. In a chapter entitled "Class Firmness in the School and Socially-useful Labor" the author thus formulates the purposes of this feature of Soviet education:

1. Socially-useful work draws school children into the class struggle and thus enables them to take a definite place in the socialist camp.
2. Socially-useful work enables the school to participate realistically and prac-tically in the solution of the daily problems confronting the country in the present stage of development.
3. Both of these considerations indicate the tremendous role of socially-useful work in holding the school to the class line.[7]

Socially useful labor also served to fill the lives of the young after school hours with interesting and exciting exploits and thus weaken the influence of traditional forms of social control. Of the same general import were the numerous institutions established for children and youth, some within and some outside the school—circles and clubs designed to appeal to a great variety of interests—literature, art, music, library, handicraft, natural science, social science, sport, and many others. Although each circle or club was supposed to be a "free union of children," it was al-ways the Young Communists and the Young Pioneers who assumed positions of control and leadership. And these organizations were under the strict tutelage of the Party. Also every classroom was supposed to have its Lenin Corner and pictures of Marx and Lenin, and perhaps some other revolutionary leader or leaders, on the walls. As we have said, the entire regimen of the school, in so far as possible, was saturated with the ideas and spirit of the revolution.

In the formal curriculum of the 1920s, if one could say that such a curriculum existed in the complete middle school in those years, a subject called *obshchestvovedenie,* which may be translated inaccurately as "social science," occupied a central position in the fifth, sixth, seventh, eighth, and ninth grades. This was social science, however, not in the Western sense; it was rather a loose and shifting organization of materials designed to promote political understanding and build political convictions in the younger generation in accordance with Bolshevik ideology. According to M. Pistrak of the department of social education in the Commissariat of Education, it was a "synthesis of a number of disciplines —history, economics, geography, political economy, economic policy, sociology, etc.," but with a new content. Thus the facts presented "in courses of history in the prerevolutionary school had to be thrown out as incorrect, unimportant, and unnecessary." [8] History of course had to be rewritten. The same action had to be taken with all other disciplines.

Another leader in Communist education, M. S. Epstein, said that *obshchestvovedenie* was designed to "synthesize those theoretical knowledges and socially-practical skills for the purpose of arming the child and the adolescent in the school and leading them toward the Marxist world outlook and revolutionary actions." This meant the "turning of knowledge into convictions which will evoke appropriate revolutionary actions." [9] Such was the general conception which appeared in practically every account of the subject. I. M. Kataev writes that it sets itself two tasks: "First, the study and perception by children of the life of contemporary society, those foundations on which it rests, those causes which brought it to its present condition, and the basis of the future social order for the purpose of developing a Marxist world view and methodology; and second, the education of a conscious citizen and convinced warrior of the new Communist order." [10] The central role of this subject in the curriculum derives from the great task of the school: "To prepare creators and builders of the new life and warriors for a better future for all toilers . . . to create people with initiative, consciously and critically perceiving reality, capable of feeling, thinking, and working collectively, faithful warriors in the interests of the toilers." [11]

As the subject took form, the discipline of history tended to decline to the vanishing point. The emphasis was placed increasingly on the contemporary world and on political indoctrination. An ardent apostle of this position, V. N. Zhavoronkov, commenting on the new program of the State Scientific Council "from which history is not completely eliminated," casts ridicule on the hopes of historians that "history will be restored to its rights." But "their hopes are in vain," because a careful reading of the program shows that "even the great French Revolution is not treated, and, as for antiquity, there is not the slightest trace of it." The only value in historical study is its contribution to the preparation of Soviet youth to "wage warfare against capitalist society," to "understand the laws of its development," and to compare the "old order" with "contemporary life." [12] The same author in another work puts the whole matter in a nutshell. *"Obshchestvovedenie,"* he says, "must aid in the forming of a world outlook, in giving an understanding of the struggle between two worlds, two social systems—the socialist and the capitalist." [13]

The content of this subject was never fully crystallized, but its essence is revealed in the following program for the training of members of the League of Young Communists in the middle twenties:

FIRST YEAR OF INSTRUCTION

1. The Soviets in the village.
2. The contemporary peasant economy.
3. The city and the village.
4. Cooperation—the road to the new village.
5. The life of the village and the tasks of cultural work.

SECOND YEAR OF INSTRUCTION

1. The people's economy of the USSR and the industrialization of the country.
2. Our policy in the village.
3. The Party, the Komsomol, and the Pioneers.

THIRD YEAR OF INSTRUCTION

1. The USSR and the capitalist order.
2. The struggle of the toilers in the West and in the East.
3. Our current tasks.[14]

Obshchestvovedenie was introduced into the schools in 1922 with high expectations. Here was the true Bolshevik approach to the task of rearing a generation of Communists. It was hoped that the basic ideas and interpretations of social phenomena conveyed by this body of material would penetrate all the other subjects and activities of the school. Supposedly, everything was to be interpreted from its all-embracing frame of reference. According to a standing joke of the time, whenever a pupil was asked a question by a teacher in any field he would begin his response by saying: "Now, from the Marxian point of view." Yet, when the present author in 1927 asked Lunacharsky, the Commissar of Education and a man of broad intellectual interests, whether the Soviet school endeavored to *indoctrinate* the pupils with the ideas and outlooks of Communism, he replied in the negative. The Bolsheviks were opposed to indoctrination. But when asked further if the pupils became Communists during the process of education, he responded in the affirmative. Pressed for an explanation of this happy miracle, he said, with a "bourgeois twinkle" in his eye, that the Soviet school teaches children only the truth, and the truth produces good and loyal Communists.

How successful the instruction in *obshchestvovedenie* really was, it is difficult to say. At the outset there were practically no teachers prepared to teach the subject "from the Marxian point of view." The Party and educational authorities consequently undertook heroic measures to remedy the situation. They provided short in-service programs and special institutes for the retraining of the teachers of history inherited from the old regime; they recruited members of the Party lacking professional qualifications to do the job; also they turned the resources of teacher-training institutions to the preparation of a new generation of teachers "flesh of the flesh and blood of the blood of the proletariat" and the poor peasantry. But in spite of these efforts, the quality of instruction was the subject of much sharp criticism through the decade. As late as 1927, after five years of experimentation, a leading Soviet educator, T. D. Korneichik, published an article, entitled "The Pedagogical Literacy of the Teacher of *Obshchestvovedenie*," in which he made some quite unflattering remarks. "The sin," he declared, "the grievous sin of contemporary instruction in *obshchestvovedenie* resides in the fact that it has been converted into the most uninteresting, the most tedious and boring school subject." As a consequence, "children frequently run away from lessons in *obshchestvovedenie*" and they have "christened the teacher with the name of Soviet priest." Moreover, "children's knowledge of the subject is most insignificant; their answers to questions on entrance examinations to higher schools are anecdotically silly and fantastic." In his search for causes, he said that a "portion of this sin is due to lack of prepared programs, textbooks, and instructions on methodology, to general shortcomings in the work of the school." Also to the "pedagogical unpreparedness of the majority of the teachers." As a result of these deficiencies, "many, many of them conduct instruction in too formal, dry, tedious, and abstract manner." Korneichik then gives the following account of an actual case:

A teacher on the occasion of the celebration of the anniversary of the October Revolution developed for five days with pupils of the fifth grade the theme of "An analysis of the international political situation on the eve of the imperialistic world war." The analysis, moreover, abounded in the most abstract and general terms, concepts, and theses. The pupils yawned irreverently. The teacher crucified himself in his lecture-monologue.

From all this the pupils could only recall "the Sarajevo assassination in 1914." [15]

Yet the instruction seems to have left some imprint on the young. On many occasions on his trips to the Soviet Union the present author took advantage of the opportunity to peer into the minds of children. One of these occasions arose on November 21, 1929, after he had completed a six-thousand-mile journey by automobile through the European part of the Soviet Union. He accepted an invitation to speak at a conference of eighty sixth- and seventh-grade children from some thirty different regions. At the close of his thirty-minute talk the children presented in writing the following twenty-two questions, and a request:

1. For what purpose did the Professor come to Moscow?
2. At whose expense did the Professor come to Moscow?
3. Are the workers from the USSR admitted to America to study technology?
4. Are you a member of the Communist Party; if not, how did you come here?
5. I would like very much to know whether there is somewhere in America, some plan of construction like our Five-Year Plan.
6. Do you have Pioneer, Komsomol and Party organizations, and how do they work, openly or secretly?
7. Can you tell us about the children's movement in America and in general how school children live and work?
8. Are you engaged in the liquidation of illiteracy in America: what plan do you follow and what are the accomplishments at the present moment?
9. Do you have atheists in your schools?
10. Do your children study the Russian language in school, and how do they regard it?
11. Do you have socialist competition and the five-day week?
12. Now that you have seen our country, the country of workers, what is your opinion, is it very backward in comparison with yours or not?
13. Is the Professor sent to this country by the Communist Party or by the capitalists?
14. What is your opinion about those parts of the country which you have visited?
15. What is your impression of the people of our Soviet Union?
16. It would be very interesting to know about the school life in America.
17. Do your workers know about the Five-Year Plan in our Soviet State? And what do they think of it? Do they think that we will fulfill it?
18. Tell us where you think the teaching is better, in America or in the Soviet Union.
19. Who rules your country? If the capitalists rule, do the workers and peasants hope to overthrow the capitalist order?
20. In your opinion which rule is better, the Soviet or the capitalist?
21. Are Soviet holidays celebrated in America?
22. Please explain who you are and give a brief autobiography.
23. Please continue with the questions.

These questions were by no means unusual. In fact, they constitute a pattern which at the time was common to school children throughout the country. Clearly they suggest that instruction in *obshchestvovedenie* had borne some fruit. But whether the youngsters were putting on a show for the benefit of their elders or were actually revealing their own ideological orientation, we cannot know for a certainty. Quite possibly in some instances they were merely using words which they did not understand. As a matter of fact, in the years immediately to follow, the entire subject came under severe criticism on the grounds that it introduced children to highly abstract conceptions which were "entirely beyond their understanding" and consequently led to a glib kind of verbalism. And with the ending of the "experimental period" in the early thirties the enthusiasm for *obshchestvovedenie* rapidly waned, and history full of facts to be mastered returned to her own with power. In a decree on April 23, 1934, the Central Committee declared that the emphasis on "social-political tasks" in the school constituted a "perversion of the tasks of the Communist education of children and is contrary to the decrees of the Central Committee." [16] About three weeks later, on May 16, a joint decree of the Central Committee and the Soviet of People's Commissars ordered the immediate preparation of a comprehensive set of textbooks on the history of the ancient world, of the Middle Ages, of the modern world, of the U.S.S.R., and of the dependent and colonial peoples, all for the purpose of giving to the pupils "a Marxist understanding of history." These textbooks were to observe "an historical-chronological sequence in the exposition of historical events with the view of fixing in the memories of pupils the most important historical phenomena, historical figures, and chronological dates." [17] However, this does not mean that the political education of the younger generation was to be abolished. With the emphasis on the mastery of *knowledge* launched in the following period, this crucial aspect of Soviet education merely assumed a different form.

III

The new period witnessed two important changes in the political education of the younger generation in the complete middle school, in addition to the abolition of *obshchestvovedenie* and the practical elimination of socially useful labor during school hours. On the one hand, political education rapidly absorbed the content of Stalinism; and on the other, the entire process was subjected to much tighter control by the Central Committee. In spite of the monolithic logic inherent in Bolshevism, the 1920s were marked by differences of opinion among educational leaders and by some diversity in instructional materials and programs. The symbol of the new period was the "stable textbook" which was prepared in accordance with Party directives, approved by the highest educational authorities of the state, and used throughout the land for a given subject in a particular grade, except for minor adaptations to local and cultural differences. The power and effectiveness of the control were of course greatly heightened by the emphasis on examinations, school marks, rules of conduct, and a variety of rewards and punishments. One may therefore say that it was in this period that the Bolsheviks proceeded in a most thorough and systematic manner to form the political and world outlook of the New Soviet Man. The thesis will be expounded by a brief examination of the teaching of the several school subjects, but with particular attention to the teaching of history. The major source to be used in the exposition is the 1948 edition of the approved textbook in the theory and practice of education for use in the training of teachers for the secondary school in the universities and higher educational institutions. Entitled *Pedagogika,* it was prepared under the editorship of I. A. Kairov who was later elevated to the position of Minister of Education of the RSFSR. Subsequent textbooks in the same field have followed closely the pattern set by Kairov.

According to Kairov, "the Soviet school is called upon to build in the pupils the foundations of a scientific Communist world outlook," that is, "a unified system of views and convictions which express our attitude and our conduct toward nature and society." The world outlook of "Soviet man is dialectical materialism" and is "based on the firm foundation of scientific knowledge." It is "consequently irreconcilable with every kind of prejudice and superstition." It "affirms that the world is material in its nature, and was created by no one." It "repudiates the concept of supernatural forces which supposedly govern all the phenomena of nature and social life, of the immortality of the soul, and of life hereafter." It contends that "the world develops according to the laws of the movement of matter and is in need of no 'world spirit.'" Soviet society is organized in terms of this view of the universe and history: "Private ownership of the tools and means of production is abolished and with it the exploitation of man by man." The people, having been "delivered forever from age-old oppression, make their own history and hold their destiny in their own hands." In the "building of a new Communist society on scientific foundations" and in the "molding of the Soviet people in the new scientific Communist world outlook," the Communist Party is the "leading and guiding force." [18]

The entire structure of Soviet life "favors the development and strengthening of the scientific world outlook and the deliverance of people from prejudices and superstitions." Unfortunately, the "development of men's consciousness lags behind changes in the conditions of life." As a consequence, "there are not a few people in Soviet society who preserve in their world outlook some vestiges from the past, such as idealistic conceptions and religious prejudices and superstitions." Such vestiges "do not disappear of themselves" but by means of "prolonged, painstaking, and patient educational work." In short, "man must be assisted in ridding himself of prejudices and superstitions through the dissemination and strengthening of materialistic views of all the phenomena of nature and society." Only through such a process of education can pupils be "protected against the influences of idealism and all sorts of superstitions and prejudices." And the "world outlook is formed in pupils first of all in the process of the mastery of the fundamental scientific knowledges." This means that "every school subject must contribute to the development in the pupils of a materialistic conception of the phenomena of nature, social life, and the mind of man."[19] It will be illuminating to see what Kairov has to say about the responsibility of each of the more important subjects in the development of the Communist world view of the younger generation.

Mathematics develops the method of "dialectical thinking in pupils," reflects in "concepts and formulas the dialectic of phenomena in the real world," and "at each step confronts the pupil with the manifestation of such laws as the conversion of quantity into quality and the unity of opposites." Physics "acquaints the pupils with the basic properties and laws of matter and energy," teaches them "that the material world exists objectively, outside and independently of our consciousness," provides a "materialistic explanation of such complex phenomena as radio activity and atomic energy," demonstrates that "matter and energy are eternal and that one form of energy can be transformed into another," and reveals the "operation of the general laws of dialectics in manifold physical phenomena." Consequently, "physics has tremendous significance in the formation of a dialectical-materialistic world outlook." Chemistry in its revelation of the "unity of the structure of the material world," of the "laws of the conservation of matter," and of the nature of "chemical transformations" also contributes to the "formation of a dialectical-materialistic world outlook." Geology answers questions regarding the "creation of the universe" and acquaints pupils with "the evolution of the earth and life." Paleontology in particular "has tremendous significance in the formation of the pupil's world outlook." Astronomy, by acquainting pupils "with the structure of the universe, the structure, movement and evolution of celestial bodies," also "aids in the formation of a materialistic outlook." Biology gives to pupils "a genuinely scientific materialistic interpretation of the natural development of the organic world."[20] The mental sciences of psychology and logic also make an important contribution in this realm.[21]

The other subjects of the curriculum are all included in the category of "the sciences about society and different forms of art." Each is justified, not only for the more narrowly practical purposes, but also for broad political and ideological reasons. Thus, the mastery of the Russian language has "importance for all nationalities." This is due to the fact that the language contains the "basic scientific and literary riches of the peoples of our land," to the fact that its mastery "by the toilers of all the nationalities hastens the liquidation of a certain cultural lag in the national republics," and to the further fact that such mastery "helps to bring together into one brotherly family of peoples the nationalities composing the USSR." Soviet literature, "employing the methods of socialist realism," reveals the "essence of the process of our development," and "educates and arms the people with ideas." Also, it "flogs without mercy the vestiges of yesterday which prevent the Soviet people from marching ahead" and at the same time "boldly attacks bourgeois culture which is in a state of stagnation and decay." The study of foreign languages likewise has a Communist political purpose: knowledge of these languages "strengthens the international bonds of the toilers." Painting and sculpture "serve as a mighty weapon of Communist education." In music, "contemporary Soviet and old revolutionary songs offer rich material for the social-political education of pupils." [22]

This brings the account to that body of subject matter which in the middle thirties displaced *obshchestvovedenie*—geography, history, and the constitution of the U.S.S.R. The concentration on geography and history is impressive, amounting to six years of study for the former and seven for the latter. Instruction in the constitution is confined to the tenth grade. Geography, according to Kairov, "arms the pupils with systematic knowledge of the natural resources, the population, and the economy of the USSR and capitalist countries and shows the transforming influence of man's activity upon the natural environment, which is particularly mighty and planful under the conditions of socialist society." Also "geography cultivates love for the Motherland" and "educates the pupil in the spirit of the brotherly unity and friendship of peoples." It "reveals the life and condition of colonial peoples deprived of rights, oppressed and exploited by imperialist powers." It "helps pupils to understand the life about them and contemporary political events." Finally, it fosters the "acquisition of elementary skills in the field of topography, the ability to use a map and to orient oneself by means of the compass and the planets—all of this has great significance for life and particularly for the military training of youth." [23]

History, of course, is the great subject for the inculcation of Bolshevik political ideas. "In the land of victorious socialism," says Kairov, "history is a mighty weapon of Communist education." It "provides scientifically based answers to the question of whither the development of mankind is tending and by what means progressive mankind can hasten and ease the birth of a new society." The course in history "acquaints pupils with contemporary social life" and "arms them with knowledge of historical facts and events." It equips them to "understand the basic laws in the life of human society and reveals the essence of the historical movement as the struggle of classes." Study of the history of the U.S.S.R. "possesses exceptional importance," because it will "aid pupils better to understand the priceless significance of the achievements of the socialist revolution" and give them an appreciation of the "heroic struggle which their fathers and grandfathers waged for their freedom." It will also teach them to "guard carefully the victories of the revolution" and "cultivate in them the desire to devote all of their strength to continue successfully the cause of their fathers—the building of a Communist society in the Soviet Union." It will "nurture in the pupils a profound loyalty to the interests of the people and the interests of the toilers, a high Communist idealism and irreconcilability toward all reactionary forces, resolution, courage, and bravery in the struggle for the achievement of the finest ideals of mankind—for Communism." It will "imbue pupils with a deep love of the brilliant leaders of the proletarian revolution, Lenin and Stalin"—"the greatest figures of history who struggled selflessly and unwaveringly, persistently and stubbornly with all sorts of enemies of the people," and "brought our country to the victory of socialism." [24]

Although the constitution of the U.S.S.R. is studied for only one hour a week in the tenth grade, this is regarded as a most important element in the political education of the younger generation. "The sections and articles of this historic document," writes Kairov, present to the pupils, "simply and briefly, the facts of the victory of socialism in the USSR, the facts of the liberation of the toilers of the USSR from capitalist slavery, and the facts of the victory in the USSR of democracy developed to its logical end." By learning the "fundamental laws and responsibilities of the citizen, including the electoral system," they will be able to "participate consciously in the socio-political life of the country." And by "perceiving the great democratic ideas on which our constitution is founded" the pupils will be inspired with a "feeling of just pride in the victory won by the peoples of our country on the front of the emancipation of mankind." Such a study of the constitution will "increase the faith of youth in their strength and mobilize them for the struggle to gain new victories for Communism." [25] Unquestionably this is powerful doctrine.

IV

In the program for the political education of the younger generation the Soviet leaders are endeavoring to build in the minds of boys and girls two great myths—one about the Soviet Union and the other about the so-called capitalist world, and particularly today about the United States of America. The content of each of these myths is indicated by much that has already appeared in the present work and in this chapter. But the matter is of such great importance in the world struggle now going on that it merits detailed elaboration. And it is to the "stable textbooks" in history that one may turn most profitably. The reader should recall again the nature of the stable textbook. Briefly, it is a textbook prepared according to Party directives and is the only textbook for the subject and grade. Consequently, the pupil is neither confused nor enlightened by having to confront opposing or even differing points of view. In his early years he is taught the "truth," the "truth of the toiling masses of the world," as revealed, altered, and reversed by the decrees of the Central Committee. And these changes in content are to be understood, not as responses to the advancement of historical knowledge, but rather as responses to the demands of domestic and foreign policy as formulated by the Party. It should not be forgotten that in the Soviet Union history and historiography are regarded as mighty weapons in the political education of the younger generation.

Every Soviet history textbook, even a textbook in ancient history, is quite revealing. But, because of limits of space, attention will be confined here to the third volume of *The History of the USSR*, edited by Professor A. M. Pankratova, covering the period from 1894 to the date of publication, and used in the tenth grade, the last year of the complete middle school. This basic text is now, 1955–1956, in its fourteenth edition. The way in which the Party line influences the preparation of a textbook in history is clearly revealed in the treatment of a single event in four editions of the Pankratova volume—the Allied landing in Normandy on June 6, 1944. The editions are dated 1945, 1946, 1951, and 1955.

Internal evidence shows that the 1945 edition was sent to press toward the end of 1944, the year before the conclusion of the war. The account of the landing runs as follows:

> On June 6, 1944, the allied troops achieved a successful landing in the North of France in accordance with the resolutions adopted at the Teheran Conference regarding coordinated actions of the allied powers from the East and the West. In appraising the landing of the allies in the North of France, Comrade Stalin replied to a correspondent of *Pravda* as follows: "Evaluating the seven-day battle of the liberating armies of the allies during the invasion of Northern France, one can say, wthout equivocation, that the wide forcing of the Channel and the mass landing of allied troops in the North of France were entirely successful. This unquestionably was a brilliant success of our allies. It cannot be denied that the history of warfare knows no other undertaking equal in breadth of design, grandiosity of scale, and mastery of execution.

"As is well known, the 'invincible' Napoleon in his time failed shamefully in his plan to force the Channel and seize the British Isles. The hysterical Hitler, who boasted for two years that he would force the Channel, did not even dare attempt to carry out his threat. Only the British and American troops succeeded in achieving with honor the grandiose plan of forcing the Channel and making a mass landing of troops.

"History will mark this deed as an achievement of the highest order." (*Pravda*, June 14, 1944.)

The brilliantly achieved invasion by British and American troops of Northern France led to further military victories of the allies, who by the 15th of September, 1944, cleared almost all of France and Belgium of German forces and crossed the German frontier, taking possession of the first German city—the birthplace of Marx—Trier.[26]

The edition for the following year of 1946, prepared after the war was over and after a great shift in the Party line, presented a very different picture of the landing. The account was reduced quantitatively to twelve and one-half lines in the Russian text and was changed qualitatively in more striking fashion. And one may be sure that these changes were not the result of the researches of historical scholarship. Here is the quotation:

The victories of the Red Army played a decisive role in the insuring of the military successes of the allies in North Africa and Italy. The drawing of the basic strategic German reserves from the West and the destruction of the best German divisions on the Soviet-German front provided the opportunity for the successful development of large offensive operations by the allies in Europe. On June 6, 1944, allied troops achieved a landing in northern France. The second front held 75 Hitlerite divisions and, gradually, eased the fulfillment by the Red Army of the task of the final defeat of German troops. Thus, the fourth year of the war proved to be a year of decisive victories of the Soviet armies and the armies of our allies over the German forces.[27]

By 1951 the "brilliant success of our allies" approached the vanishing point in these brief lines:

Our allies in the war—England and the United States of America—in the course of three years of war delayed in every way the opening of a second front in Europe against the German troops. But when, after the tremendous victories of the Soviet Army, it became clear that the Soviet Union without the aid of the allies would occupy with its own forces the territory of Germany and liberate France, the allies decided to open a second front in Europe.[28]

Four years later, and two years after the death of Stalin, it should be noted, the tribute to England and the United States passed the zero point and entered the realm of negative quantities. "Our allies" have disappeared and presumably changed sides years after the close of the war:

England and the United States of America in the course of three years of war delayed in every way the opening of a second front in Europe against the German troops. But when after the tremendous victories of the Soviet Army it became clear that the Soviet Union, with its own forces would occupy the entire territory of Germany and liberate France, England and the USA decided to open a second front in Europe.[29]

Some of the comments in the course of the chapter on "The Great Patriotic War of the Soviet Union" convey an even more hostile attitude toward the Western Allies. It would seem that both Britain and the United States sabotaged the war from June 22, 1941, the day Hitler launched his attack on the Soviet Union. Thus the agreements reached in the Moscow Conference in 1942 with Great Britain and the United States "did not mean that the ruling circles in England and the USA would renounce their anti-Soviet policy. Reactionary elements of all kinds delayed the opening of a second front in Europe."[30] And following the Teheran Conference of 1943, Churchill "employed every kind of dodge to block the opening of a second front, in order to bring the greatest possible harm to the Soviet state. Also reactionary circles in the USA took the same position regarding the second front and supported all measures for the exhaustion of the USSR."[31] Likewise, "the decisions of the Crimean [Yalta] Conference were systematically disrupted and are being disrupted by the ruling circles of Great Britain and the USA who obstruct in every way the establishing of a genuinely democratic peace and international cooperation."[32] The Potsdam Conference fares no better. Its decisions, "in spite of the fact that they were signed by the leaders of the governments of Great Britain and the USA, were violated and are being violated by them systematically and with evil design."[33]

This hostility of the Western powers preceded the war. Thus, the Soviet government, always carrying on a "struggle for peace," "began negotiations with representatives of England and France for the conclusion of a pact of mutual aid against fascist aggression in Europe." Unfortunately, "the negotiations were rendered unsuccessful by the intrigues of extremely reactionary circles of these countries hostile toward the USSR and striving to direct aggression exclusively against the Soviet Union."[34] The Soviet-Nazi Pact followed, but for the purpose of keeping the peace. Consequently, "the wise foreign policy of the Soviet Government raised yet higher the role of the USSR in the resolution of international problems and its authority in the eyes of the toilers of the entire world."[35] The Red Army, of course, moved into western White Russia and the Ukraine to "liberate" the peoples of these lands and enable them to unite with their brothers and sisters in the Soviet Union. And the peoples of Lithuania, Latvia, and Esthonia, after being "liberated" by the Red Army, petitioned the Supreme Soviet through their freely elected representatives for admission into the Soviet Union. Their petitions were all granted. But the case of Finland was different. It seems that "the Finnish militarists, having long since entered into relations with the German fascists, and incited by the ruling circles of England, France, and the United States of America, entered into a war with the Soviet Union." [36]

In spite of all these difficulties, in spite of the powerful armed forces of Germany and Japan and the intrigues of the "ruling circles" shaping the policies of their avowed allies, the Soviet people won the war. In fact, "the Soviet Union alone carried the basic burden of the war, and the Soviet people shed their blood not only for themselves, but also for other peoples." [37] And the "Soviet Army fulfilled its liberating mission in relation to all the peoples of Europe and helped them to throw off the yoke of the German enslavers." It took only twenty-four days to bring Japan to unconditional surrender. The following lines put the last seal on this heroic achievement:

> The victory of the Soviet Union in the Great Patriotic War excited the admiration of all progressive mankind. The entire world recognized the great service of the Soviet Army which by its heroic and selfless struggle saved civilization from the German-fascist barbarians and from the Japanese imperialists. The Soviet Army emerged before the whole world as an army of liberation, and the Soviet Union as the savior of civilization and progress in Europe and throughout the world.[38]

The defeat of Hitler apparently was due entirely to the Soviet Union— its courageous people, its heroic army, its brilliant leadership, and its social system. The textbook makes no mention of lend-lease, of the perilous voyages around the North Cape, of the strategic bombing of German industrial centers, of the battle for the control of the seas, of the long struggle in the Pacific against Japan, of the sublime courage of the British people in the summer of 1940. It was the Soviet workers who supplied "the Soviet Army with arms, munitions, and equipment," and the collective farmers who "provided food and raw materials for both the Soviet Army and the country." [39] According to Stalin, the victory was a triumph of the "Soviet social order," of the "Soviet governmental order," of the "Soviet armed forces." And the Party receives the following accolade:

> The leading and directing role of the Communist Party among the masses of the people is the most important source of the strength of the Soviet Union. In the days of the Patriotic War the Communist Party was the inspirer and organizer of the struggle of all peoples against the fascist robbers. As a result of the organizational work of the Party all the energies of the Soviet people were united and directed toward the common goal.[40]

Leading the Party was Stalin, whose name "rightly stands along with the names of the greatest people in the history of mankind—Marx-Engels-Lenin." [41]

The meaning of the victory, according to the textbook, is clear. The war was "a turning point in the history of mankind." The argument runs as follows:

> The victory of the Soviet people over the strongest imperialistic beast graphically demonstrated to the entire world the tremendous superiority of the socialist system over the capitalist. This was one of the most important results of the struggle between the two systems into which the world split as a result of the first victorious proletarian revolution in the world. . . .
>
> The outcome of the Patriotic War is a great historic lesson which serves as a terrible warning to all who would attempt to set loose a new war. The Soviet armed forces, leaning on the greatly revived economic and political might of our state, on their very rich military experience, will always do their duty before the Motherland. . . .
>
> The Great Patriotic War was not only for the freedom and independence of our socialist fatherland; it was at the same time a war for the liberation of the enslaved peoples of Europe from Hitlerite tyranny. In the gigantic armed conflict with fascism, as the most beastly and predatory detachment of the imperialists of the entire world, socialism was victorious and this victory determined the entire subsequent fate of mankind. . . .
>
> The great victory of the Soviet Army not only helped the peoples of a number of countries of Europe and Asia to throw off the yoke of slavery, but also inspired them to a further struggle for a new and just order, without landlords and capitalists. In this is one of the greatest meanings of the universal-historical victory of the Soviet people in the Great Patriotic War.
>
> Forever will remain in the memory of the people the image of the Soviet warrior who with his blood, his courage, and his mastery of the military art saved world civilization from catastrophe and destruction.[42]

The war changed profoundly the "balance of political forces" in the world. "In the postwar period there have been formed two opposing political camps: the aggressive, antidemocratic camp led by the USA, and the peace-loving, democratic camp led by the Soviet Union." The balance of "forces between these two systems—the socialist and the capitalist—has been radically changed to the advantage of socialism." On the one side, "a third of mankind, more than 800 million people, has fallen away from the capitalist system and firmly entered on the road to socialism and democracy." On the other side, "within the capitalist system as a result of the war three large states—Germany, Italy, and Japan—have dropped out of the number of great powers, and England and France have lost their former positions." At the same time, "the world economic situation in the postwar period is characterized by two lines of development. One is the line of uninterrupted raising of the peaceful economy of the Soviet Union and the countries of the democratic camp. The other is the line of continuing decline of the economy of capitalism, shackled to the general crisis of the capitalist system." [43]

The countries of the camp of capitalism are "approaching a new economic crisis," according to the laws of social development as revealed by Marx and Engels. They are now engaged in a fierce struggle for markets and raw materials to keep their economies going. Moreover, "in the USA, England, Italy, Japan, Belgium, and Western Germany alone the number of fully and partly unemployed amounts to 32 million persons." The condition of the masses in the United States is particularly grievous: "From 1938 to 1952 the military expenditures of the USA grew almost 60 times, the direct taxes on the population increased more than 12 times, and the profits of the monopolists expanded 13 times. Yet the unrestrained pillaging of the population by a handful of millionaires significantly reduces the purchasing power, lowers the demand for consumers' goods, and thus hastens the coming of an economic crisis." Striving to find a way out of their political and economic difficulties, "the ruling circles of the USA and other imperialist states are preparing a new world war, directed in the first instance against the USSR and the countries of people's democracy." Already "in their drive for 'world rule' the United States of America has passed from the preparation of a new world war to a direct act of aggression, attacking the Korean People's Democratic Republic in the summer of 1950." And "the American imperialists are attempting to conceal their policy with the flag of the United Nations, thus transforming this organization, created for the guarding and strengthening of peace, into an organ to hide acts of aggression." [44] Fortunately, in this situation "the Soviet Government, expressing the hopes of all progressive mankind, unceasingly steps forward to guard peace against threats of war, to strengthen friendly relations between countries, and to promote international cooperation on the foundation of the mutual respect and independence of peoples." [45]

There is of course nothing in the textbook about the Soviet system of espionage, probably the most expensive and comprehensive in the long history of this art. There are no references to the defections of Igor Gouzenko in Canada, Vladimir Petrov in Australia, and many others which revealed clearly the magnitude and the complicated operations of the system. But, according to Communist habit and custom, they attribute to others the hostile practices in which they engage most widely and successfully. The following short paragraphs tell the story:

> The imperialists of the USA and their partners, feverishly preparing for a new world war, strenuously dispatch to the USSR and the countries of people's democracy their spies, wreckers, and diversionists, attempting to undermine peaceful, socialist construction.
>
> In 1952 the Senate of the USA passed a law for the assigning of the vast sum of 100 million dollars specifically for injurious, terroristic and spying activity in the countries of the democratic camp.

The Soviet people must not forget for one minute the necessity of raising in every way their vigilance, of keeping a sharp eye for all intrigues of the firebrands of war and their agents, of strengthening unceasingly the armed forces and the *scouting organs* of our government. [Italics mine.] [46]

Without doubt this characterization of the Soviet system of security police and espionage as "scouting organs" is the crowning euphemism of the twentieth century.[47]

The textbook concludes with a look backward and a look forward, ecstatic about past achievements and sublimely confident of the future. "In October, 1917, under the banner of Leninism, the working class of our country in union with the poor peasantry achieved the greatest victorious socialist revolution in history, and opened a new epoch in the history of mankind." In the meantime, the "march of world history brilliantly confirms the prescience of V. I. Lenin and I. V. Stalin about the universal-historical role of the first socialist state as the vanguard of the international Communist movement." The actual achievement of "socialism and the successes of Communist construction in the USSR demonstrate to the whole world the indisputable superiority of the Soviet socialist order over the capitalist order and assure the doom of capitalism." In their struggle to achieve the transition from socialism to Communism the Soviet people are led by the Communist Party. "Armed with the knowledge of the laws of social development, with the revolutionary theory of Marx-Engels-Lenin-Stalin, the Communist Party of the Soviet Union successfully resolves the problems of Communist construction." The relation between the Party and the people is frankly stated: "The strength of the Party is in its indissoluble bond with the people. The strength of the people is in its solidarity around the Party." Under these circumstances "no power on earth can stop the victorious movement of the Soviet people to the ultimate triumph of Communism." The fact is that "we live in an age when all roads lead to Communism."[48]

An interesting feature of a textbook in Soviet history is a list of the "Principal Dates in the History of the USSR" for the period covered. The pupil is expected to commit to memory the dates and the associated events. An examination of the list given in the textbook under review is most illuminating. Among important items missing are the following: the election of delegates to the Constituent Assembly in November, 1917, the freest election the Russian people have ever known; the dissolution of the Constituent Assembly by armed force when it convened the following January; the Kronshtadt uprising in 1921 and the New Economic Policy which followed; the execution of Zinoviev, Kamenev, Bukharin and other renowned Bolshevik leaders in 1936 and 1937; the Soviet-Nazi Pact of 1939; the dissolution of the Comintern in 1943; the launching of the United Nations in 1945; the liquidation of several national minorities during and after the war; and the execution of Beria in 1953. On the other hand, the list contains several events which did not occur, or at least did not occur as represented: "August, 1918—the villainous attempt of Social Revolutionaries and Bukharinites on V. I. Lenin"; "December 1, 1934—the villainous murder of S. M. Kirov by Trotzkyite-Zinovievite-Bukharinite bandits"; and "June, 1936—the villainous murder of A. M. Gorky by Trotzkyite-Zinovievite-Bukharinite bandits." It should be noted in this connection that after Stalin rose to power the history of the revolution was radically rewritten, and not to his disadvantage. In the chapter devoted to the Great Patriotic War, thirty-nine pages in length, the name of Stalin appears fifty-six times. No other living leader of the Party or any one of the great Soviet commanders is mentioned even once. It is an interesting feat in historiography to give an account of a great war lasting more than four years without referring to the outstanding military figures. And Stalin's successors are not mentioned in the account of the dictator's death. This would seem to show that a struggle over the succession was still under way at the time of publication and that Pankratova was uncertain about the outcome. Obviously she was not taking any chances.

The impact of the repudiation of Stalin at the Twentieth Congress on Soviet historiography and history textbooks will undoubtedly be tremendous. That the textbooks would be revised in accordance with the new line was made perfectly clear by Pankratova herself in an address delivered at the Congress. With thirty-two references to Lenin and nine to Khrushchev in an address of about three thousand words she demolished the "cult of personality" and proclaimed the "necessity of a struggle against the survivals of subjective-idealistic views about the role of personality in history"! She said further that the "classics of Marxism-Leninism considered the cult of personality a serious and harmful deviation from the materialistic conception of history" and that the "theory of 'heroes and crowds' disparages the role of the masses." [49] As editor for twenty years of the most important textbooks in the field of Soviet history taught in the middle school, she was well qualified to speak and expound the new line, even though it contradicted her life's work. The upshot was a decision to interrupt the teaching of history in the tenth grade until a revised textbook could be prepared. The big question, of course, is whether the new edition will be any more objective and truthful than the old. There is no suggestion in Pankratova's address that the Central Committee will abandon the Leninist doctrine regarding the preparation of materials for use in the schools "saturated with Communism." Whatever the line of the Party, it will continue to be decisive in the political education of the younger generation. *Politika* will still rule.*

* The new textbooks appearing in September, 1956, are in accord with these expectations.

V

In the present volume several references have been made to the Young Communists and the Young Pioneers. The first is an organization of youth from fourteen to twenty-six years of age, and the second an organization of children from nine to fourteen. The full name of the former is the All-Union Leninist Communist Union of Youth, and of the latter the All-Union Children's Communist Organization in the Name of Lenin. The one was launched in 1918, and the other in 1922. In the interests of economy of space they will ordinarily be designated in these pages simply the Young Communists, or Komsomol, and the Young Pioneers.

Beginning as small organizations of carefully selected youth and children, they have grown into mass organizations enrolling a near majority of the appropriate ages. They are both under the closest supervision of the Communist Party, although the Young Communists regard the Pioneers as their offspring and special responsibility. They are both organized on the closely knit and monolithic pattern of the Party. The Young Communists and the Young Pioneers are among the foremost agencies in the field of political education. It may be said that they have served four functions. In the first place, they have carried the voice, the policies, and the doctrines of the Party to children and youth and have thus been an important factor in the Party's program for the political capture of the entire younger generation. In the second place, they have kept the Party informed regarding the political beliefs and activities of their contemporaries and also of their elders—parents and teachers in particular. In the third place, they have been active helpers of the Party in the general propagation of its ideas and programs and in the actual work of socialist and Communist construction. And in the fourth place, they have served as effective agencies for training and testing members of the younger generation with a view to the recruitment of the "best" into the Party itself. Their role in the middle and higher schools has been an important one. They have provided the major part of the leadership in pupil self-government, in the school collective, and in all of the extracurricular activities of these institutions. Young Communists and Young Pioneers are always under heavy pressure from the Party and their own organizations to "volunteer" for every kind of onerous task. At the time of writing, thousands of Young Communists are being drafted into special brigades to assist the police in the struggle against juvenile delinquency and crime.

The "statutes" of the Union of Young Communists, as formulated in the 1920s, give a clear picture of the political outlook of the organization. According to these statutes, it is the duty of every Young Communist to master "revolutionary theory" as a "mighty weapon in the hands of the toilers" and to "study systematically and stubbornly the teachings of Marx,

Engels, Lenin, and Stalin." He must "fight vigorously for the general line of the Party, unmask irreconcilably and consistently deviations in both theory and practice, and give a decisive blow to opportunistic perversions of the teachings of Lenin."

He must also "fight unceasingly for the Leninist unity of the Party, cultivate the spirit of its Bolshevist tradition, and rebuff unremittingly every attempt to oppose the Party." Naturally, he must "conduct an irreconcilable struggle against the class enemy and attack without mercy pessimists, opportunists, and people of little faith." He must be a "shock worker," a "model of Bolshevik efficiency," and a "propagandist of the new Communist forms of life." He must "be ready at any minute to defend the USSR with a weapon in his hands." He must remember that "as yet the working class has conquered only one-sixth of the earth" and that the "struggle will not be concluded until the proletarian revolution is victorious throughout the world." He must remember too that the "road to Communism rests on the unbroken union of the toilers of all lands and nations" and that he must "devote his whole life to the great cause of the struggle for Communism, ready at the first call of the Party to take his place in the front ranks of the warriors of the international proletarian army." He is told that he should "prepare himself in all of his activity to become a member of the All-Union Communist Party of Bolsheviks," but that only "the best members" will be admitted "without recommendations." All others have required one or more recommendation and have been held on probation as "candidates" for longer or shorter periods.[50]

The Young Pioneers have often been called the "Boy Scouts of Russia." While there are some points of resemblance, the comparison is about as apt as the likening of the Supreme Soviet to the American Congress. The Pioneers constitute a wholly authentic element of the Soviet system, quite as much so as the Young Communists or the Party itself. While the Young Pioneer loves to go camping and take excursions and is told to be "a model to all children," to be "industrious, persistent and cheerful," he is given very positive political instruction in the "laws of the Young Pioneers"—instruction which would certainly bring trouble on the head of any leader of the Boy or Girl Scouts. Thus, the Pioneer must be "true to the cause of the workers," "an enemy of kulaks and capitalists," and an ardent supporter of the "Communist International." He must be a "friend and comrade of the children of the workers, peasants, and toilers of the entire world" and a "younger brother and helper of the Communist and the Young Communist in the struggle for Communism." He must "prepare himself to become a selfless warrior against poverty and oppression, and for socialism." To this end he must master "knowledge," "help teachers and others," and "support discipline in study and work." He must be "an active helper to the Soviet, the labor union, and the cooperative," a "friend and helper of the Red Army, and a future warrior" in the armed forces. He must assist in the advance of "technical knowledge and labor discipline" and be an "active participant in the harvest." He must oppose "national differences and hatreds" and support the "international union of all workers and toilers." He must "wage war against drunkenness and hooliganism, against religious stupefaction." Finally, he must "organize and unite children under the banner of Ilich (Lenin)." [51] Being the darling of the Party, the organization of Young Pioneers is the recipient of many privileges. Like the League of Young Communists, it has its own newspaper and literature. It has also houses and palaces, some of which are quite extravagantly appointed and in which the Pioneers may pursue a great variety of cultural and avocational interests.

In the thirties and forties the concerns and activities of both the Young Communists and the Young Pioneers took new directions, in accordance with profound shifts in the Party line. One of these shifts, as already noted, called for the mastery of knowledge on the part of the younger generation. Another involved an exaggerated emphasis on "Soviet patriotism" and the "glorious Soviet Motherland," a shift that will be reported in some detail in the following chapter. In accordance with a decision of the Central Committee of the Party on April 21, 1932, "the basic task of the Pioneer organization is the Communist education of a strong, healthy shift of Young Communists devoted to the cause of Lenin and Stalin, armed with knowledge and culture." [52] The Pioneers were called upon to "organize their work so that it would raise the ideological-political level of their members and other pupils, develop their interest in science, technology, and art, and achieve a higher level of knowledge and discipline on the part of pupils." [53] An authoritative monograph, published under the auspices of the Central Committee of the Union of Young Communists in 1947, emphasizes the new line on Soviet patriotism in these words: "Each one of us says with pride: 'I am a citizen of the Soviet Union. We love our Motherland as our own mother; we are prepared to serve her without sparing our strength or life itself because there is no other people as great as ours and no other country as great as ours." [54]

A third organization, with both adult and youth sections, merits brief consideration here—an organization dedicated to the transformation of the world view of both the younger and the older generation—The League of the Militant Godless. With its roots going back to 1921, it was organized in 1925 as "A Society of Friends of the Godless," changed its name in 1926 to "The League of the Godless," and in 1929 to "The League of the Militant Godless." The age of admission, first set at eighteen, was later lowered to sixteen and then to fourteen years. Also in 1929 the League organized a section for children aged eight to fourteen which came to be known as "The League of the Young Militant Godless." [55]

The League of the Militant Godless was very active in the middle twenties. It conducted antireligious propaganda, organized antireligious courses, published a great quantity of antireligious literature, organized antireligious discussion circles, founded antireligious museums, and employed for antireligious purposes the cinema, the theater, the library, the radio, and other agencies. In 1929 it succeeded in winning the Commissariat of Education over to a militant antireligious policy. Also it worked closely with the Young Communists and the Young Pioneers. An interesting example of the penetration of this influence into the primary school is a simple problem in arithmetic which appeared in an approved textbook for the second grade, published in 1936: "Find out how many children in your grade are members of the League of the Young Militant Godless. Treat separately the boys and the girls. Draw in your notebooks two columns of squares. One column should represent the godless boys, the other—the girls. Over the diagram write: 'The number of godless in the second grade.' Under the columns write: 'Boys,' 'girls.' Along with the diagram indicate the scale on which it is made." [56]

During the Great Patriotic War the attack on religion was moderated to a degree in the interests of national solidarity. But in the following years, and particularly since Stalin's death, the campaign to "improve" antireligious instruction in the schools has assumed the proportions of a major undertaking. The organs of the All-Union Ministry of Culture and the Republican Ministries of Education in the summer of 1954 devoted considerable space to the campaign. *Sovietskaia Kultura* on August 28 reported the results of a five-day seminar in Leningrad "on the subject of scientific-atheistic propaganda organized by the regional committee of the Communist Party." Among the themes developed by the speakers were the following: "On the Relation of the Communist Party and the Soviet State toward Religion and the Church," "Science and Religon on the Origin of the World," "The Reactionary Nature of Religious Vestiges in the Consciousness of People," "The Successes of Contemporary Cosmogony," and "The Method of Scientific-Atheistic Propaganda." The "deplorable condition" in the schools which the campaign was launched to correct is realistically described in an editorial entitled "A Weak Sector" in *Uchitel'skaia Gazeta*, September 1, 1954, at the opening of the new school year. In reporting conditions in the schools of Yaroslavl' the editorial states categorically that the quality of "scientific-atheistic training of pupils" is "intolerable" and that "many teachers do not conduct a struggle against the penetration into the midst of the children of religious survivals and superstitions." In its bill of particulars the editorial reports that "some pupils participate in religious ceremonies and are infected with all sorts of superstitions," that a fourth-grade pupil, Igor, and his third-grade sister, Galia, "wear crucifixes, attend church regularly, read prayers, and collect money for church needs," that there are "instances of the christening of children in the region," and that "teachers, knowing these things, tolerate them and look on them with indifference." It seems also that some "teachers are themselves enslaved by religious prejudices and observe church rites and holidays." One teacher, Comrade Nikolaeva, of School No. 14, was known to keep "ikons illuminated by image lamps" in her home. And then there was the case of an upper-class student in School No. 21 who "left the ranks of the Komsomol and devoted herself to prayers" in order to improve her scholarship. The account concludes that antireligious instruction should be "systematic" in character and marked by a "militant and offensive spirit," that "a most important task of all teachers is to show the absolute contradiction and irreconcilability of science and religion." Clearly antireligion has become a basic component of the religion of the Soviet state. This emphasis constitutes one of the essential elements in the political education of the younger generation.

6

THE MORAL EDUCATION
OF THE YOUNGER GENERATION

In his oft-quoted address at the Third All-Russian Congress of the League of Young Communists in 1920 Lenin told his audience that "the entire question of education of contemporary youth must be education in Communist morality." [1] This statement expresses the fundamental truth that there is a moral aspect to every element or phase of an educational program. Certainly much of the content of the chapter on political education, and of every chapter in the present volume, involves questions of morality, of right and wrong, of good and evil. A separate treatment of the subject, however, is both justified and necessary in any effort to give a comprehensive account of Soviet education. This is true in part because of the tremendous emphasis on "education in Communist morality" in Soviet pedagogical literature, programs, and philosophy—an emphasis that has increased greatly with the passage of the years, and particularly since the great change of the middle thirties. It is true also because of the special nature of the Bolshevik regime, of its purposes and methods.

The October Revolution set itself the task of transforming human society, of building a new society which would pass through the imperfect stage of socialism to the perfect stage of Communism—the ultimate form of human society toward which the entire history of man has been tending since the species first appeared on the planet—the earthly apocalypse of the race. But the transformation of society implied an equally profound change in people, a change in their moral attributes and dispositions, as well as in their physical and intellectual powers and qualities. Inherited traits of character, vestiges from the "old exploiting society," would have to be eradicated, and new traits appropriate to the "new classless society" would have to be developed. The early Bolsheviks and their precursors in the history of the Russian revolutionary movement wrote rapturously about "new people" and the "people of the future," as Soviet literature today is saturated with passages extolling the "New Soviet Man," as the highest and finest expression of the historical process. The cultivation in boys and girls of the moral traits of the New Soviet Man is the essence of education in Communist morality. Here is one of the most basic tasks assigned to the complete middle school, assisted by the family, the Young Pioneers, the Young Communists, and all the other agencies and processes for molding the minds and hearts of the younger generation.

There emerges here a certain fundamental conflict in Soviet ideology which is confronted, though not fully acknowledged, by Soviet spokesmen. According to a strict Marxian interpretation, the question of the moral education of the people and the creation of the New Soviet Man should present few difficulties. According to this interpretation, the basic reality in any society from which all else derives is "the prevailing mode of production and exchange, and the social organization necessarily following from it." [2] The evils of historical society and the delinquencies of historical man are the natural and inevitable fruit of the institution of private property in the means of production and the consequent division of society into classes. Vice, crime, prejudice, hatred, avarice, selfishness, and general sinfulness are all the product of the operation of this institution. It would be safe to assume therefore that with its abolition the "people of the future" and the New Soviet Man would quickly appear. Under the conditions of public property and classlessness the "remnants of bourgeois mentality" would wither away and children would grow to maturity fully endowed with the virtues of utopia. In the process of overthrowing the old order and building the new, the working class "purges itself of all the filth of the old society" and "changes its own nature." [3] By 1936, according to the "Great Stalinist Constitution" adopted in that year, private property in the means of production was abolished and a socialist order established. Yet great masses of the people continued to behave in the manner of economic individualists, and Soviet youth were frequently charged with "hooliganism." It was even necessary to execute most of the old Bolshevik leaders and send millions to forced-labor camps. Obviously something had gone wrong.

The difficulty doubtless arises from the nature of Bolshevism. On achieving power, the Bolsheviks, as we have noted, found themselves in the position foreseen by Tkachev. A small, tightly organized and disciplined minority, holding in its hands the absolute power of the state and its organs of coercion, sought to impose its will on a vast population and drive that population relentlessly toward the goal of Communism, ruthlessly silencing and destroying all opposition. And the difficulty was multiplied when the minority was subjected to the despotic rule of a single man and perhaps his immediate associates. It is not surprising that the great emphasis on education in Communist morality developed during the reign of Joseph Stalin. The Bolshevik apologist would probably say that the source of the difficulty is the fact that the revolution must pass through the stage of socialism before arriving at the goal of Communism, that this first stage was reached years ago, and that the Party is now leading the people to final victory. If this is so, the Party spokesmen should be speaking less of the "vestiges of capitalism" and more of the "vestiges of socialism." For the two social orders as conceived by the Bolsheviks, are profoundly different and require correspondingly different moralities. One need only repeat the words to be found in the textbooks. Under socialism the guiding principle is: "From each according to his ability, to each according to his work"; whereas under Communism it is: "From each according to his ability, to each according to his needs." In the Soviet Union today the adjustment of economic and other rewards to performance generates a highly competitive spirit which would appear to be quite contrary to the ethics of Communism. At any rate the emphasis today is on Communist and not on socialist morality.

The problem of the "vestiges" is recognized by all Soviet spokesmen. And it is interesting to observe that they employ the concept of "cultural lag" somewhat after the manner of William F. Ogburn in his *Social Change*, published in 1922. The substance of this concept is that the "adaptive" elements of the culture—the political, moral, and spiritual— lag behind the economic. There is, however, an important difference. The Bolsheviks, their professed doctrine to the contrary notwithstanding, have actually subjected economic to political power. The following quotation from M. I. Kalinin in 1945 conveys the official view of Soviet morality today and the nature of the lag:

> The Great October Socialist Revolution raised the morality of the peoples of Russia to a higher stage. It has become the highest morality in human society. This is no exaggeration: it is merely an objective deduction from the actual reality. To be sure, this does not mean that the people awoke one beautiful morning, endowed with a sudden blessing—a new socialist morality. Marx pointed out long ago that the consciousness of people lags behind economic development, that it is not possible in just one revolutionary overturn to destroy all the vestiges of capitalism.[4]

And so, "in a stubborn struggle to overcome the desperate resistance of all the traditions of the old world, the Party of Lenin and Stalin has brought the toilers of our country to the victory of socialism."[5]

II

The theoretical foundations of Communist morality are derived from the Marxist-Leninist view of the world and of human history. In Lenin's talk to the Young Communists in 1920 he explained quite clearly the nature of Communist ethics in words which are commonly quoted today wherever the subject of ethics is expounded. He repudiated scornfully the idea of universal ethical standards "stemming from the will of god," because "we believe in no god." And "we know very well that the clergy, the landlords, and the bourgeoisie have spoken in the name of god in order to advance their own exploiting interests." Such a brand of ethics is a "deception, a fraud, and a clouding of the minds of workers and peasants in the interests of landlords and capitalists." From this Lenin proceeds to the basic Marxian principle of the class struggle in history and the central ethical doctrine of the *Catechism of a Revolutionist.* "For us," he says, "ethics are subjected to the interests of the class struggle of the proletariat in the creating of a new Communist society." [6] That this conception of ethics has not been forgotten or superseded in the Soviet Union was made very clear by a Soviet educator, N. I. Boldyrov, in a broadcast from Moscow on July 7, 1955, entitled "Lenin and Communist Morality." In the course of the lecture the speaker quoted Lenin as follows: "Everything that contributes to the building of a Communist society is moral, everything that hinders this is immoral and amoral." [7] And this means that "if you are not inclined to crawl in the mud on your belly, you are not a revolutionary, but a chatterbox." [8] Of course only the Central Committee of the Party can know for a certainty what builds and what does not build the Communist society. And all Soviet citizens, including teachers and educators, must heed the voice of the Party.

Such a view of morality has some interesting and fateful consequences. Nowhere perhaps is this seen more clearly than in the writing of history. The reader is already familiar with the way in which school textbooks are written and rewritten in the interests of building Communism, of liquidating kulaks, of battling the "ruling circles" in the United States, of proving that the bourgeois world is moving to its doom in strict accord with the Marxian laws of social development. The great conception of historical truth as developed by professional historians during the past century and a half is definitely repudiated. According to this conception, the historian, whatever his hopes and fears, whatever his likes and dislikes, is expected to strive to give a truthful account of the course of events in a given place and time. To be guided by such considerations is labeled in the Soviet Union "objectivism" or "bourgeois objectivism." Thus the *Dictionary of the Russian Language,* published in 1949, gives the following definition of the word "objectivism": "Pseudo-objectivity in the study and evaluation of anything, not based on a class, Marxist-Leninist analysis." [9] And no other definition is offered. This means that the Soviet historian when writing on any subject of concern to the Party, must present a record of events which supports the "proletariat," the "vanguard of the proletariat," the "Communist Party of the Soviet Union," or the "Central Committee of the Party" in the struggle to overthrow the capitalists and build a Communist society. This means also that an individual under arrest on the charge of espionage or counterrevolutionary activity must make a "truthful" confession in this sense. The "truth" is not an account of what actually occurred, but rather a statement that will strengthen the Bolshevik state and advance the case of Communism. Undoubtedly, the "confessions" of many of the old Bolsheviks were of this order.

A striking instance of the bearing of this approach on historical writing came to the attention of the world on February 10, 1948. On that day the Central Committee of the Party issued an "ideological decree" directed at Soviet musical composers in general and at Vano Muradeli, one of the younger composers, in particular, for his opera *Velikaia Druzhba*. Among other things the decree stated that the plot of the opera, which unfolded in the North Caucasus in the years 1918 to 1921, was "historically false and fictitious." It created the "erroneous impression that peoples of the Caucasus, such as the Georgians and the Ossetians, were at that time hostile to the Russian people. This is historically false. It was the Ingushi and Chechentsi who opposed the establishment of friendship among peoples of the North Caucasus at the time." [10] As a matter of historical fact, the Bolsheviks had a great deal of trouble with the Georgians during the period of the civil war. Georgia was one of the few really strong centers of democratic socialism in those years. But to recognize this fact after the Great Patriotic War would mean the pursuit of "bourgeois objectivism" in historical writing. The ancient struggle in Georgia must be forgotten and erased from the record. But the Ingushi and the Chechentsi, two small nationalities of the North Caucasus, had been disloyal to the Soviet government when Hitler's armies marched into the region and, as a consequence, "were resettled in other parts of the USSR." Muradeli failed to realize that the severe punishment visited upon them should have been justified in the opera, even though it dealt with the earlier period.

It should be said, on the other side of the question, that the Bolsheviks regard this resort to Machiavellian principles as temporary. So long as society is divided into classes and one class is engaged in exploiting the other, the exploited class is entirely justified in employing any means to overthrow and destroy the exploiter. So, until the classless society is established throughout the world, the ethics of battle must prevail. Their morality of deception is superior to the bourgeois because they are employing it to create conditions for the emergence of a universal morality. Thus, according to an editorial in the authoritative official organ of the Academy of Pedagogical Sciences, the "Communists set themselves the loftiest aim ever known in the world, namely, the liberation of all peoples from oppression and violence, from the horrors of ravaging predatory wars." They also seek "to create conditions for the all-round and harmonious development of personality." These "ideals express the hopes and aspirations of the overwhelming majority of mankind." Consequently, "the struggle for Communist morality in the last analysis is the struggle for a universal morality." [11] The initial conditions for such a morality have already been established in the Soviet Union, so the argument runs, because social classes have been abolished. But the ultimate triumph of the universal morality will come only after all nations have taken the road to Communism.

Communist morality is also founded on a conception of human nature. The position taken by Tkachev on this question has become a dogma to be repeated on every occasion. "Deeply mistaken and reactionary," writes the Soviet philosopher Zis', "are the theories circulated abroad that moral laws and principles bear an eternal and unchanging character, and have a self-sufficient meaning, independent of nature and the level of social development. Thus, for example, John Dewey in his work *Problems of Men* writes that the fundamental moral principles and attributes of 'human nature' are unchanging and that the customs and traditions of people can alter only the manifestations of these principles." [12] This, he says, is a "metaphysical notion." Whether the writer had read the book or was merely castigating "bourgeois objectivism" is an interesting question, because Dewey actually expressed quite the opposite view. In fact, in answer to the question "Does Human Nature Change?" he replied: "I think the proper answer is that human nature *does* change." Also he wrote that "belief in the eternal uniformity of human nature is thus the surviving remnant of a belief once universally held about the heavens and about all living creatures." [13] Quite possibly Zis' used John Dewey in this connection because he is widely known in the U.S.S.R. and is officially regarded as "an enemy of the people" and the archrepresentative of "bourgeois education" in the Western world.

Soviet pedagogical literature is full of assertions, not only that human nature can be changed, but also that the possibility has been fully demonstrated by the Bolsheviks. "There is no doubt," declared Zis' in 1948, "that during the 30 years of Soviet power our people have been radically changed, their moral views and norms of conduct. Soviet reality has blown completely asunder the legend about the so-called 'eternal' and 'unchanging' human nature." [14] Another Soviet educator, addressing himself to parents, writes that "the Party of Bolsheviks conducts a grandiose work for the education of the toilers of our country in the spirit of Communist morality," that "the results of this work are evident," and that "our Soviet people in their moral qualities stand immeasurably higher than the people of bourgeois society." [15] The most frequently quoted and most authoritative affirmation of the position is this statement made by A. A. Zhdanov speaking for the Central Committee to the assembled literary writers of the Soviet Union in August, 1946:

> Where will you find such a people and such a country as ours? Where will you find the magnificent qualities which our people displayed in the Great Patriotic War and which they display in their daily work as they pass to the peaceful restoration and development of economy and culture? Every day our people rise higher and ever higher. Today we are not what we were yesterday, and tomorrow we shall not be as we are today. Already we are not the same Russians we were before 1917, our Russia is different, our character is not the same. We have changed and grown along with the great reforms which have profoundly changed the face of our country.[16]

Reference has been made already in this volume to the fate of pedology and Paul Blonsky. In the 1920s pedology was regarded as a fundamental science in the field of education and was generally taught in teacher-training institutions. It constituted an attempt to develop a science of child growth and employed the methods of the laboratory, physical and mental measurements, and objective study of the conditioning factors of family and environment. On July 4, 1936, the Central Committee issued a decree condemning and abolishing pedology. The heart of the decree, which follows, is directed in part toward the question of the nature of human nature:

> These (numberless and harmful questionnaires, tests, etc.) so-called scientific "investigations," conducted with a large number of pupils and their parents, were directed, for the most part, against those who are unsuccessful or do not fit into the frame of the school regimen of the pupils. Their aim was to reveal, from the so-called "scientific" "bio-social" point of view of contemporary pedology, the hereditary and social conditions of the failure of the pupil or of individual deficiencies in conduct, and to discover a maximum of negative influences and pathological perversions of the pupil, his family, relatives, ancestors, and social environment, and thus to find grounds for the removal of pupils from the normal school collective.[17]

Ever after in Soviet educational literature pedology has been called a pseudo science. It tended to overemphasize, according to Bolshevik theory, the hereditary and deterministic factors and thus raised doubts about the possibility of changing human nature. It was condemned also because it removed from the shoulders of teachers responsibility for failures in the educative process. From the opposite side, the case of T. D. Lysenko twelve years later in the field of genetics is relevant here. That human nature can be changed is Bolshevik dogma. But with the repudiation of Lysenko after Stalin's death, it is just possible that pedology will be "rehabilitated."

III

In the 1920s the subject of Communist morality received very little explicit attention in Soviet educational literature and discussion. To be sure, there were profound moral implications in socially useful labor, in *obshchestvovedenie*, in the school collective, in the self-government activities, in the freedom allowed the child, and in the relations between the pupils and their teachers and parents. But the emphasis was narrowly political and ideological rather than moral.

An examination of two of the most widely used textbooks in pedagogy reveals the outlook of these early years. The first is Paul Blonsky's *Pedagogika*, which went through several editions. This volume contains no reference to education in Communist morality or to Lenin's pronouncements on ethics. In his chapter on the "Cultivation of Instincts and Emotions" he devotes about four and one-half pages to the inculcation of "self-restraint," "courage," "truthfulness," and "altruism," and to the related subjects of "punishment as a means of education" and the "ethics of the child." He also has a good deal to say about "labor." But when he expounds his ideas on the moral education of the younger generation, he fails to mention a single Communist or Bolshevik authority. To be sure, he reveals his knowledge of the relevant literature on the subject, but for the most part in what would be called today in the Soviet Union the "bourgeois" tradition. He presents quite sympathetically the ideas of Aristotle, Locke, Froebel, Richter, Paulsen, Havelock Ellis, and G. Stanley Hall. In response to the question of how to make the child courageous he says: "Locke gives the answer." Only in his discussion of the "school, as a labor commune" does he refer to Marx.[18]

The other volume is the English translation of the text by Albert Pinkevich, an important member of the Party and president of the Second University of Moscow. In a book of about four hundred pages he allots two and one-half pages to what he calls "Moral Evaluations." Having just concluded a discussion of "Aesthetic Evaluations," he writes: "Of a yet more arbitrary or conditional character is the conception of morality and, consequently, of moral education." However, being a good Communist of the 1920 variety, he accepts in full the Marxian position in the realm of ethics. There is no morality "common to all mankind," "appropriate for all times and peoples," "applicable to all social classes," and founded on the revelations of religion. In history there is only class morality. And the bourgeoisie "impose on the overwhelming majority of the population the morality which insures their own life, property, and capital." The morality of the proletariat, on the other hand, must serve the interests of workers in their irreconcilable struggle against landlords and capitalists. He accepts the dictum of Lenin that "everything that serves the laboring classes in the struggle is moral." In the "realization of the 'ultimate ideal' of humanity" it is ethical to practice deception, to confiscate property, and to take life. But with the creation of the classless society the morality of the proletariat will become the morality of all mankind—the first universal morality in history. Interestingly enough, Pinkevich always speaks of "proletarian morality," and not of "Communist morality." Moreover, he seems to think in terms of the Marxian conception of the "workers of all countries" uniting in a struggle to overthrow the world bourgeoisie. Consequently, he has nothing to say about "Soviet patriotism" and "love of the Soviet Motherland." He even tends to look with a hostile eye on the idea that one should kill "in defense of one's country." [19] Such a view could scarcely be found in a pedagogical museum in the Soviet Union today.

With the profound changes in Soviet society and in Soviet education in the thirties and forties Communist morality emerged as a central concern in the rearing of the younger generation. Indeed, Kairov devotes seven chapters and 121 pages to the subject in his *Pedagogika* published in 1948! Moreover, the question of moral education permeates the entire volume from beginning to end. The sources of this great change are doubtless many and complex. The setting of the "mastery of knowledge" as a major objective of the school certainly played an important role. Such mastery required a disciplined generation of children and youth. The failure of the "proletarian revolution" in other countries and the decision to "build socialism in one country" also had an influence. And then the Great Patriotic War, which tested Soviet institutions and generated a non-Marxian outlook on the world, opened new perspectives to Communist aggression and aroused the apocalyptic visions of the Bolshevik leadership. All this had a powerful impact on education and directed attention to the problem of the moral education of the younger generation. It seems quite likely, too, that the failure of the New Soviet Man to appear on schedule was an important contributing factor.

Since the Great Patriotic War the basic elements in education in Communist morality have become standardized. Though the treatment varies in some measure from one textbook in pedagogy to another, depending on the age of the children to which it is directed, the fundamental principles remain the same for all levels of school instruction and for all the agencies for the rearing of the young, including the family. The overarching conception in the education of the younger generation is, of course, the inculcation of fidelity to Communism, to the "cause of Lenin." This conception was stated quite succinctly in an authoritative article on "Communist Education" in the December, 1946, issue of *Bol'shevik*: "The content of all ideological work," says the writer, "is determined by the task of instilling in the youth the spirit of fidelity to the idea of Communism, unselfish devotion to the Soviet Motherland, and readiness to strengthen her freedom and independence by every means." And such "inculcation of Soviet ideology in the masses of youth presupposes a struggle against the survivals of capitalism in the consciousness of people and the formation of a new consciousness with a new Communist morality." [20] This broad conception is commonly broken down into education in Soviet patriotism, in socialist humanism, in collectivism, in conscious discipline, and in qualities of will and character. The content of each of these elements will be developed briefly, with particular attention to education in Soviet patriotism.

Soviet educators seem to agree that "Soviet patriotism," "love of the Soviet Motherland," is the most important ingredient of Soviet morality. Yesipov and Goncharov in their approved textbook for the training of primary school teachers tell their readers that "the cultivation of the spirit of Soviet patriotism in the younger generation is the most important task of moral education in our country." [21] Kairov in his approved textbook for the training of secondary school teachers declares that "the education of Soviet youth in the spirit of Communist morality means first of all education in the spirit of Soviet patriotism." [22] And Zis' makes the even broader claim that "the sources of Soviet morality, the new feelings and dispositions in our country, are rooted in love of the Motherland, in life-giving Soviet patriotism." [23] In the post-Stalin era "patriotism" is linked with "proletarian internationalism." [24]

This emphasis merits a word of comment. In the first decade and a half of the revolution the words for Motherland or Fatherland and patriotism were proscribed. They were "bourgeois" and anti-Marxian words, employed by the capitalists to mesmerize the workers and lead them into wars in the interests of private property and profits. And so it was until June 9, 1934, when *Pravda* published an editorial on "patriotism" which summoned all Soviet citizens "to struggle for the Motherland, for her honor, fame, power, and prosperity," and proclaimed the doctrine that "the defense of the Motherland is the supreme law of life." No event in the whole history of the Bolshevik state marks so clearly the end of one epoch and the beginning of another. Up to this time Russian historiography had been ruled by Michael N. Pokrovsky, a close friend of Lenin and an historian of purest Marxian vintage. From this time the writing of both Russian and world history was profoundly changed. During the period of Pokrovsky's dominance the history of old Russia was presented in the darkest colors in strict accord with the "iron laws" of historical materialism. In the words of Klaus Mehnert, prerevolutionary Russia was portrayed as "a prison in which the peoples languished under the brutal cruelty of Tsarist oppression." [25] And the author well remembers his experience in Soviet schools in 1927 and 1929 which fully support this judgment. Both pupils and teachers almost brought tears to the eyes as they painted the dismal picture of Russia before October, 1917. The only bright spots in the past were provided by rebels and revolutionists. All else was black.

The source of the great reversal was Stalin. No sooner had he established himself in power than he launched a program for the rewriting of history. Naturally this involved first of all a drastic revision of the account of the period of the rise of the Bolsheviks and the growth of Soviet power, and particularly the glorification of Stalin and the degradation of his opponents. But the new policy went much further. The entire Russian past was recovered and clothed in garments of grandeur. Every figure of that past, whether tsar, soldier, statesman or administrator, explorer, scientist, educator, writer or artist, who had shed luster on Russian genius or increased the power of the Russian state was brought into the gallery of heroes.

The measure and character of this reversal are clearly revealed in the rehabilitation of Ivan IV, who in life violated most of the Ten Commandments and in death was called the "Terrible," even under the autocracy of the tsars. The new interpretation of the man who launched the long career of the political police in Russian history is given briefly in an official textbook published in 1945 and used throughout the country in the eighth grade. "Ivan IV," so runs the summation, "died . . . in 1584. He was a talented and wise man. He was well-educated for his time; he loved and knew how to write; he had a sharp and fine mind. In both domestic and foreign policy he formulated his aims correctly and clearly, and pursued them with tenacity and perseverance. His recognition of the necessity of seizing the shores of the Baltic reveals his great vision." [26] The 1955 edition of the textbook used in the fourth grade closes the account of his reign with these "patriotic" words: "The possessions of Russia under Ivan IV expanded many times. His kingdom became one of the greatest states in the world." [27] The failure of the world-renowned moving-picture director, Sergei Eisenstein, to sense or at least to recognize in one of his films this complete reversal in the estimation of Ivan IV led to his disgrace and possibly to his death. Perhaps Ivan IV is destined to follow Stalin into the category of tyrants. The two rulers had much in common.

The substance of Soviet patriotism is unlimited love of, pride in, and

devotion to the Motherland. Perhaps the best way to convey this conception is to quote at length from the short preface to this fourth-grade history textbook "approved by the All-Union Governmental Commission."
Entitled "Our Motherland," it contains the following passages:

> The USSR is the land of socialism. Our Motherland is the largest country
> in the whole world. In the north there is eternal ice, and in the south it is so
> hot in summer that oranges and lemons ripen, tea and cotton grow.
>
> In natural riches our country occupies first place in the world. Everything
> that is needed for life exists in our country.
>
> In the 16 Union Soviet Republics live 60 different nations, approximately
> 200 million people. All are united in one brotherly union—the *Union of
> Soviet Socialist Republics,* or simply the USSR. All the peoples of the USSR
> live in one united friendly family and work for the general welfare. In the
> USSR there are no capitalists and landlords, as in other countries. In the
> USSR there is no exploitation of man by man. All of us work for ourselves,
> for the whole society.
>
> From a backward country our Motherland has become the most advanced
> and powerful.
>
> This is why we so love our Motherland, why we are so proud of our USSR
> —*the land of socialism.*
>
> *The Great Party of Communists-Bolsheviks* showed us the way to social-
> ism. It led the struggle of our fathers and mothers, the struggle of workers
> and peasants, when they overthrew the rule of tsars, landlords, and capital-
> ists. Under the leadership of the Communist Party we have created the
> worker-peasant power, we have built socialism.
>
> The peoples of our country have repelled all attacks on the USSR. The
> Soviet Union smashed German Fascism and Japanese robbers. Our country
> has become yet more powerful. . . .
>
> We love our Motherland and we must know well her history.[28]

Soviet patriotism, as the above statement suggests, means devotion to
the Party. It is always the Party and its great leaders, Lenin and Stalin(?),
that are responsible for the unprecedented achievements of the Soviet
state and the Soviet people. For, as Yesipov and Goncharov say, "our best
men and women are banded together in our Communist Party which
directs the entire life of the country. Soviet patriotism is expressed in
devotion to the Communist Party and supreme readiness to serve the
cause of Lenin and Stalin." It was the Communist Party that organized
"the toiling masses for the construction of a new Communist society," that
through the five-year plans "transformed our land into a mighty industrial
country, the most advanced and most cultured." It was the Communist
Party that rallied "all the peoples of the Union in the struggle for the
freedom and independence of the Motherland during the Great Patriotic
War." In a word, to employ the orthodox phraseology of the Soviet Union
prior to the Twentieth Congress, the "Party of Lenin and Stalin is the

organizer and inspirer of all of our victories." The younger generation is told in school and out that there is and there can be no conflict between the interests of the people and the interests of the Party and the government, because the Party is the "vanguard of the working class," and all Soviet citizens are workers. Social classes have been abolished. Yesipov and Goncharov, moreover, in expounding the cause of Lenin and Stalin, declare that the "education of the young in the spirit of Soviet patriotism means also to plant in their consciousness the understanding that the interests of our people and the interests of the toiling masses of the entire world are indivisible." [29] And "our truth is the truth of the toiling masses of the entire world." All of this leads to the development in the consciousness of youth of "love of oppressed peoples" everywhere. Perhaps it is unnecessary to add that Soviet textbooks and pedagogical literature contain not the slightest shadow of criticism of the Party, its leadership, and its policies. At a given moment the Party is always right, even when it confesses the errors of the past.

Love of country means love of the people of the Soviet Union. This sentiment, of course, is implied in the feeling of patriotism in all lands. But it assumes a special character in Russia. On the one hand, the Russians constitute a superior people because they were the first in the world to establish socialism, and they did this in spite of a condition of technical backwardness. Marx and Engels had few kind words to say about the Russians and scarcely expected to see the "First Worker's Republic in History" established in the land of the tsars. So there must have been something in the people and their culture which enabled them to overtake and surpass the most advanced countries of the West in such a brief historical period. And, as Zhdanov asserted in 1946, Soviet people vastly improved themselves after the Great October Revolution. This, says Kairov, places a heavy and glorious responsibility on the teacher in the middle school. He "must give special attention to the task of showing concretely the greatness of the Soviet people." He "must prove and convince by means of vivid facts and examples that the Soviet people, by virtue of the character of their ideas, their world outlook, and their deeds, stand immeasurably higher than the people of bourgeois society." Then Kairov quotes from Stalin's report to the Eighteenth Congress of the Party in 1939: "The least Soviet citizen, free from the chains of capital, stands a head higher than any foreign high-ranking bureaucrat who drags on his shoulders the yoke of capitalist slavery." [30]

Patriotism must be given expression in deeds. Words are not enough. Indeed, a true patriot is one who gives himself wholly to "the general good" and to the advancement of the "interests of the Soviet state," striving to be of "the greatest possible usefulness to the Soviet Motherland." He works "devotedly for society" and is "ready when necessary to give his life for the Motherland." But it is in his "attitude toward labor" that we see the "basic mark of the new man—a member of Communist society." He must develop a "Communist attitude toward labor." No longer, as in capitalist society, should labor be regarded as "a grievous burden" to be borne or to be "performed under compulsion." In the words of "Comrade Stalin," labor in the Soviet Union "is a matter of *honor,* a matter of *glory,* a matter of *valor* and *heroism.*" According to the Communist attitude, "labor is associated with man's desire to serve society more fully, to work consciously and with highest productivity for the general welfare." In the Soviet school this means for the pupil "the cultivation of discipline," the "conscious striving for perfect knowledge," and "preparation for organized and disciplined labor in higher schools, in production, and in the service of the Red Army." Closely linked with the Communist attitude toward labor is the "*communist attitude toward public ownership,*" toward "socialist property produced by social labor." And teacher and pupil are reminded of these words from the Soviet constitution: "It is the duty of every citizen of the USSR to safeguard and strengthen public, socialist property as the sacred and inviolable foundation of the Soviet system, as the source of the wealth and power of the Motherland, as the source of a prosperous and cultural life for all working people." [31]

There is yet another very important element in Soviet patriotism which is emphasized in all the literature on education in Communist morality. "The pupils of the Soviet school must realize," write Yesipov and Goncharov, "that the feeling of Soviet patriotism is saturated with irreconcilable hatred toward the enemies of socialist society." The authors point out that "hatred gives birth to class revolutionary vigilance and creates a feeling of irreconcilability toward the class enemy; the weakening of such vigilance undermines the cause of the socialist revolution." One must "learn, not only to hate the enemy, but also to struggle with him, in time to unmask him, and finally, if he does not surrender, to destroy him." But "to vanquish the enemy is impossible without the most burning hatred of him." [32] Kairov, a one-time Minister of Education of the Russian Republic, speaks precisely the same language. "Love of the Motherland," he writes, "is inseparably linked with deep hatred of the enemies of the Motherland." This means, concretely, hatred "of oppressors, of exploiters, of enslavers of man," of people "who live on the labor of others," of people "who foment hatred and enmity among nations," of people "who preach the morality of man-hatred." [33] Such hatred should be no "fortuitous outburst of passion" but rather an "expression of the conviction of a person and his world view." The enemy to be hated, however, is not a matter of private judgment. The enemy, whether domestic or foreign, is whomsoever

the Party wills. It could be Stalin, as it once was Trotsky or Bukharin.*
From the standpoint of understanding Communist morality, this theme
is so important that one further quotation is justified. The following statement from an editorial in the official organ of the teaching profession on
the eve of Stalin's death is clearly aimed at the leaders of the free world:

> Love of one's socialist motherland is linked inseparably with hatred of her
> enemies. It breeds in the hearts of Soviet youth abhorrence and contempt
> for slavery and oppression, for the dark forces of reaction, for all enemies
> of progress, civilization, and democracy. These sentiments were well ex-
> pressed by the distinguished writer, Sholokhov, in his flamingly-inspired
> article, A WORD ABOUT THE MOTHERLAND: "Let our hatred not cool toward
> the enemy, even when defeated! And let it [hatred] boil and bubble in our
> hearts with a tenfold fury toward those for whom there is no name in a
> human tongue, who as yet are not satiated by the profits derived from the
> blood of millions and who with blind satanical madness prepare a new war
> for mankind worn out with suffering." [34]

IV

A second basic ingredient of Communist morality is called "socialist
humanism." By this is meant respect for the "rights and dignity of personality." In contrast with bourgeois society, which rests on human exploitation, Soviet society makes possible the realization of "genuine
humanism" for the first time in history. Since there are no social classes and
all men are equal, each individual is free to develop his own personality
to the fullest. Since all work for the general welfare and consequently are
not divided by conflicts of interests, there is no foundation for individual
rivalry and jealousy. Unfortunately, antihumanistic vestiges from the past
tend to persist in the minds of the people. This calls for a systematic
education of the younger generation in humanistic morality. The "Rules
for School Children" constitute an attempt to achieve this purpose, along
with others. "Education in the spirit of socialist humanism," write Yesipov
and Goncharov, "has as its task the leading of children to a consciousness
of the high value of human personality and the inculcation in them of
respect for the rights and dignity of man." This means the development
of "love for mother and father." How beautiful are these words! The
Soviet state has "established the title of 'Mother-heroine'" and bestows
"orders and medals on mothers of many children." With the word "'father'
we address the Great Stalin when we wish to express to him the feeling
of filial nearness and of love and respect." Children should "obey parents
and help them," "be always polite toward their school director and

---

* The author wrote this sentence before the Twentieth Congress.

teachers," "respectful toward their elders," and "considerate of and attentive to their elders, the sick, the weak, and the little ones." They should also have "a feeling of respect for one another": the older children should not "bully the younger," the strong should not "taunt the weak," boys should not "treat girls scornfully," and the well should not tease and ridicule those with "certain defects." On the other hand, "a sense of duty and responsibility, a sense of honor and personal dignity should be cultivated in the individual." All of this constitutes education in the "spirit of socialist humanism." [35]

One might think that socialist humanism is in conflict with the doctrine of inculcating hatred and mercilessness toward enemies. From the Communist point of view, however, this seems not to be the case. According to the authors quoted above, "hatred of the enemies of the socialist Motherland by no means contradicts the principle of humanism, since it is devoted to the protection of the rights and liberty of the workers from the designs of beasts of prey." Thus, "the heroic fulfillment by the Soviet people of the mission of liberating freedom-loving peoples from inhuman fascism is the highest expression of humanism." [36] If humanism is to triumph, its enemies must be destroyed, and this requires hatred. The official organ of the teaching profession puts the case in these terms: "Humanism is not the abstract gospel of a sentimental 'love of man.' The touchstone of all humanism is the question of the application of violence and the tolerance of severe measures toward enemies of the people." [37]

There is also no conflict between socialist humanism and Soviet patriotism. Indeed, the two are closely linked together. Only in the Soviet Union, under the conditions of socialism, can humanism achieve universal application. Here "the working people of all nationalities are completely liberated from exploitation." In the Soviet Union, as the elementary textbook tells the children in the fourth grade, all the nationalities are "united in one friendly union." This means that there are no superior or inferior peoples, that all peoples live together on a plane of complete equality, that the Great Russian enjoys no rights or liberties which he does not share with a Samoyed or Yakut. The Soviet school, in the words of Kairov, cultivates in the youth the "noble ideas of friendship and mutual aid among peoples, the ideas of national and racial equality." [38] And this is Soviet patriotism. In contrast the "imperialistic countries" have transformed love of the Motherland, which is fine and good, into chauvinism and race hatred. Ogorodnikov and Shimbirev, in their *Pedagogika* for teachers' institutes, present the United States as an example of such perversion. In the United States, they write:

> . . . racial discrimination against the Negro is now being extended to other
> nationalities. While eulogizing intensively the so-called "American way of
> life" and everything American, contemporary bourgeois ideologists laud in-

every possible way the "superiority" of the Anglo-Saxon race over other peoples. On this is based the idea of world domination or, to use the terminology of Truman, "the mission of leading the world," imposed presumably by "destiny" on the imperialist bourgeoisie of the USA.[39]

Consequently, genuine humanism is possible only in the Soviet Union and in the countries of people's democracy.

At the same time, an interesting contradiction runs through Soviet pedagogical literature, historiography, literature, and politics. The ambitious project for the rewriting of history which was launched in 1934 led eventually to an extravagant glorification of the Great Russians, the people who built the empire and today constitute approximately one-half of the population of the U.S.S.R. This tendency was given great force in the remarks of Stalin on May 24, 1945, at a reception in honor of Red Army commanders in the Kremlin. Drinking toast after toast to the Great Russians, he declared them to be "the most outstanding nation of all the nations composing the Soviet Union," to merit recognition "as the leading force of the Soviet Union among all the peoples of our country," to possess "a clear mind, steadfast character . . . and faithfulness." [40] Five years later, on May 24, 1950, *Pravda* celebrated the event with a long editorial by Vs. Vishnevsky entitled "The Word of the Leader about the Russian People." Here Stalin's toasts are repeated and their meaning elucidated in the following and other words:

> Sublime is the history of Russia. From time immemorial the Russian plains were inhabited by our ancestors, of remarkable endurance, of great vitality, of inquiring mind, of active disposition, of rare tenacity. During the entire course of their history the Russians never submitted to foreign usurpers. They never bowed their head before the enemy.
>
> Sublime is the history of the Russian people. They have enriched mankind with immortal creations of mind and talent.
>
> The Russian proletariat, the most revolutionary in the world and led by the great Party of Bolsheviks, by the Party of Lenin and Stalin, brought the peoples of our country to the victorious socialist revolution and opened a new era in the history of all mankind.

The tide of the Great Russians in Soviet historiography was flowing with considerable power even before Stalin drank his toasts. In 1944 the Russian historian, Ivan Bulavin, published an article entitled "Russians Struggle for the Freedom of Soviet Peoples" expounding an interpretation of history which has become orthodox in the Soviet Union. According to this interpretation, the Great Russians came to possess their vast empire by protecting weaker peoples against attacks from their enemies. "They protected the nations of the West from invasion by the Mongols, they protected the peoples of Asia from enslavement by the Teutonic Knights." In the case of the Tartars, "the selfless struggle of the Russian people . . .

for the first time performed its universal-historical role—Russia saved European civilization from the menace of the East." Gradually the "surrounding non-Russian tribes" came to see in the "Russian state their natural and only defender from numerous foreign enemies." While never engaging in aggression themselves, "whenever the national existence of Russia was threatened by some external foe, the Russian people rose as one man in defense of their native land." [41] This is a glorious portrayal. But in subsequent years many a non-Russian historian fell into disgrace when he persisted in telling the story of the conquest of his people by the Great Russians. All Soviet educators and writers must realize that the patriotism of the Great Russians is the humanistic patriotism of the Soviet state, which "is based on the recognition of the equality of all the peoples of the world, their rights to liberty and independence, their rights to manage their lives in accordance with their own wishes and without interference from the outside," including, of course, interference from Soviet power.[42] To paraphrase George Orwell, while all the peoples of the Soviet Union are equal, the Great Russians are more equal than the others.

Soviet education is saturated with this interpretation of the role of the Great Russians in history. Every Soviet pupil will read a number of times the celebrated statement by Vissarion Belinsky, the father of Russian literary criticism, which appeared in the *Almanac of 1840*: "We envy our grandchildren and great-grandchildren who in 1940 are destined to see Russia standing at the head of the civilized world, giving laws to science and art, and receiving reverent tribute from all enlightened humanity." This quotation is commonly followed with the comment: "These remarkable words have been fulfilled." Yesipov and Goncharov, after quoting this "prophecy," pay their own tribute to the Great Russians in the epoch of the revolution:

> The Russian working class, in the struggle for the building of a new socialist society, has stood at the head of and has led the entire people. We are filled with a feeling of national pride because the Russian nation created this revolutionary class and proved itself capable of giving to mankind the great models of the struggle for freedom and for socialism. The numerous peoples of the Soviet Union were liberated from national oppression, from the oppression of landlords and capitalists, through the direct aid of the Russian proletariat. The services of the Russian people are exceptionally great, not only to the peoples of the Soviet Union, but also to all mankind. The Soviet Union by its example inspires the workers of the entire world for the struggle against exploiters and ravishers. The history of the Russian people proves to all mankind their political wisdom, their military valor, and their genius.[43]

As one reads these passages he is inevitably reminded of the "Russian messianism" of the empire, until he recalls that this particular form of "love of people and country" never received the full support of the state. It would seem clear that the Great Russians are prepared to continue to sacrifice themselves without hope of reward until "all mankind" and the "entire world" are "liberated." And then one recalls how national minorities are treated in the Soviet Union when they object to "liberation" under the guidance of the great Party of Lenin and Stalin. One recalls the Tartars of the Crimea, the Kalmuks of the Volga, the Ingushi and Chechentsi of the North Caucasus, and others who, during and following the war, were transported from their "native" lands to distant places still unknown to the world. One recalls also the liquidation of millions of peasants at the time of the collectivization of agriculture in the early thirties. And one can never forget the millions upon millions of political dissenters who through the years have been consigned to forced-labor camps. These tragic events are not mentioned in the pedagogies or in the history textbooks. Nor are they included in any listing of important dates to be committed to memory by the younger generation. Perhaps the degradation of Stalin will bring a complete rewriting of the history of his reign.

The role of the Russians in history is matched by the role of the Russian language in education and culture. As the reader knows, the tsars pursued a policy of Russification of the national minorities of the empire. This policy was excoriated by the Bolsheviks as an evil expression of imperialism. Lenin and his associates declared on coming to power that there would be no "first language" in the new order, that all languages would be equal. But with the growth of the Soviet state and Soviet ambitions a great reversal took place. For many years now, the Russian language has been taught from the third or an earlier grade in the schools of the other nationalities. And a continuous propaganda is conducted to improve the quality of instruction in the "language of our big brother" and the "only general language for all the peoples inhabiting the territory of the Soviet Union." According to the Moscow organ of the Young Communists, "the future belongs to the Russian language as the world language of socialism," as "the world language of internationalism." Consequently, "democratic peoples are studying the Russian language."[44] The organ of the Union of Soviet Writers declares that "no one can call himself a scholar in the full and genuine meaning of the word if he does not know the Russian language, if he does not read the works of Russian thought in the original."[45] It is perhaps relevant to note in this connection that, according to an American observer, in Central Asia separate schools are maintained for children of Russian parentage and children of the native population.[46]

V

The remaining components of Communist morality—collectivism, conscious discipline, and qualities of will and character—will be treated briefly. "Collectivism," writes Bushlia, "constitutes the most important distinguishing trait of the life and labor of the workers of our country." Only through their collective efforts "were the Soviet people able to overcome many, many difficulties and obstacles." Collectivism, however, does not involve any contradiction "between society and the individual." In fact, it "affords all opportunities for a complete and rounded flowering of individual abilities and aptitudes." At the same time, education in the spirit of collectivism means the rearing of "people capable of working together in organized fashion and always subordinating their conduct to the general interests of the collective." Children must be trained to "subject their own interests to the tasks of the collective." [47] Yesipov and Goncharov see collectivism founded on "comradeship and friendship among children" and the joining of the humanistic qualities of "personal dignity and honor" with a "sense of the honor of the collective." Friendship, being an expression of intimacy, is more limited than comradeship and may develop at the expense of the collective; whereas "all pupils of a class are comrades and should be comrades." They are comrades because they are engaged in a common undertaking devoted to the welfare of all. The class, the Pioneer formation, the pupils' circle, and all other children's groups and organizations "may be regarded as collectives only if the members are aware of common tasks, devoted to common purposes, conscious of complete mutuality of interests, and willing to direct their strength and work toward the general good." A genuine collective must be marked by "guiding and executive organs, good management and subordination, and distribution of obligations and responsibilities." This means submission to group discipline and obedience to the leader.[48] In a word, it means preparation of the "best" for membership in the Communist Party.

What is called "conscious discipline" is a closely related element of Communist morality. Here is one of the most important tasks in the moral education of the younger generation. "Without discipline," write Yesipov and Goncharov, "one cannot study, one cannot work." But this is not merely a matter of the school years. The teacher faces "a much deeper task" of "the cultivation in children of a *state of discipline*" as "one of the most important traits of character" which will endure through the decades of adult life. For without discipline one "cannot achieve high productivity of labor" or "conquer in war." The substance of this element of Communist morality is put most concisely by the two authors in the following paragraph:

> The discipline which we cultivate in our children under socialist conditions is characterized by the following qualities: In the first place it is *conscious*, that is, it is founded on an inner conviction of the necessity of following definite rules and regulations in conduct which in turn are based on an

understanding of their meaning and significance. In the second place, discipline is *self-initiated,* that is, it is not a discipline of simple obedience, but rather a discipline which is linked with the desire to fulfill in the best possible manner a given assignment, order, or commission. More than this, it is linked with a readiness always to do one's duty, not waiting for an order or a reminder, but displaying initiative. In the third place, discipline is *firm,* that is, it is unquestioned obedience and submission to the leader, the teacher, or the organizer. Without this there is no discipline; submission to the will of the leader is a necessary and essential mark of discipline. In the fourth place, discipline is *organizational,* that is, it is a discipline which prompts and habituates the pupil to the precise organization of individual and collective work, to organization in games and life. In the fifth place, discipline is *comradely,* that is, it is founded on mutual respect of the members of the collective. In the sixth place, discipline is *resolute,* that is, it surmounts difficulties, prompts the completion of every task, subjects conduct to high purposes, and conquers motives of low degree.[49]

A final ingredient of Communist morality involves traits of will and character. Patriotism, humanism, collectivism, and discipline are not enough. It is necessary also, writes Kairov, to "cultivate in the young strong will and firm character so that they may be able to overcome difficulties," just as the will of the Soviet people is hardened "by overcoming all and every kind of obstacle on the road toward the great goal—Communism." By presenting this sublime goal to the pupils they will understand its greatness, and by "practical participation in its realization" they will acquire "strong will and character." [50] A frequently quoted and paraphrased passage in Soviet pedagogical literature is a sentence from the speech by Andrei Zhdanov before the Union of Soviet Writers in August, 1946. "The younger generation," he said, "must be educated to be steadfast, cheerful, unafraid of obstacles, eager to meet and able to overcome all obstacles." "The chief volitional qualities of man," say Yesipov and Goncharov, "are purposefulness, resolution, persistence, initiative, courage, and endurance." [51] The object of Soviet education is to develop all these qualities in Soviet youth to the maximum. The true Bolshevik is one who "formulates his purposes clearly and to the point and pursues them without wavering." In such words the character of Stalin was described before his downfall.

VI

The process of education in Communist morality is highly complex. It involves every teacher, every subject, every pupils' collective, every worker, and the entire regimen of the school. Everything must be organized and administered for the purpose of achieving the common goal.

The organization of instruction is particularly important. The way pupils study influences the development of conscious discipline and traits of will and character. Each subject has a special contribution to make in the shaping of attitudes, the acquisition of interests, and the forming of convictions. The roles of language, history, geography, and the sciences are fairly obvious. But even aesthetics has a contribution to make. "Understanding the beautiful," observes Kairov, "has an historical and a class character." He then reminds his readers that the Central Committee of the Party "has demanded that workers in literature and art direct their energies to the rearing of a Soviet youth cheerful, buoyant, devoted to the Motherland, and confident in the victory of our cause, not fearing obstacles, able to overcome all difficulties." The teacher must reveal to the young "the fallacy of the position that art exists for the sake of art, that there is a special form of 'fine' art." He must relate art to the "interests, problems, and demands of the people" and help educate "Soviet man in the spirit of Communism." He must foster patriotism by cultivating "love of the beauty of our native land, of the great works of native art, of literature, of the beautiful traditions of the people's life, customs, and culture." [52] And of course physical education not only develops bodily strength and agility but also cultivates discipline and pride in the Motherland.

The regimen of the school is basic in all moral education. For it is in the actual conduct of the pupil that words are translated into deeds. And here the rule of consistency should be strictly followed. This is particularly applicable to obedience to the "Rules for School Children." "Consistency," according to Yesipov and Goncharov, "must be observed by all adults who share in the rearing of the young." The several teachers of the child in a given grade "should follow a single line" and not "contradict each other." And when a child passes from one grade or school to another he should experience no change in the enforcement of the Rules. "It is injurious also if the child experiences a duality or even a trinity of educative influences, if, for example, the elders in the family say one thing to him and the teacher tells him something else, if one teacher follows one line and his comrade in work another."

For the pupil, violation of the Rules is a most serious matter. On February 29, 1944, the Commissar of Education of the RSFSR issued an "instruction" to all teachers in the complete middle school which included a section on the "evaluation of the conduct of pupils." According to this instruction, a "grade of 5 is given for flawless conduct both in the school and outside the school." For a "noticeable violation of conduct" a grade of 4 is given, but such a grade is "permitted only during one quarter." If the pupil fails to improve, the "pedagogical soviet" may lower the grade to 3. This grade is "given for serious violations of conduct and serves as a warning of possible expulsion from school." The "pedagogical soviet then reviews the case" and may lower the grade to 2. Expulsion follows auto-

matically, if "approved by the regional department of people's education."
Certificates and diplomas are issued "only when the pupil's conduct is
excellent (grade of 5 with the following remark: 'with excellent (5) conduct')." [53] Thus, although all pupils are not expected to make 5—the highest mark—in every subject, they are expected to make such a mark in
conduct. In fact, flawless conduct is demanded of every pupil both inside
and outside the school. According to the decree of the Central Committee
of the Party on August 25, 1932, "incorrigible pupils who behave like
hooligans, offend the teachers, disrupt the school regimen, destroy or steal
school property are to be expelled from school and deprived of the right
to re-enroll during a period from one to three years." [54] In order to educate the younger generation in the spirit of Communist morality, the
Soviet state has made and is making use of a comprehensive and graduated system of both rewards and punishments.

A method recommended universally for inculcating in pupils the ideas
and ideals of Communist morality is the presentation of examples of
highest conduct. To be sure, the teacher is expected in his life and work
to set such an example before the children. But, in addition, much attention is given to the great figures in the history of Russia and in the history
of Communism—Lenin and Stalin. These men, "the leaders of our Party,"
write Yesipov and Goncharov, "are models of people with clear aims,
persistence, inflexible will, and resolute character." A study of their lives
and deeds shows "how stubbornly and persistently they worked to create
the Party and to temper it in battle with enemies and in struggle with
difficulties, how stubbornly and persistently they overcame all obstacles
to achieve the clearly formulated aim—the victory of the socialist revolution and the building of a Communist society." And "the best people of
our country embody the traits of the new man, the traits of Bolshevik
character." [55] The official organ of the profession advises teachers that
they can find no "better means of influencing pupils" than the following
characterization of the spiritual figure of Stalin given in the *Short Biog-
raphy* and before the action of the Twentieth Congress: "Everyone knows
the irresistible, shattering power of Stalin's logic, the crystal clearness of
his intellect, his iron will, his devotion to the Party, his hot faith in the
people, and his love for the people. His modesty, his simplicity, his solici-
tude for the people, and his mercilessness toward enemies of the people." [56] The history of the Party of course supplies appropriate materials
in abundance. And Marx and Engels should not be overlooked.

VII

This brief account of the moral education of the younger generation
may well be closed with an account of the presentation of the first passport to a group of boys and girls on reaching the age of sixteen. The system of internal passports, as we know, was employed in old Russia to aid

the police in combating subversion and revolution. It has generally been regarded as a mark of autocracy and despotism. Abolished at the time of the revolution, it was revived when Stalin was well advanced on the road to power. And now an effort is being made to convert the passport into a thing of honor, a badge of citizenship, a credential of maturity. An entire page of the December 4, 1955, issue of *Komsomol'skaia Pravda*, the official organ of the League of Young Communists, is devoted to reporting the giving of passports to sixteen-year-olds in Ivanovo, an important industrial center. The day is declared a holiday; parents, relatives, and friends are present; some old Bolsheviks grace the occasion; and the hall is draped in flags and flowers. The major speech, delivered by F. E. Titov, First Secretary of the Provincial Committee of the Communist Party, follows:

> Dear Young Friends!
> Today you receive your first passport. This is a great event in your life.
> A Soviet citizen!
> How proudly and majestically this sounds! An honorable and responsible title. We are proud that the creator of the first socialist state in the world and its great citizen was Vladimir Ilich Lenin.
> Everything that is advanced and progressive is linked with the title of Soviet citizen. Guard then the high honor of this title!
> You are happy that you live in the land where the Basic Law is our Constitution, the most democratic in the world. In our country Soviet man enjoys, not only the greatest rights and civic responsibilities, but also all conditions for the realization of these rights.
> Before you are bright roads. For you doors to schools, colleges, institutes, mills, and factories are wide open. Take advantage then of these great rights —study, work, harden yourselves!
> Prepare yourselves to enter life. You are receiving the first passport in a heroic time, when our multi-national free people-creator selflessly struggles for the building of a Communist society. Mighty is the spectacle of this gigantic construction. In mills and in factories, on collective farms and virgin lands, in lumber mills, in institute laboratories, at the helm of the ship and the wheel of the locomotive, millions of Soviet people create their happy present and future.
> Much is being built also in our Ivanovo province! Already has begun the filling of the bed of the Gorky sea, which will feed a tremendous electric station on the Volga; work on the Volga-Ivanovo canal is started, new machine-construction mills and textile factories are being erected, blocks of new homes are being built, cities are being improved.
> Young friends, these deeds await your hands!
> You are receiving your first passport at the time of the glorious fifty years of the first Russian revolution. Fifty years ago the older generation of the working class, your grandparents, under the leadership of Vladimir Ilich Lenin raised the banner of the struggle for a bright future. To the lot of

your generation falls the joy of carrying the banner to a victorious conclusion.

So, guard, preserve and develop the glorious traditions of your people, of our great Communist Party! Herein lies the guarantee of your success.

You receive your first passport in the city of Ivanovo, in a city of glorious revolutionary tradition of the working class, about whose heroic struggle Vladimir Ilich Lenin not infrequently spoke with admiration. The working class of Ivanovo created the prototype of the Soviet power—one of the first of the Soviets of workers' deputies in Russia. The toilers of the city with their own hands transformed Ivanovo from a wretched backward city into a great industrial center. During the years of the civil and Patriotic wars Ivanovo gave thousands of heroes who selflessly defended their socialist Motherland.

Years will pass, many of you will become highly trained and distinguished workers, engineers, teachers, pilots, tankists, navigators. Perhaps life will scatter you over the wide reaches of your Motherland, but you received your first passport in Ivanovo. Be proud of it. Do not disgrace the glorious name of this revolutionary city.

The response to the Secretary of the Party was made by a girl, Ira Shaldina, under the title "I Am a Citizen of the Soviet Union: I Am Sixteen Years Old." It suggests clearly that the occasion partook of the nature of an initiation ceremony into adult life. But let Ira speak:

I hold here in my hands my first passport. Now I am no longer a little one and everybody will treat me as a grownup. And this means that I too must from now on treat everything in life seriously, evaluate all my actions correctly, be more strict toward myself and my comrades.

With this passport I will be admitted as an equal in any mill, in any factory. There I shall be able to strengthen with my work the might of my Motherland. On reaching the age of eighteen I will go with this passport to the polling place and exercise my right of electing the organs of my government.

I am now mature and the demands made upon an adult will be made upon me everywhere—at home or in school. Heretofore, when a serious request was made to me and I was not inclined to act upon it, I usually said: "I am still a little one."

And I was left alone. What could be expected of a little one? But now, from today, I shall be unable to say to anyone: "It is too hard for me, I am a little one." The young guardsmen and the young builders of Komsomolsk-on-Amur had exactly the same passports. To them the Soviet passport and the Komsomol card were the civic conscience of the Soviet man. These people feared no difficulties, they knew no fear, and during the years of the great ordeals of their Motherland, they said they were grown up and could help their people, their country in her hour of trial.

On the first page of my passport the name of my city is given, a city of revolutionary traditions, a city of glorious textile workers; and I want to carry the esteemed labor honor of our Ivanovo through the entire great country, no matter where I may happen to live and work. Everywhere I shall proclaim with pride: "I am from Ivanovo where I first received my passport."

Sixteen years! How many times have I dreamed about this! I wanted to be sixteen faster. Not infrequently I would go to the library and ask for some interesting book, but I would receive the offending words: "You will understand nothing in this book; when you are older, then if you please, you may read it." Or in the summer, I would ask for a boat—no permission; they would say: no boats for children under sixteen. And how many times in school when we were noisy during recitation, the teacher would reprimand us: "Aren't you ashamed of yourselves to behave thus; you will soon receive your passport." But we consoled ourselves in the meantime with the thought that we were still children, and much would be forgiven us.

And at last today this carefree time of childhood is gone. Everybody will regard us now as adults, respect our opinions, and even consult us. For we are no longer children.

Today is the usual work-day, not even Sunday. But I noticed from early in the morning that the people of our city talked about today's celebration of presenting the first passport, and were making preparations for the occasion. The entire city rejoiced in this celebration, rejoiced for us, the sixteen-year-olds.

I would like to see everywhere in our province, in all other provinces and regions of our Motherland, the same celebration marking the day of presenting the first passport. Let this day serve as a good beginning, an example to all. The warm attention given us, young boys and girls, obliges us to study yet harder and to be worthy of the high honor paid us today in this hall.

Here several hundred people are gathered. And everyone present will now remember us, remember our faces and know that we are grownups. This puts great demands upon us. When I was coming here this evening I somehow forgot about the school. All of us girls talked on the way about the concert, about dances, and in general thought of nothing but the pleasant time we anticipated. But now as I hold my passport and look into the warm faces of the people, I feel ashamed for my grade of 3 in literature. This I myself admit to you honestly. I promise to correct this 3 and in the future shall try with all my strength never to receive such a mark either in school or in my work.

In a year I shall be in the tenth grade. I know from my older friends that in the tenth grade they write essays on the theme of the Soviet man, what sort of person he should be, what it means to love one's Motherland. If I should write an essay on this theme, I would certainly begin with a description of today's celebration. I would write about the concern of our Motherland for us, the sixteen-year-old ones, about what our Motherland and the entire Soviet people expect of us, about how we shall carry our first passport throughout our lives with honor.

Among the honored guests were several old Bolsheviks. They chatted with the sixteen-year-olds about life in prerevolutionary times. They related how they had "passed their youth" in stifling and damp factory buildings, in conspiratorial quarters, in jails, in *katorga*. One of them, a participant in three revolutions, addressed the youth formally. Here are a few of his remarks:

> We, old men, are happy in your happiness. It appears that our struggle was not in vain. You were born in the Soviet time, you did not experience forced labor, you did not hear the clanking of chains. We lived differently. Listen to this old document of prerevolutionary life—a contract of the sale by a peasant of his son, a sale into slavery to a factory owner of Ivanovo, one Grachev. . . .
>
> To what desperation could capitalism lead a man if he is forced to sell his own son into slavery! . . .
>
> And so, my friends, guard with honor your Soviet passport, carry it with honor. May it ever remind you of the great rights and duties of a free Soviet citizen.

One can only wonder if these young people had ever read Lenin's castigation of the system of internal passports. In the fateful year of 1903, when he was laying the foundations of Bolshevism, he characterized as follows this instrument for controlling the movements, the behavior, and the mind of the Russian peasant:

> What does this mean, this *freedom to move from place to place*? It means that the peasant must be free to go where he pleases, to move wherever he wishes, to choose for himself the village or the town he prefers, without having to ask for permission. It means that passports must be abolished in Russia too (in foreign countries passports were abolished long ago), that no police officer, no Zemsky Nachalnik must be allowed to stop any peasant from settling down or working wherever he pleases. The Russian peasant is still the serf of the officials to such an extent that he is not free to move to a town, or free to settle in a new district. The Minister issues orders that the governors should not allow *unauthorized* settlement! The governor knows better than the peasant what place is good for the peasant! The peasant is a child who dares not move without authority! Is this not serfdom, I ask you? [57]

Where and when in previous history has man transformed an instrument of tyranny into such a glorious symbol of freedom? Perhaps the Bolsheviks are actually changing human nature, in accordance with their boasts, and they are doing this under the banners of the sacred "cause of Lenin."

7

THE TRANSFORMATION

OF THE INTELLECTUAL CLASS

Members of the intellectual class, as here considered, are people who in exceptional measure work in the realm of words, symbols, ideas, theories, and evaluations. They perform many functions and engage in many activities. They play a central role in the transmission of the old and the creation of the new in a given culture. They are the articulate spokesmen of diverse and conflicting interests. They bear a heavy responsibility in the formation of public opinion and the shaping of popular ideals. They interpret and criticize life, society, history, and the world. Ordinarily they are writers, artists, scientists, and philosophers, editors, journalists, lectures, actors, politicians, teachers, lawyers, and clergymen. They are commonly found in the professions even the technical callings, but if narrowly devoted to their specialties they belong on the margin of the group. Also, in most instances they are regarded as "educated" men and women, graduates of colleges and universities, although they may be persons who on their own initiative have risen from the ranks of agriculture, labor, business, finance, bureaucracy, and the armed forces. As a rule, they prize independence in the realm of things of the spirit and consequently tend to resist discipline and regimentation.

The intellectuals constitute an important element in any society above the most primitive. Even at the level of tribal society, the shaman, the medicine man, or the storyteller is a significant social force. In his study of the great revolutions of modern times Lyford P. Edwards assigns to them a key role in both the maintenance and the undermining of an established order. Indeed, he argues that "the first master-symptom of revolution is the 'transfer of the allegiance of the intellectuals.'"[1] As long as they play their traditional role of justifying and defending inherited institutions, even though there may be discontent among the masses of

136

the people, these institutions will endure. Popular revolts and rebellions led by untutored men may occur, and autocrats may be defeated in battle, but the social system will remain without substantial change. However, when people of ideas become discontented because of resentment regarding their own status, because of the call of conscience incited by conceptions of right and justice, or for any other reason whatsoever, the very foundations of society are placed in peril. And they are in peril because of the creative formulation by imaginative minds of policies and programs for the reconstruction of society and the redistribution of power.

II

Whatever the general merits of Edwards' theory, the Russian intellectuals, particularly the so-called "radical intelligentsia," played a tremendous role in the revolutionary movement which overthrew the tsars and launched the Bolsheviks on their fateful course. The policy of the Bolsheviks toward the intellectuals down to this day has been influenced profoundly by traditions, conceptions, and outlooks formed in the long revolutionary struggle.

In Soviet histories this struggle is traced back to the second half of the seventeenth century. From 1667 to 1671 Stenka Razin, a rough, untutored Cossack leader without ideology or program, headed a bloody revolt against the autocracy in the valley of the Volga. A century later, from 1773 to 1775, another Cossack leader, Emilian Pugachev, led a rebellion in the same spirit and in the same region, proclaimed the abolition of serfdom, and for a time challenged the rule of Catherine the Great. Both of these popular uprisings were waged with savagery and put down with ferocity and brutality. It was not until the nineteenth century, however, that the struggle took on a definitely revolutionary character, with more or less clearly developed doctrines and programs. In the first quarter of that century elements of the intellectual class, army officers among them, entered the arena of political struggle. In December of 1825 an organized group of these men, influenced by the ideas of the French Revolution and by knowledge of the more advanced institutions of Western Europe, attempted to overthrow the autocracy by violence. Although they were unsuccessful, they gave birth to a movement which was destined to bear abundant fruit a century later. The radical intelligentsia was thus launched on its long march to a victory which most of its members in 1917 failed to anticipate and probably lived to regret.

Alexander I, a relatively liberal monarch according to the standards set by the Romanovs, was followed in 1825 by Nicholas I, who established an unsurpassed reputation for tyranny. Reacting against the revolutionary attempt of the Decembrists, he resorted to harsh measures of repression. At the same time, he nourished a tradition of fear and hatred of intellectuals, of novel ideas, and of the foreign world from which, as he thought, evil had come—a fear and hatred shared in considerable measure by all his successors. He sought to isolate Russia from the West and forbade foreign travel on the part of his subjects. He introduced a severe censorship over the expression of ideas and looked with suspicion on all institutions of learning. He called the University of Moscow a "den of wolves," distrusted both professors and students, and set a limit to enrollments. He even regarded voluntary discussion clubs as dangerous. But the radical intelligentsia had appeared as a force in Russian history. It became the fashion for the young intellectual to cultivate revolutionary ideas and espouse revolutionary causes.

Throughout the nineteenth and during the early years of the twentieth century the radical intelligentsia dominated and directed the revolutionary movements against the autocracy. But in the manner of true intellectuals everywhere, while generally agreeing in their criticisms of the old order, they differed violently in their proposals for the building of the new. They differed particularly on questions of method, on how the autocracy was to be overthrown and how a better society was to be built. They differed also regarding the roles in the revolution of the various elements of the population—the liberal aristocracy, the middle class, the peasants, and the proletariat. They differed vigorously regarding their own role. But, as we have seen, the idea that finally triumphed was the idea of a revolution guided both before and after the conquest of power by a small, closely organized and tightly disciplined party of professional revolutionaries fanatically devoted to their cause, certain of the correctness of their programs, sure of the righteousness of their acts, committed to the subordination of means to ends, and loyal to their version of the interests of the people or the working class. Such was the Party of Bolsheviks when, under the leadership of Lenin, they overthrew the provisional government, dissolved the Constituent Assembly, and concentrated all power in their own hands in 1917 and 1918.

The leadership of the Bolshevik Party was composed of intellectuals. And the Party membership contained a fairly high percentage of such people. It has been estimated that at the time of the revolution seven or eight thousand of the old Bolsheviks had enjoyed the privilege of university study. Moreover, the foremost leaders of the Party—Lenin, Trotsky, Bukharin, Zinoviev, Kamenev, and Radek—had spent years abroad perfecting their ideas and debating with the leaders of radical movements in the West. Though always dominated by the revolutionary purpose, they enjoyed historical study, philosophical speculation, and the clash of mind with mind. The very conception of revolution elaborated by Lenin gave the leading role to the intellectual. He took every opportunity to pour scorn on all who contended that the proletariat through its own efforts would or could achieve socialism. The idea that the intellectuals should follow or sink themselves in the mass of workers he ridiculed as "tailism," bringing up the rear of the movement. The workers by themselves, even the industrial proletariat which according to Marx was destined to destroy capitalism and bring in the epoch of civilization, could only achieve "trade unionism" and liberal reforms which would destroy their revolutionary zeal and make them content with their lot as "slaves of capital." Again and again Lenin stressed the point that a revolutionary movement without a "correct revolutionary theory" would be without significance in history. And the only people who could elaborate such a theory were the intellectuals. Indeed, to him this was the distinctive function of the radical intelligentsia, even though he was contemptuous of this group as a whole. Practically every one of its members could formulate a theory of his own, but only he himself and those who agreed with him could formulate the "correct" theory of revolutionary strategy and tactics.

III

After the seizure of power the Bolsheviks soon discovered that they had inherited from the autocracy the prerevolutionary intelligentsia. Although a few members of this class emigrated to other countries, the great majority remained and decided to take their chances under the new regime. It may be well, therefore, to say a few words about the characteristics of the old Russian intelligentsia. Many of them had worked actively for a revolution and many others had been sympathetic. They were highly educated men and women—educated in both the formal and the genuine meaning of the term. Even the specialized scholar or professional man had broad artistic and philosophical interests. They were familiar, not only with the culture and institutions of their own people, but also with the culture, the institutions, and the languages of the West. While there were Russophiles among them imbued with the doctrines of Great Russian messianism, they generally admired the cultural, political, and technological achievements of European countries, and particularly France, Germany, and England. Not a few of them might be classed as cosmopolitans, citizens of the world, who sometimes insisted on speaking French or German at home. And if sufficiently affluent, they employed nursemaids of foreign origin to teach these languages to their children from infancy. Also they were proud of their work, placed a high value on the life of the mind, and cultivated all the arts. Learning for learning's sake and art for art's sake were ideals to be fostered. They prized particularly the tradition, always pursued precariously under the autocracy, of intellectual and artistic freedom. In their thought the revolution would bring more of all these good things and make them accessible to wider strata of the population.[2]

Even the Bolshevik leaders of 1917 were nurtured in some measure on this tradition. Lenin, though absorbed in the revolutionary cause, possessed a wide-ranging mind and could tolerate differences among his associates. Trotsky was always a maverick, high-spirited in character, brilliant in speech and writing, arrogant toward men of lesser mold, moving in and out of the Party during his career. Bukharin, scholar and theorist, had his own ideas about most things and did not hesitate to challenge the propositions of Lenin. Zinoviev, proud, ambitious, and unprincipled, was a consummate politician and the first head of the Communist International. Radek, sharp of wit and cynical in expression, enjoyed making unflattering remarks about the behavior and character of his comrades. Stalin, however, in those early days was a man of different stamp, a Georgian by birth, relatively gray and colorless in the presence of his more talented comrades who had traveled and lived abroad. But he also was ambitious, a man of iron will and a ruthless genius in the organization and the use of power. Perhaps for these reasons he succeeded in destroying all the old Bolshevik leaders of the first rank who did not die from natural causes before he established his dictatorship.

The reaction of the Russian intelligentsia to Bolshevik rule was diverse. A few went over to the Soviets immediately, joined the Party, and rose to moderately high positions in the new state. Andrei Vyshinsky was a good example of this group. Others adopted a sympathetic but critical attitude, placed their talents and services at the disposal of the Bolsheviks, and hoped that the more violent features of the dictatorship would quickly pass into history. Yet others assumed a neutral position, refused to take sides in the struggle, and awaited the swift overthrow or collapse of Bolshevik power. But the great body of the intellectuals, professionals, and technical specialists were openly hostile in the early years. The strike of the teachers, already mentioned, was characteristic of the class. Even the more friendly elements were quickly disillusioned and were swept aside by the revolutionary excesses of the dictatorship. Being men and women of rich personal culture, committed to the ideals of human dignity and intellectual freedom and averse to the shedding of blood and the exercise of terror, they found themslves forced into opposition and sabotage. Consequently, the radical intelligentsia soon sensed that this was not the revolution for which they had hoped and struggled. Nevertheless, with the abandoment of the policies of Military Communism and the launching of the New Economic Policy in 1921, many comforted themselves with the belief that a regime of liberty was on the way.

Intellectuals working in the cultural apparatus—writers, artists, teach-

ers, and scientists—were particularly offended by the demand for Bolshevik orthodoxy in all that they did. They revolted at the thought of
converting works of art, materials of instruction, and programs of research into weapons of the Party. This attitude was well expressed by
a short-story writer, Mikhail Zoshchenko, in 1922. In an article published
in the literary journal *Literaturnye Zapiski*, entitled "About Myself and
about Some Other Things," he expressed these thoughts concerning the
function of the writer—thoughts which in later times other members of
the literary guild doubtless cherished but did not dare to utter:

> All in all it is very difficult to be a writer. Consider the matter of ideology.
> . . . Today they demand ideology from the writer. . . . Really, what a
> nuisance. . . .
> What, tell me, can my "precise ideology" be, if not one party as a whole
> appeals to me?
> From the point of view of party people I am a man without principle.
> What of it? I can only say about myself: I am no Communist, no Socialist
> Revolutionary, no monarchist, but simply a Russian and politically amoral
> besides. . . .
> I give you my word of honor—to this day I don't know, well, let us say,
> Guchkov. . . . To what party does Guchkov belong? Only the devil knows
> to what party he belongs. I know he is not a Bolshevik, nor a Socialist
> Revolutionary, nor a Cadet—I don't know and I don't want to know, etc. etc.[3]

This confession of lack of faith was destined to overtake Zoshchenko
just twenty-four years later when the Central Committee subjected him
to most severe censure and degradation by an uncomprising decree.
Apparently he was able to remain "politically amoral" through all the
years. Many of his colleagues were not so fortunate.

The Bolsheviks understood well the role of the intellectuals in the
revolutionary movement which undermined the old regime. Being intellectuals themselves, moreover, they were familiar with the type of mind
that encourages doubt and passes all things under critical review. Also,
being practiced from youth in the arts of conspiracy and deception, they
were profoundly suspicious of all who were not completely with them.
Consequently, they knew better than Nicholas I how dangerous such
people are to any established authority. Intellectuals would naturally
oppose the imposition by political fiat of any Party line or body of doctrine. In fact, the more radical wing of the Russian intelligentsia, the
Bolsheviks included, had made a virtue of attacking, ofttimes savagely,
the established order in all its manifestations. Obviously, unless they could
be placed under severe discipline, they would constitute a threat to the
revolution, with its rigid doctrines and preconceived goals. Moreover, in
accordance with the Bolshevik analysis of capitalist society, they were
closely bound to the old order, even though they had subjected it to

merciless analysis and criticism. Linked by the ties of birth and the bonds of education to the middle and upper classes, they could never be trusted to build a classless society. Only the Bolsheviks had completely broken with the past and emancipated themselves from bourgeois influences.

Lenin was ever fond of ridiculing and castigating the intellectuals as an unstable and untrustworthy element in the population, belonging clearly to no social class and incapable of forming a class of their own. "No one will undertake to deny," he wrote in 1904, "that the intelligentsia, as a special stratum of contemporary capitalistic societies, is precisely characterized in general and as a whole by individualism and incapacity for discipline and organization." [4] After coming to power in 1918, he, while recognizing the value of the knowledge possessed by the "educated man," pointed to the "necessity of control by the 'plain' workers and peasants" because of the "*slovenliness,* so present among 'educated' people." The weakness of the latter was their tendency "'to replace deeds with discussion, work with talk, a tendency to undertake everything under the sun and to bring nothing to a conclusion." [5] Peter Tkachev expressed precisely the same view.

The Bolsheviks were caught in a dilemma. Although they did not trust the "bourgeois intelligentsia," they could not follow the precedent set by Nicholas I. They required these men and women, with their technical and professional knowledge, to assist them in the achievement of their purposes. They were committed, not only to the maintenance of all the services which the "educated," and only the "educated," could provide, but also to the building of a powerful industrial economy. Also they were committed to the swift expansion of educational facilities and the rearing of a new generation in the spirit of Communism. They were even committed to the transformation of the people and the changing of human nature itself. The Bolsheviks were consequently dependent on the intellectuals. As Lenin put the matter in 1919, "we have bourgeois specialists and that is all we have." By this he meant there were no proletarians properly trained to man the cultural apparatus and the technical posts in economy and government. These bourgeois specialists, he continued, were the only "bricks" with which the structure of socialism could be built. Yet, "socialism must triumph, and we, Socialists and Communists, must prove in practice that we are able to build socialism with these bricks, with this material." The job confronting the Bolsheviks was the creation of a "socialist society with proletarians having only the slightest culture and with bourgeois specialists." [6] This proved to be a formidable task.

In confronting the dilemma, the Bolsheviks followed two courses—a short-term course and a long-term course. The one took the form of a many-sided effort to persuade, cajole, coerce, and capture the "bourgeois intelligentsia"; the other took the form of a positive and an equally many-sided effort to create a new intelligentsia "flesh of the flesh and blood of the blood of the proletariat." The first will be treated briefly.

A common practice of the Bolsheviks during the first years of the revolution was to attack the intelligentsia with words. Lenin referred to them again and again as "saboteurs," "lackeys of capital," "servants of the moneybags," and "agents of the White Guards." Speaking before the First All-Russian Congress of People's Education on August 28, 1918, Lenin referred to "sabotage on the part of teachers of the higher school" and charged them with the desire "to monopolize our school, to make it a weapon of the class struggle, to make it a weapon directed against workers and peasants." [7] On August 1 of the following year, in an address before the All-Russian Congress of Workers of Enlightenment and Socialist Culture, he told his audience that he was "not surprised at the long and stubborn resistance on the part of the teachers, whose organization in an overwhelming majority, if not in its entirety, stands on the platform of hostility to the Soviet power." He stated, moreover, that "the same difficulties" had been "faced in other fields of organization." [8]

In meeting this situation Lenin proposed a variety of measures in a speech at the Eighth Congress of the Russian Communist Party on March 19, 1919. He pointed out that they could "force" bourgeois specialists "to refrain from participating actively in counterrevolution" and "so threaten them that they would not dare to stretch out a hand at the call of the White Guards." All this was being done. But something more was necessary. He proposed that they "be surrounded by an atmosphere of comradely cooperation, by worker's commissars, and Communist cells" and thus be "placed in a position from which they could not extricate themselves." But, he said, "it is impossible with a stick to compel an entire social stratum to work." It is necessary to provide these people "with better working conditions than they enjoyed under capitalism." Otherwise, they "will not work." Lenin also held out the olive branch to the "bourgeois specialists." They are committed to the "advancement of culture," and when they see that the "leading elements of the working class" have the same interest, "their attitude toward us changes." All this will cost money, but "even two billion is a trifle." He advised strongly against "petty fault-finding with respect to specialists." And again he recommended that "during this period of transition we must provide for them the most favorable living conditions possible." In the long run it "will be the best politics" and "the most economical management" even to "overpay the specialists." [9] In 1927 the author visited a school in a small town far from Moscow. An instructor in physics told him that the teachers were generally hostile to the Soviet power during the early years but that this attitude had changed to one of friendliness. When asked for an explanation, he replied that the change was probably due to an increase in salaries.

The use of intellectuals educated under the old regime continued to be a problem through the twenties and even into the thirties. In a "Resolution on Anti-Soviet Parties and Movements" adopted at a conference in August, 1922, the Party declared that "anti-Soviet parties and movements are attempting systematically to convert the chair of higher institutions of learning into a tribune of open bourgeois propaganda, a legal publishing house into an instrument of agitation against the worker-peasant government, etc." And under the New Economic Policy, which encouraged the kulaks, "anti-Soviet elements of the village intelligentsia strive to penetrate the cooperatives" and "exert influence on the village soviets." The Party is called upon to guard with particular care "the press, the higher school, and the cooperatives." These institutions constitute "the 'commanding heights' which the Party must seize or conquer absolutely." While every effort must be made to win the support of "non-Party elements among representatives of science and technology, teachers, writers, poets, and so forth," "one should not repudiate the use of repressive measures" against those "who engage in politics" and promote "counterrevolutionary aims." [10] In May, 1924, the Party posed the question of whether the "socialist economy" or the "capitalist order" would be victorious. It even suggested that the "cultural superiority and skills of the trained functionaries" of the latter may "force us to retreat." [11] At the same time, the Party declared that the situation in the institutions of higher education "remains acute." This is revealed by the fact that in the "majority of cases, even in the departments of social science, the chairs are occupied by old bourgeois professors." The only remedy for the condition described was the "creation of a staff of Communist professors as quickly as possible." [12] This struggle with the "remnants of capitalism," as we have seen, has continued to the present time.

IV

The long-term task of the Party was the rearing of a new Soviet generation of specialists and intellectuals "flesh of the flesh and blood of the blood of the proletariat." In the course of years, provided the Bolsheviks remained loyal to their original purposes, this objective would be reached without resort to extraordinary measures designed to speed the process. With the control of all educational institutions firmly in their hands and with the extension of the opportunities of schooling to the great masses of the people, according to announced plans, it would appear that the ultimate outcome could not be in doubt. Within thirty or forty years the

Bolsheviks would have prepared their own staff of technicians, engineers, and professional workers. But they could not wait. In order to commit the younger generation to the revolutionary cause and the world outlook of Lenin, the school and all other cultural institutions had to be converted into faithful servants of the Party. And the essence of the school is the teacher. Consequently, if the revolution was to be held on its course, the old Russian intelligentsia, the old "bourgeois" specialists, had to be replaced in all haste.

The first measure undertaken by the Soviet state to transform the social composition of this class was as radical as the revolution itself. It was a decree issued in August, 1918, by the "Workers' and Peasants' Government" and signed by Lenin.[13] According to its provisions, the doors to all higher institutions of learning were to be opened to all persons of either sex or any nationality over sixteen years of age, regardless of previous education or academic qualifications. Tuition fees, entrance examinations, and graduation diplomas and certificates were abolished. And tuition fees already paid for the first half of the academic year 1918–1919 were "subject to refund." In quarters sympathetic to Bolshevik rule the decree was hailed as a measure to break the monopoly of the bourgeoisie in the realm of higher education. One enthusiastic supporter doubtless expressed the sentiments of many with these words: "The workers' and peasants' republic should open wide the doors of the university to her youth—create her own truly democratic intelligentsia of workers and peasants—to replace those 'intellectuals' of the bourgeoisie who now hate with such a cruel hatred the government of workers and peasants." [14]

The great part of the instructors and students in the higher schools were naturally outraged by this measure. They protested vigorously against the "forcing of the street into the higher school." The provisional government, during its brief career from March to November, 1917, had guaranteed autonomy to the universities and had proclaimed the ideal of "culture for culture's sake." However, because of the hard conditions induced by civil war, intervention, and famine, drastic reforms were not put into effect until 1921. During the next three years the plan to proletarianize the higher school was tested and found wanting. Great numbers of ill-prepared young people did indeed flock to the university. They flocked, however, not from the proletariat and poor peasantry, as hoped, but from the "city bourgeoisie," from the professions, the traders and merchants, and the white-collar workers.

By 1924 the "open door" policy was recognized as a failure from the standpoint of both academic standards and class orientation. Special committees were formed to investigate each and every student and to conduct a sifting process designed to raise the intellectual level and

eliminate "hostile elements." In 1929 entrance examinations were restored
and attendance of children of the "former people" was proscribed. At the
same time, children of proletarian or poor peasant origin were provided
with maintenance stipends. In applying for admission to a higher school,
a candidate was required to fill out a long and detailed questionnaire
about himself and his parents. Documents had to be presented "proving
the social class of the candidate, and that of his parents," and also "proving that neither the candidate nor his parents had ever been disfranchised." Also he had to present documents giving his labor record, his
role in the civil war, and his party affiliations. Severe penalties were
attached to any effort to falsify the record.[15] In spite of these negative
and positive provisions for the proletarianization and Communization of
the student body, many "enemies of the people" did succeed in gaining
admission to the higher school by falsifying documents, by adopting
proletarian parents, and by resorting to other forms of subterfuge. The
author knows personally of the case of a young woman of proscribed
parentage who in 1929 was refused admission to a conservatory of music
in Leningrad. She eventually evaded the "rules of admission" by working
for a year in a china factory and thus, as she said, "establishing her own
ancestry."

During the twenties and early thirties the Party devoted itself without
surcease to the task of capturing the higher school. Decree after decree
was issued to increase the number of Communists in important posts and
to strengthen the influence of Communist and Young Communist organizations in the institutions of higher learning. In 1928, at the time of the
launching of the First Five-Year Plan, it resorted to the extraordinary
measure of recruiting large numbers of Party members directly into the
student body of these institutions. In July of that year the Plenum of the
Central Committee resolved "to direct into the higher technical schools
1,000 Communists, who have gone through the serious school of Party,
Soviet, and labor union work, and provide for them the necessary material
assistance." It resolved also to "follow this practice annually during the
next years." [16] The number was doubled in 1929 and tripled in 1930. The
following year the Central Committee raised the number to five thousand,
to be composed of persons having had "leadership experience in Party,
industrial, governmental, and labor union work." Industrial workers selected were to have a "Party record of not less than four years," farm
laborers and collective farm workers "not less than five years," and white-
collar employees "not less than seven." [17] The labor unions followed the
example set by the Party and recruited from their numbers additional
thousands for the higher schools. They were all expected to have the
equivalent of secondary schooling. However, since many were deficient
in academic preparation, special courses were organized for them.

V

The decree of 1918 which opened the doors of the higher schools to all youth over sixteen years of age regardless of academic qualifications had many unanticipated consequences. Young men and women of proletarian origin quickly discovered their deficiencies and asked for the organization of special preparatory lectures and courses of instruction. Out of this situation came a most extraordinary social invention, which was destined to play a central and continuing role in the proletarianization of higher education and the modification of the intellectual class. This institution, called the *rabfac,* or workers' faculty, originated in Moscow in 1919 and developed into a major educational institution in the late twenties and early thirties. It reached its peak in the academic year 1932–1933 with 1,025 institutions and a total enrollment of 339,517 students.[18] Thereafter, because of the growth of primary and secondary schools, it rapidly declined and practically disappeared in the early forties. It was in 1936 that the Soviet state officially ended discrimination against the "former people." By that time the new Soviet intelligentsia had arrived in considerable numbers.

Perhaps no other Soviet educational institution, apart from the Communist Party itself, the Party organizations for children and youth, and the Party schools and universities, expressed so uniquely the spirit and purposes of the Soviet state. The *rabfac* was a preparatory institution for the universities and higher technical schools organized and administered to serve the new privileged class of workers and peasants. Since the sons and daughters of the bourgeoisie and the "former people" could not be trusted, since the "children of the revolution" were deficient in educational and cultural background, and since the Bolsheviks were in a hurry, a special institution to bridge the gap between the old and the new had to be created. The *rabfac* was peculiarly symbolic of the Bolshevik conception of the class struggle, and was regarded as a powerful weapon to be employed by the proletariat in that struggle. It was a weapon to be used against the "bourgeois intelligentsia" entrenched in the higher schools. Its basic purpose was to pour a proletarian and Communist contingent into those institutions and eventually into the new Soviet intelligentsia.

In the early days, admission to the *rabfac* was largely a matter of class origin and political reliability. Recommendation from a Party organ, a trade union, a village soviet, or a "poor peasants' committee" was ordinarily sufficient. But it was soon learned from experience, as in the higher schools, that class origin and political reliability were not enough. As a consequence, minimum academic standards were soon established and preparatory courses were organized for the benefit of the ill-prepared.

Eventually fairly elaborate rules of admission were adopted, which resembled closely the rules of admission to the higher schools. The applicant was required to answer a list of some twenty-five questions. Although the sponsoring organization or agency was assumed to be entirely loyal to the regime and the Party, the applicant had to give in considerable detail an account of his life—date and place of birth, employment both before and after the revolution, social status of parents both before and after the revolution, membership in labor unions, military activity during the civil war, work done for Soviet and Party organizations, membership in political parties now and in the past, ownership of property by himself and his parents. His age was supposed to be between eighteen and thirty years. A false statement in this record could have serious consequences for both the applicant and the sponsoring authority.[19]

The question of the social origins of the *rabfac* student was regarded as a matter of crucial importance from the standpoint of the original purpose of the institution. It is also complicated for three reasons. In the first place, the temptation to falsify tended to exaggerate the contribution of the proletariat and the poor peasantry, the favored classes of the regime for which the *rabfac* was established. In the second place, the line between the industrial worker and the peasant was often blurred, since an individual parent might have been born in the village and become a factory worker in his youth. In the third place, since every applicant had two parents and since they may have had different occupational backgrounds, he might identify his parentage with the preferred occupation. Nevertheless, the evidence seems to support the thesis that the *rabfac* did fulfill its mission to a large extent—the mission of preparing young men and women of the desired social origin for the higher schools. Tandler presents the statistics available, all of course from Soviet sources. According to these data, 40 per cent of the students in 1921–1922 were of working-class origin, and 32 per cent of peasant origin. The remaining 28 per cent were classified as nonmanual workers—a category which included white-collar workers of many kinds. By 1928–1929 the percentage of manual workers rose to approximately 69 per cent, the peasants just about held their own, and the nonmanual workers declined to less than 5 per cent. During the remaining years there was relatively little change. In terms of membership in the Party and the League of Young Communists, the percentage rose from 20 in 1920–1921 to between 75 and 80 at the end of the decade. Thereafter a fairly sharp decline ensued.[20]

The social composition of the teaching staff might appear to be important, in view of the purpose of the institution. However, from beginning to end, the major category in terms of origins was that of intellectual worker. Merchants and businessmen were scarcely represented at all.

Peasants ranked second and workers third. The total pattern was not unlike that found in other educational institutions. More significant is the question of Party membership. In 1923–1924 all *rabfac* directors were reported to be Communists. About 19 per cent of the teachers were members of the Party or the Young Communist League. But these figures probably fail to tell the whole story. Teaching in the *rabfac* was comparatively onerous and demanded a rather high degree of dedication to the revolutionary cause. Moreover, the watchful eye of the Party was directed with especial vigilance toward this institution, because it was here more than in the other agencies of people's education that the new Soviet intelligentsia was being reared.[21]

In the sphere of the curriculum, after some experimentation with courses of a few months' duration, the program crystallized by the middle twenties into three or four years of study. In 1928 the curriculum included four years of the Russian language, three years of a foreign language, four years of mathematics, one year of mechanical drawing, one year of design, four years of biology, two years of chemistry, three years of physics, one year of physical geography, two years of economic geography, four years of history of the class struggle, and about thirty weeks devoted to the subject of political literacy. Practically all of the divisions of the curriculum were supposed to be closely related to the cause of Communism and to develop the Marxist-Leninist world view. The four-year course in the history of the class struggle followed the orthodox interpretations of historical materialism from ancient times down to the October Revolution and the launching of the Communist International. Naturally a great deal of attention was devoted to the class struggle in tsarist Russia and the rise to power of the Bolsheviks. The course in political literacy was designed to convey to the students an understanding of the fundamental concepts, institutions, and policies of the Soviet state and the Bolshevik Party. In like fashion it sought to illuminate the international situation in terms of imperialism, war, revolution, and national defense. Interestingly enough, it contained a section on "the Chinese revolution." The final division of the course was devoted to a study of "the international organization of the working class—the Profintern, the Amsterdam International of Trade Unions, and the Comintern and the Second International." [22] The point should be stressed that Party cells and organs were particularly active and powerful in the *rabfac*.

The important question remains: To what degree did the *rabfac* and the many other measures undertaken to proletarianize the higher schools succeed? The only answer which can be given to this question must be found in Soviet statistics. Data from prerevolutionary Russia should provide a kind of bench mark. According to S. Kaftanov, Minister of Higher

Education of the U.S.S.R. at the time of writing, "under the conditions of tsarist Russia higher education was limited to the wealthy stratum of the population." He then documents his generalization as follows:

> In 1914 in eight Russian universities children of the nobility and government officials constituted 38.3 per cent of the students, children of the clergy and the bourgeoisie 43.2 per cent, children of rich peasants 14 per cent, and children of workers, poor and middle peasants, and working intelligentsia 4.5 per cent. It was practically impossible at the time for worker and peasant youth to receive higher education.[23]

The situation in the higher technical schools was approximately the same. In 1921 over 30 per cent of the graduates of Soviet higher schools were workers and peasants. In 1930–1931 the figure stood at approximately 75 per cent, and the remainder was composed almost wholly of children of persons employed in the economic, governmental, military, and Party apparatus.[24] The Soviet statistical yearbook of 1936 shows the swift rise and the beginning of the decline of the contingent of workers in the total student body. According to this source, the percentage was 25.4 in 1928, 46.4 in 1931, and 45.0 in 1935.[25] From the middle thirties the "employee" group grew rapidly and soon became the leading element among students in the higher schools. E. N. Medynsky, the leading educational historian in the Soviet Union, gives the following data for 1938: employees and their children, 42.2 per cent; workers and their children, 33.9 per cent; collective farmers and their children, 16.1 per cent; individual peasants and their children, 5.6; and all others, 2.2 per cent.[26] These data show that by the late thirties the struggle to create a "new Soviet intelligentsia" had been completed to the satisfaction of the Bolshevik leaders. Such is the official interpretation prevailing in the Soviet Union today. With the achievement of socialism all social classes were abolished and a great cultural revolution achieved. In March, 1939, at the Eighteenth Congress of the Party, Stalin put his stamp of approval on the matter.

> As a result of tremendous cultural work a new Soviet intelligentsia has been born among us, an intelligentsia which has emerged from the ranks of the working class, the peasantry, and the Soviet employees, flesh of the flesh and blood of the blood of our people—an intelligentsia which has never known the yoke of exploitation, which hates exploiters, and which is ready to serve the people of the USSR honestly and faithfully. I think that the birth of this new people's socialist intelligentsia is one of the most important consequences of the cultural revolution in our country.[27]

One more word might be said about the *rabfac*. The inquiring visitor to the Soviet Union in 1936 was ofttimes surprised to discover so many persons in responsible posts who had come by this route. Nikita Khrushchev himself was once a student in a *rabfac*!

A general comment on this radical transformation of the intellectual class may be appropriate. No one should make the mistake of confusing the "new people's socialist intelligentsia" with the old Russian intelligentsia. As we have seen, great numbers of the latter were liberal and even cosmopolitan in their outlook, familiar with the languages, the arts, and the thought of the West. Not a few traveled and studied in the countries of Europe and other continents. The Soviet intelligentsia, according to design, at least, has come largely, as the Russians would say, "out of the midst," perhaps "out of the depths," of the people. They have not traveled and studied abroad, and their contacts with the cultures of lands outside the "camp of socialism" are heavily restricted and carefully controlled by the Party. Here is an achievement of the Soviet system of education which, joined with the "iron curtain," may have most fateful consequences for both Russia and the world—consequences which were quite unforeseen by the early Bolshevik leaders who opened the doors to the higher schools and launched the *rabfac* on its course. Cultural relations with both the Russian past and the outside world were systematically weakened. The ideal member of the Soviet intelligentsia is a person technically trained for his specialty, committed to the cause of Lenin, and profoundly ignorant of the life and institutions of the Western world.

VI

The consummation of the long struggle to create the new intelligentsia was marked in striking fashion in 1940. As a necessary aid in the program for bringing youth of proletarian and poor peasant origin into the higher schools, the maintenance stipend was provided from the early days for students of the preferred classes. By the late 1930s this practice seemed to have established itself as a permanent feature of the Soviet system of vocational and professional education. Originally designed to change the composition of the student body, it was later justified on the ground that it eliminated the economic condition of the parent as a factor influencing attendance at the higher schools. Then on October 2, 1940, an all-Union decree ordered the introduction into the higher schools of tuition fees ranging from 300 to 500 rubles a year.[28] At the same time, the maintenance stipend was converted into an instrument for raising the level of scholarship. The practice now, writes Kaftanov, is to provide stipends to all students who "do well in their studies." And "students who make excellent marks in all subjects have twenty-five per cent added to their stipends." [29] There is no mention of assisting children of the proletariat and poor peasantry. In the field of education, as well as in other sectors of economy and life, the Soviet state overlooks few means of motivation.

By far the most unexpected provision in the decree was the introduction of tuition fees into the senior division of the secondary school, into the eighth, ninth, and tenth grades. In the schools of Moscow, Leningrad, and the capital cities of the Union Republics, the fee was set at 200 rubles a year, elsewhere at 150 rubles. The reasons given in the decree for this reversal of the practice of granting free tuition to all, a practice that had been written into the Great Stalinist Constitution of 1936, were two: "the rise in the material well-being of the workers" and "the heavy expenditures of the Soviet Government on construction." The explanation in its first variant was, of course, incorrect. Students of the Soviet economy are generally agreed that the standard of living of the masses of the people increased very little, if at all, under the first three five-year plans.

The true meaning of the decree is perhaps revealed in a second decree issued on the same day, October 2, 1940. This decree created what is called the "state labor reserve."[30] Under its provisions, from 800,000 to 1,000,000 male youth ranging in age from fourteen to seventeen years were to be mobilized or drafted under a quota system each year, for industrial training in special six-month and two-year schools established for the purpose. Instruction was to be free of charge and the pupils were "to be maintained by the state during the period of their studies." On graduation they were "to work four years continuously in state enterprises" under the direction of a specially designated authority. According to a decree issued three months later, voluntary withdrawal from the schools or systematic violation of discipline was made punishable by a one-year sentence to a labor colony. In December, 1953, this system of recruiting and training was extended to agriculture. Also, it should be noted, female youth are now subject to the draft. As A. S. Shcherbakov, a high Party member, observed in *Pravda* on January 22, 1941, the labor reserve schools constituted an answer to those "who mistakenly understood the right to work to mean the right to choose one's own place of employment in disregard of the interests and needs of the state."

The decrees of October 2, 1940, taken together, would seem to mark the crystallization of the postrevolutionary society. A new intellectual, professional, technical, managerial, and political elite had been created. This class was highly privileged in terms of both material and spiritual rewards, and probably for the most part loyal to the regime. The tuition charges in the secondary school and higher schools, while large enough to constitute a serious financial burden for most families, presented no obstacle to the educational advancement of the sons and daughters of the new elite. The fees therefore have played some role in driving underprivileged Soviet youth into the ranks of the "labor reserves." The fact is that, in spite of the systematic and intensive propaganda for a full generation of the idea of the heroism of manual labor and the doctrine of the great historic mission of the proletariat, the Soviet secondary school for many years has been oriented toward the university and the professions, and has associated a stigma of inferiority with the occupations by which the great masses of the people gain their livelihood. It would seem that the portfolio is still more to be desired by Soviet youth than either the hammer or the sickle. According to criticisms appearing in the Soviet press as late as May 15, 1956, Russian parents, like their American opposite numbers, want their children to go to college and "wear a white collar." And this outlook is shared by Soviet youth.

The provisions of the decrees will doubtless undergo radical modification during the coming years. According to the Sixth Five-Year Plan, universal compulsory education up to the age of seventeen will be achieved by 1960. Moreover, the plan itself calls for the eventual abolition of tuition fees in the secondary school. And Khrushchev announced in his speech at the Twentieth Congress that this would be done "at the beginning of the new academic year." [31] The return to the earlier practice, however, will probably lead, not to any radical change in the selective and sifting process, but rather to the raising of the general level of educational qualifications for entrance into the lower vocational schools. But this is speculation. The basic fact is that a new intelligentsia has been created and that its children will occupy indefinitely a preferred position in the realm of higher education. Only another proletarian revolution or a reduction of the great inequalities in compensation among the occupations could seriously alter the situation.

VII

That the new intelligentsia occupies a preferred position in Soviet society is well established. The Party long ago abandoned and repudiated the principle of equality of compensation as "rotten egalitarianism." In fact, it has pursued the policy proposed by Lenin in dealing with the "bourgeois intelligentsia" inherited from the old regime. He operated on the theory that the specialist should be paid enough to ensure his loyalty to the Soviet regime. And so it is today. A member of the intelligentsia is generally given a salary well above the wage rates of manual workers. And if he holds an important post in the economic, cultural, governmental, military, or Party apparatus, he receives many times the compensation of the "worker at the bench." Also, for "fulfilling or over-fulfilling the plan," he is awarded a substantial bonus. If he is a writer, he may receive large royalties; if an inventor, large fees. And the top-ranking intellectuals in the realms of science, history, philosophy, literature, drama, music, and theater may receive prizes valued up to 100,000 rubles. The Soviet philosopher, M. Prots'ko, was scarcely exaggerating when he wrote in 1950 that "in the Soviet land the most favorable condi-

tions are established for the fruitful creative work of the intelligentsia. . . .
In socialist society cultural workers are surrounded with the fatherly care
of the Party and the socialist state." The latter "spare no means" to this
end. They "raise their salaries," "improve their material living conditions,"
and "establish Stalin prizes for the best works and inventions." [32]

The administering of these rewards, material and psychological, is
contingent on one very important condition: the individual must be
loyal to the Party and follow the Party line in all matters. The one thing
which the intellectual prizes next to life itself is denied. He does not
have freedom. The Party leaders, of course, know this. Consequently,
they do not trust him, even though he may be "flesh of the flesh and blood
of the blood of the proletariat." They must keep him under close surveillance, make clear to him from time to time the Party line in his special
field of endeavor, and punish him severely if he shows "bourgeois" tendencies or "bows down before the West." He is always sensitive to the fact,
moreover, that an abrupt change in the line may leave him stranded on
a hostile shore. This part of the story will be related in a subsequent
chapter.

8

THE TRAINING
OF SPECIALISTS

The development of the Soviet program for the training of specialists can be understood only on the background of the social structure, the character of the economy, the traditions of the people, and the general cultural level of Russia at the time of the revolution. The condition of backwardness has been referred to many times in the present volume. It influenced profoundly the struggle for power in 1917, the conception of the role of the Bolshevik Party, the program for the general education of young and old, and the entire course followed by the Soviet state. Lenin set the pattern in proclaiming and lamenting the heritage from the past. In fact, he stated without qualification on a number of occasions that the revolution itself would not and could not stand if it failed to spread to more advanced countries, and particularly to Germany, the very symbol to the Bolsheviks of modern science, technology, and efficiency.

At the time of the revolution Russia was primarily a land of peasants and rural artisans. Machine industry, though advancing rapidly in some sectors, was confined to a few urban centers and mining regions. Sixty or sixty-five per cent of the people were illiterate in the formal meaning of the term. If judged from the standpoint of knowledge of science and technology, they were grossly illiterate. In their efforts to deal with the forces of nature, with pests, drought, and fertility, the peasants resorted to various magical practices which had been handed down from generation to generation through the folklore of the village. As for familiarity with machines, they were living in the age of the hand tool, human muscle, and the horse. Between the small privileged class and the masses of the people there was a wide cultural gulf which was difficult to pass in either direction. The typical intellectual lived in a world of the mind divorced from the world of practical affairs, with little interest in raising

155

the productivity of the economy. Even the specialist in some technical field was often more interested in theory than in practice. To be sure, not a few sensitive souls experienced a sense of guilt as they contemplated the lot of the people and the backwardness of their country. But it was this general condition among the intellectuals that led Lenin to emphasize repeatedly the necessity of bridging the gap between theory and practice, between mental and physical labor. And the theme of the integration of theory and practice runs through the whole history of Soviet education from the earliest days. The emphasis on socially useful labor in the twenties constituted an attempt to apply this principle.

This does not mean that Lenin had only contempt for the "bourgeois specialists" trained under the old regime. In fact, he was dependent upon them for the achievement of his purposes, both cultural and technical. He endeavored to capture them by persuasion, bribery, and terror. His major difficulty was that there were so few of them. A measure of their number may be found in the statistics of technical and higher education in the closing years of the tsars. In 1915 the number of higher educational institutions of all types in the Russian empire with a population of over 180,000,000 was only 91 and the total student body approximately 125,000. While there were 233 middle technical schools, the enrollment was under 50,000, little more than one-third of the attendance in the higher schools. For the training of skilled laborers, 2,644 institutions enrolled less than 220,000 pupils.[1] The curricula of the higher schools gave little attention to the training of specialists, except in a few fields. "The historical-philological faculty of a university," for example, "prepared secondary school teachers in the ancient languages, the Russian language and literature, and history. Consequently the deeper specialization had to be acquired on the job. Technical and polytechnical institutes graduated mechanical and chemical engineers without further specialization." [2] The Soviet program for the training of specialists has moved toward the other extreme.

The fact to be emphasized at this point is the poverty of trained specialists and scientists in the Russia of 1917. Though not fully aware of the magnitude and complexity of the task, the Bolsheviks were committed from the beginning to the conversion of a backward society into a modern industrial state, the most advanced in the world. This meant the development, sooner or later, of a vast and comprehensive program for the training of specialists and the mastery of science. Here was the secret of both power and abundance. Here also was the secret for the building of a socialist society. In the romantic twenties they apparently assumed that the expropriation of the capitalists and the proclamation of socialist ideals would quickly overcome all obstacles. Much that has been reported in preceding chapters on educational reforms, socially useful work, and proletarianization of the intelligentsia lends support to this view. Consequently, it was not until the initiation of the First Five-Year Plan that their program of training was really launched on the course that eventually brought anxious thoughts to the minds of leaders in the Western countries. Every day or week now someone breaks into print on the subject of the large number of engineers being trained in the Soviet Union.

A second consideration which has played an important role in the evolution of the Communist program of both middle and higher education is the Marxian dogma of the relation between science and religion. The two, according to the dogma, are in irreconcilable conflict, and have been since the emergence of science in human culture. On the one hand, the findings of science inevitably undermine the intellectual foundations of religion and expose the "falsehood" of all idealistic and theological outlooks on the world. On the other hand, only a socialist society, only a society founded on dialectical materialism, can fully liberate science and bring its blessings to mankind. In the Soviet Union today one of the great aims of education is the inculcation in the mind of the younger generation of a "scientific-atheistic" world view. The two conceptions are invariably linked together. So the great emphasis on science in both the lower and the higher schools serves a double purpose. It serves the practical purpose of multiplying the material strength of the Soviet state and the eschatological purpose of defining the destiny of man.

The role of technical education in the development of the materialistic world view was expressed quite clearly, if somewhat naïvely, in a pronouncement of the All-Union Communist Party at its Thirteenth Congress in 1924. "Antireligious propaganda in the village," it read, "should bear exclusively the character of a materialistic explanation of the phenomena of nature and social life with which the peasants come in contact. The explanation of the origin of hail, rain, thunder, and drought, of the appearance of pests, of the nature of the soil, of the action of fertilizer, etc., is the best form of antireligious propaganda." This bit of advice was republished in an authoritative Party organ as late as 1945 in an editorial on "methods of propagandizing against religion through education in science." [3] The article reminded the author of an experience he had in Magnitogorsk in October, 1936. There he spoke to a group of 250 teachers of the middle school on the subject of American education. Among the thirty-four written questions addressed to the speaker at the close of the talk was the following: "Are pupils taught the truth about natural phenomena such as rain, thunder, and wind?" The Party instruction and this question reveal something of the level of religious teachings and conceptions in old Russia. The antireligious propaganda of the Bolsheviks took the form of telling the peasants to abandon resort to religious incantations and the sprinkling of holy water around the fields to combat pests and ensure good harvests. All this was supposed to demonstrate that there is no God.

II

The general institutional pattern for the training of specialists was established in the 1920s. It should be added, however, that the pattern is one of great complexity and is always undergoing change in its details. Some agencies organized in the early period and designed to meet a temporary condition are gone. The *rabfac* is a good illustration. Moreover, old institutions have altered their programs and functions in response to Party decrees, Soviet achievements, and changing tasks and purposes. Thus, the schools for the training of the "state labor reserves" of conscripted youth established in 1940 represented adaptations of existing institutions. And new agencies have been added from time to time, such as the schools for worker and peasant youth organized during the war. The entire story cannot be told in these pages. It must suffice to confine the account to the main lines of development. Also, chief attention will be devoted to the period following the launching of the First Five-Year Plan, which marked the beginning of the vast program for the industrialization of the Soviet Union.

The system evolved in the first ten years of Soviet power recognized three levels of occupational qualification and training—lower, middle, and higher. The first corresponds roughly to the category of semiskilled and skilled labor, the second to that of semiprofessional, and the third to that of professional. Based on the schools of general education and articulating with them at various points, a wide range of institutions was established to prepare youth for the three levels of qualification. According to the prevailing theory, the individual proceeded to his special training from any one of three critical points in the full middle school, which at that time embraced nine instead of ten years. If he was to become a worker of lower qualification in industry, agriculture, mining, or transportation, he was supposed to enter the training school after having completed the first four grades. The factory-mill school, with many variations, was the recognized type for this level of training. An aspirant for semiprofessional service commonly left the middle school at the end of the seventh grade and entered an appropriate institution. The type here was commonly called the "technicum." Training for the third level was based on the completion of the nine-year program of general education and was provided in the universities and higher technical schools. Here were trained secondary school teachers, agronomists, physicians, surgeons, engineers, historians, linguists, mathematicians, scientists and others engaged in the higher forms of professional service. The training programs and facilities in all these institutions, lower, middle, and higher, were marked by a high degree of specialization.

The factory-mill school, in the Soviet pattern, was created in 1920, but grew rather slowly before 1930. It began with a three- or four-year program and was linked functionally with some industrial enterprise. The pupils were largely semiliterate youth who had been reared "under pre-revolutionary conditions." At first, large attention was given to training in the elementary subjects of the primary school. An eight-hour day was divided into four hours for general instruction and four hours for productive labor. Later, because of the "cultural growth of the country" and the extension of educational opportunities, the division of time was changed to two and six hours respectively, the program was shortened to one and one-half or two years, and the age of entrance was established at fifteen to eighteen. In 1940, under the system of State Labor Reserves, the curriculum was reduced to six months "for the preparation of workers in mass production." At the same time, a two-year school was established for the training of railroad workers, and a three-year school for artisans in the fields of metallurgy, chemistry, mining, and the oil industry. And institutions of the factory-mill type were organized for rural youth in agronomy and animal husbandry. All through the years training agencies were developed by labor unions and large enterprises, for the purpose of raising the level of technical skill and knowledge in industry and agriculture.[4] Another interesting institution which appeared in the twenties was the machine-tractor station. This is a state enterprise equipped with tractors and agricultural machines which enters into contracts with entire villages for the plowing of fields and the sowing, cultivating, and harvesting of crops. But it is also an important educational agency for training peasant youth in the use of farm machinery and modern techniques.

The technicum was developed in the early twenties, with antecedents in prerevolutionary times, to prepare youth for occupations of middle qualification or semiprofessional grade in "various branches of industry, construction, transport, communications, and agriculture." In the field of medicine, the institution was called a medical school and trained nurses and midwives; in the field of education, it was called a pedagogical school and trained teachers for the primary school and preschool agencies. The courses were three to four years in length and the students from fourteen to thirty years of age. Graduation from the seven-year school or the equivalent was a prerequisite for admission. In the later years entrance examinations were introduced and a severe regimen was established. In the early period "out-of-class and out-of-school work—lectures, excursions, circles—was broadly developed." "Successful students" are now provided with maintenance stipends. Graduation is "contingent on the taking of a state-examination or the defense of a project before a state-approved commission." Graduates of the technicum must "work three years in their field of specialization." Thereafter they may apply for admission to the higher school. However, if a student completes his work with a rating of "excellent," he "has the right to enter a higher school immediately." Many technicums organize evening and correspondence courses.[5]

Specialists of higher qualification are trained in the universities and higher technical institutes. These institutions also have their antecedents in prerevolutionary Russia. But the Bolsheviks changed them profoundly and directed them toward the tasks and goals established by the Party. That this was not achieved without a fairly prolonged and bitter struggle has already been made abundantly clear. Nevertheless it was achieved. The university and the higher technical institute ordinarily rest on the complete middle school. The university is distinguished by the number of its separate faculties or schools and by the breadth of its program. In fact, it is only in the Soviet university that anything approaching the curricula of American universities and colleges of liberal arts may be found, and the number of universities in 1956 was only 33 out of a total of almost 900 higher institutions of all kinds. The technical institute, though it may have several faculties, provides a highly specialized form of training. The purposes of Soviet higher education have been well stated by Medynsky:

> The chief tasks of our higher educational institutions are as follows: (1) the ideological-political education of the students and instructors in the foundation of the teachings of Marx-Engels-Lenin-Stalin; (2) the preparation of cultured specialists of high qualification for all branches of the people's economy and culture; (3) the conducting of scientific-research for the purpose of assisting in the solution of the most important problems of socialist construction; and (4) the popularization of scientific and technical knowledge and the newest achievements of science and technology among the broad masses of the population.[6]

This pattern was well established in theory in the 1920s. But it was developed and perfected on the operational side during the next two decades. Much of the remainder of the present chapter will be devoted to telling the story of the subsequent period and outlining in some detail the Soviet program for the training of specialists of higher qualification—the number of institutions and students, the organization of the curriculum, the regimen of work and study, the methods of entrance, promotion, and graduation, the whole system of rewards and punishments, and the relation of the higher school to society.

One more word regarding the entire system for the training of specialists of all degrees of qualification during the first decade would seem to be appropriate. As in the middle school, more attention was given to political indoctrination than to the mastery of science and technology. Along with this emphasis went the drive for the proletarianization of all specialists in training. Political loyalty and class origin were generally regarded as more important than scholastic achievement. Party activity and socially useful work often demoralized the teaching staff and disorganized the program of study. The brigade, the laboratory, or the project system ruled the classroom—a system under which group rather than individual accomplishment set the standard. Moreover, even though the revolution and the civil war were still fresh in the minds of all, the feeling of tension and urgency was moderated. The New Economic Policy was in full career, the "temporary stabilization of capitalism" was official doctrine, the world revolution was postponed to a more or less distant future, and the very idea that Stalin was soon to destroy all his old comrades in the Party leadership and send millions of dissenters to a life worse than the *katorga* of the tsars was unthinkable. Also, the program of forced industrialization and collectivization lay in an unforeseen though near, future.

III

In October, 1928, the Party launched its Plan of Great Works, which, with its successors down to the present time, was destined to change the face of the Russian land, transform the economy, and give a powerful impetus to the program for the training of specialists. It was indeed a *plan* of great works. With the broad directives given by the Party leadership and the details elaborated by the State Planning Commission, it outlined goals of achievement during a period of five years which seemed quite fantastic in the light of all the negative factors. It proposed an increase of annual production in state industry of 180 per cent, a fourfold increase in the annual production of oil, a more than twofold increase in the annual production of pig iron, a fourfold increase in the annual production of machines, a raising of annual production of tractors from practically nothing to 53,000 in the year 1932–1933, a raising of the production of chemical fertilizers from close to zero to 400,000 tons annually. The Plan also called for comparable changes in the fields of agriculture, transport, and "cultural construction." [7]

This is not the place to assess the achievements of the Plan except to say that they were certainly much greater than was anticipated by most Western observers. The announcement of the launching of the Plan was generally hailed in Europe and America with ridicule and derision. The program outlined was so gigantic and the country so backward that the whole undertaking appeared to some as an occasion for laughter but not for sober study and thought. The very idea that Russia would "overtake and surpass the most advanced capitalist countries" in a brief historical epoch was nonsense. Many certainly regarded the Plan as political rather than economic in purpose and an eleventh-hour bid for popular support by a toppling regime. According to this interpretation, the Soviet government, having consumed the savings accumulated under the capitalist institutions of the empire and then having reduced the peasants to extreme poverty, found itself on the brink of complete moral and political bankruptcy. In order to avert disaster it bethought itself of the Five-Year Plan and the dramatic challenge to capitalism to take the minds of the people off their miseries. That the costs in human suffering were tremendous cannot be denied. Yet the Plan did take the Soviet state a considerable distance on the road to industrialization. It is introduced here because of its impact on the training of specialists.

The Soviet supply of specialists in 1928 seemed far from adequate to ensure even the partial success of the Plan. The institutions for the training of such people had not expanded radically since prerevolutionary times, in spite of Soviet propaganda to the contrary. Thus, between 1915 and 1928 the number of higher schools had grown only from 91 to 129 and the student body from 124,700 to 159,800. In the case of technicums and schools for training specialists of middle qualification, the growth was more impressive—from 233 to 1,650 institutions and from 48,000 to 253,600 students. These years, moreover, witnessed an actual decline in the realm of preparing skilled workers. In number of institutions, the decline was from 2,644 to 1,814, and in pupil enrollment from 219,000 to 178,300.[8] And almost one-half of the people were still illiterate,[9] as contrasted with 35 or 40 per cent at the time of the revolution.

A comparison of the Soviet Union and Germany with respect to the degree of training of industrial workers is revealing. In the year 1928–1929, the year of the launching of the Plan, only 41.3 per cent of the workers in Soviet industry were skilled, whereas in Germany the corresponding figure was 62.6. In the case of engineers the condition was yet more unfavorable. For industry as a whole the percentage of engineers to the entire number of workers was 0.37 in the Soviet Union and 1.38 in Germany.[10] The execution of the Plan demanded specialists of all grades and types. This general situation led the Soviet authorities to employ large numbers of foreign engineers, technicians, and even skilled laborers. Not a few American citizens assisted the Bolsheviks in the great program of construction. This fact goes unrecorded in the history textbooks used in the Soviet schools.

The Plan itself called for a great expansion of the training of specialists at all levels. According to the original estimates, which later were revised upward, large state industry would require during the five-year period

1,535,800 additional skilled workers, transport 145,000, and construction 235,800. The number needed in small industry and handicrafts was approximately 1,300,000. For the rural economy 5,000,000 peasants would be given the rudiments of agricultural knowledge, and 250,000 would be trained in the use of the new agricultural machinery. At the level of technical and professional personnel the Plan was even more ambitious because of the longer period of training required. In 1927, according to the data of the Supreme Economic Council, the Russian Republic, with a population of more than 100,000,000 persons, had in 1927 only 45,200 such specialists in all branches of the economy. Moreover, but 9,400 of these had enjoyed the privileges of higher education and only 10,200 had finished the middle school. The education of the remainder must be left to the imagination. On this slender foundation the Plan proposed the preparation of 50,000 engineers and 80,000 technicians, figures which were raised in 1929 to 60,000 and 120,000 respectively. For the rural economy 30,000 specialists of higher qualification and 20,000 of middle qualification were to be trained. The need for physicians was placed at 17,500. And then there remained the "commanding heights" of science. The number of highly trained workers in the various branches of science was to be increased from 26,000 to 85,000. These data, which give only the highlights of the story, were checked by the State Planning Commission for the author at the time.[11]

This gigantic commitment naturally had its parallel in the field of education. Every institution for the preparation of specialists, as well as the primary and secondary school, was placed under great strain. Many new and supplementary schools and courses, evening, part-time, and correspondence programs, were established. The Plan called for the training of 56,200 additional teachers of higher qualification and 163,700 of middle qualification. For the purpose of propagating the Plan, many thousands of organizers and agitators were needed. As a consequence, the Soviet Party schools and the Communist universities were greatly expanded.[12] In these institutions members of the Party and the League of Young Communists were trained to carry the Plan and the Party line to every nook and corner of the Soviet Union. During this period Stalin coined an expression that was repeated in the press, over the radio, and by every agitator: "Trained personnel decide everything." And a statement by the "Great Leader" at the Eighth All-Union Congress of the Young Communist League in May, 1928, four months before the official launching of the Plan, became a kind of theme song for the program of industrialization and for the development of the entire system for the training of specialists. He challenged the picked youth of the country in these words:

Before us stand the greatest tasks of the reconstruction of our entire public economy. . . . The working class cannot become the true mentor of the country if it is unable to free itself from ignorance, if it is unable to master science and manage the economy on the foundations of science. . . .

Before us stands a fortress. This fortress is called science with its many branches of knowledge. This fortress we must capture at any cost. This fortress youth must capture, if it wants to be the builder of a new life, if it wants to become the genuine shift of the old guard. . . .

To master science, to forge the new personnel of Bolshevik specialists in all branches of knowledge, to study, to study, to study most stubbornly— such now is the task.

*The march of revolutionary youth toward science—*this is what we need now, Comrades.[13]

This statement by Stalin expressed quite unequivocally the bias which was to mark the development of both secondary and higher education during the next quarter of a century. It was in the early thirties that the theme of the mastery of knowledge and particularly scientific knowledge came to dominate the upper grades of the middle school. It was during this period also that the Soviet state expanded and diversified its program for the training of specialists of higher qualification. The mastery of science, moreover, did not merely mean the intellectual comprehension of the findings of science and the prosecution of scientific research. It also meant the application of science to all branches of the economy. It meant the *practical* mastery of technology.

The impact of the First Five-Year Plan on the program for the training of specialists is clearly and extravagantly reflected in Soviet statistics. Consider the quantitative changes which took place between 1928 and 1932. In the former year there were 129 higher schools of all kinds, with an enrollment of 159,800 students. The corresponding figures for 1932 were 645 and 394,000. In schools of the technicum type the number of establishments grew from 1,650 to 3,096 and the number of students from 253,600 to 754,100. The factory-mill schools and others of similar grade and purpose expanded in like measure, from 1,814 to 3,970 institutions and from 178,300 to 975,000 pupils.[14] However, in the next three or four years the authorities retreated and the enrollments declined. The expansion outran material facilities and properly qualified teaching personnel. But the recovery starting in 1935, though severely interrupted by the war, carried the enrollment in higher institutions, including extension students, to over 1,600,000 in 1954. The technicum followed a similar course, reaching an enrollment of more than 1,800,000 students.[15] In this same year the higher schools of the Soviet Union graduated 173,000 persons. Because of the emphasis on specialized training in both the universities and the technical institutes, practically all of these graduates were specialists. Among them were 53,000 engineers, 24,000 specialists in medicine, and 20,000 in the various branches of the rural economy.[16] Between 1928 and 1954 the higher educational institutions graduated approximately 2,660,000 specialists. Schools of technicum grade gave to the country in 1954 more than 250,000 specialists of middle qualification.[17] According to the directives of the Party for the Sixth Five-Year Plan, "the general output of specialists of higher and middle qualifications will be increased by fifty per cent" by 1960, and the output of such specialists "for the branches of heavy industry, construction, transport, and rural economy by one hundred per cent, in comparison with the Fifth Five-Year Plan." [18] Quantitatively, the achievements since 1928 constitute an impressive record. The question of quality remains to be considered. Attention from here on will be confined to the higher schools.

IV

The quality of instruction and achievement in the Soviet higher schools has long been a subject of debate and controversy. This is due in part to radical changes in policies and conditions in the course of Soviet power. In the 1920s, according to all accounts, the level of scholarship left much to be desired. This was the inevitable result of the emphasis on political indoctrination, the distrust of "bourgeois professors," the emphasis on proletarian origin, the inadequacy of material facilities, the disorganization of programs of study, the poor preparation of entering students, the brigade or laboratory method of teaching, the weakness of discipline and regimen, the emphasis on extra-class activity, and the domination of Party and Komsomol organizations. Then, during the period of the First Five-Year Plan, as we have observed, the forced expansion of the system of higher schools led to a degree of chaos and the lowering of standards. However, the middle thirties were marked by a vigorous stocktaking and the opening of a new period in the history of the training of Soviet specialists. The question of quality will be considered in relation to the developments of the last two decades.[19] The subject will be elaborated in terms of programs of study, methods of admission, examinations and marks, maintenance stipends, and position of the specialist in Soviet society.

The program of study in Soviet higher schools, whether in the university or in the technical institute, is designed to prepare specialists of high qualification rather than to give a broad education in the sciences and the humanities. It is closely linked with the program of construction. In 1953–1954, 295 specialties were represented in the total system. Of these, the industrial-engineering branch embraced 188, education and the arts 53, socioeconomics 24, agriculture 22, and health 8. In some cases the specialties are further divided, with the result that training is provided altogether for 450 specializations.[20] The length of the undergraduate course, to employ an American expression which is not wholly appropriate, ranges generally from four to six years, with an exception in the case of the two-year pedagogical institutes. Resting on this course, in many specialties a program is conducted for advanced training and research, which may be carried on in the universities and the training institutes but which also may be provided in special research institutes and laboratories. After graduation, a student may be chosen to pursue a three-year course in a given specialty as an *aspirant* and, if successful, receive the degree of *candidate*. He may then proceed on a doctoral program to be concluded in four years. He prepares a dissertation under professorial guidance, defends his dissertation in public before a special committee, and, if successful, may be awarded the degree of doctor of science by a state certificating authority.

The methods of admission are deliberately and carefully designed to bring into the higher schools the ablest young men and women, within the limits of political loyalty and reliability. Graduation with academic distinction from the complete middle school has become the generally accepted route to study in these institutions, although other roads are recognized. The reforms introduced into the secondary school in the thirties and early forties have played an important role here, notably the emphasis on marks and examinations, the tightening of discipline, the rules of conduct, the tuition fees in the eighth, ninth, and tenth grades, the gold and silver medals, and the reduction in time devoted to political subjects and activities. Since the higher schools, as a rule, have more applicants,sometimes many more, than can be admitted, a relatively severe selection is possible. Except for those who hold medals, comprehensive and competitive entrance examinations have become the universal practice. Those who do badly in the secondary school, who are financially unable to afford further education, or who fail to excel in the entrance examinations are forced into the lower vocational schools and the occupations of lower and middle qualification. In theory, only the best of the younger generation, as measured by Soviet standards, win the coveted prize of gaining admission to the universities and higher technical schools. Playing their part, however, are the harsh conditions of life of the masses of the people and the great diversity from one locality to another in the extent and quality of training in the middle school. It should be added that the prestige and excellence of the higher schools vary greatly from one institution to another. As a consequence, the pressure to gain admission to one rather than to another is heavy and persistent.

There is one feature of Soviet admission practice that merits special attention. Since the early 1920s the Soviet state has pursued the policy of drafting young men into the armed forces for two to five years at about the age of eighteen. This draft supposedly has been universal in its application. However, for many years various categories have been exempted for reasons of state policy, and particularly in relation to educational status and prospects. The call to the colors has been postponed to enable young men to complete their study in secondary schools. It has been known for some years that young men in highly important lines of study and research have been exempted from the draft. This practice was followed even during the Great Patriotic War. "Today," writes Nicholas DeWitt after making a careful study of the laws and regulations, "the Soviet Union has a clear-cut policy of preferential treatment toward higher education students concerning the military draft." [21] And a secondary school pupil completing the tenth grade at seventeen or younger may enter a higher school and thus be relieved indefinitely and perhaps permanently from the conscription. Although the Soviet child is taught from earliest years that the defense of the Motherland in battle against her enemies is his most sacred duty, apparently many young men regard compulsory military service as an onerous task which interferes with personal advancement in their chosen careers. Undoubtedly, here is a reward for study in the higher school which must influence many to follow the injunction of Stalin to "study, study, study" and "capture the fortress of science." If the individual falls behind his classmates, he will find himself outside the walls of learning and in the ranks of the conscripts.

As in the lower schools, marks and examinations have been converted into a powerful means of motivating the work of students. Except for young men and women with outstanding records in the secondary school, they are admitted by competitive examinations in the basic subjects of language, history, mathematics, and science, with some adjustments to the diverse demands of specialization in the higher schools. After gaining admission, the student is subjected to a regimen of "mandatory attendance" at from thirty-two to forty hours of instruction in a six-day week. During the semester he is subjected to various tests, and at the end of a course he must take a final examination. In a five-year program of training, he must take approximately fifty such examinations. If a student fails more than three subjects, he is automatically dismissed; if he fails three and does not succeed in removing his "debts" by the end of the year, he is subject to dismissal.[22] In order to be admitted to *aspirantura* training a student must pass examinations in his chosen specialty, one foreign language, and the principles of Marxism-Leninism. At the end of two years of study he again has to pass a broad and detailed examination, which embraces Marxism-Leninism, two foreign languages, the general field of science covered by his training, and the special subject proposed for his dissertation. The third year closes with the acceptance or rejection of his research project. If successful, he then proceeds to his study for the doctorate.[23] In the Soviet higher schools, marks and examinations accompany the student from the beginning to the end of his academic career.

The stipend also must play an important role in the motivation of the student. Originated in the twenties as a means for changing the social composition of the intelligentsia, as a means of developing a "new Soviet intelligentsia," it survives today as an instrument for stimulating and rewarding excellence in scholarship. The decree of the Central Committee on October 2, 1940, which established tuition fees, with numerous exceptions, for study in the higher schools, also affected the stipends. While the latter were by no means abolished, they were directed toward a different end. They were made contingent on success in study as determined by marks and examinations. The number and size of stipends are also employed to encourage prospective students to choose one institution rather than another, one specialization rather than another. DeWitt is of the opinion that at the present time from 70 to 75 per cent of the students in Soviet higher institutions receive maintenance stipends ranging perhaps from 140 to 315 rubles a month. In addition there are approximately 7,000 "personal stipends" of 400 to 1,000 rubles per month for "the most outstanding students" in special fields.[24] Such stipends are given "in the name" of almost everybody of note and respectability, from Comrade Stalin (Comrade Khrushchev?) to the Kazak folk minstrel-poet, Dzhambul Dzhabaev, and for almost every subject from philology to soil science. They are given "in the name of" somebody or other to "persons preparing to defend doctoral dissertations." [25]

The entire process of granting stipends is of course conducted strictly within the limits of political loyalty and orthodoxy. Both students and instructors must give every outward evidence of unqualified devotion to the Communist Party and its Central Committee. To those young men and women of talent and industry who conform positively in ideology and conduct the future is full of promise. All others, and they probably constitute a distinct minority, live under the shadow of failure, disgrace, exile, and penal servitude. In the realm of higher education particularly, the Soviet state is fully committed to the use of both the carrot and the stick.

This suggests yet another broad type of motivation which must play a central role in Soviet higher schools. Apart from the power and prestige of Party affiliation, the members of the new intelligentsia of engineers, managers, physicians, scientists, teachers, writers, artists, and bureaucrats constitute a privileged class in the Soviet Union. To these people go the highest material and spiritual rewards of society. And if any one element in this class were to be singled out for a special mention in this connection, it would undoubtedly be the engineers and scientists. These specialists are the most favored of the favored in the Bolshevik state. It should be made very clear that there is a well-marked road to privilege and distinction, and that road runs through the higher school. The time has long since passed when the Communist Party followed the rule of preferring simple proletarians for membership in its sacred ranks. The "worker at the bench," though not forgotten in Party literature, does not occupy the position which he enjoyed when the revolution was young.[26] The great program of industrialization launched in 1928 led almost inevitably to this end. The program demanded engineers and scientists; and the Sixth Five-Year Plan continues the course set by its predecessors. The purpose of "overtaking and surpassing the most advanced capitalist countries" remains dominant in the Soviet Union. And in terms of the *rate* of training engineers and technicians, Russia has already overtaken and surpassed quantitatively the United States of America. To the old slogan of 1928 Stalin added a new dimension or gave a new emphasis in his speech of February 9, 1946. "I have no doubt," he said, "that if we give the necessary assistance to our scientists they will be able not only to overtake, but also to surpass in the nearest future the achievements of science beyond the borders of our country." [27] That this is a goal of the Soviet Union today cannot be questioned, Stalin or no Stalin.

DeWitt, at the close of his study of the Soviet higher schools, offers the following estimate of the quality of instruction in these institutions:

> Throughout this volume many reservations have been made concerning the training, supply, and utilization of professional personnel in the U.S.S.R. Despite these reservations, we must bear in mind that during the last two and a half decades the Soviet Union has made enormous strides towards building up its specialized manpower resources. As a result of its efforts, it has reached a position of close equivalence with or even slight numerical supremacy over the United States as far as the supply of trained manpower in specialized professional fields is concerned. The Soviet effort continues. Our own policies in the field of education and in regard to specialized manpower resources will decide whether within the next decade or so the scales will be tipped off balance.[28]

Another bit of testimony from a scholar competent to speak with some authority will be added. Eric Ashby, an English biologist, spent a year in the Soviet Union in 1944–1945. While there he devoted himself to the study of Russian science. In the final paragraph of his account he draws the following tentative conclusion:

> The quality of scientific work, in the Soviet Union as elsewhere, is no better than the quality of the worker. There are many first-class men whose work is important, but the general level of accomplishment is lower than one might expect, because of the greater dilution of first-class men by hack workers. Nevertheless science in the Soviet Union is ambitiously planned, well endowed, vigorous, and healthy; and even if its record over the last

twenty-five years is not astonishing, its promise for the future can hardly be overestimated.[29]

While Ashby made some mistakes in forecasting the future of Lysenko, his study warrants careful reading today—ten years after. And during these ten years the world knows that Soviet science has had many achievements to its credit. Of course, the fact must be recognized that much of the spectacular advance of Soviet science and technology during the past quarter of a century was due to the relative backwardness of Russia and the utilization by various means of the knowledge and skills, the inventions and discoveries, imported from Western countries. By employing engineers and scientists from these lands, by purchasing great quantities of books and journals, by taking German scientists captive after the war, and by a comprehensive program of scientific espionage, the Bolsheviks have profited greatly from Western genius. Without this assistance from the year 1928 on, Russia would doubtless have remained a comparatively backward country.

V

It may be well to bring together in this concluding major section of the chapter some of the distinctive features of the Soviet system for the training of specialists. Among these features are central planning, integration of theory and practice, the program of military training, the position of women, the worship of science and technology, emphasis on Marxism-Leninism, loyalty to Party and Motherland, and the desired traits of the Soviet specialist. Each of these features will be treated briefly.

Since the launching of the First Five-Year Plan, central planning has involved not only the several branches of the economy but also the entire cultural apparatus and particularly the institutions for the training of specialists at all levels. Although the State Planning Commission was founded in 1921, it operated feebly during the period of the New Economic Policy, that is, from 1921 to 1928. The Bolshevik leaders contend that over-all planning of the development of a society is possible only in a socialist state. Indeed, they are fond of saying that such planning is the "little child of socialism." And so it was not until they embarked seriously on the building of socialism that the system came into full operation.

The impact of central planning on the agencies for the training of specialists has already been indicated. But much more should be said. It is obvious that the planned expansion of the various branches of the economy requires a corresponding expansion of the training facilities and the number of specialists in the indicated categories. The development of the vast network of higher schools after 1928 was a direct response to the demands and the perspectives of the First Five-Year Plan. The types of institutions created and the places chosen for their establishment were all determined by the needs of the Plan. No university or technical institute in the Soviet Union ever springs into being on the free initiative of some individual, group, or locality. It comes into existence only if the central plan requires it. To be sure, political considerations both within the Union and beyond the borders play their role. An existing institution does not launch a new department because its rival across the street or in another province has done so. Service to the Soviet state and its planned program of development are always the decisive factors in the situation. The Soviet state, of course, means the Party and its Central Committee. The entire program of development is under the monolithic direction of the Party.

The size of the student body in general and for a given institution or faculty in particular likewise is not left to chance or the urge of the young "to go to college." Such matters are determined by the number of specialists of each type and grade required. Soviet spokesmen boast of the great increase in the number of young men and women attending their higher schools, but the Party is not committed to an unlimited growth in this realm for its own sake. Although the individual receives personal benefit from his studies, the overriding objective is service to the state. Consequently, on completing his program of instruction he is expected to follow the occupation for which he was trained by the state. Under a series of decrees and regulations, beginning in 1933, the young specialist is assigned to a job within five days after graduation for a minimum of three years. He may be assigned to some distant or inhospitable region of the Soviet Union.[30] The system of workbooks and passports assists in limiting the freedom of choice and movement of the individual. The idea that the graduate should be allowed to seek his place of employment and shift from one post to another according to his own desires is utterly foreign to Soviet theory and practice. This could only lead to waste of talent and training. As the author was writing these lines, he noticed a dispatch in *The New York Times*, February 14, 1956, reporting with great satisfaction that 78 per cent of the students graduating from the teacher-training courses of the city colleges of New York in 1955 had become teachers. This was regarded as remarkable, because five years before "only 57 per cent went into teaching soon after they had finished their college programs." It is well known that many graduates from engineering schools in the United States, even from the world-famous Massachusetts Institute of Technology, do not become engineers. The point should be made perhaps that the Soviet graduate is not only assigned to a job but also guaranteed a job somewhere in the country after graduation.

A second characteristic feature of the Soviet system for the training of specialists is the integration of theory and practice. Lenin, aware of the overemphasis on theory in pre-Bolshevik Russia, stressed this point on every occasion. The result in the twenties and early thirties was the tipping of the balance too far in the direction of practice. Socially useful work and polytechnical training in their more romantic forms represented this extreme tendency. Today an effort is made, on the one side, to give to the student a fairly comprehensive grasp of the sciences basic to his specialty and, on the other, to relate instruction to practice in industry, agriculture, or some other branch of the economy. In the industrial schools of the factory-mill type this is easily done because the training institution is commonly attached to a productive enterprise, whether in manufacturing, mining, or agriculture. The two are in a measure under a common management. In the higher schools the instructor is expected to relate the work of the classroom to practice, and provision is made for the student to gain some actual experience in a productive enterprise during the course of his training.[31] And here, as in the lower schools, the fact that the educational institution and the productive enterprise are both creatures of the state tends to facilitate the process.

It was said earlier that the student in the higher schools is commonly exempted from military service. This was correct only in the literal sense of the term. As in the secondary school, every male student must undergo a measure of military training during the period of his study. For this purpose he is required to devote several hours each week to "military drill, the use of small arms, tactics, map-reading, etc." Physical training is a formal part of the curriculum and in its emphasis on gymnastics rather than sports is viewed as an important factor in the training of the soldier. Also, the relation of the natural sciences to the development of the armed strength of the country is not overlooked, either in the higher or the lower schools. The student is expected to participate in some "paramilitary organization" during out-of-class hours. Though supposed to be voluntary, this activity is practically compulsory, like much else in the Soviet Union. In addition, provision is made to train military specialists of the rank of commissioned officer.[32] The eager discharge of these duties is regarded as evidence of love of the Motherland. In December, 1933, the author received a letter from the "Model Industrial Pedagogical Technical School in the Name of Lenin" in Moscow describing the life of the institution. It contained the following passage:

> There is one thing more which adorns the life of our technicum—a model post of defense which was opened recently. We have agreed to attend it faithfully and to study all means of defense in case any imperialistic country should attack us. We are fulfilling our task honorably so that everything conquered by our fathers will never be given to anyone.

In *those* days of long ago, Nazi Germany was the "imperialistic country." The particulars have changed, but the substance remains the same.

The position of women in the higher schools is a fourth significant feature. As everybody knows, the Bolsheviks proclaimed the equality of the sexes at the time of the revolution and declared as a major objective the "abolition of the exploitation of woman by man." They consequently established the practice of coeducation from the bottom to the top of their system of education. Although they abandoned this practice from 1943 to 1954 in a limited number of middle schools, they still maintain that only in the Soviet Union and the lands of "people's democracy" do women enjoy opportunities equal with men. The available data on higher education appear to support the original Bolshevik position. During the first twenty years of Soviet power the percentage of women attending higher schools of all kinds rose gradually to 43 per cent in 1938. While they were particularly strong in education and health, they constituted over one-fourth of the students in engineering. For the postwar period the evidence is partial and inadequate. After reviewing the literature, however, DeWitt estimates that the percentage today is not far from 50.[33] The author recalls visiting an engineering technicum in Rostov in 1929 in which the members of the staff were particularly sensitive to the question. He was told by the director that as a matter of institutional policy fifty women were admitted each year for every fifty men. He was told also that the former were just as competent as the latter. Certainly there has been a big change in this area since prerevolutionary days, and the "other sex" now constitutes a most important reservoir of talent to be tapped in the selection and training of specialists at all levels.

The prestige position of science in the Soviet higher schools and in the Soviet Union in general is another striking feature. Next to Marxism-Leninism, it is a word to conjure with. "Scientific" is a term of fulsome approbation. Of course, it must be "true science" and not the "pseudo science" which prevails in many areas of investigation in the "bourgeois countries." It must be a science devoted to the interests of the "people," and not "science for science's sake." To be sure, whether in a given instance it is the one or the other, only the Party hierarchy can know. Moreover, as S. V. Kaftanov, Minister of Higher Education at the time, made clear in a brochure published in 1947, it must be "patriotic science," that is, science loyally committed to the service of the Motherland.[34] As we have noted, Soviet science serves a dual purpose: it is the source of strength in economy and defense and also the support of the materialistic outlook on the world. Both of these ends are consciously advanced in science instruction from the primary school. The authors of the most recently published textbook in pedagogy present the Soviet position in these words:

> One of the basic principles in the contruction of teaching programs is the *principle of scienceness*. In contrast with the bourgeois school, which falsi-

fies and distorts knowledge, the content of instruction in the Soviet school is built on the foundation of science. In the teaching programs is included only authentic and scientifically verified material, truthfully and faithfully reflecting the development of nature and society.[35]

Of especial interest to the student of Soviet education is the Academy of Pedagogical Sciences. Founded in October, 1943, it seeks to direct and coordinate all research activities in the field of education. It is organized in thirteen great departments or institutes devoted to the following fields of inquiry: the theory and history of pedagogy, methods of instruction, psychology, defectology, physical nurture and school hygiene, schools of the nationalities, art education, pedagogy, natural science, the library, the museum, the pedagogical archive, and the museum of toys. According to Medynsky, the Academy directs its researches to the solution of a series of problems: "The aims and tasks of Communist education, the process of nurture and its nature, the process of teaching, the problem of polytechnical instruction, preschool education, questions of educational psychology, history of Soviet pedagogy and school, and the most important problems of the history of Russian pedagogy and the pedagogy of the non-Russian peoples of the USSR."[36] It was early assigned the task of investigating methods of developing habits of obedience and courage in the young. In 1954 its staff consisted of "34 active members and 59 corresponding members." It organizes many lectures and publishes many reports of studies.[37] Its entire program of research is "distinguished from bourgeois and petty bourgeois theories of pedagogy" because it is "built on the foundations of dialectical materialism."[38] In the words of its official organ, "no other country has such an institution as the Academy of Pedagogical Sciences."[39] This statement is probably correct.

Very important in the Soviet educational system is the search for scientific talent in the younger generation. In the secondary school, science and mathematics are basic subjects of study. And a youngster who is truly gifted in any branch of science will be encouraged to proceed to the higher school. If he fulfills his early promise, he will receive stipends and honors and be inspired to work for an advanced research degree. "In 1954," writes DeWitt, "Moscow University told its applicants that those who studied hard would become good research scientists and those who were just average would become school teachers upon graduation."[40] And in Russia a talented and productive scientist stands in the upper-upper stratum of Soviet society. To the Bolsheviks science is power, and they are the foremost students of power in the contemporary world.

A sixth feature of the program of the higher school which has marked all of Soviet education throughout its career is systematic indoctrination in the teachings of Marxism-Leninism. Although the professional training provided in universities and institutes is highly specialized, every student

is expected to achieve a degree of mastery of this basic body of doctrine
which supposedly guides the entire course of the Soviet state at home and
abroad. In Communist pronouncements the classics of the Bolshevik revolutionary tradition are regarded as sacred documents. They reveal without question the nature of the universe, the "laws of social development"
through the ages, and the future of all mankind. This aspect of the training of the specialist was once stated with precision by Stalin in these
words:

> There is one branch of science whose knowledge must be compulsory for
> all Bolsheviks of all branches of science—this is the Marxist-Leninist science
> of society, of the laws of development of society, of the laws of development
> of the proletarian revolution, of the victory of Communism. For it is impos-
> sible to consider him a genuine Leninist, who calls himself a Leninist, but
> who is cloistered, let us say, in mathematics, botany, or chemistry, and who
> sees nothing beyond his specialty.[41]

Though Stalin has been officially repudiated, the pronouncement still
stands.

The Central Committee of the Party has given unremitting attention
to this question through the years. It has issued countless decrees on
raising the level of instruction in Marxism-Leninism. A critical point was
reached in 1938 with the publication of the *Brief Course of the History
of the Party* prepared by a special commission of the Central Committee
and approved officially by the Central Committee. In November of that
year the Committee issued a decree ordering that "instruction in
Marxist-Leninist theory in the higher schools be based on a profound
study of the *Brief Course of the History of the Party.*" The decree also
ordered the introduction into these institutions of a "uniform course" and
a "uniform department of Marxism-Leninism." [42] In the intervening years,
decree after decree has been issued demanding the improvement of the
quality of instruction. The Party and Komsomol units in the higher schools
have always been directed to give special attention to this part of the
program. While some observers have concluded that in these later years
the instruction has lost its vitality and assumed the form of a disagreeable
chore to be performed, the Marxist-Leninist line, which at a given time
is always the Party line, must be understood and respected by the Soviet
specialist. More than one Soviet scientist has learned this to his regret.
Moreover, the boredom, if it exists, may be due to the success of a program of indoctrination conducted vigorously for more than a generation
by all the agencies of propaganda. To the student in the higher school it
may be "old stuff." The emphasis will doubtless continue with the forthcoming post-Stalin revised version of the *History of the Party*.

Marxism-Leninism, as we have observed, is sometimes referred to as
the "science of the sciences," the science which underlies, envelops, and

directs all the other sciences. Any change in interpretation or in application of doctrine can be made only by the Party hierarchy. And when this
happens all involved must speedily confess their errors and step forward
in vigorous support of the Party decision. In 1936 a considerable company
of educators were informed by the Central Committee that pedology was
reactionary pseudo science. Paul Blonsky, the leader in this field of inquiry, in spite of a confession of error, disappeared from the ranks of
educators. In 1948 the Central Committee established truth by political
fiat in the field of genetics, approved the ancient doctrine of the transmission of acquired characters, and raised a poorly trained scientist, T. D.
Lysenko, to the very pinnacle of power and influence in the field. Scientists who found themselves on the wrong side of the issue promptly made
their confessions, but nevertheless suffered demotion. One of them, A. R.
Zhebrak, a geneticist known and respected beyond the borders of the
Soviet Union, sent an abject letter to *Pravda* which contained the following sentence: "But now, since it has become clear to me that the basic
theses of the Michurin school in Soviet genetics are approved by the Central Committee of the All-Union Communist Party, I, as a member of the
Party, cannot defend positions which have been declared mistaken by the
Central Committee of our Party." [43] The decision on genetics had its reper-
cussions immediately in biology, physics, and even mathematics. The fact
that after Stalin's death the theories of Lysenko went into eclipse does not
in itself greatly alter the situation. It merely demonstrates that what the
Party gives, the Party can take away. Unless there is a profound change in
the role of Marxism-Leninism in Soviet cultural affairs, the scientist, particularly if he is working in the realm of theory, must be ever on his guard.
A former professor of history at the University of Kiev who defected to
the West at the close of the war once told the author that "every Soviet
professor expects some day to meet his Golgotha." Of course, the passing
of Stalin may be marked eventually by a new dispensation in this department of Soviet life. But, as yet, only the most superficial evidence points
in this direction. In his speech at the Twentieth Congress of the Party on
February 14, 1956, Nikita S. Khrushchev called on the delegates "to raise
the level of ideological work" and to "enhance in every way the role of the
Party as the leading and guiding force of the Soviet people, in all fields of
political, social, economic, and cultural life in the USSR." [44] This is Leninist as well as Stalinist doctrine.

As the foregoing account makes clear, the Soviet higher school is
designed to prepare specialists of a particular type—a type required by
the Party in the achievement of its apocalyptic goals of building Communism in Russia and of bringing victory throughout the world. The
authors of an official pedagogy describe the Soviet specialist in these
words:

He must not be a specialist, locked in some narrow specialty, detached from Marxist-Leninist theory, from general problems, problems of science and technology. Culture, literacy, and political orientation, sound knowledge of science and technology, and devotion to the cause of socialist construction—such are the basic traits of a Soviet specialist.[45]

There seems to be no good reason for thinking that the higher schools are not preparing a rapidly growing number of specialists of this type. The task of the Party, however, has been put in these words by a defecting member of the new intelligentsia: "The Soviets want people to be brilliant in their fields, such as engineering and medicine, but nonthinking in so far as politics and propaganda are concerned. When they succeed in creating a brilliant man who cannot think, they will have achieved their ideal society."

VII

The training of teachers in the Soviet Union must be brought briefly into the picture. From the early days of the revolution the Party, driven by the logic of its position, has given the closest attention to this problem. The crucial role of the teacher in changing the character of the people is evident throughout the present volume. Moreover, as a Soviet educator of the twenties put the matter, "because of the low degree of literacy and the remoteness from the rest of the world, so characteristic of many sections of our country, the teacher in an overwhelming majority of cases is almost the sole bearer of culture." And the Soviet teacher must be a bearer of culture in the language of Bolshevism. The first task was to capture and retrain the old teachers in the spirit of the revolution. For this purpose all sorts of courses and institutes were organized. The second and long-term task was to prepare a new generation of teachers drawn from elements loyal to the Soviet regime and thoroughly indoctrinated in the ideas, outlooks, and purposes of the Party. The feverish expansion of the system of people's schools from decade to decade made imperative a corresponding expansion of the institutions for the training of teachers.

After several years of experimentation the general pattern of these institutions was established in 1924. Three levels of training were recognized and an appropriate institution was established for each. Although there have been minor changes involving both names and programs, the levels remain. The institution for the preparation of teachers for the kindergarten and the four grades of the primary school is called a "pedagogical school" and is essentially a technicum. Students are admitted on completing the seven-year school of general education and the course of study is four years in length. Teachers for the fifth, sixth, and seventh grades are prepared in a two-year "teachers' institute," which rests on the ten-year middle school. And a two- or four-year "pedagogical institute" trains graduates of the complete middle school for instruction in the eighth, ninth, and tenth grades. In addition, there are training institutions of special bias, such as agriculture, industry, physical culture, art, and foreign language. Like all programs in Soviet educational establishments today, the curriculum and regimen of these institutions are supposed to be severe. Emphasis is placed on the subjects taught in the middle school, pedagogy, psychology, and school observation and practice. In other respects they follow the characteristic patterns developed for the training of the Soviet specialist in general. [46]

VIII

The meaning of this story for the free world is not difficult to grasp. Within a single generation the Bolsheviks have converted a backward country into a powerful industrial state. While many factors have entered into this program of construction, Soviet power rests immediately and in large measure on the vast army of specialists trained in the higher schools. The Sixth Five-Year Plan calls for further and impressive expansion in this realm. It would appear, as many students have observed and as Soviet spokesmen have proclaimed, that the Bolshevik revolution is entering a new and fateful phase. No longer will the Soviet leaders confine themselves to the exporting of Communist doctrine and political agitators. Indeed, they have already embarked on a program of technical and economic assistance to backward countries—a program which will doubtless grow in volume in the coming years. In his speech at the Twentieth Congress, Khrushchev boasted that the Soviet Union is "helping the people's democracies to build 391 enterprises" and "China to build in one five-year period alone 156 enterprises." [47] At the same time, alluring proposals are being made to many other countries. All of this, in so far as it is genuine, means specialists, specialists, and more specialists. But it does not mean that the training institutions have produced so many specialists that the Soviet Union now finds itself embarrassed by a surplus. The system does not work in such fashion. If specialists are prepared beyond the defined needs of the domestic economy, they are prepared according to plan to advance the cause of Communism in the countries chosen for attention—to enhance the prestige and influence of the Soviet Union wherever they may go. The Soviet specialist, as we have seen, is not only a technician; he is also committed to the cause of Lenin. And one may be sure that every specialist, before crossing the borders of the Soviet Union, will be carefully trained for his *komandirovka* (mission) and subjected to the most severe tests of political loyalty, outlook, and understanding. This new form of the outward thrust of Bolshevism is a product of the swift development of Soviet educational institutions.

9

THE POLITICAL EDUCATION
OF THE PEOPLE

The great masses of the people of Russia had only the vaguest notions of the real aims of the Bolsheviks when they seized power in 1917. They doubtless liked Lenin's promise of peace, land, and bread—peace for everybody, land for the peasants, and bread for the town and city dwellers. That is, those who heard the promise liked it. The condition of the country at the time should be recalled. The vast distances, the primitive means of communication, and the low level of popular culture made general participation and understanding impossible. The author was told in 1927 that not a few of the inhabitants, far removed from the towns, cities, and railroads, learned of the revolution only years after it had occurred. It should be stated, too, that many rank-and-file members of the Party could only repeat the slogans of the leaders. And, as the event proved, most of the latter did not foresee the road to the execution chamber which they were destined to traverse. They failed to grasp the full meaning of the "dictatorship of the proletariat" of which they spoke so glibly—a meaning which only history would reveal.

As soon as they had silenced their critics, defeated their enemies on the field of battle, and taken into their own hands the full power of the state, the Bolsheviks found themselves in the position envisaged by Tkachev. The people generally lacked the qualities of mind and heart necessary to support the revolutionary cause. This nineteenth-century revolutionist, as we have noted, proposed in one of his wilder moments the extermination of all persons over twenty-five years of age. At another time, he had turned to education as the way out of the difficulty—to the education of the young and the reeducation of the old. The Bolsheviks combined the two approaches of Tkachev. On the one hand, they destroyed, incarcerated, silenced, or drove from the country all who actively opposed them. On the other, within the limits set by circumstance, they launched with great energy a comprehensive program for the molding of the minds of the people. Naturally this program, though directed primarily at the adult population, has played a central role in the education of children and youth. The influence of a newspaper or a moving-picture theater, for example, cannot be confined to any single age group. That the task proved more difficult than anticipated is clear today. The sacrifices required and the punishments administered generated dissatisfaction and hostility from the beginning. Lenin's conviction that the ideal of socialism would inspire the loyalties and evoke the energies of the people proved to be utopian. As a consequence, the degree and rigor of Party control were somewhat less during the first decade than later.

II

The first great task assumed by the Party in the realm of the political education of the people was the "liquidation of illiteracy." The motivating principle was stated by Lenin: "An illiterate person stands outside of politics; he must first be taught his ABC's." However, Lenin had something more in his mind than the development of the independent informed citizen of the liberal tradition of the Western world. Although he talked about the right of the workers to participate freely in the election of their officials and even proposed that soldiers should choose their officers in this manner, he actually regarded literacy as an instrument or a weapon employed by the Party to mold the minds of the people. A person who could not read was beyond the easy reach of Communist propaganda. At any rate, reliance on the techniques of oral persuasion before the days of the radio was costly and limited in its sweep.

Incidentally, while the Bolsheviks distinguished themselves from their rivals by stressing *deeds* rather than words, history records no group of men who placed greater emphasis on the importance of the printed word. Their vast system of propaganda is grounded on faith in the efficacy of the press. That this system embraces all other agencies and processes for informing and shaping the mind is true. Yet both Lenin and Stalin, as well as lesser Bolsheviks, stated again and again that the press is the sharpest weapon of the revolutionary cause. Whether this faith in the printed word has been justified by events is a question which will not be argued here. The point to be made is merely that the Bolsheviks regarded the development of a literate population as absolutely essential to the achievement of their purposes. Of course, the fact is recognized that they were committed, not only to the political education of the people, but also to the building of a modern industrial society. In such a society a general condition of literacy is indispensable. But in these pages the question will be considered primarily from the standpoint of its bearing on political and perhaps moral education.

The task of liquidating illiteracy which the Bolsheviks confronted in 1917 was a truly staggering one. This theme has been stressed a number of times in the present volume. Wholly precise and dependable data on the degree of illiteracy at the time of the revolution are not available. According to the official Soviet figures, the rate of literacy in European Russia for both sexes combined in 1920 was 330 per 1,000 persons. The rates in the Northern Caucasus and Western Siberia were somewhat lower; and the rate for the entire Russian Empire was 319.[1] Everybody knows, of course, how treacherous statistics of literacy are, because of the difficulty of defining and applying a common standard. But the condition measured by any standard was bad enough to challenge and perhaps dishearten the most optimistic. The Bolsheviks launched a stupendous program, employing all existing agencies and creating many new ones. In the execution of the program, they undoubtedly had the enthusiastic support of hundreds of teachers and educated persons of liberal and humane outlook who did not share the political objectives or approve the harsh methods of the Party. Certainly the campaign to wipe out illiteracy aroused the enthusiasm of the majority of those who had worked in the tradition of the "enlightenment" stemming from the liberation of the serfs in 1861.

The campaign was launched in earnest by a decree issued on December 26, 1919, by the Soviet of People's Commissars and signed by Lenin, entitled "On the Liquidation of Illiteracy among the Population of the RSFSR." The basic directive of the decree read as follows: "The entire population of the Republic from 18 to 50 years of age unable to read and write must be taught reading and writing in their own or in the Russian language, according to desire. Instruction is to be conducted in government schools, existing and to be established, for the illiterate population according to the plan of the People's Commissariat of Education." [2] "Hundreds of thousands of workers" responded to the call of the Party. "Old and young began to learn. Broad strata of the population were drawn into" the campaign—"teachers, engineers, secondary school pupils, Communists, Komsomols, and literate workers." The "working day was shortened by two hours without loss of pay" for those who were being taught. Physical facilities were provided in "people's homes, clubs, and private houses," in "factories, mills, and Soviet institutions." The decree was printed in "hundreds of thousands of copies" and distributed "throughout the land." [3]

The campaign naturally had its slogans. The most popular perhaps was simply: "Down with illiteracy!" But there were many others designed to involve every facet of Party ideology and programs. Most of these carried a strong political coloration. "Poets, writers, and artists" worked them into placards for mass distribution. Here are some of the more common slogans:

> Illiteracy is the blood sister of ruin.
> Illiteracy is the reserve of counterrevolution.
> Literacy is a sword vanquishing dark forces.
> It is the right and duty of every citizen to be literate.
> Literacy is the road to Communism.[4]

The campaign was supported with vigor by all Party organizations. The Party itself was, of course, the leading and directing force everywhere. The Young Communist League and the Society of Young Pioneers were active in both school and community. Members of these associations played an important role in the 1920s in directing the socially useful work of the pupils into the battle to liquidate illiteracy. The Pioneers in their All-Union Conference in Moscow in August, 1929, besides binding every member to "destroy five rats and ten mice annually" and to "wage unrelenting warfare on mosquitoes, bedbugs, roaches, and flies," pledged themselves to "assume special interest in the liquidation of illiteracy" and "to teach thousands of adults to read and write." [5]

In February, 1922, the First All-Russian Congress for the Liquidation of Illiteracy was held. The Congress outlined a broad program of attack, including the "preparation and publication of instructional materials, the organization of facilities and points for the liquidation of illiteracy, and the conducting of a series of courses for the preparation of workers in both centers and localities." [6] The second congress in 1923 led to the founding of the "Society 'Down with Illiteracy'" which proceeded to coordinate divergent forces and efforts. M. I. Kalinin was elected president of the society. By the time of the meeting of its first congress in August-September, 1925, it "enrolled 1,600,000 members in 28,000 cells" and had "published 5 million primers." [7]

Special mention should be made of the contribution of the Red Army. In this institution, because of the discipline exacted, the Party directives seem to have been followed energetically. At the First All-Russian Conference for the Liquidation of Illiteracy it was reported that "in the Red Army by November, 1921, the percentage of illiterates had been reduced from 65–70 to 5–6." [8] The soldiers "learned reading and writing under all conditions: in intervals between battles, on guard, at the roster. For instruction newspapers, self-made primers, placards, and brochures were used." Under the conditions of universal military service eventually adopted, the armed forces came to constitute a major educational institution, not only for the teaching of reading and writing, but also for raising the general cultural level and liquidating "political illiteracy."

The First Five-Year Plan embraced a cultural, as well as an economic and social, program. It gave particular attention to the task of liquidating illiteracy among adults. According to its provisions, from eighteen to nineteen million persons between the ages of eighteen and thirty-five years were to be taught reading and writing. In addition, millions of older persons were to join the ranks of the literate. The five-year goal was the raising of the level of literacy of the population above eight years as a whole to 82 per cent. In the city the percentage was set at 93 and in the village at 79. In driving toward this objective, every conceivable agency was to be called into service. The number of schools and "points" for the liquidation of illiteracy was to be increased from 1,380 in 1927–1928 to 4,778 in 1932–1933. Also, the trade unions and cooperative organizations, the Communist societies for children and youth, and numerous "voluntary" agencies were to join in the work.[9] In 1930–1931 all these organizations, along with the institutions of government, entered into an agreement to make a carefully planned and coordinated attack on the problem.

In 1934 Kalinin reported the triumphant conclusion of the long and arduous struggle. "The liquidation of illiteracy in our country," he wrote, "is at bottom finished. More than nine-tenths of the population are able to read and write in their own language."[10] This statement was of course an exaggeration. The struggle was destined to continue for a number of years and, in spite of Soviet denials, is probably continuing down to the present time in the more backward parts of the Union. Moreover, although the official position is that the job was done by 1939, Soviet educational statistics tell a slightly different story. In that year, according to Ivanova, the percentage of literates for the entire country stood at 81.2. However, after making full allowance for exaggeration—something that must be done for all Soviet statistics—the student must concede that in this realm the Bolsheviks registered a truly remarkable triumph.

The task was greatly complicated by the diversity of peoples and cultures in the Soviet Union. While the Great Russians constituted approximately one-half of the population, the Soviet Union is a land of many nations and races. According to the *Large Soviet Encyclopedia,* "more than 200 languages" are spoken in the country. Some of these languages, notably among the small tribal societies inhabiting the northern regions, had not been set to writing in 1917. The Soviet philologists were assigned the task of devising the needed scripts. Interestingly enough, they employed the Roman alphabet for this purpose. Also they abolished the Arabic alphabet in use among the Moslem peoples of Central Asia and replaced it with the Roman. As late as 1927 leading Soviet educators told the author that in the Russian language the Cyrillic alphabet was to be abandoned in favor of the Roman, because the latter was superior. This, however, was not done, probably because of the difficulties involved and the development of Great Russian nationalism and patriotism. In 1937 the Soviet leaders conducted a second linguistic revolution among the minorities by substituting the Cyrillic alphabet for the Roman. In these events Olaf Caroe, a close student of Central Asia, discerns a calculated and subtle motive on the part of the Bolsheviks—"the realization that change upon change in the medium of education would tend to sever the generations one from another and help to usher in the new age." [11] He also sees in the abandonment of the Arabic alphabet an attempt to isolate Soviet Moslems from their brothers beyond the borders in the Middle East. By 1934 appropriate reading materials were being published in "104 languages." [12] The First Five-Year Plan called for a large increase in the proportion of newspapers, journals, and books printed in the non-Russian languages. [13]

The question of the ideological content of the textbooks employed in the liquidation of illiteracy remains to be examined. The directive was laid down unequivocally by a decree of the Eighth Congress of the Russian Communist Party in March, 1919. In this decree teachers working in the village were told that they "must regard themselves as agents not only of general but also of Communist education as well." This meant that "they must be subjected to control, not only by their immediate centers, but also by the local Party organizations." The conduct of the work among illiterates must be based on "a compulsory draft of the literate," and the subject matter "must be the decrees and decisions" of the Party. [14]

On November 3 of the following year Lenin provided the wider interpretation. "Throughout the entire program of our work of enlightenment," he said, "we cannot stand in the old position of political neutrality, we cannot conduct the work of enlightenment unrelated to politics." [15] He then justified his declaration by saying that "this idea has ruled and does rule in bourgeois society." It is therefore the duty of all educational workers to assist in "overcoming the old customs and the old habits which remain with us in the heritage from the old order." This conception was a guiding principle throughout the entire campaign for the liquidation of illiteracy. When an individual learned to read, he learned Party doctrine and policy at the same time. Here are some leading lines from an early primer:

> We will be victorious.
> We will not be slaves.
> We bring freedom to the world.
> He does not die who dies for a great cause.
> The stronger the Red Army, the nearer the end of the war.
> The union of workers and peasants is invincible.
> To protect the revolution is the duty of all toilers.

Communism is our torch of victory.
We will not give up, we will stand, we will be victorious.
We are not slaves. We are not masters.[16]

The programs of the Party and the government always constituted a basic element in the reading materials. After 1928 the provisions of the First Five-Year Plan saturated the textbooks. A volume prepared for use in the teaching of peasants to read included short articles on such subjects as the following: "We Build a New Life," "The Past," "The New Village," "How to Raise the Harvest," "Cooperation—the Way of the Village to Socialism," "The Commune of Red October," "Grain Factories," "The Electrification of the Soviet Union," "The Five-Year Plan," "We Build New Factories and Mills," "What We Will Build During the Five Years," "To the Struggle for the Five-Year Plan," "The Protection of Health in the Village," "To the Struggle with Drunkenness," "The Plan of Great Works." [17] Because of the system of monolithic control, the content of instruction could be and was changed swiftly in accordance with the desires and decisions of the Party leadership.

III

The tremendous campaign for the liquidation of illiteracy was one of the most fundamental features of the struggle on the part of the Bolsheviks to capture and mold the minds of the people. It was one of the ingredients of a systematic and all-embracing effort to eradicate the "remnants of capitalism" from the consciousness of the people and build a Communist world view and conception of society in all ranks and categories of the population. It was designed, not to liberate the mind of the individual, but to hold it captive. The Party, of course, was well aware of the dangers residing in literacy. Obviously, unless it could exercise control over the materials read, literacy would breed differences on every question and thus undermine the authority of the tiny group of professional revolutionists which had overthrown the provisional government. This meant that a free press in the historical meaning of the term could not be tolerated. It was necessary to bring under the control of the Party all media of communication. Although none of these media was overlooked, attention was concentrated in the early years on the press in all its forms. Literacy without a free press can scarcely be a truly liberating force in society.

One of the first and last concerns of the Bolsheviks down to this day has been the creation of a Party press, that is, a press which propagates Party purposes, doctrines, and policies. This course is justified or rationalized on the grounds that the Party is the "vanguard of the workers," can have no interest apart from the interests of the people, and consequently expresses the true will of the people through the press. In the "Program of the All-Union Communist Party" adopted at the Eighth Congress in March, 1919, "the Comrades" were reminded that "the press is a mighty weapon of propaganda, agitation, and organization and is an indispensable means of influencing the widest masses." It was for this purpose that "the Soviet power expropriates from the bourgeoisie buildings, presses, supplies of paper, and so on, and makes them available to the toilers and their organizations." [18] To this position the Party has returned again and again from year to year. At the Eleventh Congress in April, 1922, the Party declared that "the press is one of the mightiest weapons in the struggle of the Party to influence the masses, their Communist education and their organization." [19] Two years later the Party decreed that "under present conditions the press assumes exceptionally great significance as a weapon in the education of the masses," that its "most important aim is education in the spirit of Bolshevism," and that "it is necessary to begin work on the creation of children's literature under the most scrupulous control and leadership of the Party." [20]

From this basic position there has been no significant deviation down to the present time. Nothing is printed in the Soviet Union, whether newspaper, magazine, pamphlet, or book, without the approval of the Party. To be sure, Article 125 of the Stalinist Constitution guarantees "freedom of the press" by "placing at the disposal of the working people and their organizations printing presses, stocks of paper, public buildings, etc." The fact of the matter, of course, is that the Party through its network of cells and committees controls all of these so-called "people's organizations." On May 5, 1948, *Pravda* carried an editorial commemorating the thirty-sixth anniversary of the founding of this official organ of the Central Committee, entitled "The Sharpest and Strongest Weapon of the Party." The editorial praised the entire Soviet press as "the freest in the world" and expressed its central theme in these words: "Every line of our newspapers and journals, every word of the Bolshevik press must be devoted to the raising of the level of ideological work, to the task of educating the mass of toilers in the spirit of Communism, in the struggle with survivals of capitalism in the consciousness of people." [21] That the death of the great dictator has altered the situation in any fundamental respect is not evident today.

The interest of the Party in the press led to a swift expansion of the publication of newspapers, journals, and books comparable in every way to the drive to liquidate illiteracy. Naturally, the two lines of development proceeded in close harmony, the one responding to and stimulating the other. A few facts and figures from Soviet sources, always to be viewed with some skepticism, will give some measure of the growth of the press. In 1913 old Russia published 859 newspapers and journals, with a total circulation of 2,729,000, and 28,132 books with 113,400,000 copies.[22] A volume of the *Large Soviet Encyclopedia,* published in March, 1955, reports the "publication in the USSR of approximately 7,000 newspapers and about 1,500 journals." The total circulation of the former is 47,000,000. "Over 200 publishing houses print books in all languages of the peoples of the USSR and in many foreign languages." The encyclopedia states further that "for almost 400 years from the date of the appearance of the first printed Russian book to the Great October Revolution 550 thousand titles of books were published in Russia, whereas during the years of Soviet power 1,210 thousand titles of books were published with a total circulation of over 17 billion copies." In 1954 "eleven times as many books" were published as in 1913. Moreover, the Soviet publishing houses have printed "more than one billion copies of the works of Marxism-Leninism." Publications in the field of science have increased thirty times and, in the department of children's literature, fifteen times. Socio-economic subjects and belles-lettres are not neglected. And "almost 300 million copies" of books by 1,675 foreign authors were published between 1918 and 1954.[23] Even after full discount is made for exaggeration, the record is impressive. Clearly the Bolsheviks do regard the press as a "sharp and mighty weapon."

A Soviet newspaper, the reader should know, is not a *news* paper in the traditional sense. Although it prints news, it is first of all a *propaganda* paper. Everything it publishes is viewed, as the Soviet dictionary would say, from the standpoint of a "class-Marxist-Leninist analysis," from the standpoint of Party policy. And control is monolithic. One may read the 7,000 Soviet newspapers in vain to find a genuine clash of opinion on, or a genuine criticism of, the policies of the Central Committee at a given time. While there are adaptations to local conditions, the daily press throughout the land follows a single line, a line set ordinarily by *Pravda,* the organ of the Central Committee. Moreover, a Soviet paper does not feel impelled to give an account of any event, however important it may be, just because it happened. Such action would be condemned as "bourgeois objectivism." The board of editors must await authoritative instructions regarding the way the event should be presented and interpreted. Ofttimes the report is delayed; sometimes an event is never recorded at all.

An interesting illustration for the American reader of the procedure followed by the Soviet press is the case of the United States Supreme Court's decision on May 17, 1954, on the desegregation of the races in public schools in the United States. The action of the Court ran directly counter to one of the major lines of Communist propaganda throughout the world regarding American democracy, namely, the discrimination against the Negro. Although the case had been under consideration for many months, the judgment handed down apparently caught the Soviet editors unawares. To the best knowledge of the author, who followed the Soviet press closely at the time, it was not until June 23, more than five weeks later, that the event was acknowledged. On that day a long article appeared in *Izvestia* under the title of "Judges and Governors" which labeled the decision a "demagogic gesture" made by "the ruling circles of the USA" and "designed for export." It then proceeded to quote from the public utterances of Governor Byrnes of South Carolina, Governor Talmadge of Georgia, Governor White of Mississippi, and others, to the effect that segregation would be maintained even if it meant the "liquidation of the system of public schools." In conclusion, the article stated that the "noise surrounding" the decision "proves once more to the entire world that racism penetrates all the pores of the social system of the USA, that it comprises an inalienable component part of the reigning bourgeois ideology, that in the central as well as the local organs of government there are ardent defenders and zealous champions of savage race theories." And even if the decision "were to be formally introduced, in reality everything would remain as before."

Even a scholarly journal will follow faithfully the Party line in the realm of domestic and world politics. A striking instance is found in a long article appearing in the November, 1949, issue of *Sovietskaia Pedagogika*, the authoritative theoretical and scientific organ of the Academy of Pedagogical Sciences. The article was entitled "The School and Pedagogy in the USA in the Service of Reaction," and the author was N. K. Goncharov, a leading Soviet educator and coauthor of a state-approved textbook on the theory and practice of Soviet education. Goncharov makes an impressive parade of scholarship with forty citations and quotations from American journals and educational literature. The uninitiated and uninformed Russian teacher or citizen could only conclude that the picture presented is wholly accurate and trustworthy. Yet a careful checking of the author's citations and quotations, some of them quite extended, shows that he had not the slightest hesitation in completely distorting the facts. The article as a whole is a tissue of fabrications. He would even remove or insert a negative to prove his basic thesis—that all schools and educators in the United States were serving the cause of the "American monopolists" bent on world conquest and domination. Such is scholarship in the service of the cause of Marx and Lenin. At one point he quotes correctly a passage from John Dewey's *Problems of Men*, but a passage which expresses a position that Dewey proceeds to refute in the very next paragraph.[24]

In the field of book publication the same principle prevails. Every book will be scrutinized, not only in the process of publication through the publishing houses, but also after publication by the sharpest eyes of the

Party. This watchfulness will be applied with especial care to works dealing even remotely with history, social science, and philosophy. Many a distinguished scholar has fallen into disgrace after the appearance of some work which had been heralded as an important contribution to Soviet scientific literature. Mention need only be made of Eugene Varga's *Changes in the Economy of Capitalism Resulting from the Second World War,* completed near the close of the war and G. F. Alexandrov's *History of Western European Philosophy,* in 1947. Both of these men were recognized leaders in their respective disciplines, but the "line" had changed. Moreover, textbooks to be used in the schools and works for mass distribution are subjected to the closest censorship. Even books in natural science, particularly if they touch the realm of theory, must support the fundamental positions of dialectical materialism as currently interpreted by the Central Committee of the Party. With the general repudiation of Stalin at the Twentieth Congress of the Party in February, 1956, a radical rewriting of history is to be expected. In fact, this was clearly implied in the remarks of First Deputy Premier Anastas I. Mikoyan. But that the new books will be prepared by trained historians following the canons of "bourgeois objectivism" without precise Party directives can scarcely be expected. It seems quite probable that the reputation of Khrushchev, if he survives, will not suffer in the process.

Soviet works of reference are also regarded as sharp weapons in the political education of the people. In the *Large Soviet Encyclopedia,* for example, which expresses the highest standards of Soviet scholarship, the grand plan of the work and all relevant articles are written from the perspective of the "class-Marxist-Leninist analysis." With a change in the Party line, subjects given large space in the preceding edition may be omitted altogether. In March, 1949, the Soviet intelligentsia, "scientists, publicists, writers, artists, and other workers on the cultural front," were mobilized for the purpose of bringing out a new edition of the encyclopedia, for the "purpose of illuminating the decisive victories of socialism in our country, the achievements of the USSR in the fields of economics, culture, science, and art." This great work of more than fifty volumes "must show with conviction and in full the superiority of socialist culture over the decadent culture of the capitalist world" and, "proceeding from the Marxist-Leninist theory . . . must expose imperialist aggression and apply Party criticism to contemporary bourgeois movements in the realms of science, technology, and culture." The intelligentsia is told that the encyclopedia "must be saturated with Bolshevik Party spirit." [25] The new edition, which is now available in New York down to the thirty-ninth volume, shows clearly that those who prepared it followed faithfully the directives of the Party. Unfortunately, the editors are confronted now with the task of the fundamental revision of the text of many articles.

A striking instance of the omission of subjects treated in the preceding edition of the encyclopedia is found in the allotment of space to the several minor nationalities liquidated for lack of patriotism in the Great Patriotic War—the Kalmuks of the Volga Valley, the Ingushi and Chechentsi of the North Caucasus, and the Tartars of the Crimea. In the first edition of the encyclopedia, published in the 1930s, the history, the land, and the culture of each of these minorities received generous and extravagant attention as a member of the "brotherly union of peoples." The Kalmuks were allotted seventeen pages, the Ingushi and the Chechentsi fifteen, and the Tartars forty-four. The new edition of the encyclopedia includes not a single line on any of these peoples. They were not only liquidated—they were erased from the historical record. It should be added, however, that there is an account of the Crimean Autonomous Soviet Socialist Republic which occupies the territory formerly inhabited by the Tartars. The account states that its "population is mainly Russian and Ukrainian" and that "after the war the Crimean province began to be populated by migrants" from Russia and the Ukraine. The reader can only wonder how this rich land remained uninhabited down to 1946. The fortunes of yet another national minority should be mentioned. The German settlement on the Volga, dating from the reign of Catherine the Great, achieved the status of an autonomous republic under Soviet rule with a population in 1939 of approximately 600,000. When Hitler's troops marched into the Soviet Union in 1941, these peoples were transported to eastern regions. The first edition of the encyclopedia devotes nine pages to them; the second is completely silent about both their history and their fate. They have apparently joined the "lost tribes of Israel."

An incredible instance of revision involves the person of Lavrenti P. Beria. One of a triumvirate formed following Stalin's death on March 5, 1953, to direct the affairs of the Soviet state, he was arrested in June and executed as a traitor from early youth in December of that year. Unfortunately for the editors, Beria's name begins with "B," and consequently his biographical sketch appeared in an early volume published in 1950. The sketch included two pages of print and a full-page portrait. From beginning to end it was a glowing tribute to "the loyal student and companion-in-arms of Stalin: member of the Politburo of the Central Committee of the VKP(b), vice-president of the Council of Ministers of the USSR." He had been awarded "the title of Marshal of the Soviet Union," "five Orders of Lenin," "the Order of Suvorov First Class," and many minor orders and medals. Obviously, something had to be done. Instead of calling in all copies of the guilty volume, the State Scientific Publishing House addressed the following instructions to subscribers: "[We] recommend the removal from Vol. 5 of the B.S.E. pages 21, 22,

23, and 24, also the portrait between pages 22 and 23 and the replacing of these pages with the pages of a new text being mailed to you. With scissors or razor blade cut out the above mentioned pages, leaving sufficient margin near the spine of the book onto which the new pages can be glued." These new pages gave accounts of the Bering Sea, the life of Admiral Bering, and other matters which the editors had failed to include in the original printing. What will happen to the biographical sketch of Stalin, M. D. Bagirov, and perhaps some other persons destined for demotion lies in the realm of mysterious things. A new edition is clearly needed to meet the unfolding situation—an edition that might bring back into history the foremost leaders of the October Revolution executed by Stalin.

This very brief analysis of the basic Soviet work of reference documents with fidelity the following quotations from an authoritative Communist source: "A Soviet encyclopedia cannot be a mere compilation of knowledge expounded in an objectivist, neutral, and apolitical manner. It should illuminate all aspects of human activity and cognition from the standpoint of a militant Marxist-Leninist world outlook." [26]

Even the dictionary is employed in the political education of the people in the spirit of Communism. Important words in the realm of Bolshevik ideology and policy are commonly defined in Leninist terms—words like "capitalism," "fascism," "social democracy," "people's democracy," "imperialism," "dictatorship," and so on. And the meaning of an old word may be completely changed in successive editions of a dictionary in response to shifts in Party policy. The case of the word "cosmopolitanism" is illustrative. In old Russia and in the Soviet Union down to 1948 the term carried the meaning that it had borne for centuries throughout the Western world. In the large four-volume *Explanatory Dictionary of the Russian Language,* which was prepared by a group of Russian scholars during the years 1935 to 1940 and which was issued without revision as late as 1947, "cosmopolitanism" is defined as "the views and convictions of a cosmopolite," and a "cosmopolite" as "a person who does not regard himself as belonging to any nationality, who regards the entire world as his fatherland." The 1935 edition of *Webster's New International Dictionary of the English Language (Unabridged)* is in substantial agreement: "Cosmopolite—One at home in every country; a citizen of the world; one without national prejudices or attachments."

So it was until 1948. In that year, following the establishment of the Republic of Israel, there was apparently an upsurge of Jewish national sentiment, many Jews seeking permission to leave their Soviet Motherland and join their kindred in the ancient home. The Party leadership responded with a savage attack on "antipatriots" and "homeless cosmopolitans." Starting in the field of theatrical criticism, the attack moved swiftly through the entire cultural apparatus, through literature, the drama, scholarship, and science. The great majority of these "cosmopolitans" were Jews. The Jewish press and theater were closed. And out of this episode emerged a new definition of "cosmopolitanism." This definition appeared immediately in the new *Dictionary of the Russian Language* in 1949. "Cosmopolitanism," as here defined, is "an antipatriotic bourgeois outlook, hypocritically accepting the entire world as one's fatherland, denying the value of national culture, and repudiating the idea of defending one's fatherland." This is all. The ancient definition is gone without a trace.

There is yet another product of the press which should be brought into the picture—the calendar. This document merits special emphasis because it reveals the attention to detail which marks the Soviet program for the political education of the people. It shows that the Bolsheviks overlook nothing which can be directed toward their purposes. One might think that the calendar would be permitted to be nonpolitical in content, confining itself to the weeks, the months, and the seasons, to meteorology, astronomy, and the movements of the heavenly bodies. It does include these matters, but they seem to be incidental to the main objective. It devotes far more attention to the movements of Communists and Communist ideology and programs. In fact, it reflects faithfully the line of domestic and foreign policy presented by the Party to the peoples of the Soviet Union and the world at the time of publication.

The calendar is five inches long, three inches wide, and one and one-half inches thick. One leaf is allotted to each day of the year and every page is crowded with pictures, quotations, graphs, and commemorations of events. It contains about two thousand items, and every item is carefully selected to support the Party interest. The margins are so narrow that little space is available on either the front or the back of a leaf for notes or memoranda. It is the one and only calendar for mass distribution in the Russian language. Until 1949 it was issued under the auspices of the Council of People's Commissars or Ministers of the RSFSR. In that year responsibility for its publication was transferred to the august Ministry of Culture of the U.S.S.R. The calendar has grown from 2 million copies in 1946 to 25 million in 1956. Thus, it would appear that on a given day all Soviet citizens who possess the calendar, have a command of the Russian language, and feel the need to check the day of the week, month, or year, look at the same pictures, note the same anniversaries, and read the same quotations from the same men and women of past and present included in the Soviet gallery of heroes at the moment. And they must know that everything appearing on its pages bears the stamp of truth, because it is endorsed by the highest authority in the field of culture. At any rate, the Bolshevik leaders doubtless hope this is so.

The political use of the calendar can best be indicated by noting some of the changes in emphasis since the Great Patriotic War. During the war there were many favorable references to the coalition of the Allied Powers, to Britain and the United States, to Churchill and Roosevelt. Then came the great shift in Soviet policy, the erection of the iron curtain, and the launching of the cold war. Swiftly every friendly mention of the United States was eliminated, and America was presented in terms of the most severe Marxist interpretation of capitalism on the eve of collapse. The masses of the people lived in dire poverty and the entire economy was controlled by and for the "monopolists." The rich were growing richer and the poor poorer. Unemployment was increasing rapidly and an American mother puts up a sign in the window of her apartment: "Four Children for Sale—Inquire Within." The harsh conditions, the general popular discontent, and the decline of markets force American capitalists to launch an aggressive foreign policy designed to start a "third world war." And the lot of the Negro is worst of all. "He is not regarded as a man. Here there is no penalty for beating a Negro or raping a Negro woman. This is protected by the law, forgiven by the church. Parents teach this to their children." And "with people subjected to lynching, it would be possible to populate a large city."

With the death of Stalin many people expected radical changes in Soviet domestic and foreign policy. Malenkov, during his brief moment of power, promised to increase the production of consumers' goods and raise the standard of living of the Soviet people. What happened is revealed in the 1954 calendar. It suggests that Stalin's immediate successors did indeed intend to launch a new economic policy along the lines indicated. It conveyed the impression that the production of consumers' goods was to be the first domestic concern of the Party and that the golden age of abundance was just around the corner. In this respect it was radically different from all its predecessors. It contained forty-eight full-page graphs portraying the fabulous advance of the Soviet economy since the war and the rich perspectives of the coming years. Particular emphasis was placed on consumers' goods and services, on food, clothing, shelter, education, and health. Moreover, no one could peruse this calendar without gaining two impressions: first, that the Soviet peoples were already the most favored of mankind, and second, that the future was incomparably bright. However, these promises were belied by the fact that there was no suggestion in the 730 pages that the Soviet leaders were seriously intending any substantial reduction in the proportion of productive energies assigned to the basic industries and war potential.

In the sphere of foreign policy no change was indicated. The nations of the free world were in a state of chronic and growing crisis which would continue until capitalism is overthrown. The picture of the United States presented in the calendar was dismal almost beyond description. American industries, for example, were marked by reliance on "heavy physical labor." Thus, "in the coal industry—eighty-two per cent of the miners work without the help of machines; in the building industry—seventy-eight per cent." This condition was attributed to the "fact" that "manual labor is cheaper" and consequently "more profitable for the capitalists." "Scientific and technical achievements are employed chiefly for military purposes." America was therefore marked by dire poverty, and "the lot of the great masses . . . is growing worse yearly." Thus in 1953 there were "thirteen million full and part-time unemployed workers in the United States." The Korean War brought "enormous profits" to the American "imperialists," while "prices and taxes grew fabulously." According to a letter from an American worker, "two of my children were born after the war [World War II]. Not once have they eaten butter, and, as for meat, they don't know what it is." The reader of the calendar is told also that "in the USA more than two million orphans sleep in the streets" and that "about six million children are unable to go to school." The treatment of the Negro is presented in terms of savage cruelty and brutality. Negroes are shot down, even by the police, without compunction. "Enjoying complete immunity from punishment the American racists attack Negroes on the slightest provocation or on no provocation at all. . . . Such are the 'rights of man' in the land of the dollar." Negro children "work on the plantation of a white master from four o'clock in the morning until nine in the evening." When a little Negro girl "drops from exhaustion . . . the white overseer strikes her with a whip and calls her a 'lazy nigger brute.'" A delegate from Korea "related how American soldiers tore an infant from the arms of a Korean mother, killed the child, then cutting out the eyes of the dead child forced the mother to eat them. The unfortunate woman threw herself upon the depraved attackers. They shot her down." Also "the American troops in Korea killed hundreds of thousands of children" and "the American army of occupation brought hunger, poverty, and ruin to the toilers of Japan." The calendar contains not one friendly reference to anything in America except the Communist leaders and fellow travelers. Even the discovery of America by Columbus, which in past years had been recorded, was there no longer.

The calendar for 1955 told approximately the same story to the Soviet readers. Then, in the issue for 1956, possibly because of the so-called "Geneva spirit" or a basic shift in the Party line, a great change came over the calendar. It does contain an unflattering "letter from an American worker" and a commemoration of the "attack of American imperialists and their servants on the Korean People's Democratic Republic." And that is about all. To be sure, it boasts in figures of the superiority of the Soviet system of production over the capitalist. Also, it contains no friendly references to America, beyond the exploits of Columbus. Yet it is quite unlike any other postwar calendar. It breathes peace and tranquillity, emphasizing the everyday interests of the people. It displays twenty cartoons lampooning various deficiencies in Soviet life. It gives much advice to housewives on cooking and cleaning, and tips to citizens on hunting and fishing. It counsels parents on child care, gives a number of pages to children's interests, makes suggestions on health and first aid, includes hints on gardening, and allots considerable space to puzzles, chess, and sports. Another interesting feature of the calendar is the decline of Stalin since his death. This is revealed in the number of times his picture appears in its pages. In 1953 his picture appeared thirteen times. The following year the number was reduced to three, and in 1956 to two. This placed him on a plane of equality with Lenin, Marx, and Engels. No member of the present Presidium has more than one picture. What all of these shifts mean for the political education of the people is a question that can only be answered by the process of dubious inference. Incidentally, the ninety-seven-page article on the United States in Volume XXXIX of the *Large Soviet Encyclopedia* published in April, 1956, includes the American Declaration of Independence!

The problem of the distribution of the products of the press has received the close attention of the Bolsheviks from the early twenties. There is, of course, a network of bookstores, shops, and stalls which reaches out from the cities and towns into every village, every railroad station, and every army encampment. An interesting feature of the Soviet bookstore is the practice of fixing prices of books, not in terms of cost of production, but rather in terms of Party policy. If a certain book or pamphlet is designed for wide popular reading, a nominal price will be asked. From the standpoint of political education, this practice has distinct advantage. The basic institution, however, to make the products of the press accessible to all ranks of the population is the library, with its primitive variants, the club and cottage reading room. The heritage from the old regime in the realm was impoverished. The number of libraries in 1914 was 12,600; of clubs and cottage reading rooms, 222.[27] In 1924 the Commisariat of People's Education of the RSFSR issued a general instruction on the organization of central libraries and their relations with local units designed to "bring book and newspaper within the reach of the deafest corners of the localities." [28] By 1954, according to the 1956 issue of the calendar, the number of libraries of all kinds had grown to 380,000, with more than one billion copies of books.

From the standpoint of the political education of the people, the selection of the books to be placed on the shelves of the libraries was the question of most vital concern to the Party. The instruction of the Commissariat cited above stated that "particular attention" should be given to the subjects of "political literacy, Marxism, Leninism, history of revolutionary movements, Youth and Pioneer movements, labor and woman questions, literature on campaigns, etc." Also "natural science and antireligious propaganda." The Central Committee of the Party issued several decrees during this period. The most important, in the judgment of the editors of Volume V (1950) of the *Large Soviet Encyclopedia*, was issued on October 30, 1929, and marked a "new stage" in the development of the Soviet library. The launching of the First Five-Year Plan and the bitter internal Party struggle were the immediate occasion of the decree. It called upon the Party and state authorities immediately "to conduct a revision of books in all libraries and to purge the libraries of ideologically injurious books." Also they were told to "check within six months the existing personnel of library workers from the point of view of their political and professional qualifications." This required the "reeducation of the old personnel and the training of new librarians" drawn increasingly from "workers and peasants." [29] The policies here formulated were followed down to the rise of Khrushchev to power.

The point should be made that a truly free library is dangerous to any authoritarian or totalitarian system. If the people were permitted to read books containing materials subversive of the system, literacy itself could scarcely be tolerated. Consequently, the Bolsheviks have followed the policy of the "permanent purge" in the realm of books as well as in the realm of personnel. As the Party line has changed, as "truth" has been altered by political fiat, books have been removed from and placed on the shelves of both bookstores and libraries. Moreover, some books which cannot be put into general circulation may be placed at the disposal of certain categories of people, such as Party members of a given grade and trusted scholars working in special fields. In 1955, according to a reliable source, an article appeared in *Kommunist Tadzhikistana* which put the question quite bluntly. Entitled "The Soviet Library Has Cast Aside Impartiality and Objectivity in Catalogues," it included the following paragraph:

> The Soviet library catalogue is a tool for the Communist education of the masses; therefore, it is necessary to be very careful in the selection of material to be listed in the catalogues. To propagandize the most advanced literature in the world—the works of the great leaders of science: Marx, Engels, Lenin, and Stalin, the decrees of the Party and the government, the advanced ideas of native public workers—means strictness in the selection of books to be listed for the readers' catalogues.

The library, being a component part of the Soviet system for the education of the people, is a political weapon. It therefore cannot be allowed to develop according to its own laws. It must always be held tightly in the hands of the Party.

There are other institutions of mass influence which should be included in the present account, notably the museum, the radio, and the cinema. Since the history of the museum parallels that of the library, and the history of the radio that of the press, attention will be confined here to the cinema—an institution recognized by the original Bolshevik leaders as a powerful weapon of Communism. *see Inkeles .*

The legacy from prerevolutionary times in the realm of the cinema constituted a slender foundation on which to build a powerful and wide-reaching system of moving-picture facilities. The total number of moving-picture projectors in the Russian Empire in 1914 was only 1,412. The Bolsheviks, however, grasped fully the potential of the cinema in the field of the political education of the people and turned with their customary energy to its development. By 1936 the number of projectors reached 29,758.[30] According to the *Large Soviet Encyclopedia,* despite the devastation of the war, this figure increased to 39,961 in 1953. Of these, approximately 24,000 were "portable projectors." It became possible therefore "to arrange cinema presentations at least two to four times a month in all villages, collective farm brigades, field stations, and remote animal-breeding points. Also for timber workers, for fishermen, for builders of canals and irrigation systems, for workers on geological surveys, for the inhabitants of the far north, etc." The encyclopedia might have included the millions of men and women in the forced-labor camps. Unquestionably the Soviet state has built a powerful film industry and a vast network of moving-picture stations in a very brief period.

The effort to bring the cinema under Party control began at the Eighth Congress in March, 1919, with a decree "On Political Propaganda and Cultural Enlightening Work in the Village." "Cinema, theater, concerts, exhibits, etc.," read the decree, "must be utilized for Communist propaganda." While these agencies should "strive to bring the illumination of many areas of knowledge into the dark village," their main purpose was "to assist in the development of consciousness and clear world outlook." [31] The Thirteenth Congress in May, 1924, decreed that the "cinema must become a mighty instrument in the hands of the Party of Communist education and agitation" and penetrate "the widest proletarian masses, Party and labor organizations." To achieve these purposes, it was declared necessary "to draw into the work of the cinema in the shortest possible time a sufficient number of Communists." [32] With the liquidation of the New Economic Policy, the launching of the First Five-Year Plan, and the consequent sharpening of the "class struggle" in town and village, the Party turned again to the cinema. In January, 1929, the Central Committee characterized the cinema as "one of the most important weapons of the cultural revolution" and as "a mighty weapon of mass agitation and propaganda for the Communist education and organization of the broad masses around the slogans and tasks of the Party." It warned against the "desire on the part of the petty bourgeoisie to exert influence" on the cinema and to direct it into the service of the "ideology of non-proletarian strata." [33] It took the Party many years to capture the cinema, but in time success was achieved.[34] The ideological aspect of this struggle will be presented in the following pages.

IV

In the political education of the people the creative writer and artist, the poet, the novelist, the dramatist, the painter, the sculptor, and the musical composer constituted a problem for the Bolsheviks throughout the first twenty years of Soviet power. On the one hand, the Bolshevik leaders could not tolerate open hostility on the part of these people, or the veiled teaching of counterrevolutionary doctrines through the medium of the arts. On the other hand, the more sensitive among them to humanistic values, such men as Lunacharsky, Bukharin, Radek, and Trotsky, realized that great art can flourish only under conditions of freedom. They knew that an artist could not create according to specifications laid down by a dictatorial state. And so through the years a genuine struggle was carried on within the ranks of the Party and among factions of artists. The reader will recall the apolitical approach to literature expressed by Mikhail Zoshchenko in 1922.

Fanatical advocates of *proletkult*, or proletarian culture, formed a militant society known as the Russian Association of Proletarian Writers, RAPP for short, which waged uncompromising warfare on all "bourgeois" tendencies. The members of the organization endeavored to arrogate to themselves the right to set and enforce standards in all realms of art. They failed, however, because they were unable to get the solid support of the Central Committee. The more talented artists for the most part formed a group called the "Fellow Travelers" who accepted the revolution but refused to convert their art into a naked political weapon. Most of them had, of course, started their professional careers under the old regime and cherished even the limited freedoms allowed them by Nicholas II. Moreover, having been accustomed to more or less censorship from the imperial authorities, they possessed a degree of experience in evading political dictation without betraying conscience and forsaking the guidance of the inner light. As a consequence, works of great merit were produced in the Soviet Union during the twenties and early thirties in literature, music, and the drama. The artist in various realms was able to maintain a degree of integrity.

The truce, however, if it could be so described, was an uneasy one. At one time RAPP seemed to have the advantage and at another the Fellow

Travelers. But the rise of Stalin to power, the liquidation of the New Economic Policy, the collectivization of the village, the purging of the old Bolshevik leaders, and the sending of millions to forced-labor camps led eventually to the virtual destruction of freedom for the artist. Not a few writers and dramatists were silenced completely, some of them being sent into exile, and the brilliant young composer, Dmitri Shostakovich, was subjected to savage criticism by the Party in 1935 for his opera *Lady Macbeth of Mtsensk County* and his ballad *Bright Brook*. The result was, in the words of Max Eastman, the spectacle of *Artists in Uniform* or, as Juri Jelagin put it, the *Taming of the Arts*.[35] Eventually the Party established as official doctrine to govern all the arts, the conception of "socialist realism." This conception has been given the following definition by the highest theoretical organ of the Central Committee:

> Socialist realism, resting on the tradition of classical realism, establishes as the foundation of artistic creation, not the subjective-arbitrary fancies of the artist, but his comprehension of objective reality. The degree of artistic representation of Soviet realistic writers is determined first of all by the degree to which they reproduce accurately and faithfully in artistic forms the course of the life process. . . .
>
> In their creative work Soviet writers are guided by the policy of the Bolshevik Party and the Soviet state. This constitutes the strength of Soviet literature, because it gives to writers the opportunity to understand the course of reality more profoundly and to reflect it truly. Also it opens before the writer the perspective of active participation through his work in the building of a new life, inspired by the ideal of Communism. The best works of Soviet literature assist actively in the reeducation of the broad masses of the people in the spirit of Communism and in the liberation of the consciousness of the toilers from the vestiges of capitalism. The most important task of Soviet writers is to propagate the idea of Communism. . . .
>
> Fidelity to the living truth, a conscious Party Communist direction, service to the socialist Motherland, and ability to behold the tomorrow of his people —such are the basic conditions of the writer who desires to follow in his work the method of socialist realism.[36]

The period of the Great Patriotic War witnessed a measure of relaxation on the cultural and ideological front. The Bolshevik policy toward religion and the church was moderated, the Federal Constitution of the United States received sympathetic comment, English and American music was presented and praised in Moscow, and Stalin assigned Great Britain and the United States to "first place among freedom-loving countries." And then, immediately after the closing of the war, a devastating storm swept through Soviet literature, drama, music, and the entire cultural apparatus— a storm raised and directed by the Central Committee. A brief examination of this phenomenon will reveal in its most intense manifestation to date the use of the arts and artists for the political education of the people in accordance with the conception of socialist realism. Of course, the reader should know that this conception means whatever the Central Committee says it means at any given moment. It seems quite possible, after the Twentieth Congress of the Party, that a new definition may be forthcoming in the not distant future.

The occasion of this storm was a fundamental change in the policies of the Party. During the closing months of the war, perhaps from December, 1944, but certainly from February, 1945, the Central Committee made one of those unheralded and fateful decisions which the student of Soviet affairs has come to expect. It decided to reverse completely the wartime policy of relatively friendly relations with the Western democracies and to revive the policy of revolutionary aggression against "capitalism" and "bourgeois ideology" in the spirit of 1917. The reasons for this tragic action cannot be developed here, except to say that the political and military triumphs achieved in the struggle greatly increased the power, prestige, and authority of the Soviet state throughout the world and convinced the members of the Central Committee that history was marching with rapid pace at their side. They decided to take full advantage of the opportunity. Not to have done so would have been to betray the most basic principle of Communist morality enunciated by Lenin, and by Nechaiev before him: "Whatever aids the triumph of the revolution is ethical; all that which hinders it is unethical and criminal."

Following the shift in policy, the Party launched a mighty ideological offensive designed to support the new policy and to erase all friendly feelings toward the West in general and toward America in particular aroused by collaboration in the war. Although there had been intimations of coming events in speeches by Stalin and other leaders for several months, the storm did not break in full fury until August 14, 1946. On that day, doubtless after long deliberation in secret chambers, the Central Committee issued the first of a series of powerful and forthright decrees which commanded the entire intellectual class to participate actively in the battle against enemies of Communism at home and abroad. The initial decree was directed at literary writers and journals. It was followed during the next two years by similar decrees in the fields of the drama, the cinema, music, and humorous magazines. In the Soviet Union these have been referred to collectively as the "decrees on ideology." [37]

All the decrees carried two emphases which had first appeared in moderate form and tone in a speech by Stalin on February 9, 1946. On the one hand, they called for an unbounded glorification of Soviet institutions, the New Soviet Man, and the "great Stalinist epoch." On the other, they demanded an equally unbounded denunciation of everything Western and "bourgeois." Intellectuals were ordered to "lash out boldly and attack bourgeois culture which is in a state of emaciation and depravity." Ideological indifference and political neutrality were placed under the curse of the Party. "Art for art's sake" was condemned in most scathing terms. A humorist was warned that "his humor over the radio is nothing but laughter for laughter's sake," that this is "bourgeois," and that, if he does not take care, he will soon be "out of Soviet radio." Even the clowns in the circus were harnesed to *politika*, the policies of the Party, and given their marching orders. Writers were warned that "they have forgotten that our journals are a mighty instrument of the Soviet state in the cause of the education of the Soviet people, and Soviet youth in particular." Andrei Zhdanov, the spokesman for the Committee, told the Union of Soviet Writers that "all of our ideological workers are standing today in the front line of fire." [38] And Konstantine Simonov, the noted dramatist, in an address before the All-Union Conference of Theatrical Leaders and Dramatists on November 18, 1946, declared: "The people of our Soviet art must be in the foremost rank of the warriors for Communism; we and our *kind of weapon* have our *place* in this foremost rank." [39] "Writers," said Stalin, "are engineers of human souls," and they are expected to build only good Communist souls. And Khrushchev has employed this expression since his attack on the old dictator.

These decrees, and the associated speeches by the Party leaders, should not be regarded in the nature of literary, artistic, and philosophical criticism from a professionally competent source. They were directives which could be ignored only at great personal risk. This brings the account to the methods employed by the Party to enforce its will and "protect the people" from the vagaries and corruptions of the creative mind.

First of all, it should be noted, the decrees are never couched in purely general terms. On the contrary, they invariably single out particular individuals and their works for unrestrained excoriation, and generally persons and works of exceptional distinction or popularity. This lends to the entire proceedings a sense of high, but tragic, drama. Thus the decree on literature held up to savage ridicule and cruel threat two writers whose works had received widest distribution—Mikhail Zoshchenko, a short-story writer, and Anna Akhmatova, a poetess. The former, it will be remembered, avoided politics in the first years of Soviet power. The remaining decrees attacked in similar fashion distinguished dramatists, moving-picture producers, musical composers, and humorous writers.

The response to an ideological decree has become completely stereotyped. An all-Union meeting of the class of intellectuals immediately involved is called within a few days or weeks. The meeting is opened with a long address by a high Party spokesman who interprets the decree in the blunt and extreme language of Bolshevism, in the language made familiar to the West by the speeches of Molotov, Vyshinsky, Gromyko, and Malik and by the Soviet verbal assaults on "American warmongers" and the "enemies of all progressive mankind."

At the meeting of the Union of Soviet Writers, Andrei Zhdanov, so closely associated with the decrees that they have been labeled *Zhdanov-shchina*, interpreted the decree on literature and passed judgment on the two writers condemned by the Party. Here is the essence of his appraisal of Zoshchenko: "Only the dregs of literature could produce such 'works'. . . . In this tale Zoshchenko turned his vulgar and mean little soul inside out. . . . In Soviet literature there can be no place for putrid, empty, vulgar, and ideologically indifferent works. . . . With cynical frankness he continues to remain a preacher of ideological indifference and vulgarity, an unprincipled and unscrupulous literary hooligan." Observing that Akhmatova is also a "representative of this ideologyless reactionary swamp," Zhdanov charges that "she preaches the theory of 'art for art's sake,' of 'beauty for beauty's sake.'" He then characterizes her work as "the poetry of a frantic little lady, rushing back and forth between the boudoir and the chapel. . . . Not quite a nun and not quite a fornicatrix, but rather a fornicatrix and a nun in whom fornication is mingled with prayer." [40] The crucial words in this indictment are "ideologyless" and "ideologically indifferent."

All who heard Zhdanov's voice knew that it was the voice of the absolute state, of the court of last resort from whose judgment there was no appeal. Not one of the great writers present, or anyone else, rose to defend or console Zoshchenko or Akhmatova. On the contrary, all who spoke joined the chorus of denunciation. According to the record in *Literaturnaia Gazeta,* Zhdanov's speech was interrupted from time to time by bursts of "tumultuous applause," and even by "laughter of approval in the hall." At the close of his address he is honored with "tumultuous applause. All rise." The only suggestion of criticism in the whole course of the decree comes in the form of a query from an obscure Ukrainian writer by the name of Petro Panch. He apparently raised the question of the "right of the writer to make mistakes." The answer of the Presidium of the Union of Soviet Writers by formal resolution was clear and unequivocal: "This 'theory' opens the door to the penetration into literature of harmful influences." [41] Only the Central Committee of the Party enjoys the "right to make mistakes," and of course it is always correct at any particular time.

More grievous, perhaps, and certainly more degrading to the free mind of the creative artist than public censure is the ritual of confession of error or guilt. Following the address of the representative of the Central Committee, those responsible directly or indirectly for the "dreadful" state of affairs in a given field of art as defined by the decree, with almost no exceptions, confess their "sins" eagerly and extravagantly, accept their punishments without open protest, and promise to mend their ways immediately. Nikolai Tikhonov, who on grounds of negligence was "liberated from his duties" as president of the Union of Soviet Writers, recognized the justice of the indictment, added some details of delinquency not mentioned by the Central Committee, and declared that the decree outlines the "program for our future activity." The great Eisenstein, condemned for his interpretation of Ivan the Terrible in a moving picture, welcomed the "severe and just criticism" of the Party and thereafter went into decline and death. The world-renowned composer, Sergei Prokofiev, declared that the "decree separates the decayed from the healthy cells in the creative work of composers," confessed a second time a year later following the condemnation of a new opera, and promised to try again to please the Central Committee. The gifted Dmitri Shostakovich accepted the criticism "as evidence of a severe but fatherly concern for us, Soviet artists." And the brilliant Aram Khachaturian, with "a feeling of great satisfaction," assured the world that "the decree sets us musicians free." [42] These are just a few examples of the response of the artists to the decrees.

After all the personal confessions are in, the assembled intellectuals pursue further the path of self-abasement. Unanimously they pass a resolution which accepts without qualification the censure of the Central Committee and outlines measures designed to correct the "evils" set forth in the decree. Thus, the Union of Soviet Writers resolved that "it is necessary to propagate systematically the policy of the Party on the fundamental issues of domestic and international affairs" and to "saturate all of their work with the militant spirit of the active and aggressive ideology of Communism." The resolution stated further that "Soviet writers must lash those works which express any manifestation of servility toward the bourgeois West" and must expose the "nature of capitalist encirclement, struggle against its corrupting influence, and reveal the character of contemporary imperialism which conceals within itself the threat of new blood-letting wars." [43] The other groups of artists passed resolutions of similar import.

A word should be said here regarding the decision of the Central Committee in August of 1948 which established the "truth" of T. D. Lysenko's theory in genetics of the transmission of acquired characters. In this case the Presidium of the Academy of Science itself rallied to the support of the Party and sent a letter to Stalin which contained these words: "We promise you, Comrade Stalin, to take a leading position in the struggle against idealistic reactionary teachings and to clear all ways for the unhampered development of Soviet science in the name of the

great purposes of our people, in the name of the victory of Communism." [44] A few weeks later the Division of Biological Science of the
Academy addressed a letter to the "Leader of the Soviet People" assuring
its unqualified support. "We are obligated steadfastly and decisively,"
the letter read, "to unmask reactionary, idealistic perversions of biology
and to conduct an active struggle against servility toward bourgeois
science unworthy of a Soviet scientist." [45] The Academy also resolved
"to struggle actively for the further flowering of patriotic science, to revise the staffs of the scientific councils of biological institutes and the
editorial boards of biological journals, to remove advocates of the Weis-
mann-Morgan tendency in genetics, and to appoint representatives of
progressive Michurinist biological science." At the same time, the Academy
called for the revision of textbooks in conformity with the line laid down
by the Party.

Following the All-Union meeting, the entire process is repeated in the
Union Republics, in towns and cities, and in divers forms throughout
the land. Groups of intellectuals, whether directly or indirectly involved,
see the handwriting on the wall, meet under the guidance of the Party,
make their confessions of error or guilt, and pass their conforming resolutions. Thus, although no decree was addressed directly to teachers or
medical workers, they saw immediately the meaning of the decrees for
themselves and drew the obvious inferences. Needless to say, when the
Central Committee speaks, its pronouncements receive not the slightest
word of public criticism from any source within the borders of the Soviet
Union. Newspapers and magazines do indeed publish columns of "responses from the people." But every communication supports, often in
hysterical tones, the position of the Committee. Consequently, the total
impact of this process on any individual under the displeasure of the
Party must be overwhelming. Whether artist, writer, scholar, or scientist,
he must feel terribly lonely and forsaken. It is little wonder that only the
most courageous and tough-minded refuse to prostrate themselves before
the dictatorship and plead forgiveness. Yet, to anyone living in a free
society this whole pattern of confession and recantation, of groveling and
sycophancy, must ever remain something of a mystery.

Every Soviet citizen is aware that behind the decrees stands the
absolute and ruthless power of the Soviet state. The individual subjected
to direct attack by the Central Committee knows well that he can save
himself only by the ordeal of public confession and acknowledgment of
error. But even after such confession and acknowledgment, he knows
that he must expect demotion and then begin the arduous climb back to
status and acceptance by *deeds* which demonstrate that he has taken the
criticism to heart and become a "new man." For those who fail at any
point along this road, unless the Party line changes, the gates to exile

or the forced-labor camp loom in the distance, a fate which in the course of the years has swallowed millions of Soviet dissenters and alleged dissenters, among whom he is almost certain to number associates, friends, or relatives. They know that they are being watched day and night by the sleepless eyes of the members of the political or security police. There is small wonder, therefore, that on all things, both great and small, where the Party has spoken, there is virtual unanimity in public within the borders of the Soviet Union. But it is by such means that the Party has sought to direct and mold the political education of the people.

Whether the death and degradation of Stalin and the proclamation of the principle of collective leadership will bring a fundamental change in the realm of psychological regimentation is a question which cannot be answered with assurance today. The passing of the great dictator was followed almost immediately by pleas on the part of writers and artists for a relaxation of political controls. Ilya Ehrenburg, Dmitri Shostakovich, and others raised their voices. Even Mikhail Zoshchenko appeared in print again after a silence of almost a decade. However, the political wind quickly turned and blew in the other direction. The decree of the Central Committee on literary journals and writers of August 14, 1946, and the birthday of Andrei Zhdanov, director of the whole ideological purge, on February 26, are commemorated in the 1956 calendar. The somewhat ambivalent condition of the artist in 1953–1954 has been summarized in a recent study as follows:

> Soviet literature of 1953–54 gives the reviewer a painful feeling of regret that literary talents are regimented into mediocrity. The novels are long; the ideas, characters and scenes stereotyped. The official attitude permeates the pages and leaves no room for humor. But as we have seen, a few of the more gifted writers have consciously or unconsciously raised some awkward questions. At times one senses a feeling of rebellion and suspects that even in the monolithic Soviet society the creative artist is fighting for those human qualities which we cherish in the West.[46]

It is possible that the Twentieth Congress of the Party held in February, 1956, will usher in a fundamental change. Khrushchev, in an obvious reference to Stalin, condemned "the cult of the individual" and the making of a "particular leader a hero and miracle worker." The name of the dead dictator was mentioned by some speakers at the Congress and then usually in derogation. Mikoyan criticized Stalin's last important work and called for the rehabilitation of Bolshevik leaders condemned of treason and executed on Stalin's orders. A. M. Pankratova, editor of high school history textbooks for two decades, admitted the falsification of history in these books and suggested that the historical record be set straight. Mikhail A. Suslov, one of the younger members of the Presidium of the Central Committee, spoke out against the stifling and crushing of the "creative initiative" of the artist. And in secret session Khrushchev made a savage attack on his former boss and benefactor. Yet this Congress acted very much like its predecessors held under Stalin's iron rule. In spite of the fact that most of those present had been raised to power by Stalin and had praised him and his policies without restraint, no one of them rose to defend his old leader. The same unanimity prevailed as in the past; only policies and personalities had changed. In this confused and confusing situation it might be appropriate to let Khrushchev have the last word. One of the three great tasks confronting the Party, he said, is:

> To raise the level of ideological work of all Party organizations and direct it to the resolution of the practical tasks of Communist construction; to ensure the creative mastery by Communists of the theory and historical experience of the Party; to increase vigilance in our ideological work and to conduct an irreconcilable struggle against bourgeois ideology; to strengthen the work of the Communist education of the masses and the eradication of the vestiges of capitalism in the consciousness of people; to utilize more fully and actively to this end all the media of ideological influence—propaganda, agitation, the press, the radio, cultural and educational organizations and institutions, science, literature, and art.[47]

To the student of Soviet affairs this sounds very familiar. Indeed, it is the precise language of the "decrees on ideology." One should realize that the "collective leadership" of eleven like-minded men might be as coercive and ruthless as rule by a dictator. Absolute power can corrupt eleven members of an oligarchy only less completely than it can corrupt a single individual. And the struggle over the succession may not yet be concluded. The question will possibly be illuminated in the calendar for 1957.

That the essence of Bolshevism remains after the repudiation of Stalin is unambiguously proclaimed in an editorial in *Pravda* on July 6, 1956, entitled "The Communist Party—The Inspirer and Leader of the Soviet People." After rejecting without qualification the multiple Party system and the principle of political liberty of free societies, the editorial thus endorses the central doctrine of Lenin and Tkachev in the realm of the mind:

> As for our country, the Communist Party has been, is, and will be the sole master of the minds, the voice of the thoughts and the hopes, the leader and the organizer of the people in their entire struggle for Communism. Armed with Marxist-Leninist theory, strong in its unity, solidarity, and discipline, unrivaled in its ability to organize the millioned masses and to lead them in a complex situation, the Communist Party from the first days of Soviet power confidently directs the ship of our political and social life toward Communism.

V

In concluding this account of the political education of the people, the role of organizations will be treated briefly. There are first of all the so-called voluntary organizations which come and go, organizations which arise to perform some limited task or conduct some particular campaign. The "Society—Down with Illiteracy," the "Society of the Militant Godless," and various associations to promote aviation, defense, or some other interest are examples. However, not one of these organizations is "voluntary" in the sense in which the term is used in a free society. Every organization that comes into being in the Soviet Union is inspired and directed by the Party. The All-Union Society for the Dissemination of Political and Scientific Knowledge, organized in June, 1947, merits special attention here.

The launching of this organization was related to the wartime dissolution of the Society of the Militant Godless, the great postwar shift in foreign policy, and the issuing of the decrees on ideology by the Central Committee. Its purpose was to carry on a vigorous and aggressive campaign to propagate throughout the Soviet Union the positions proclaimed in the decrees. The organizers of the society addressed the following appeal to "all leaders of Soviet science, literature, and art, and to scientific, social, and other organizations and institutions of the Soviet Union":

> We call upon all leaders of Soviet science and culture to work yet more actively in order to raise the socialist consciousness of the working people. Members of the Society must interpret through public lectures the foreign policy of the Soviet state, resolutely expose provocateurs of a new war and aggression, reveal the falsity and limitations of bourgeois democracy, and unmask the reactionary essence of the ideology of the contemporary imperialistic bourgeoisie and its reformist lackeys. It is necessary to show in the lectures the advantages of the Soviet social and state order over capitalism, the successes of economic construction in the USSR, the achievements of Soviet science, literature, and art, and the tasks confronting the Soviet people. We must show the grandeur of our socialist Motherland and cultivate in the Soviet people a feeling of pride in the Soviet land, in our heroic Soviet people. At the same time we must conduct a decisive battle against the tendency of some citizens of the USSR to grovel before the contemporary bourgeois culture. The duty of the members of the Society is to explain the most important questions of Marxist-Leninist ideology, to propagandize a materialistic world outlook, and to struggle against all kinds of unscientific views and all vestiges of foreign ideology persisting in the consciousness of the people.[48]

Apparently the Society has been well financed. Certainly it has been very active and has devoted itself to the purposes outlined in the appeal. It has organized many lectures and issued a veritable flood of propaganda pamphlets. These pamphlets are from 10,000 to 15,000 words in length and are published in first editions ranging from 65,000 to 150,000 copies. They sell for 60 or 75 kopecks, 6 or 7 cents per copy. The following titles convey a fairly good idea of the range and emphasis in the pamphlets: *The Party of Lenin and Stalin—The Guiding and Directing Force of Soviet Society; The Soviet Union—The Leading Force in the Democratic Camp; The Soviet Union in the Struggle for the Freedom and Independence of Peoples; The Marxist-Leninist World View—The Greatest Conquest of Mankind; The Great October Revolution and the Formation of the New Man; On Soviet Patriotism; On Soviet Patriotism in Literature; On the Patriotic Duty of the Soviet Intelligentsia; The Crisis of Bourgeois Democracy; The Philosophizing Henchmen of American Reaction;* and *Race "Theories" and Discrimination in Anglo-American Countries.* These pamphlets of the Society are supplemented by a large volume of publications on similar themes under other auspices.

It is of course the great mass organizations embracing millions of Soviet citizens which receive the most vigorous, systematic, and sustained attention of the Party. One of the most important of such organizations is the Soviet armed forces. During the twenties and thirties the Red Army was a powerful agency for the liquidation of illiteracy and for the acquisition of various practical skills and knowledges. But most important of all its responsibilities on the cultural front was the promotion of "political literacy" and the inculcation of loyalty to the ideals and leadership of the revolution. Three measures were introduced to achieve these purposes. In the first place, membership in the Red Army was originally limited largely to young men coming from the proletariat and poor and middle peasantry. In the second place, more than 40 per cent of the soldiers and 50 per cent of the officers were members or prospective members of either the Party or the Komsomol. In the third place, during their period of service in the army the soldiers were subjected to a program of intensive study of the revolutionary literature and the policies of the Soviet state. They were even taught to obey their officers only so long as the commands were in the interests of the revolution, as determined of course by the political commissar and the Party organization in the army. That this training was not without influence on the youth from the village is suggested by the fact that the older peasants commonly referred to "that devil's blood with which they have been inoculated." [49] But the fuller story of the political education of the soldier will be told in a later chapter.

The mass organization which, according to Bolshevik ideology, is most important from the standpoint of the political education of the people is the "professional union," and particularly the professional unions which enroll members of the proletariat or working class. In the Soviet state every worker, whether machinist, collective farmer, miner, teacher, physician, writer, musician, or scientist, is expected to be a member of his professional union. However a Soviet labor union should never be confused with its counterpart in a free society. Although the industrial proletariat is the "chosen class" of Marxist ideology, it is not allowed to direct the course of the Soviet economy and state. Lenin made this very clear in his doctrine of the "vanguard of the proletariat," the Communist Party. According to this doctrine, the proletariat plays its creative role in history only when it is led and directed by the Party. Consequently, the labor union, or any professional union, is wholly under the direction of the Party leadership. It is supposed to be an instrument, not for protecting and advancing the immediate interests of its members, but for promoting the purposes of the Party, and particularly for raising the productivity of labor and for fulfilling or overfulfilling the goals of the current five-year plan. Mikhail Tomsky, an old Bolshevik, friend of Lenin, and first head of the Soviet labor unions, fought all through the twenties to establish the traditional right of collective bargaining and opposed the integration of the unions into the state apparatus. In 1929 he was removed from the Central Committee of the Party. Seven years later he committed suicide, a thoroughly disillusioned Bolshevik.[50]

The educational role of the labor union was established early in the history of the Soviet state. A decree of the Ninth Congress of the Party in the spring of 1920 declared that the professional union should be regarded "as a school of Communism and a link connecting the most backward masses . . . with the vanguard of the Communist Party." [51] The next congress of the Party, convening just one year later, stated that "the most important role of the professional unions in Soviet Russia remains their role as a *school of Communism.*" The Party members in the unions were told to reach the "millions of non-Party workers" by all means possible, by "organizing meetings, conferences, exhibits, moving pictures, music, clubs, etc." [52] The following year the Eleventh Congress told "all Communists in professional unions" to "pay much greater attention to the ideological struggle with petty bourgeois conceptions, currents, and deviations in the unions." The situation was particularly critical because "the New Economic Policy cannot but lead toward a certain strengthening of capitalism." [53] Again, in 1931, a Party resolution calls the professional union "a true school of Communism." And one of the slogans of the thirty-eighth anniversary of the revolution in 1955 repeated the injunction of 1920: "Long live the professional unions—school of Communism." [54] Unquestionably, this institution has been a major agency from the beginning for the political education of the people by the Party. In 1946 the organ of the professional unions stated the matter simply in an editorial appealing for a "higher ideological level in the mass cultural work" of the unions: "The professional unions, as the most massive social organizations of the working class and the closest aids of the Party, are charged with the great and responsible duty of the Communist education of the masses." [55] In the conduct of educational work intimate relations are maintained between the unions and the several divisions of the cultural apparatus.

The institutions of government from the local organs to the Supreme Soviet are also regarded as a mighty weapon in the political education of the people. The basic fact must be recognized, of course, that every one of these institutions is held firmly in the hands of the Party, including the police and the courts. Attention will be confined here to the process of electing members of the Supreme Soviet. The uninitiated, reading the Soviet press during the weeks prior to an election, would conclude that tremendous issues of policy and personality were at stake. The newspapers are filled with materials relating to the election. Vigorous appeals are made to the citizens to turn out, go to the polls, and exercise their "battle-won rights" guaranteed in the Soviet constitution, "the most democratic in the world." They are told that special provision will be made for the sick and the infirm, so that not one eligible citizen will be denied the opportunity of helping to elect his rulers and shape the policies of his government. Then on election day, according to Soviet data, over 99 per cent of those eligible cast their ballots and, with almost no exception, for the same candidates, because there is only one list of candidates on the ballot. It is a strange proceeding. Its value would seem to lie in its contribution to the political education of the people. The election is converted into a dramatic occasion for presenting to the citizens over a period of weeks and by means of every agency of propaganda the doctrines and policies, domestic and foreign, of the Party.

The role of the Party organizations in the realm of political education need not be elaborated. Indeed, this constitutes a theme that must run through any authentic account of Soviet education at every level and in every form. Of course, the Party has always been, is now, and will remain, unless it changes its character completely, extremely sensitive to all aspects of political education. Assisted by the 13 million members of the Society of Young Pioneers and the 18 million members of the Young Communist League, it penetrates everywhere, except perhaps a few remote villages that have scarcely been discovered. But the Party and its associated organizations of children and youth do not simply control and direct the educational process from the inside. At the time of the Twentieth Congress the Party was reported to have a membership of more than 7 millions. This vast army is organized at the base into 300,000 or 400,000 units, or cells. When the Central Committee issues a decree, all Party members and organizations are expected to regard themselves as shock troopers or detachments in the struggle to achieve the goals outlined in the decree. Besides working in organized agencies and institutions, the Party member engages in what Alex Inkeles has called the "process of oral persuasion." [56] Wherever he is and whatever he does, he is *supposed* to put Party interests first. The good Party member has no loyalty higher than loyalty to the Party. Indeed, treason in the Soviet Union has long been defined in Bolshevik practice as disloyalty to the Party, even though the individual is actually moved by love of country or devotion to the revolutionary cause. That many Party members are timeservers, social climbers, and fortune hunters is doubtless true. But this could be said of any priesthood or military brotherhood in history. It is the Party that maintains the Soviet state, that educates its people, and leads the world Communist movement to some end not yet disclosed.

10

THE REEDUCATION

OF THE OFFENDER

The reeducation of the offender is an important aspect of the education of the people. It is important, first of all, because it involves directly some part of the people, and a part of considerable dimensions in the Soviet Union. If the offender is not exterminated or incarcerated for life, his treatment apparently rests on the assumption that he can be reeducated or reformed, that he can become a changed or a "new" man. The implication of a limited sentence seems to be that the experience will "teach him a lesson" and thus develop in him a disposition not to commit the criminal act on regaining his freedom. There is, of course, the ancient doctrine of *lex talionis,* the law of retaliation, which demands an "eye for an eye," as an expression of a kind of primitive or natural justice. Related to this doctrine, perhaps, is the idea that the violation of the laws of society places the individual in the position of a debtor. In order to return to his status as a full member of the group, he must pay his debt. And the magnitude of the debt for a given offense is determined by the state in terms of suitable forms and degrees of punishment. In a word, an effort is made to "make the punishment fit the crime." But underlying all theories and practices which fall short of finality, there is the assumption that the individual will be affected by the experience and deterred from committing the offense again.

In the second place, the treatment of the offender is a factor in the education of all the people because it is a fact of life which cannot be concealed. Indeed, punishment of the offender has always been justified on the grounds that it will deter others from violating the laws. Very severe punishments in many societies have been defended by this logic. Public tortures and hangings have sometimes been thought to have a deterrent influence on the people generally. In the Soviet Union the

212

public spectacle has been employed with great power at times for the purpose of impressing on the population the dangers inherent in certain types of action, behavior, and thought. Such procedure has been followed, however, not in relation to crimes against the person or private property, but for certain crimes against the state and the Party. In cases involving political dissent and opposition, as every reader knows, the process of public trial, confession, and conviction of the offender is made an occasion for striking terror into the hearts of opponents and potential opponents and for arousing the sympathies and passions of the people in support of Party judgment. The press, the radio, and other means of communication not only report the news according to the desired pattern; they are also expected to propagate Party doctrine and policy. In fact, the people are encouraged in a sense to participate in the event, to hold meetings and pass unanimous resolutions demanding the application of the most severe measures of punishment to some designated "enemy of the people." At the same time, no newspaper, no radio, and no assemblage of citizens comes to the defense of the accused. The influence of this entire procedure must be regarded as an important element in the Soviet program for the education of the people in the spirit of Communism.

One of the basic dogmas of Bolshevism is that almost anything can be accomplished by means of education, if correctly conceived and efficiently administered. This is revealed clearly in the vast and all-embracing program of education briefly reported in the present volume. The challenge issued by Tkachev long ago that human nature itself can be transformed through educational institutions and processes has been accepted by the Bolsheviks. They have rejected the old Russian proverb that "only the grave can straighten the hunched back of an old man." In fact, they claim to have demonstrated the contrary. The supreme test of the doctrine perhaps is presented by the offender, and particularly by certain types of offenders. But here Lenin acknowledged a degree of failure among the "class enemies" bequeathed from the old regime. Among "parasites, scoundrels, and hooligans," he acknowledged in an article written in the spring of 1918, there were some "uncorrectable ones." He proposed therefore the "correction of the correctable" and the employment of extreme measures against the "uncorrectable." It was difficult, however, to distinguish the one category from the other by any known method of inspection.[1]

The Soviet provision for the reeducation of offenders grew from very small beginnings in the twenties into a gigantic enterprise, into an enterprise far surpassing in scope and diversity the practice of the autocracy, even under the most despotic of the tsars. This growth was due to the fantastic increase in the number of "offenders," as defined by Soviet

power. And the increase was the fruit of the rise of the Stalin dictatorship, the launching of the five-year plans, the purging of all opponents
in Party and government, and the inauguration of a prolonged "time of
troubles" which touched in one form or another the entire population.
At one time, and perhaps even down to this day, "places of detention"
held in bondage from 5 to 10 per cent of the adult inhabitants of the
Soviet Union, as well as a considerable number of persons of foreign
birth. Some of the details of this story will be related in later pages of
the chapter.

II

The theoretical foundations of the Bolshevik approach to the reeducation of offenders are derived from the teachings of Marx. According to
the doctrines of historical materialism, the behavior of men is determined
by "the prevailing mode of economic production and exchange, and the
social organization necessarily following from it." Consequently, the
source of crime is to be found, not in the nature of man, but in the
"economics" of each particular society. The Marxists therefore repudiate
the theories of the famous Italian criminologist, Cesare Lombroso, who
expounded the idea that the criminal is a distinct physical and hereditary
type with definite and easily discernible bodily "stigmata." In the epoch
of capitalism, crime, prostitution, and other delinquencies are an inevitable product of the institution of private property and the resulting division of society into classes. It is the poverty, exploitation, and humiliation
of the laboring masses which drive men to criminal acts, acts which are
called criminal merely because they violate the laws of the capitalist
state, laws designed to protect the interests of the exploiting class and
hold the worker in a condition of subjection and slavery. Indeed, the
entire coercive apparatus of the capitalist state, with its laws, its courts,
its police, and its army, is a weapon directed against the proletariat.

All who resist or seek to escape exploitation are arrested by capitalist
policemen, convicted and sentenced by capitalist courts and judges. The
jails and prisons are thus filled with rebellious proletarians. The history
of crime is one phase of the history of the struggle against oppression.
Under the tsars all revolutionists were regarded as criminals and were
often subjected to cruel and inhuman punishments. The Bolsheviks who
led the October Revolution had all been arrested, some of them several
times, and sentenced to penal servitude or exile. Lenin was banished to
Siberia for three years, from 1897 to 1900. And most of the leaders of
first rank were forced to live abroad for many years. Marx was banished
from his native land at the age of twenty-five, and lived most of his life
in Paris, Brussels, and London. It was in the British Museum that he

produced his greatest works, made his studies of capitalism, and elaborated the doctrines of international revolutionary socialism. How this could have been permitted by the system of world capitalism is never fully explained by Bolshevik writers. Perhaps the only explanation is found in the chronic stupidity of the Englishman, or perhaps in his love of liberty! But this would be contrary to the teachings of Marx and the inexorable laws of social development.

Old Russia was notorious in the Western world for its system of penal servitude, or *katorga*. The current *Dictionary of the Russian Language* defines *katorga* as "heavy forced labor for persons confined in prisons or other places under a particularly harsh regimen." Introduced by Peter the Great in 1691, according to the *Large Soviet Encyclopedia*, it became a characteristic Russian institution—"the highest form of punishment (next to execution) for criminal offenders and fighters against the social and political order." The great part of the prisoners involved were "exploited for the building of fortresses, ports and roads" and for "work in state mines and factories." Because of "inhuman treatment" and "cruel conditions" the prisoners engaged in "innumerable riots and jail breaks." Until the second quarter of the nineteenth century most of those sent into *katorga* were the survivors of "cossack and peasant revolts." Thereafter they became increasingly "political offenders and revolutionary elements" from the "upper classes," the "intelligentsia," and the "petty bourgeoisie." It is interesting to note that at times, when the authorities applied particularly severe measures to the prisoners, such as corporal punishment, waves of protest swept the country and forced the amelioration of conditions.[2] Some of the leading revolutionists, moreover, were able to maintain contact with their followers through the medium of letters and pamphlets. The guards often allowed them unauthorized privileges. Lenin, while in exile in Siberia from 1897 to 1900 though not in *katorga*, was supported by a government stipend, spent his leisure hours swimming, fishing, and hunting, carried on correspondence with revolutionary associates, completed his *The Development of Capitalism in Russia*, and translated Sidney and Beatrice Webb's *Theory and Practice of Trade Unionism*.[3] The reader can easily imagine what would happen to an inmate of a Soviet forced-labor camp who attempted to engage in such activities. He should note also that the highest number of persons held in all the prisons of Russia during the decade prior to the First World War was 183,949 in 1912.[4]

According to official Soviet doctrine, *katorga* was abolished by the Bolsheviks. "The Great October Revolution," says the first edition of the *Large Soviet Encyclopedia*, "completely liquidated all forms of Forced Labor in the USSR." It then adds that the "free labor of workers and peasants has become a matter of honor, a matter of glory, a matter of

valor and heroism." [5] This would seem to mean that when men convicted
of crime under the tsars were forced by armed guards to build roads,
canals, and ports, and work in state mines and factories, it was *katorga*,
but that when the same thing happens under Soviet rule on a vastly
greater scale, it is "corrective labor." By definition, *katorga* is associated
with the operation of capitalist institutions.

This is precisely the position taken in the second edition of the encyclopedia. Here *katorga* is defined as "the most severe form of prison confinement employed in capitalist countries." In such countries it is a
"weapon of terror used by imperialist reaction for dealing with progressive leaders, revolutionary workers, anti-fascists, Communists, and defenders of peace." And the "most cruel *katorga* regimen prevails in the
jails and concentration camps of the USA, England, France, Greece,
Spain, Yugoslavia, other capitalist countries, and colonial lands, where
millions of fighters for peace, freedom, and socialism are imprisoned."
The encyclopedia states further that "historically *katorga* is linked with
the development of capitalism." Consequently, the United States played
an important role in the perfection of this form of punishment. America
"is the birthplace of the Pennsylvania system, a system of solitary confinement and absolute silence." Also the "Auburn system of *katorga* appeared first in the USA and later spread through the whole of Europe.
Under this system the prisoners work most of the day under a regimen
of the knout and absolute silence. The rest of the day is spent in solitary
confinement." And generally in the United States "disciplinary and punitive measures are employed which were unknown even in the Middle
Ages—steam cells with intolerably high temperatures, ice baths, corporal
punishment with whip and knout, etc." [6] Thus conditions in America
would appear to be worse than they were in Russia before the October
Revolution.

Under fascism, which by definition is the last stage of capitalism,
katorga is transformed into its most barbarous form—the concentration
camp. This institution was perfected by Hitler as a regimen of "bloody
terror" for "war prisoners and civilians under suspicion." Also it was
directed against "progressive workers," "scientists," and "German pa-
triots." After the Soviet armies "destroyed Fascist Germany and liquidated
Hitler's concentration camps," the "center of Fascist reaction was transferred to the USA." Concentration camps, which "exist in many states, are
a means of monstrous exploitation of prisoners and constitute a source of
tremendous profit to capitalists." The camps "follow the methods and
practices of the Hitlerites." The American "intervention in Korea" led to
the founding of seventy-seven concentration camps in which "were confined hundreds of thousands of peaceful Korean citizens, including women,
children and the aged." In 1952 "American interventionists shot down

unarmed war prisoners." [7] Such is the course of crime and punishment under capitalism. It will be interesting to see whether the encyclopedia will be revised after the repudiation of Vyshinsky and under the "collective leadership" of Khrushchev.

If crimes and prisons are the natural offspring of capitalism, then the establishment of socialism should lead to the disappearance of these social phenomena. Under socialism the basic causes of crime will be removed. There will be no more exploitation of man by man because the division of society into antagonistic classes will be abolished. There will be diverse occupations, but the distinction between manual and intellectual labor will disappear. There will be no parasites living on the labor of others, and all will work for the common good, for society as a whole, and thus, in the last analysis, for themselves. Women, too, will not be driven into prostitution by the peculiarly harsh and unjust conditions of life for the sex under capitalism. And prejudice of race and nation will vanish, because all will be treated equally and no one group will hold power over another by reason of the ownership of private property in the tools of production. Moreover, since the laws will be formulated in terms of the interests of all the people, there will be no rational grounds for criminal acts and political opposition. If such were to occur, they would merely testify to the survival of vestiges of capitalism in the minds of men. This, of course, is a utopian picture, and the early Bolsheviks were not utopians in a political sense. They prided themselves on their ability to face realities.

Firmly convinced that crime would eventually wither away under socialism, they nevertheless realized that they were confronted with a heritage from the past. In this situation the leading spokesmen of Bolshevism during the first decade committed themselves to the teachings of the humane penology which had been evolving during the preceding century in advanced countries. Not a few Russian revolutionists who rejected Marxism and Bolshevism had adopted the environmental approach to crime and punishment. According to this approach, society, and not the criminal, was guilty. If the individual transgressed the moral or legal code, he did so not because of a destiny prescribed by his germ cells but because of faulty education, denial of opportunity, and unjust treatment. Dallin and Nicolaevsky, in their study of the "first decade," report that the men charged by Lenin with the task of reforming the system of justice deleted the term "guilt" from the "official vocabulary," prescribed an adjustable scale of penalties for offenses, "fixed the maximum penalty" at imprisonment for five years, abolished the words "prison" and "punishment," and substituted "place of detention" and "measures of social protection." [8]

In attacking the problem of the offender, the Bolsheviks adopted two policies—a short-range and a long-range policy. The latter has occupied a central position in the text of the present volume. It involves the comprehensive program for rearing a new generation marked by unalloyed devotion to the cause of Communism and possessing all of the traits of the New Soviet Man. By this process, it was hoped and expected that the "vestiges of capitalism" would be eradicated from the consciousness of people and the qualities of Communist morality inculcated. The fact that the persistence of these "vestiges" constitutes a major problem of Soviet education down to this day is evidence of at least a partial failure. But this subject has been treated already from diverse perspectives.

The short-range policy was to "correct the correctible," to use Lenin's phraseology. This meant the inauguration of measures designed to educate and reeducate the offender. The professed goal was the transformation of every "place of detention" into an educational institution. "Education and not punishment" was the slogan. The spirit of this conception survived into the thirties and is preserved in the title of a book on Soviet jurisprudence edited by no other than Andrei Vyshinsky, the great public prosecutor, *From Prisons to Educational Institutions*.[9] The basic principle to guide the reeducation of the offender was fundamentally the same as that which governed or dominated the work of the school at the time, a principle rooted in the teachings of Marx and Lenin, the principle of socially useful labor. The offender could be reformed and rehabilitated, converted into a useful and dependable citizen, by working under discipline for the general welfare. The experience, long or short, depending on the character of the individual, would both develop steady habits of work and change for the better his attitude toward his fellows and society. If he lacked vocational skills, these would be given to him.

That an earnest effort was made to apply this principle in the twenties cannot be denied. Although, to the surprise and disappointment of the authorities, the prison population grew from 87,800 in 1924 to 198,000 in 1927,[10] many claims of success were advanced. Extravagant reports appeared in the press of the successful reeducation of old offenders, even political adversaries and "class enemies." "Corrective labor" was made to appear as a kind of magic for the creation of the "new man." Vyshinsky, who a few years later was to be the agent of the Party in sending the foremost Bolshevik leaders of 1917 to the execution chamber, romantically and boastfully proclaimed in 1934: "In Soviet corrective-labor institutions genuine human labor triumphs in all of its manifold creativity. This labor, combined with the special characteristics of Soviet power and socialist construction, is precisely that magician who out of thin air transforms nobodies into heroes." [11] Not a few foreign visitors were impressed by this "humane system" for treating offenders and restoring them to the ordered life of society.

One of the most celebrated instances of the use of "corrective labor" in a large project of construction was the building of the canal between the White and Baltic Seas under extremely harsh conditions. Begun in August, 1931, it was completed in approximately two years. Almost 300,000 prisoners labored on this project under the direction of the GPU, the Soviet political police. At the conclusion of the undertaking, the Soviet state proclaimed a day of celebration. The Central Committee of the Party issued a resolution of triumph on August 4, 1933, stating that 12,484 persons had been "completely corrected" and given their freedom and that 59,516 had had their sentences reduced because they had "shown themselves to be energetic workers in construction." Also a "number of former saboteurs and recidivists had been reborn to such an extent in the process" that they were awarded the "Red Banner of Labor." Two such people, due to their outstanding performance, were given the Order of Lenin, the highest award of honor in the Soviet Union.[12] The author witnessed a play in Moscow in the autumn of 1936 which portrayed the theme of the redemptive power of "corrective labor" in the building of the canal. How many of the prisoners perished in the process, however, is not in the public record. According to Dallin, the majority, to their great disappointment, were transferred immediately to other construction projects. As a consequence, "scores of prisoners mutilated themselves" and "others tried to resist transfer." [13]

Although the humane conception of genuinely corrective labor was swiftly overwhelmed by the return of *katorga* and the rise of the vast network of forced-labor camps, the version of the treatment of offenders given to the world has not changed. In neither the first nor the second edition of the encyclopedia is there any reference to the "punitive camps" launched by a decree of 1919 which will be reported later. A volume of the second edition, published in 1955, contains only the following few lines on "Corrective-labor Camps": "Corrective-labor Camps in the USSR have the aim of protecting society against socially dangerous offenders by isolating them, by combining isolation with socially-useful labor, and by adjusting the offenders to the conditions of labor-collective living." [14] The account devotes a few more lines to "Corrective-labor Policy in the USSR" which could be read only with amazement by the millions who have been sentenced to hard labor in the camps. Soviet policy, says the encyclopedia, "has nothing in common with the prison policy of capitalist countries which is based on the physical and spiritual crippling of the class offenders of the bourgeoisie and their destruction by means of a terroristic prison regimen." It pursues rather "the aim of the punishment, the correction, and the reeducation of the condemned." It does not "repudiate punishment" but employs it "as a necessary element of education." At the same time, it "does not tolerate torture and the degradation of human dignity." It is based on a "sound combination of labor and cultural-educational work" designed to achieve the "correction and the reeducation of the condemned." [15] This is a beautiful picture. The reality, according to numerous and authentic accounts, is something quite different. It is nothing less than *katorga*. The rise and nature of this phase of the Soviet order will be briefly reported.

III

Along with their humanitarian and idealistic professions, the Bolsheviks from Lenin through Stalin to Khrushchev have been ruthless and tyrannical in the pursuit of their objectives. Constituting a small minority of the population in 1917 and confronted with hostile elements on all sides, the Bolsheviks resorted to the most extreme measures in the struggle to vanquish their enemies and establish their rule. Out of this struggle emerged the practices and institutions which were to evolve into the Soviet system of penal servitude surpassing immeasurably in its sweep the *katorga* of the tsars and anything known to the modern world outside Hitler's concentration camps.

During the years of the civil war the Bolsheviks created an agency comparable to the secret political police of the tsars, the Cheka, or Extraordinary Commission for Combatting Counterrevolution, sometimes called the "guillotine of the revolution" or the "unsheathed sword of the revolution." In 1922 its name was changed to the GPU, in 1936 to the NKVD, and later to the MVD, but its essential function remained substantially the same through the years. From the first it was commissioned with extraordinary powers for seeking out, arresting, convicting, and passing sentence on offenders. And the offenders were always defined by the Party in terms of individuals or categories of persons. In the beginning the offenders were "White Guards" and members of hostile parties and classes. In the course of time they became kulaks, wreckers, Trotskyites, Bukharinites, Fascists, cosmopolitans, conspirators, and American spies.

The question arose at once regarding the disposition of these "enemies of the people." Lenin set the pattern in an article written in March or April, 1918, under the strange title, "How to Organize Competition." A full paragraph from this amazing document merits quotation:

> Thousands of ways for checking and controlling the wealthy, the swindlers, and the parasites must be elaborated and tested experimentally by the communes themselves, by small cells in both city and village. Variety here is a guarantee of vitality, an assurance of success in the achievement of the general goal: the *purging* of the Russian land of all sorts of harmful insects, of fleas-scoundrels, bedbugs-rich, and others. In one place ten rich ones, a dozen scoundrels, a half-dozen shirking workers will be jailed. . . . In

another, they will be assigned to clean toilets. In a third, on being released from jail, they will be given yellow tickets so that all of the people can watch them until their *harmful* tendencies are corrected. In a fourth, one out of ten guilty of parasitism will be shot. In a fifth, a combination of all these devices will be used—for example, a conditional release may achieve the swift correction of the correctible among the wealthy, the bourgeois intelligentsia, scoundrels and hooligans. The more varied, the better and richer will be the general experience, the surer and sooner will be the success of socialism, the easier will be devised the *best* ways and means.[16]

It was soon realized that this process of "purging the Russian land of all sorts of harmful insects" required organization. The Cheka has already been mentioned. Much more was needed. In April, 1919, a decree was issued in the name of the "Worker and Peasant Government" for the establishment of "Forced-labor Camps," not, it should be noted, "Corrective-labor Camps." Here apparently is the official revival of *katorga* and the beginning of the Soviet system of penal servitude. The "initial organization and management of the camps," according to the decree, "is to be entrusted to the Provincial Extraordinary Commissions," institutions which apparently preceded the all-Russian Cheka. Not only "persons" but also "categories of persons" were to be subjected to "confinement in the camps." The prisoners were to be "put to work immediately to satisfy the demands of Soviet institutions." "Runaways" were "subject to the most severe punishments." Also, "for the purpose of managing all camps of forced labor, the cooperation of the All-Russian Extraordinary Commission" was ordered.[17]

Detailed instructions for the conduct of the camps were outlined in a decree issued about one month later. The camps were to be "isolated from other buildings and construction projects." For camps of less than three hundred persons "two guards are prescribed for every fifteen prisoners," and "one guard for every ten prisoners" above three hundred. "Newly arrived prisoners and prisoners returning from work" were to be searched. "Women and children under age must be kept" in a special camp "for each category." The prisoner was to "be paid according to the scale of his professional union," and the "expense of maintaining the camp" was to be borne by the prisoners—food and clothing, maintenance of buildings, cost of administration, and pay of guards. "All prisoners must be assigned to physical labor immediately on arrival." The penalties for attempts to escape were to be severe: for the first attempt, "an increase up to ten times the original term of sentence"; and for the second, a trial before a "Revolutionary Tribunal which reserves the right to pronounce punishment up to the highest form." If a prisoner refuses to work, he "is subject to punishment in accordance with a special instruction." The nature of this instruction is not revealed.[18]

The expectation of Lenin and his associates was that both the Cheka and the forced-labor camp were temporary institutions, created to meet an *extraordinary* situation. That situation was marked particularly by the severe struggle for power and the campaign to liquidate the "harmful insects" bequeathed to the Bolshevik state from the rule of capitalism and the autocracy. But the building of the new order was not merely a matter of the firm establishment of Soviet rule. In fact, it was an undertaking destined to require decades and to involve fatal struggles within the Party hierarchy. The *extraordinary* situation, while assuming diverse forms from year to year and decade to decade, has continued down to the present era of "collective leadership." Consequently, although the Cheka has changed its name several times, it has continued in its original essence and has vastly extended its scale of operations. And the system of forced-labor camps has certainly grown far beyond the expectations of its creators. The genuineness of the relaxations after the death of Stalin and the Twentieth Congress remains to be demonstrated over a period of time.

Before Lenin died, enemies of the Soviet regime emerged from a wholly unanticipated quarter. The sailors of the Kronshtadt naval base who had played a basic role in the overthrow of the provisional government and the establishment of the Bolshevik dictatorship rose in rebellion on March 1, 1921. The rebellion was put down with savage slaughter and the survivors were sent to the harshest camps of forced labor above the Arctic Circle. This experience warned the Bolsheviks that even proletarians and poor peasants with guns in their hands could not be trusted. Like the members of the old middle classes, they had to be born again and be transformed into "new men," according to the pattern set by the Bolsheviks.

The period of the New Economic Policy, which was Lenin's response to the Kronshtadt rebellion, was relatively quiet, as it was a period of some freedom for the individual. In those years the *extraordinary* situation gradually tended toward the *ordinary*. But the Party leaders soon realized that this tendency boded them nothing good. Under the new policy a petty bourgeoisie was appearing in towns and cities, and the threat of the peasantry loomed before them in the distance like a dark cloud. Trotsky and others saw this clearly. The peasant loved the land and, in spite of the tradition of the *mir*, wanted to hold under the institution of private ownership what he had gained from the revolution through the confiscation and division of the estates. It appeared, therefore, that the future belonged to the peasants, because of their overwhelming numbers, unless something was done and done quickly. The peasants for the most part were not Communists; nor were they attracted by the beautiful picture of life in the collective, as painted by the Bolsheviks. In order to bridge the gap between village and city, between agriculture and industry, between peasant and proletarian, the village had to be urbanized, agriculture industrialized, and the peasant proletarianized. Indeed, in order to save the revolution, a second revolution was required—a revolution which would socialize the village. While the First Five-Year Plan had diverse goals, this was certainly one of the most crucial. If the peasants were allowed to continue on their course, capitalism would eventually be restored in Russia. Also, the Bolsheviks argued that until they developed a powerful industry the Soviet Union would be dependent on the advanced capitalist countries and occupy a quasi-colonial status among the nations. This theme was repeated over and over again in the late twenties and early thirties.

The rise of the system of forced labor into an important segment of the economy was a product of the "Plan of Great Works." Under the twin slogans of "building socialism in one country" and "overtaking and surpassing the most advanced capitalist countries," the Party proceeded to marshal all the human resources of the country in the name of industrialization. This called for the forced mobilization and distribution of labor beyond anything attempted since the revolution. Peasants were drafted from the village for the building of giant mills, hydroelectric stations, mines, and canals. No labor could be wasted; unemployment disappeared; and the "labor of the condemned" assumed a new significance. In the words of P. P. Postyshev, one of the Soviet leaders, this form of labor "could be included from the beginning in the general mass of socially useful work in so far as it contributed directly to socialist construction." Consequently, "institutions for corrective labor achieved a firm economic base through the incorporation of their enterprises into the general system of our economy." [19] This means that the "condemned" became an important source of labor for projects which had to be administered under peculiarly harsh conditions of life and work.

The forced industrialization of the economy had another consequence which in time affected profoundly the system of forced labor. The Soviet state enjoyed little credit in the money markets of Europe and America in 1928. It could not therefore follow the usual course of an undeveloped country and move into the industrial age by borrowing from the more advanced nations. The only other course open was to reduce the standard of living of the Soviet people and export consumer goods badly needed at home to purchase technical assistance and machinery from abroad. During these years, for example, great quantities of grain were exported, even though many millions were living on the verge of starvation. Also, the "turnover" or sales tax on the necessities of life was greatly increased. This amounted to a system of "compulsory savings" for the accumulation of needed capital, a system which prevails down to the present day. Thus, 60 per cent of the cost of a loaf of bread is a tax which goes into the state budget. Under the system of "compulsory savings" the Party has been able in an extraordinarily short period of time to build a powerful heavy industry and military potential, while holding the mass of the people near the margin of subsistence. These are the essentials of the Communist method of industrializing a technically backward country. Although Malenkov, following the death of Stalin, apparently advocated the shifting of a larger portion of the resources and energies of the economy to the building of the light industries and the production of consumers' goods, the policy was quickly abandoned under Khrushchev.

If the Plan had merely called for swift industrialization of the economy and the mechanization of agriculture, the most severe hardships might have been avoided. However, as noted above, the program of construction had a political as well as an economic motive. The village had to be socialized, if the revolution itself were not to be placed in jeopardy. And so the country passed through a period from 1928 to 1935 of *forced* collectivization of the land. The method of persuasion by means of huge state farms and "ideal" village communes established in the twenties by the Party had failed to move the peasants to abandon their individual holdings. By 1928 the state farms and communes accounted for only about 7 per cent of the total grain production of the country. In the light of what happened, the program outlined in the Plan was modest in its provisions. It merely called for the collectivization of 20 per cent of the total cultivated area by 1933.[20] However, this phase of the Plan came under the very same compulsions which have attended every program of construction or achievement in the Soviet Union. All agencies of propaganda were mobilized to inspire efforts to "overfulfill" the announced Plan. The following slogans printed in *Pravda* in October, 1930, and copied by practically all other papers in the land are illustrative of the method:

RAISE HIGHER THE BANNER OF SHOCK WORK!
RAISE HIGHER THE BANNER OF SOCIALIST REVOLUTION!
WE WILL FULFILL THE FIVE-YEAR PLAN IN FOUR YEARS!

The drive for the collectivization of the village quickly assumed the character of a revolutionary struggle. The Party pushed the campaign by means of its local units and agents with its customary energy and ruthlessness. By the first of May, 1930, the Plan was already surpassed in the great agricultural regions of the lower Volga, the steppes of the Ukraine, and the North Caucasus.[21] At the end of the five years practically the whole of Soviet agriculture was operating under some form of collectivization. The Party had achieved the "socialist reconstruction of the village."

The relation of the First Five-Year Plan to the development of the

Soviet system of forced-labor camps is fairly obvious. Although the imagination of millions of persons, and particularly of youth, was captured by the great ideal of deliberately building and strengthening their country, probably the great majority of the older generation were hostile, disillusioned, and embittered. The sacrifice of material comforts, the regimentation of life, and the constant urge to exceed the norms of labor undoubtedly placed a grievous moral strain even on those who had been loyal to the revolution and inspired by its promises of justice, equality, and abundance. Many who had fought in the ranks of the Bolsheviks in the civil war lost their faith and joined the opposition in spirit if not in deed. In his trip through the Soviet Union in his Ford car in 1929, the author encountered not a few such people. He recalls particularly a man of thirty-five, an educator, who accompanied him from Rostov to Odessa by way of the Caucasus Mountains and the Black Sea. On one occasion this man opened his soul and revealed a sense of deep bitterness. "When," he asked, "will I have a chance to live? My youth was consumed in the fires of the First World War, the revolution, the civil war, and the famine. Then, before life could improve greatly under the New Economic Policy, I am required to sacrifice for the First Five-Year Plan. Sacrifice, sacrifice, and more sacrifice is all I have ever known." This outlook was by no means rare at the time.

The deepest and most abiding hostility developed among the peasants. Although the Bolsheviks addressed their appeal to the poor and middle peasants and sought to arouse in them class hatred toward the rich peasants, or kulaks, the opposition almost wrecked Soviet agriculture. This story has already been told briefly, and will not be repeated here, except to say that the peasants as a body slaughtered approximately one-half of their farm animals, refused to plant crops, and thus induced a famine in the richest agricultural region of the Soviet Union. Having no political power and no weapons, they could express their hostility to Party policies only by such desperate measures. One can easily imagine the passions that seethed in the breasts of these helpless people.

It is well known that some of the top leaders of the Party, such as Bukharin, Rykov, and Tomsky, favored a more gradual program of industrialization and even doubted the wisdom of collectivizing the village by state power. In the face of the known widespread opposition and hostility, the Party, under Stalin's dictatorship, was confronted with the necessity of making one of those fateful decisions which have marked the history of the Bolshevik state from the beginning. It either had to retreat to a more moderate position, as Lenin did in 1921, or had to resort to extreme punitive measures. It chose the latter course. It turned to the political police, to the policy of arrest, conviction, exile, forced labor, and execution. As in their struggle for power in the first years of the revolution, they labeled all critics and opponents counterrevolutionists, capitalists, petty bourgeoisie, and enemies of the people. In the case of the kulaks, the entire class was condemned. During the winter of 1929–1930 the Party adopted the slogan: "The Liquidation of the Kulaks as a Class." According to Dallin, "the official statistics had listed 5,859,000 kulaks in 1928." [22] And probably every kulak represented several people. Moreover, at the time of the struggle for the collectivization of agriculture, any peasant who opposed collectivization was regarded as a kulak. The important consideration here, as in the case of the capitalist, was not how much he owned, but rather what he believed. Party literature today, as the reader knows, is replete with references to the "vestiges of capitalism in the consciousness of people." Vestiges of *kulachestvo*, the desire to own land in fee simple, also persist among the peasantry.

The "liquidation of the kulaks as a class" marked the great transformation of the Soviet practice and philosophy of the treatment of offenders. Millions of peasants died of starvation from the politically induced famine of 1933.[23] Many were killed in the struggle against collectivization, and millions more were arrested and committed to penal servitude in improvised camps in the Far North. But this was only the beginning. Ever since the death of Lenin in 1924, Stalin had conducted a struggle for power, first against one group in the Central Committee and then against another. Leon Trotsky, his most brilliant opponent, was exiled to Central Asia in 1928, deported from the Soviet Union in 1929, and assassinated in Mexico in 1940. In December, 1934, Sergei Kirov, member of the Politburo and close associate of Stalin, was murdered. This event sparked the great purge which in the years 1936 to 1938 culminated in the execution of the surviving leaders of the 1917 revolution. But this was not all. The friends and sympathizers, and the suspected friends and sympathizers of these men, were purged from the Party, the government, the army, the police, and the economic apparatus. All who were permitted to live went to join the ranks of the prisoners sentenced to penal servitude. By this time the last vestige of the humane outlook of Soviet jurisprudence had vanished, except for the words "corrective labor." Andrei Vyshinsky, after sending his predecessor Nikolai Krylenko to his death, remarked: "Punishment cannot be reduced to education, and let us not pretend that prisons are no different from schools!" [24] Political dissent became the most heinous crime in the Soviet Union, and anyone who opposed or criticized Stalin and the directives of the Central Committee became a counterrevolutionary and an enemy of the people. The fact should never be forgotten that "mercilessness" toward an enemy is one of the most basic principles of Bolshevik morality.

By the end of the thirties the forced-labor camp had achieved the status of an important sector of the Soviet economy. But it was destined to grow yet larger. In the autumn of 1939 the Red Army marched into Poland and the Western Ukraine and "liberated" the Baltic states of Lithuania, Latvia, and Estonia. Immediately the Party proceeded systematically to purge the populations involved of dangerous and "unstable" elements. A deportation order of the new Communist government of Lithuania listed the following categories of persons to be arrested and deported to the east:

1. Members of Russian prerevolutionary parties—Mensheviks, followers of Trotsky and anarchists. *(note primary position.)*
2. Members of contemporary Lithuanian political parties, including students belonging to student organizations.
3. Members of the state police, gendarmerie and prison staffs.
4. Officers of the former Tsarist Army and other anti-Bolshevik armies of 1918–21.
5. Officers and military judges of the contemporary Polish and Lithuanian armies.
6. Volunteers of all armies other than Bolshevik.
7. Persons removed from the Communist Party.
8. Refugees, political *émigrés* and contraband runners.
9. Citizens of foreign states, representatives of foreign firms, etc.
10. Persons who have travelled abroad. Persons who are in contact with representatives of foreign states. Persons who are Esperantists and philatelists.
11. Officials of Lithuanian Ministries.
12. The staff of the Red Cross.
13. Persons active in parishes; clergymen, secretaries and active members of religious communities.
14. Aristocrats, landowners, wealthy merchants, bankers, industrialists, hotel and restaurant proprietors.[25]

Following the Great Patriotic War, hundreds of thousands of persons of divers categories were sent to the camps. All Soviet citizens who had shown any tendency toward disloyalty during the struggle were included. Among these were soldiers in the armies of General Vlasov and the minorities already mentioned—the Tartars of the Crimea, the Germans and Kalmuks of the Volga, the Ingushi and Chechentsi of the North Caucasus and others. Also doubtless thousands of Soviet citizens who had been seized by the Nazi armies and forced into labor of various kinds in Germany during the war. These men and women were subject to "forced repatriation," according to an agreement negotiated between Stalin and the Western Allies after Yalta. In addition, there were the returned soldiers who had seen the West and had become unstable in their convictions and loyalties. Another contingent came from elements of the Jewish population of the Soviet Union who had given evidences of "cosmopolitanism," or lack of devotion to the Soviet Motherland, after the establishment of the Republic of Israel in 1948. That there has been some relaxation and moderation of the Soviet system of penology is probably true. Yet, the fall and execution of Beria in 1953 and of his associate Bagirov in 1956, have been followed with a purge of the Party and government apparatus. And if Khrushchev should stumble in his leadership a purge of vast proportions might follow.

Ever since the middle thirties the question has been raised continuously regarding the number of prisoners in the forced-labor camps. Since the Soviet state issues no statistics on the subject and endeavors to throw a veil of secrecy over the entire enterprise, precise knowledge is unavailable. Yet an astonishing amount of data has accumulated through the years—from those who have escaped and from Soviet secret documents which have passed the borders of Russia. The estimates have ranged all the way from 2 or 3 million to 24 million. David Dallin, who has made the most comprehensive and scholarly study of the question, estimated the number in 1947 "at from 7 to 12 million." [26] The same writer places the number of known camps after the war at 125, and then adds that the list is "far from complete." [27] The problem is complicated by the Soviet institution of "free exile," under which the individual is banished to some distant region but is allowed to live and pursue his occupation as any other Soviet citizen. In a letter to the author dated October 18, 1955, Dallin gave the following reply to the question of the number of persons sent to the forced-labor camps in the course of twenty-five years: "To avoid exaggerations, I would roughly estimate the total at from 20,000,000 to 30,000,000." This does not include those "deported to cities and towns of the East to live in comparative freedom." He recognized this as a sixty-four-thousand-dollar question which nobody could answer with assurance.

IV

In the course of time, and very swiftly after 1931, the forced-labor camp developed into a basic economic institution, with its productive potential recognized in the five-year plans. The number of prisoners was too large to live at the expense of the state. Moreover, since launching the program of feverish industrialization the Soviet regime has suffered from a scarcity of human labor. To Stalin and his associates the enemies and suspected enemies of "socialist construction" had to be put to work. And the principle of the reeducation of the offender through the magic of "corrective labor" provided a moral foundation for the policy of building the great network of forced-labor camps. These men and women were to be rehabilitated.

But what work should they perform, and where? This was the question. Obviously, the entire operation should be conducted as secretly as possible and far from the eyes of even the Soviet people. Also the camps should be established in regions never visited by foreign travelers. Undoubtedly, a consideration which led Bulganin to reject Eisenhower's proposal of "open sky inspection" of military installations was the clear perception on his part that the pilots of planes flying over the Soviet land might see a great many "installations" which the Soviet spokesman would have difficulty in explaining. Fortunately for the Party, Russia embraces, and has always embraced, vast regions sparsely populated and relatively isolated from Europe. These regions lie to the east in Central Asia and Siberia and to the north in the vicinity of the Arctic Circle and beyond. Fortunately also, these regions were endowed with valuable resources of minerals and forests. It was in this great expanse that most of the camps were established.

There was a sound economic reason for locating the camps in the northern spaces. The case of *Dalstroy,* "Far Construction," well illustrates the point. The region contains vast reserves of gold, some of the richest in the world. Yet the climate is so harsh that only the strongest of men can survive its rigors. During the long polar night of six to ten weeks the temperature may drop to ninety degrees below zero, Fahrenheit. The rivers are icebound eight or nine months of the year, and in the brief summer the frost in the ground recedes only a few inches. Under such conditions few men indeed would choose to labor at fixed wages for a distant state. They might be attracted by the hope of huge rewards in the spirit of the gambler, a spirit which has played an important role in the history of gold mining. Even members of the Young Communist League would probably hesitate to accept a prolonged assignment in such a world of snow and ice and cultural poverty. But the regime needed gold, probably for export in the cause of the revolution. Here, obviously, was the place to establish a network of forced-labor camps. And this was done in the thirties under the direction of Stalin. If gold is mined, and it has been mined in large quantities, it matters little that the "majority" of the prisoners "never come back from the 'land of white death.'"[28] For they were "enemies of the people."

Dalstroy is only one of the great projects in the program of socialist construction carried through by the forced labor of men and women. And life there is exceptionally severe. Yet the great camp of Vorkuta above the Arctic Circle in the west is much like it, developed on the foundation of rich coal reserves amid harsh natural conditions. Also there are others. As under *katorga* in the time of the autocracy, forced labor is employed largely in mining, lumbering, and the construction of ports, highways, canals, railroads, and even towns where hard labor is required. Such labor has had a very special value in the Soviet Union because of the low level of industrialization and the lack of power-driven machinery. This situation has, of course, changed greatly since 1928 and may be expected to change rapidly in the years ahead. The role of forced labor in the economy may be altered considerably in the future.

The part that forced labor has actually played in the development of the economy is shrouded in mystery. Yet facts are by no means entirely wanting. Perhaps the most significant body of information is the testimony of an employee of the State Planning Commission who escaped to the West after the war. The data presented are derived from the economic plan of the Soviet Union for 1941. According to this testimony, the MVD, that is, the political police which was charged with the administration of the camps, "and its agencies were assigned 14 per cent of all capital construction—a greater amount than that allotted to any other ministry." The MVD constructed not only camp buildings, mining facilities, logging camps, and defense installations, but also canals, highways of "national importance" and "railroad lines through isolated regions." It was charged with "the extraction of timber, gold, coal, chrome, ore, oil." It was given "sole responsibility for the building and operation of all atomic developments." Forced-labor "projects accounted for one-eighth of the total product of the timber industry, 10 per cent of all furniture and kitchenware production, 25 per cent of the total USSR Arctic freight towage, and over 40 per cent of the total Soviet chrome production." And "since 1938, 75 per cent of all gold production was by prison labor." In addition, under the 1941 plan the MVD "was also assigned certain production quotas for machinery, cement, and the operation of oil fields in the Komi ASSR near Ukhta." [29] Even if these estimates are above the mark, they reveal the far-reaching economic significance of the Soviet system of forced labor. It could scarcely be dismantled quickly without serious consequences to the economy.

On the life of the people in the camps a vast amount of testimony is available. It is to this question that the reports of escaped prisoners are largely addressed. Only a brief summation is possible here. While conditions have changed from time to time and vary from camp to camp and from region to region, the general picture is essentially the same everywhere, except perhaps when the "places of detention" are located near centers of population or amid relatively mild climatic surroundings. Those who are sentenced to the severest punishments short of execution are likely to find themselves committed to camps above the Arctic Circle where the chances of survival are slender. Yet the similarities are to be expected, since the political police has been the responsible agent for the administration of the camps. One of the most authoritative accounts is that given by the author of *The Dark Side of the Moon*, because it is based on firsthand experience related by hundreds of articulate Polish citizens who were sent to the camps during the brief period of the Soviet-Nazi Pact and were slowly released under the Stalin-Sikorski Agreement of 1941. Incidentally, the great majority never returned to either Poland or the West. The author thus describes the conditions in the vast empire of forced labor to the north and east:

> All the way to the north, from the railway line of Vologda-Kirowa to the Urals, and to the north again, up to the Arctic Ocean and in the Far East, along the reaches of the Kolyma river . . . , in Kamchatka and in the territories running inland from Khabarovsk, Sakhalin and Vladivostok, it may be said that there is practically no normal human life whatever; that there exist only guarded and guards. The whole is one vast N.K.V.D. state, divided into "zones," each territory enclosed within barbed wire, patrolled by armed guards and their dogs and made doubly secure by lookout towers and storks' nests containing sentries. Each zone covers hundreds of kilometres, and there is generally at least one camp on each kilometre.[30]

There are innumerable accounts of the whole process of arrest, inquisition, and life within these camps by former prisoners. In order to convey to the reader the human side of the Soviet system of forced labor, the story of one of these people will be briefly summarized—the story of a man who spent six years in a camp on the Kolyma River and is now on the faculty of Yale University.[31]

Vladimir Petrov was two years of age at the time of the Great October Revolution. He consequently knew nothing at first hand of the old order. Until his arrest at nineteen he lived under Soviet institutions, was educated in Soviet schools, and regarded himself as a loyal citizen of the Soviet state. He was, as the saying went in Russia in the twenties, a true "child of October." And he was destined to suffer long and terribly before his basic loyalties were shaken.

Petrov was struck down at the very beginning of a promising career in engineering. He was a victim of the Stalin-inspired terror which swept the Soviet Union from border to border following the assassination of Sergei Kirov in December, 1934. Framed by a rebuffed female agent of the NKDA, he was arrested and held in the jails of the "City of Lenin" for six months. During this period he was subjected to incredible privations, indignities, and tortures, physical and psychological. Denied all the rights of a free society, he was eventually convicted without trial, as the term is commonly understood in a democratic state, by the military tribunal of the Leningrad District. He was sentenced to six years of penal servitude.

A few days later he left the city of his youthful hopes and entered a world of nightmares. Amid the sobbing and screaming of women and children, who had come to the station to bid a last farewell to their loved ones, he boarded the prison train which was to take him to Vladivostok. After forty-seven days of traveling in a closed and crammed freight car, in stifling air and human filth, without once washing his face, after forty-seven days of lying on a bed of planks, of eating food "unfit for dogs," he arrived at the great Far Eastern port. Thence he went by boat to Magadan, and by road and trail to the gold fields of Kolyma. Here, in deep anguish of body and spirit, he began his long struggle for physical survival and the maintenance of his sanity. The story of Petrov's life in the gold mines, of the hardships and privations of the prisoners, of the brutality and arrogance of guards and officials, of the corrupting influence of unlimited power, of the degradation of human beings all in the name of Communism—this story cannot be told here. It must suffice to mention a few of the most characteristic features of the Soviet labor camp and penal system.

Under the Party dictatorship the worst of all crimes is actual or suspected political dissent or opposition. From this basic principle the structure of that strange society of convicts, in which Petrov lived for six years, is largely derived. At the top are swindlers, speculators, forgers, rapists, and others convicted of criminal breaches of trust. Next come "thieves of every description, from burglars to pickpockets." Immediately below are murderers and gunmen, all loyal to the Soviet state. These three upper strata constitute the privileged classes, whose members generally receive favored treatment and are regarded as capable of reformation through "corrective labor." From them, moreover, the authorities recruit persons for positions of responsibility in the administration of the camps.

Separated by an impassable gulf from this relatively small company of the privileged are the political prisoners of all shades, "the irreconcilable enemies of the Soviet regime." But here also there are gradations. Standing at the top of this structure, but below the "ordinary criminals," are so-called "agitators against the Soviet regime"—persons convicted of incautious political conversation, of telling anti-Soviet anecdotes, of concealing their social origins, or of failing to get along with local representatives of government or Party. On about the same level are those convicted of plundering or destroying "socialist property," even when the value of the article involved does not exceed 10 rubles. Finally, at the very bottom of the social scale are prisoners convicted of "espionage," "terrorism," "wrecking activities," "diversionary acts," "failure to give information," "concealment of a prerevolutionary past," and "membership in counter-revolutionary groups." But even this class has its pariahs whom all shun as they would shun the plague—persons convicted of "treason," of "preparing an insurrection," and of "having ties with foreign countries." Such an analysis of forced-labor society is not found in either edition of the *Large Soviet Encyclopedia.*

Women prisoners, according to Petrov, occupy a special social category. While they have their separate camps, their guards are men. The fate of a woman, therefore, particularly if young or comely, is beyond tragedy. Every man in the administration, from the highest official to the chef in the kitchen, has an inalienable right to violate the woman of his choice, unless perchance she is regarded with favor by some man of greater power. She is quite without defense or recourse beyond her own talents and qualities. Consequently, though a man may live out his term of years in the camp without losing "his human image," a woman can never do so.

At the time of Petrov's arrest, many who fell into the toils of the political police maintained for months a steadfast loyalty to the Soviet government and the Party leadership. They simply could not bring themselves to abandon their illusions and see the true nature of the dictatorship. They contrived ingenious apologies and invented all sorts of reasons for the defense of their faith. Some of them imagined that counterrevolutionists had found their way into the local headquarters of the NKVD; others that foreign agents bent on the overthrow of the Soviet regime were responsible. A persisting riddle in their minds was how they, "honest Soviet citizens, could be imprisoned as criminals." Petrov himself for a long time was certain that his case would be reviewed by some higher authority and his innocence established. The program of education had been remarkably successful. The situation, of course, may be different today.

Another feature of the Soviet system revealed in *Soviet Gold* may surprise the reader, but nevertheless is easily understood. It would appear that the labor camp is the only place in the Soviet Union where complete freedom of expression may be encountered. This does not mean that such exercise of freedom is general among the prisoners. Quite the contrary. The overwhelming majority, nourishing the hope of ultimate liberation from the camp, guard their conversations with extreme care and "laud to the skies" the Soviet order, the Party, and the Great Stalin. They know that among the prisoners there are some who would seek favor by reporting to the authorities and betraying their comrades. Yet there is an occasional prisoner like Prostoserdov, who had spent ten years in the camps and had just been given an additional ten years to serve. Boasting that he didn't "have to be afraid of anything," he cursed Stalin and the whole Soviet regime and defiantly proclaimed himself a "Social Democrat," a "Menshevik." Apparently freedom of expression emerges in the Soviet Union only among those who have abandoned all hope. Such people are to be found occasionally in the forced-labor camps, and probably nowhere else.

A crowning irony of this system is the propagation in the camps of Party policies and doctrines, apparently as part of the program of reeducation. Here are a few samples of slogans adorning the archways to the

camps: WELCOME TO OUR PLACE! LABOR IN THE SOVIET UNION IS A MATTER
OF GLORY, HONOR, COURAGE, AND HEROISM! THE WAY TO FREEDOM IS
THROUGH HONEST WORK! LONG LIVE THE SECOND FIVE-YEAR PLAN! EVERY-
WHERE AND ALWAYS WE ARE INSPIRED BY OUR GREAT LEADER, COMRADE
STALIN! Today some of these slogans are doubtless gone. But unless the
regime has been profoundly changed, they would be replaced by slogans
dedicated to Khrushchev, "collective leadership," and the Sixth Five-
Year Plan.

The management of a camp has one over-all objective—the fulfillment
or overfulfillment of the program of production assigned to it. To achieve
this objective, manuals to guide the administration have been very carefully prepared. At least one such manual has found its way across the
Soviet border and into the United States. It was issued by the NKVD in
1937 for the "Ukhta-Pechora Labor Camp" above the Arctic Circle. A
great deal of attention is given in the manual to the subject of food. It is
evident that the allotment of food is designed to drive the prisoner to
apply himself most fully to his task. If he should refuse to do this, he
would starve to death. The first article of the "General Regulations" concerns food. It reads in part as follows:

1. Food is supplied to the camp for the following purposes:
    a. to ensure a normal diet for the prisoners:
    b. to stimulate the prisoners to do better work and to favor an increase in
       labor productivity.

The minimum daily allowance for those doing heavy physical labor is
1,292 calories, but this may be raised for surpassing the norm. The American standard recommended for such work is 3,000 calories. In order to
live, therefore, the prisoner must exceed the norm. It is interesting to
note, moreover, that the dogs are not forgotten in the manual. "Duty-
bound search dogs" are allotted 1,184 calories per day. Then there is an
additional allotment for "pregnant and nursing bitches." And there must
be one "duty-bound search dog" for every 1,500 inmates. Provision is
also made for "sentry dogs." The manual fails to indicate the food ration
for a guard or the director of the camp.[32]

The inmates of the camps, like slaves in the galley or on the plantation
since ancient times, compose ballads which express both their frustra-
tions and their yearnings. Here is a sample of the creative art of the prisoners in the well-known camp at Vorkuta under Arctic skies:

Eeeee—Rrroom! Rrroom! Rrroom!

O'er uneven birch-covered trails
        Rrroom! Rrroom! Rrroom!
Three bold daring and desperate men
        Rrroom! Rrroom! Rrroom!

> With all might they are running
> 　　Rrroom! Rrroom! Rrroom!
> To rejoin their beloved ones.
> 　　Rrroom! Rrroom! Rrroom!
>
> To faraway places they sent them
> 　　Rrroom! Rrroom! Rrroom!
> Where life is barren, swampy, and harsh.
> 　　Rrroom! Rrroom! Rrroom!
>
> For a mistake they have long since paid for
> 　　Rrroom! Rrroom! Rrroom!
> They were jailed in an ancient convent.
> 　　Rrroom! Rrroom! Rrroom!
>
> For three days and three nights they were running
> 　　Rrroom! Rrroom! Rrroom!
> When in the distance they heard the alarm.
> 　　Rrroom! Rrroom! Rrroom!
>
> With swift dogs the guards overtook them
> 　　Rrroom! Rrroom! Rrroom!
>
> Farewell, freedom, farewell![33]

V

A basic and essential feature of the Soviet system of political education is the purge. This process is designed not only to correct offenders but also to regiment the thinking of all Soviet citizens. Beginning in a small way and in a limited form in the days of Lenin, it has grown into a powerful institution which is carried by the Communist Party to all lands. Every so-called national Communist Party has engaged in the purge of its own ranks in accordance with the line laid down in Moscow. At this very moment the purge of Stalinists, in the spirit of the Twentieth Congress, is proceeding throughout the world of Bolshevism. And wherever the Party has captured the state in the countries of "peoples' democracy," from Czechoslovakia to China, the purge has become a mighty weapon of government. In its most extreme manifestation, when hardened leaders of the revolution abjectly confess to the committing of acts which they never contemplated, the whole question assumes the character of a "riddle wrapped in a mystery inside an enigma." Ever since the great architects of the Bolshevik revolution, men of undoubted courage and strength of will, appeared in court and made their confessions of error and treason, writers and scholars have sought for some rational explanation of this strange manifestation of Communist totalitarianism.

The purge resides in the very logic of Bolshevism, and perhaps of any modern totalitarian system. It resides in the conception of a small, tightly organized, disciplined, and centralized body of revolutionists dedicated to the overthrow of an old order and the building of a new one. It lies at the heart of Leninism and the Russian revolutionary tradition shaped by such men as Nechaiev and Tkachev. It is found in the life and doctrines of the author of the *Catechism of a Revolutionist*. It is an indispensable arm of a monolithic party or state under which a clearly defined policy must be pursued without wavering or doubt. Under such a system there can be no place for opposition, indifference, or even lack of enthusiasm. The center must continuously purge the Party ranks of enemies, critics, doubters, waverers, careerists, shirkers, and all unstable elements. And in the bitter struggle for power which recurs from time to time, members of the opposition must be liquidated or rendered harmless. Otherwise the monolith is shattered and transformed into the polylith of a free society with its pattern of limited and distributed powers. Brzezinski concludes his scholarly study of the phenomenon with these words: "The purge and totalitarianism have been linked in an indissoluble union, and the Soviet system may rightly be called one of the permanent purge." [34]

In the first days of Bolshevik rule Lenin endeavored to purge the government, the army, the police, the "commanding heights" of the economy, and posts of power in the cultural apparatus of all hostile elements. But it was in the Party that the true purge evolved. Before Stalin consolidated his rule it assumed a moderate form and followed a simple routine. Periodically an effort was made to purge the Party of those elements who were either out of sympathy with Bolshevik practice, program, and doctrine, or who had grown weary or self-seeking through the years of struggle. One of the most thorough and systematic purges was conducted in 1921 in the period of the Kronshtadt rebellion and the launching of the New Economic Policy. Both of these events aroused criticism and opposition in the ranks of the Party. The next purge of this militant character occurred during the entire year of 1929 in connection with the First Five-Year Plan. The author was in the Soviet Union at the time, and he recalls a slogan inscribed on the walls of a factory in Kharkov which expressed well the central theme of the purge then in progress: EVERY GOOD BOLSHEVIK IS WILLING TO CONFESS HIS ERROR. In accordance with the spirit of the slogan, each member was supposedly brought before the bar of both Party and public opinion to give an account of his stewardship. The process was as follows: An examining committee for a particular district was formed of three of the oldest and most active Party members from a nearby region. Then one member after another within the district was called before the committee and required to reveal his social origins, tell the story of his life from birth, confess his errors, and show why his name should be retained on the roll. These meetings were open to the public, and anybody, whether a Party member or an ordinary citizen, was permitted to attend and even participate in the questioning of the member under examination. In some cases, if the victim was widely known, the number of persons in attendance reached into the thousands. There was a current joke that people seeking entertainment would weigh carefully the relative attractions of one of these sessions and the theater, and then decide in favor of the former.

In the twenties the purge was conducted in and by the Party, and about the worst that could happen to the ordinary member was expulsion. Even in the early struggle over Lenin's mantle, the idea that an important Party leader would be done to death or even expelled was repudiated. Any suggestion of this kind reminded the leadership of the terror of the French Revolution—something to be avoided at all costs. In a bitter battle at the Fourteenth Congress of the Party in December, 1925, Zinoviev and Kamenev of the left made a savage attack on Bukharin on the right. Stalin, after relating the efforts of the New Opposition to exclude Trotsky, uttered these words:

> We did not agree with Zinoviev and Kamenev, being fully aware that an amputation policy is full of dangers to the Party, that the amputation method, the method of bleeding—they demanded blood—is dangerous and infectious; to-day, one is amputated, another tomorrow, a third the day after. What will be left of the Party in the end? . . . Now, what do they want to do with Bukharin? They want his blood. That is what Zinoviev demands, in his embittered concluding speech. You demand Bukharin's blood? We will not let you have it; be sure of that.[35]

Yet within a few years Stalin himself first expelled these former leaders and then sent them to the execution chamber. Moreover, he turned to the political police and conducted a purge that embraced not only the Party but also the entire social structure. And treason came to be defined in practice as opposition to the person and the policies of the one and only "Great Leader, Comrade Stalin." Rarely, if ever, in history was such an all-embracing and uninterrupted purge conducted.

This brings the account to the most extraordinary phenomenon in the strange world of Bolshevism—the ritual of confession. The Communists have developed a method of extracting confessions of anything and everything under the sun, according to their desires, from Party leader to simple workman, from artist to scientist, from a cardinal of the Church to an officer in the Army of the United States. The power and the effectiveness of the method were first revealed in all clarity to the outside world in 1936 to 1938, when the close associates of Lenin in the October Revolution stood up in court and admitted criminal acts against the Soviet state. Consider the case of Nikolai Bukharin, a man of exceptional intellectual capacity and stability of character. In the following words, after rejecting every form of defense, he said precisely what the Public Prosecutor demanded:

> I am kneeling before the country, before the Party, before the whole people. The monstrousness of my crimes is immeasurable especially in the new stage of the struggle of the U.S.S.R. May this trial be the last severe lesson, and may the great might of the U.S.S.R. become clear to all. Let it be clear to all that the counterrevolutionary thesis of the national limitedness of the U.S.S.R. has remained suspended in the air like a wretched rag. Everybody perceives the wise leadership of the country that is ensured by Stalin.[36]

Had this man been arrested and tried in public for violent revolutionary activity under the tsars, his behavior could have been easily predicted. In accordance with the Russian revolutionary tradition, he would have taken advantage of his last opportunity on earth to denounce the cruel oppression of the autocracy and to appeal to the people to revolt. Bukharin had proved by his life from the younger years that he was a man of courage.

Why he confessed, and why nearly all confess, remains something of a mystery. Yet much is known. Perhaps the most scholarly and comprehensive account of the entire process is found in a book written by a Russian professor of history and a German scientist who found themselves together in a Soviet prison in the late thirties and agreed to collaborate in the preparation of a serious volume on the purge, should they ever escape. They did escape during the war and they did write the book—*Russian Purge*.[37] In this work, as well as in many other accounts, the general pattern is clearly revealed.

If the individual is not a Party member and incurs the moderate displeasure or arouses the suspicion of the authorities, he may find himself the subject of attack at a meeting of his professional union or at some other gathering. The attack will be launched by a known Party official or spokesman. Thereafter he will see his associates and even his friends rise against him, probably to protect themselves. He becomes an isolated and condemned man. But if the individual is a person of consequence and if he is suspected of "counterrevolutionary activity," a category which, as Vladimir Petrov makes clear, may cover almost anything having the slightest political significance—if he is such a person, he may be awakened at two o'clock in the morning by the political police and hustled off to prison. And it is here that the process for the extraction of confession begins. He is usually held in confinement for several months or even longer, depending on his own response and the seriousness of the alleged offense.

The methods employed for the extraction of confessions are many and diverse. According to Khrushchev, who was in a position to know, false confessions were obtained by means of "cruel and inhuman tortures." In his terrible and terrifying indictment of Stalin at the secret session of the Twentieth Congress on February 24 and 25, he added some details. A person confessed to crimes he had never committed "because of application of physical methods of pressuring him, tortures bringing him to a state of unconsciousness, deprivation of his judgment, taking away of his human dignity." [38] We know, of course, that the testimony of Khrushchev can scarcely be trusted. His record for telling the truth is not without blemish.

In the light of the testimony of those who survived the ordeal, it would appear that the main reliance is placed on the inquisitor or a panel of inquisitors, working in relays. A confession is demanded immediately. If he refuses to comply, he is subjected to the ritual. Sitting on a high stool with a strong electric light bearing on his eyes, he is subjected to a line of uninterrupted questioning which probes his past with utter ruthlessness, involving both relevant and irrelevant matters, but all designed to break his will and shatter his personality. If he proves to be a stubborn case, this process may continue without rest day and night for weeks. Threats against his person and members of his family constitute an important factor. Eventually the poison generated in the body by fatigue and sleeplessness makes a "new man" out of him. He is ready to confess, but he still doesn't know of just what he is supposed to be guilty. If he asks for specific charges, the inquisitor replies that he knows well what he has done. The only assistance offered him is pencil and paper and the instruction to get busy. If he is intelligent, informed, and imaginative, he proceeds to set down a confession to acts he never committed. Ordinarily the first effort is not successful. He is told that he is concealing some very important facts and that he should not endeavor in this fashion to deceive the political police. He is commanded to name his accomplices. So he tries again, and perhaps again and again, until he has made an acceptable confession, one which will serve the Party and the people and which he may even believe himself. Godin, the Russian professor of history, went through this process. He wrote a good but false confession, yet he told the author on one occasion that he still does not know why he was arrested. It is interesting to note that after the long ordeal of inquisition the prisoner accepts with a genuine sense of relief the sentence of a term of years in a forced-labor camp.

If the prisoner is not guilty, and if he is not an intelligent, informed, and imaginative person, he may find himself in real trouble. He may want to escape the inquisitor and confess, but he lacks the creative talent required to prepare a truly good confession—a confession that will meet the specifications of the inquisitor. Consequently, according to Godin, there emerges in the prison a group of specialists who assist the less gifted in the writing of confessions. Such a specialist must be not only intelligent and imaginative but also informed. He must know the history and ideology of the Party and be acquainted with current events. In particular, he must know all the "enemies of socialism." If, for example, he is unacquainted with the "established fact" that the United States supports a comprehensive network of spies in the Soviet Union or that the Trotskyites endeavored to betray the Soviet Motherland to Germany and Japan, he can scarcely be of much assistance in preparing a confession that will stand up against criticism or that will be useful to the Party. The value of real talent in this situation is suggested by the case of Joseph Scholmer, a German physician who was arrested in East Berlin in 1949 and eventually sentenced to forced labor in Vorkuta. Under the questioning of the inquisitor he finally admitted to having been both a British and an American agent. But this was not enough. He was required to name all his associates and finally to give the location and the architectural details of the headquarters of the espionage service. He accommodated the inquisitor by drawing a kind of blueprint of a house he had contemplated but never built. This was precisely what was required.[39]

VI

The educational influence of this entire system of purge, confession, and forced labor on the people, and particularly on the younger generation, must be substantial. The system must be present in the minds of millions almost constantly—free men, women, and children committed to neither prisons nor camps. There is always present the conflict of loyalty to the Party and loyalty to family and friends. The state, of course, is a jealous state and commands that loyalty to the Motherland and the Party be put first. To be sure, Rule No. 17 of the "Rules for School Children" instructs the pupil "to obey his parents." Yet the well-known case of Pavlik Morozov, a young Pioneer, who betrayed his father to the political police, is celebrated throughout the Soviet Union. The exploits of this young "patriot" were immortalized in a poorly written epic poem of five thousand words by Stepan Shchipachev in 1951. The poem was published in a first edition of 100,000 copies by the State Publishing House of Children's Literature of the Ministry of Education of the RSFSR.[40] It consequently falls in the category of children's literature along with "Jack and the Beanstalk" and "Little Bopeep."

Also, a well-known educational institution established in the early years of the Soviet regime, the "children's home," is related to the purges. This institution was organized, in the first instance, to provide a home for hundreds of thousands of children made homeless by "the imperialistic war of 1914–1917, the civil war of 1918–1920, and the calamitous famine which befell the Volga Region."[41] With the liquidation of the kulaks, the purging of the Soviet apparatus, the losses in the Great Patriotic War, the liquidation of minorities, and the general expansion of the camps of forced labor, the number of homeless children must have increased considerably. The lot of a child whose parents disappear in the night can easily be imagined. A personal account of such a tragedy may be found in a book entitled *The Waif* and written by a man whose mother died in his infancy and whose father, an engineer, was arrested in 1929 when the son was six years of age.[42] This little book is a moving report on an important phase of the education of the offender in the Soviet Union.

But the point to be emphasized in these pages is the fact that the treatment of the political dissenter has exerted a molding influence on all persons in Soviet society for decades. Whether the repudiation of the famous Public Prosecutor, Andrei Vyshinsky, and his notorious method of "trial by confession" in April, 1956, will alter radically the Soviet system of jurisprudence remains to be determined. It is deeply rooted in the folkways and mores of Communism. The Bolsheviks have traveled a long distance indeed from their original conception of "corrective labor."

11

THE POLITICAL EDUCATION
OF THE SOLDIER

The political education of the soldier is an essential part of the Soviet program of education. Indeed, it has played a crucial role in the whole history of the regime—in the seizure of power in 1917, in the achievement of victory in the civil struggle, and in the maintenance of Bolshevik rule through years of strain and crisis. It was of course a vital factor in the winning of the Great Patriotic War, although, as we shall see later, the political education of the Soviet soldier revealed certain weaknesses in the months immediately following the Nazi invasion in June, 1941. An effort will be made in these pages to present the main features of the Bolshevik program for the creation of an armed force loyal to the revolution, the Party, and the cause of Marxism-Leninism.

The reason for this concern over the political education of the soldier is not difficult to discern. It is found at the very root of historical materialism. Bolshevism rests on violence and armed force. This is one of its most basic doctrines. Lenin always opposed those who would revise the harsher teachings of Marx in favor of peaceful methods of achieving revolutionary goals. Consequently, he and all true Bolsheviks were and are close students of the organization, capture, and use of military power. In fact, they rank among the most profound students of this question in history. In the last analysis, they argue, he who controls the weapons of warfare, he who holds in his hands the means of taking the lives of his fellows, is the arbiter of history in a given epoch. Shortly after World War II, Molotov modestly proclaimed to the world that "we Bolsheviks are not pacifists." This undoubtedly is the understatement of the twentieth century. Communism stands where it does on the earth today because of its immense power and its readiness to use that power. To be sure, there are other factors, moral, ideological, and organizational, which have

242

played their indispensable roles. But in the absence of their armed forces the Bolsheviks would not now dominate an empire reaching from the Elbe to the Yellow Sea and threaten the future of all free nations.

Karl Marx taught his followers that the moving and creative force in history is the struggle between social classes, the struggle between the oppressed and the oppressor, the struggle in the present age between the proletarian and the capitalist. Because of the eternal laws of social development, this struggle is irreconcilable. It must continue until either the one or the other is victorious, and history is on the side of the proletarian. "The history of all hitherto existing society," proclaims the *Communist Manifesto*, "is the history of class struggles." The adversaries in this struggle from the days of slavery have "stood in constant opposition to one another, carried on an uninterrupted, now hidden, now open fight, a fight that each time ended either in a revolutionary reconstitution of society at large, or in the common ruin of the contending classes." According to the next to the last paragraph of this document, Communists "openly declare that their ends can be attained only by the forcible overthrow of all existing social conditions." The last words of the *Manifesto* constitute the famous battle cry of international revolutionary socialism: "Workingmen of all countries, unite!" All Soviet newspapers and popular journals have carried this battle cry on their mastheads down to the present day.

This absorption in the theme of violent struggle moved Marx and Engels to give much thought to military weapons, science, strategy, and tactics. Of the two leaders Engels seems to have devoted particular attention to the question. In the Marxian tradition he is reputed to have been one of the very foremost students of military affairs of his age, far superior to the army commanders serving the capitalist states in the second half of the nineteenth century. It might be interesting for the reader to know that Marx and Engels grasped at the outset the essential elements of strategy and tactics necessary for the winning of the Civil War in the United States by the Northern armies. The point is well illustrated by the following quotation from a chapter on the war found in a Soviet high school textbook on modern history:

Twice the Southern forces almost captured the capitol, but the Northerners defended themselves and adopted the plan of drawing a ring around the Southerners (the plan of the "strangling encirclements"). Marx and Engels had pointed out that the plan was ill-starred; that for victory it was necessary to penetrate deeply behind the rear of the enemy and cut off the railway trunk lines in the state of Georgia. Marx and Engels calculated that the victory of the North required revolutionary measures and first of all the abolition of slavery. The course of the war compelled the Northerners to adopt this plan advocated by Marx and Engels at the beginning.[1]

The Marxists, like the Bolsheviks, have always placed high on the agenda of their program the abolition of war. The present line of the Russian Communists calling for the union of "all peace-loving peoples" for the prevention of a third world war contains little that is novel. This is an old line, indeed, even though the tune is played with variations to suit time and circumstance. But here again the key to Soviet intentions is found in the class struggle and the institutions of capitalism. According to their outlook on the contemporary world, these institutions are the ultimate source of all conflicts and wars among the nations. Consequently, those who are truly sincere in their desire to abolish war must be equally sincere in their desire to abolish capitalism. A true Bolshevik may express regrets that it is so, but he is helpless before the inexorable laws of history. The only ray of hope in the situation derives from the growing might of the Communist world and the declining strength of capitalism. If the former should become overwhelmingly strong, then the latter might capitulate without resort to violence. Such would seem to be the burden of Khrushchev's relevant remarks in his seven-hour speech at the Twentieth Congress of the Party in February, 1956.

These remarks merit a few additional words. Khrushchev repeats the Marxist dogma that "in the competition between the two systems—the capitalist and the socialist—the socialist system will win." Regarding the final outcome, there is no doubt. But he says this does not mean that "armed interference of socialist countries in the internal affairs of capitalist countries" will be necessary. Also he states that the "change from capitalist to socialist society" need not "be accompanied by civil war under all conditions." It seems that "the use or nonuse of violence" in the process "depends not so much on the proletariat as on the degree of resistance on the part of the exploiters, on the use of force by the class of exploiters." In other words, if the "exploiters" should capitulate of their own volition, resort to violence would be unrealistic and foolish. It is well to remember here that the Bolsheviks never did believe in violence for the sake of violence. They merely contended that, in Khrushchev's words, "ruling classes will not voluntarily surrender power." Of course, if they refuse to do this, they will simply be run over by the laws of historical development. The point should perhaps be made that Lenin never proposed the use of armed force unless he thought he possessed enough of it to make victory probable. On several occasions he retreated before superior strength.

The most interesting feature of Khrushchev's speech was his suggestion that "fundamental changes have occurred in historical conditions" and that consequently the "possibility arises of passing to socialism by means of the parliamentary method." [2] The student of Marxism, however, has heard this before. In addressing the Amsterdam branch of the First International in September, 1872, and after declaring that the workers "must overthrow the old political system," Marx said:

> Of course I must not be supposed to imply that the means to this end will be everywhere the same. We know that special regard must be paid to the institutions, customs, and traditions of various lands; and we do not deny that there are certain countries, such as the United States and England, in which the workers may hope to secure their ends by peaceful means. If I mistake not, Holland belongs to this same category.[3]

Moreover, shortly before his death in 1895, Engels subjected the more extreme positions of his earlier years to sharp criticism. Influenced by changes in the weapons of warfare and the development of democratic political institutions, particularly in Germany, he declared that "our former position has been proved an illusion" by "history," that "universal suffrage" is a "new weapon of the struggle, one of the most powerful," that "revolt of the old type . . . has now in significant measure become obsolete," that the time of "revolutions by unconscious masses led by conscious minorities is past," and that "we revolutionists" are "advancing more surely toward our goals by legal than by illegal methods."[4]

It should be recalled that Marx and Engels developed their original position regarding violent overthrow before the invention of the mitrailleuse and the machine gun. Perhaps Khrushchev has really been influenced by the perspectives revealed to mankind by the atomic and hydrogen bombs. Although he has for the moment adjusted the classical doctrine of Leninism to a reexamination, he has scarcely repudiated the doctrine of violence in the social struggle. Neither has he moved to transform the monolithic power base of Soviet society supported by armed force.

II

Bolshevism has been the most violent offspring of Marxism, unless it be Maoism. It brought together into a single mighty synthesis all of the elements in Marxism which supported the use of armed force in the achievement of its objectives. Also, as the record shows, the Bolsheviks in their morals and methods were the direct heirs of the most extreme and violent elements of the Russian revolutionary tradition. While they repudiated in theory the doctrines and practices of individual assassination advocated by the "Populists," they evolved a corresponding doctrine of their own. They regarded their precursors in the advocacy of violence as ideologically naïve in their thought that a revolution could be achieved by the extermination of a few individuals in positions of power in the state. According to their teachings, the social system itself had to be destroyed. This required the organized use of violence against opposing social classes and political parties, and the employment of terror on a mass scale against the bourgeoisie.

The organized use of violence means an army. Lenin saw clearly the relation between the goal of violent revolution and the means of armed force. As early as 1905, at the time of the unsuccessful revolution of that year, he put the matter quite concisely in these words: "A revolutionary army is necessary because great historical decisions can be decided only by force, and the organization of force in the contemporary struggle is a military organization." [5] In 1920, just as the Bolsheviks were consolidating their rule in Russia, Lenin made a statement before the Second Congress of the Communist International which seems to have presaged the signing of the Warsaw Pact more than a quarter of a century later, which openly coordinated the armed force of the Soviet Union and her satellites. "Everywhere," he said, "we have proletarian armies . . . we can organize them into a unified detachment, into a unified force." If this is done, "then no philosophizing, no guesswork as to what cannot be known and what no one can know, no one can prevent us from accomplishing our task; and this task will be the task of leading on to the victory of the world revolution and the creation of an international proletarian Soviet Republic." [6] In those days, at the dawn of the "dictatorship of the proletariat," Lenin envisaged a great international proletarian army dedicated to the overthrow of world capitalism. The Red Army constituted the pioneer contingent of this world force.

The development of the Bolshevik conception of the soldier of the revolution is deeply rooted in World War I and its aftermath. The theoretical position of the Marxian or Social Democratic parties of Europe was that wars are waged between capitalistic states for the protection and promotion of the economic interests of the bourgeoisie of the nations involved. According to their view, therefore, the proletariat should lend no support to such wars and should do everything possible to oppose and cripple the national effort. When the war began in August, 1914, many thought that the appeal of social class would prove stronger than the appeal of fatherland and that the socialist parties of Germany, Austria-Hungary, France, Italy, and perhaps Britain and Russia would present a united front to the warmakers and paralyze the war effort. Of course, this did not happen. The event proved that for the overwhelming majority of workers and socialists patriotism triumphed over class consciousness and loyalty. Yet there was a small minority on the extreme left which remained true to the socialist faith of the *Communist Manifesto*. Under the leadership of Lenin these remnants of international revolutionary socialism met in Zimmerwald, Switzerland, in September, 1915, and resolved that the war was contrary to the interests of the working class and that socialists should engage in a revolutionary struggle against the main enemy—capitalism. This corresponded to the position taken by Lenin at the very outbreak of hostilities in a famous declaration: "To turn the contemporary imperialistic war into civil war, that is the only correct proletarian solution." It is interesting to note that during the brief period of the Soviet-Nazi Pact, Communists throughout the world proclaimed the same position regarding World War II.

From August, 1914, to March, 1917, Lenin viewed the war and conducted his revolutionary propaganda from the vantage point of Switzerland. Greatly to his surprise, the Russian Imperial regime collapsed and the stage was set for the launching of a civil war which he fondly hoped and believed would spread far beyond the borders of Russia and engulf the whole of Europe in a revolutionary struggle against capitalism. He hastened to Russia in April and assumed the leadership of the Bolshevik faction of the All-Russian Social Democratic Labor Party. It was in this situation that the foundations were laid for the development of the Soviet armed forces. It was in the days of the struggle for power in 1917 that the conception of the political education of the soldier emerged as a basic and unique feature of the Soviet system. If Lenin had failed to grasp or resolve the problem of force, he would not have triumphed in November. And the pattern established by the Bolshevik leader at that time persists in its essential elements down to the present day. In terms of the ideal, the Soviet soldier has always been both technically and ideologically proficient.

Lenin seems to have had two objectives in April, 1917. On the one hand, he sought to turn the "imperialistic war" into a "civil war" in the major European countries involved. He appealed to the workers to overthrow their governments, and to the soldiers, particularly the Germans, to refuse to obey their officers. He also proposed the fraternization of Russian and German soldiers on the front line of battle. On the other hand, he endeavored to demoralize and disintegrate the Imperial army as a fighting force. He advocated the "democratic" doctrine of the election of officers by the soldiers and thus introduced the class struggle into the military world. But most effective of all his maneuvers was his twofold slogan: "End the war" and "All land to the peasants." The first appealed to the great body of the soldiers who had been poorly equipped, inadequately fed, and often badly led. Also they had suffered many humiliating defeats at the hands of the German armies. The second slogan had a powerful appeal to the average soldier because, as Lenin once said, a Russian soldier was a "peasant in uniform." And, proverbially the peasant was hungry for land. Obviously, if the estates were to be divided and distributed among the peasants, he wanted to be on hand when this was to be done. Neither the peasant nor the worker understood Lenin's abstruse speeches on the subjects of Marxism and historical materialism, but they had no difficulty whatsoever in grasping the meaning of peace and land.

As Lenin was busy undermining loyalty and discipline in the Imperial army, he was also active in building a new armed force loyal to the Bolshevik Party and committed to its announced program. This was clearly necessary if he was to achieve the purpose which he outlined immediately on his return to Russia—a purpose which at first was not shared by his Bolshevik comrades. The latter had assumed, in accordance with the teachings of Marx, that it would be contrary to the laws of social development to pass from a simple agrarian economy immediately into a system of socialism. Before the achievement of this ideal state, capitalistic economy and bourgeois government would first have to develop and make their essential contributions to the historical process. The March Revolution had cleared the way for precisely this stage of development. But Lenin rejected the thesis without openly repudiating the Marxian analysis, and proposed the immediate transference of "power into the hands of the proletariat and the poorest strata of the peasantry." This required a second revolution, and a revolution which could not be accomplished without a violent struggle for power.

To prepare for this struggle, the Bolsheviks proceeded to create their own armed force—the Red Guards. These were battalions composed for the most part of industrial workers. The first consideration was unquestioned loyalty to the cause of Lenin. Some of the guards had been soldiers in the Imperial army and had been converted to Bolshevik doctrine. But for the most part they were without military training or experience. Consequently, they had to acquire the special skills and knowledges required for combat. According to an eyewitness in Petrograd in the fateful summer of 1917, V. Bonch-Bruyevich, they drilled daily, "studying all battle exercises, the use of weapons and the military formations, with the greatest eagerness." [7] In July, with their assistance, the Bolsheviks staged an unsuccessful uprising. Lenin and Trotsky went into hiding, but were not dismayed. They continued to build up their military strength and, on November 7, seized power. At the same time, the other political parties, though knowing well the intentions of the Bolsheviks, failed to organize countervailing military power. Lenin's observation in 1905 that "great historical questions can be decided only by force" was proved entirely correct in this instance.

The forcible overthrow of the provisional government and dissolution of the Constituent Assembly were accomplished primarily by the Red Guards. But these successes only plunged the revolutionary state into a bitter and prolonged struggle with opposing Russian forces and Allied armies of intervention. If the Bolshevik regime was to survive, it had to prepare for and engage in military operations on a large scale. The Red

Guards, though adequate for a coup in the capital and the centers of communication, were scarcely equal to such tasks. Consequently, in February of 1918 the Party resolved to build a genuine army and Leon Trotsky was charged with the task—a task of vast dimensions. It is scarcely possible to recruit and train an army without officers, and there were very few officers indeed in the ranks of Bolshevism. As a matter of fact, the officers of the Imperial army, practically the only masters of military science, strategy, and tactics in the country, were by definition "class enemies." Yet their knowledge and techniques were absolutely essential in the process of transforming the Red Guards, common soldiers, and raw recruits into an army. They were used precisely as the "bourgeois intellectuals" were used in other fields.

Trotsky, the architect of the Red Army and certainly a man of genius, gave an account of the process in his work *How the Revolution Armed Itself*. On the basis of a "Marxist analysis of the immediate needs of self-defense," he asserted that the working class, "having disarmed the bourgeoisie, had to arm itself in order to hold its power." The immediate task was "to lead the peasants against the landowners and prevent the kulak democracy from arming the peasants against the workers' state." This required the "creation of a staff of reliable commanding officers." In building the Red Army, he continued, "we used Red Guard detachments, as well as old personnel, peasant headmen and former tsarist generals." [8] The welding of such diverse and conflicting elements into a fighting force required the invention and adoption of various measures. According to Trotsky, "Soviet Russia built her army anew from workers and peasants." Members of the exploiting and disfranchised classes were not admitted. Yet "thousands of former officers were drawn into the building of the army to provide training and correct leadership." At the same time, "new commanding officers, linked by the ties of blood to workers and peasants, were being prepared in military schools." Also the entire process was conducted in close association "with the toiling masses, the local Soviets, the trade unions, the League of Communist Youth, and the organizations of the Communist Party." Political education was assigned a crucial role from the very beginning. "Forward-looking proletarians," wrote Trotsky, "in the capacity of commissars, agitators, and political leaders enlightened the army, united and inspired it in the most difficult hours." The result was an army "surpassing all armies of the past" in its devotion to the "struggle for the welfare of the toilers against their exploiters." [9]

The first consideration in building the Red Army, as noted above, was the inculcation of unquestioned loyalty to the Party and its leadership. This required all the measures mentioned by Trotsky. But there were others. The position of the officer was reduced, because he was least to be trusted. The salute was abolished for the soldier while off duty, along with the old class distinctions. The pompous uniforms of officers, with their broad epaulets, were discarded, to be revived extravagantly, however, a couple of decades later. And standing by the side of the commander was always a political commissar, a member of the Party, endowed with the authority to watch over the former and even to countermand his orders. In case of a conflict between them, the soldiers were instructed to obey the commissar. Trotsky testifies, however, that among the officers trained under the tsar there were "not a few honest and loyal servants who devoted themselves wholeheartedly to the cause of the workers." [10] Many of these features of the Red Army established in the days of the civil struggle persist to the present time.

III

The need for a thorough and comprehensive program for the political education of the soldier was clearly recognized by the Bolsheviks from the moment of the seizure of power. They constituted a tiny minority in a hostile world. There were enemies on every side both within the country and beyond the borders. The entire industrial proletariat in whose name they professed to speak was but a small fraction of the population. To be sure, they called the new government at the outset the "government of workers and peasants." Yet the peasants, in so far as they had political affiliations, belonged for the most part to the rival Socialist Revolutionary Party. The so-called left wing of this party did cooperate with the Bolsheviks in the overthrow of the provisional government and were allotted some representation in the organs of rule. But they were speedily disillusioned by the policies and practices of the Communists. The forced requisitioning of food from the peasants by armed detachments from towns and cities aroused bitter hostility in the villages, in spite of the fact that many peasants had profited from the Bolshevik policy of the redistribution of the land. In the absence of decisive striking power in their hands, the proletariat and its "vanguard," the Party, would have been overwhelmed in a sea of peasants. Trotsky himself once said at first the peasantry "did not want to go into the Red Army." [11] And of course a decade later the forced collectivization of agriculture and the "liquidation of the kulaks as a class" sharpened and intensified the old antagonisms and hatreds. Under these circumstances only a soldier thoroughly imbued with the spirit of Communism could be trusted.

While a strong military force was indispensable to the maintenance of the dictatorship, the Bolsheviks had reason to fear armies. They knew that men with weapons in their hands are dangerous, because they realized that they could never be certain that the weapons would not be pointed in their direction. They knew also that an army can be disintegrated by means of propaganda. Had they not employed precisely this tactic on the Imperial army in their struggle for power? And if they feared an army, they feared able and ambitious military commanders even more. They were close students of history and particularly the history of revolutions. With especial care they had studied the great French Revolution and the counterrevolution led by Napoleon. They consequently feared the emergence of some form of Bonapartism which would establish a military dictatorship and turn back the march toward socialism. Trotsky himself, though not a professional soldier, was sometimes charged with having Bonapartist ambitions. Consequently, the Bolsheviks proceeded to take all possible measures to keep military commanders loyal or at least subservient to the Party. In July, 1937, eight Soviet generals of highest rank, the famous Marshal M. N. Tukhachevsky among them, were found guilty of "espionage and treason to the Fatherland" and executed. The fear of an army commander with a popular following probably accounts for the fact, mentioned in another chapter, that the official history textbook for the tenth grade gives an account of the Great Patriotic War without naming a single general. In this connection the rise of Marshal Zhukov to candidate membership in the Presidium of the Party may have political significance.

To meet and forestall these hazards, the Bolsheviks advanced along four major lines, already suggested in the quotation from Trotsky. First, they guarded with extreme care the process of recruitment to make certain that the Red Army would be composed of the most "stable elements" in the Soviet population. Second, they endeavored to bring into the army a sufficient number of Party members and Young Communists to permeate the army from top to bottom and establish their special pattern of organization at all levels. Third, they organized a system of political education embracing all ranks, from the high command to the common soldier. Fourth, they developed a comprehensive and all-pervading system of police control for the purpose of detecting the slightest manifestation or suggestion of disloyalty to the Party and its leadership. All four of these approaches to the problem are closely interrelated. Each will be developed briefly.

According to Bolshevik doctrine, the industrial worker, the proletarian of Marxist ideology, should make the most reliable soldier of the revolution and consequently should be recruited in the largest possible numbers. It was in their name that the revolutionary struggle was waged, and if there was a privileged class outside the ranks of the Party, they were that class. However, in 1920 they constituted but 14.9 per cent of the Red Army, a higher percentage, to be sure, than they represented in the population as a whole, but not particularly impressive. According to the official reports, the percentage of workers was above the average "in the divisions that had distinguished themselves in action" and below the average "among the deserters." [12] During the years of the First Five-Year Plan the percentage of workers rose rapidly, probably because of the widespread discontent among the peasantry. In 1932 the figure reached 38.7 per cent,[13] far above their representation in the population. However, all through the years the army, of necessity, was recruited largely from peasant youth. This fact raised the importance of the program of political education.

Even the proletariat, however, was never completely trusted by the Bolsheviks. Consequently, they consistently emphasized the importance of bringing into the army as many Party members and Young Communists as possible. In the early years, of course, this contingent constituted but the smallest fraction of the population. The Party leadership, recognizing the weakness inherent in dependence on tsarist officers, moved vigorously to prepare Party members to assume the responsibilities of command in the Red Army. By 1928, 100 per cent of the corps commanders were members of Party or Komsomol, 71.9 per cent of the division commanders, and 53.6 per cent of the regimental commanders.[14] At the Nineteenth Congress of the Party in October, 1952, Marshal Vasilevsky reported that "86.4 per cent of all officers and generals are Communists and Komsomols." [15] While the corresponding percentage among the soldiers is not available, it may be assumed that the number is large enough to provide a network of Party cells and organs completely embracing the armed forces of the Soviet Union. According to the testimony of three former Soviet army officers, these institutions "operate on all levels of the Army and embrace all members and candidates of the Communist Party on active military service. Every Communist serving in the Soviet Armed Forces, from a high-ranking staff officer to a rifleman, is a member of a Party cell. Within the cell the Party members are subject to Party discipline and to their own Party officials, without regard to their military rank." [16] The Party members constitute a powerful educational force in the army and also serve as indispensable aids to the political police in combating disloyalty in all its manifestations.

The systematic organization of a program of political education in the armed forces dates from the creation of the Red Army. The Eighth Congress of the Party in March, 1919, issued a decree ordering the "conversion of the barracks . . . from a center of purely military training into a school of general and political education." [17] The instruction was to be "conducted on the basis of class solidarity and socialist education." The decree was elaborated at a Conference of the Party in December, 1921, in the following words: "Since the army now is composed for the most part of young heads, extremely susceptible to all sorts of influences, the Party is confronted with the urgent task of converting the barracks into a parallel division of the Party schools. The political work of the Red Army must be conducted so that within 2 years of service the Red Army recruit will leave the barracks with knowledge equal to that of graduates of the provincial Party school." [18] This meant that every soldier would be required to study the essentials of Marxism, Bolshevism, Party programs, and contemporary political events at home and abroad, all through the prism of the Party line at the moment. It meant also that every effort should be made to convert the soldier into a qualified propagandist of Communism wherever he might later find himself.

From these simple beginnings there has evolved a comprehensive system of political education and control reaching down to the company level and making heavy demands on the time and energy of the soldier. At the head of this system is the "Main Political Administration of the Armed Forces of the USSR," which is under the immediate direction of the Central Committee of the Party. Organized into many departments, it plays the role and discharges the functions in vastly expanded and perfected form of the political commissar in Trotsky's time. Lenin once observed that "without the military commissar we would not have had the Red Army." One might say with equal force that without the Main Political Administration the Soviet army would not be what it is today. Indeed, the army might have overthrown the regime.

The responsibilities of this institution are many and diverse, although its over-all task is to assure the political loyalty and political understanding of the armed forces. The former Soviet officers, quoted above, summarize its functions as follows:

> It . . . concerns itself with the preparation of educational programs for the military personnel; it directs the training of the political cadres of the Army in its special schools and academies; it edits and publishes the political agitation-propaganda publications; it supervises "cultural enlightenment" activities among the troops; it reports regularly to the Party leadership on the political morale of the troops; and it keeps in touch with the military personnel through its directives and instructions and through its "living links" of instructors, field workers and inspectors. It also supervises the operation of the various subsidiary organizations devoted to the development of political loyalty in the Soviet troops, such as the cinema theaters, rest houses, clubs, mobile libraries, etc.[19]

The program of political education administered by this organization embraces the entire armed forces and all ranks of personnel. It calls for systematic political instruction as an essential part of the daily routine. Obviously, such a program requires a professional staff of instructors running into many tens of thousands. The process of selecting and training these people is a tremendous operation in itself. For this purpose, as the quotation indicates, numerous schools and academies have been established. Naturally, those chosen for training come from the ranks of the Party and the Komsomol or are given additional instruction sufficient for membership. The courses range in length from three to twelve months for members and to not less than two years for young persons without Party experience. Graduation carries the rank of second lieutenant.[20] The curriculum includes such political subjects as the history of the Party, Marxism-Leninism, military history, economic and political geography, and historical materialism.[21] While opinions differ regarding the quality of the political workers, the Party expects them to be "the best of the best." The security of the Soviet state undoubtedly does rest in some measure on their shoulders, for they are engaged not only in the process of political education but also in the task of political supervision of the armed forces. It is reported that the promotion of an officer may be determined by the estimate of the political worker associated with him. This has been an important function of the commissar from the beginning.

The content of the political education of the soldier has varied from time to time in accordance with the interests, tasks, and purposes of the Central Committee. The program for soldiers and noncommissioned officers during the years 1948 to 1950 embraced twenty-four subjects. Among them were the following: the military oath, the safeguarding of state and military secrecy, the constitutions of the Soviet Union and capitalist countries, the Five-Year Plan, the political organs of the army, Soviet patriotism, the superiority of the socialist over the capitalist system, the division of the world into two camps, the relations between officers and men in the Soviet army and in capitalist armies, the condition of the working class in the Soviet Union and in capitalist countries, the preparation of a new war by the imperialists, and speeches by Soviet leaders.[22] Also, current events are followed closely through the newspapers during the periods devoted to political education. Programs of instruction at a higher intellectual and theoretical level are conducted regularly for officers of all ranks. A report by F. F. Kuznetsov at the Nineteenth Congress of the Party in October, 1952, covers this point quite well:

> All forms of Party-political and cultural-educational work are employed in the ideological training of the military personnel. A harmonious system of Marxist-Leninist instruction embracing all officers has been established in the army. Everybody studies, from the commander of a platoon to great military chieftains. Political instruction is conducted among soldiers and sergeants. This form of political education gives good results by cultivating a high political consciousness in our soldiers and sergeants. 135 universities of Marxism-Leninism are functioning in the army; also a wide network of Party schools, political schools and circles.
>
> It is important to note that compared with prewar years a greater propor-

tion of the top personnel is now studying in the system of Party education. During the past two years commanding officers constituted 74 per cent of the graduates from the evening universities of Marxism-Leninism.[23]

The uninitiated might assume that this all-embracing system for the political education of the soldier, particularly since it rests on carefully formulated programs for the political education of the entire younger generation from early childhood, would be sufficient to ensure the loyalty of the armed forces. But such a judgment, though quite reasonable, reflects a gross underestimation of "Bolshevik vigilance." Clearly, the heads of members of the Presidium and the Central Committee must lie uneasily on their pillows. In order to achieve a condition of complete security, they have evolved through the years a system of political police to watch over not only the military personnel but also the political workers and commissars. Parallel with the structure of the Main Political Administration and comprehending all ranks of the armed forces is the Main Administration of Counterintelligence of the Soviet armed forces. This institution is a department of the MVD, or political police of the Soviet Union, operates Special Sections (00) in army, navy, and air force, and works closely with the Political Administration. It is organized openly at the divisional level and has its hierarchy of officers beginning with the rank of "senior lieutenant." In order to reach into all levels and departments of the armed forces, it recruits a secret staff of informers. But since no informer is fully trusted, it charges one informer to report on the words and actions of another.[24] The functions of the Main Administration of Counterintelligence have been thus described by a former Soviet officer:

> The operations of the 00 are designed to combat foreign espionage and to unmask foreign agents; to fight against counterrevolution, sabotage and wrecking; to investigate the political morale of the military personnel; to check the activities of the staff and the troops; to supervise the preparedness and equipment of the troops; and to safeguard military secrecy. In general the 00 performs those functions in the Soviet Army which are carried out by the territorial organs of the MVD throughout the U.S.S.R. The 00 maintains close touch with local MVD agencies, and the two collaborate closely in their operations.[25]

In actual fact the Counterintelligence Administration is primarily responsible for "ensuring state security and the political loyalty of the Army." It assumes that "every soldier and officer is a potential enemy" and pays no regard to "rank and prestige." It even watches over the "activities of the political and Party apparatus of the Army." Its agents attend "all meetings and gatherings of the troops," as well as "lectures, maneuvers, parades, inspections, etc." It has "access to the most secret files" and unlimited power of search.[26] It is supposed to be everywhere and listen in on conversations of the smallest groups. There is a legend that the conversation of even four comrades will be reported almost verbatim to the authorities, and that if any one of them indulges in anti-Soviet jokes or remarks, the individual involved will be known and penalized.[27] All of this suggests an impressive evolution of the political commissar who disciplined the officers from the Imperial army and introduced the "revolutionary order with an 'iron' hand."

The effectiveness of this system of political education and control has long been a subject of controversy. Some former Soviet officers maintain that the effort at indoctrination is stubbornly resisted by the soldiers and that the officers in particular resent the activities of the commissars and police. Yet no Soviet officer has ever become a Napoleon, and the army as a whole or in large part has never rebelled against the regime. The former officers of the tsars did help to build a powerful armed force, even as the "bourgeois specialists" helped to build a powerful industry. At the time Stalin triumphed over Trotsky, the creator of the Red Army, and liquidated his followers, the Red Army remained in its tents. The army even stood by and watched the execution of the major part of its high command and five thousand officers in 1937. Also, although the great majority of the soldiers were rural youth, the regime weathered the storm attending the collectivization of agriculture which brought famine to the village and sent millions of peasants into penal servitude. That there was widespread discontent and hostility in army ranks at the time can scarcely be doubted. Yet the system of control prevailed.

The system, however, failed to stand the supreme test. When the armies of Hitler marched into Russia, widespread dissatisfaction and outright disloyalty became manifest. How many soldiers defected from the Red Army during the early months of the Great Patriotic War and before Hitler could apply his barbarous racial doctrines to the Slavic peoples cannot be known with precision. But sober estimates run as high as two or three million.[28] Certainly history records few instances of such wholesale desertion to the enemy in the heat of battle. In spite of a quarter of a century of intensive and systematic indoctrination in the teachings of Marx and Lenin, many youth of the Soviet Union remained hostile to the Bolshevik regime. Whether the situation will change during the post-Stalin era cannot be foreseen at this time.

IV

One of the major tasks confronting the Bolsheviks in the realm of the armed forces was the creation of a staff of officers loyal to the revolution. At first, as noted above, they were compelled to make use of the professional knowledge of the old officers through a system of hostages and political commissars. Naturally such devices were far from satisfactory. The Bolsheviks distrusted these men because of their links with pre-revolutionary society, and in the course of the civil struggle many defected to the White armies. The basic objective was the creation of a new staff of officers from those elements of the population which supported the Bolshevik cause—"flesh of the flesh and blood of the blood of the proletariat."

To achieve this goal, the program of political education in the Red Army was not enough. The officers trained and experienced in the Imperial army had to be replaced as swiftly as possible. In the light of later developments in the Soviet Union which placed the officers of the armed forces among the privileged groups in society, the early attitude toward the officers and a military caste is revealing. The word "officer" carried such a bad odor, reminiscent of tsarist oppression and class society, that for a time it was abandoned in favor of "military specialist," "instructor," "commander," or "Red commander." [29] These were the days when the principle of equality ruled Bolshevik propaganda, when the compensation of the Party member could not exceed the wage of the "worker at the bench," and when Lenin had his picture taken carrying logs for construction on his "Saturdays."

The organization of schools for the training of officers was launched with the establishing of ten so-called Command Courses by February, 1918. For this purpose the Bolsheviks took over the buildings and instructional staffs of the old military schools and colleges. The first student bodies were drawn from the more revolutionary-minded soldiers in the old army, elements from Red Guard battalions, youth of proletarian social origin, and members and sympathizers of the Party. In the first year industrial workers constituted 37 per cent of the enrollment. Partly because of distrust of the instructors and partly because of a commitment to Bolshevik democracy, the students were given responsibility for enforcing discipline and managing the institution somewhat after the pattern prevailing in ordinary schools of comparable grade. However, under the stern demands of the military struggle, these romantic notions were speedily abandoned.[30] Great emphasis was placed in the Command Courses on political education. It was expected that the young graduates would be steeped in and committed to the teachings of Marx and Lenin. From this simple beginning the Soviet state has developed a network of military schools for training commanders of lower and middle qualifications.

For preparing personnel of "higher military and military-technical" qualification for all branches of the armed forces, the Bolsheviks have developed the military academy. The first such academy was founded in 1918 and came to be called the Academy of the Red Banner in the name of M. F. Frunze, a famous Bolshevik general of the civil-war period. Precise data on the number of these academies, which in terms of level of scholarship are supposed to rank with the universities and higher technical schools, are not available, but White puts the number at eighteen or more. The aim of the academy is to "train, not a narrow specialist, but a commander—a socially conscious person in the full meaning of the word." Officially, it is supposed to be a "breeding place of military-scientific knowledge based on the Marxist method." [31] This means, of course, that the program of instruction includes the standard subjects in the field of Communist ideology and that the graduate is expected to be a good Marxist-Leninist devoted to the building of a Communist society.

In the late thirties the students in these academies were "maintained by the state" and in addition received a "monthly allowance of 50–65 rubles." To gain admittance, the applicant had to be a graduate of the ten-year school and be "recommended by the Party, the Komsomol, and the regional military commissariat." Also he had to "pass an entrance examination in the Russian language, literature, algebra, geometry, trigonometry, physics, geography, and current politics." In the last subject he was required to "show clear knowledge of the current policies of the Party and the Government; basic resolutions of recent Party and Soviet congresses, plenums of the Central Committee of the Party and congresses of the Comintern; also the most important questions in the field of international relations." In addition, he was asked to "write a detailed autobiography," give the "occupation of his parents," and answer these questions: "Did any member of your family ever serve in the White Army? Do any members of your family or any of your friends reside abroad? And do you have contact with them?" A student graduated "with the rank of lieutenant." The object of the institution was to prepare commanders of high qualification "loyal to the proletarian revolution." [32]

Perhaps the most surprising development in the program for the training of officers is the establishment of a system of military and naval boarding schools open to carefully selected boys from an early age. The schools were established by parallel decrees in June and August, 1943. They are of two types, one for the navy and the other for the army and the air force. The first is named the School of Nakhimov, and the second, the School of Suvorov. The decrees called for the organizing of two institutions of the former type and nine of the latter, each with an enrollment of five hundred boys. The pupils enter at the age of ten and pursue a course of seven years, or from ten to seventeen. For each school a preparatory institution may be provided for younger boys. Originally admission was open only to "sons of soldiers of the Red Army or Navy, of partisans of the Patriotic War, of Soviet and Party personnel, and of workers and collective farmers who had perished at the hands of German occupation troops." [33] It is generally believed that the pupils are now recruited from the sons of officers, Party members, and persons holding important positions in the economic, cultural, and governmental apparatus. On graduation they are expected to enter the military and naval academies to become officers in the Soviet armed forces. These schools, according to the decrees, are "modeled after the type of the Cadet Schools" of prerevolutionary Russia. The pupils are "maintained completely by state funds."

The curriculum and regimen of the schools are reputed to be severe. In addition to pursuing the subjects of the ordinary middle school, the boys are subjected to military training under the direction of "experienced officers." Also "military discipline is maintained in the schools, drills are conducted, and emphasis placed on physical culture and sport." They study the elementary aspects of military science and acquire the basic military skills and knowledge in the use of weapons. [34] They wear uniforms and are trained in the spirit appropriate to an officer of the Soviet armed forces. According to one qualified student, "they wear smart blue and scarlet uniforms, are taught ballroom dancing, bowing, heel clicking, and kissing of ladies' hands. They are initiated in the mysteries of the manners of the pre-revolutionary Russian upper class whose successors they are expected to become. Admission to these highly-selective military and naval academies is difficult; in 1950 one youngster out of ten applicants was admitted to the Suvorov Schools." [35] The picture seems rather remote from the Command Courses of 1918 and the egalitarian doctrines of primitive Bolshevism and the teachings of Lenin.

The Suvorov schools were opened with great acclaim on December 1, 1943. Soviet writers were called upon to be present and prepare glorified accounts of their spirit and purpose. Apparently they are housed in the finest buildings and amid attractive surroundings. The boys are made to feel that they are among the elect of their generation. Many of them are sons and grandsons of heroes of the revolution and the Great Patriotic War—"the flower of our future staff of officers." The teachers are carefully selected, and class size is limited to twenty-five boys. They are awakened at the sound of the bugle at 6:30 in the morning. "With lightning speed," wrote the famous author, Valentin Kataev, "the night silence is turned into a morning hum." In "precisely ten minutes," the boys, clothed in "gym shirts," march in company formation "down into the yard." For another ten minutes they "do their setting-up exercises, throw out their hands, stand on tiptoe." Then, as the bugle sounds again, they return to the building and, "stripped to the waist, they wash, scrub, brush their teeth, and dress" in their "dark uniforms with brass buttons and red epaulets." The bugle calls them to the dining room where they "eat with snow-white napkins tucked under their chins." And so they are sum-

moned from class to class, to singing and dancing and fencing, and
finally to bed at ten o'clock in the evening. Kataev gives the following
summation: "The rhythm of the Suvorov school, the clear, military rhythm
completely possesses all of them and carries them from bugle to bugle,
from command to command." With the first day a "new life has begun"
for each of these boys.[36] And here is a verse from one of their songs:

> We are children of Stalin,
> An eagle breed.
>
> And our song we proudly
> And clearly sing
>
> Of heroic feats of arms,
> Of glorious exploits
>
> Achieved by our fine army
> On the battlefield.[37]

The naming of these schools merits a word of comment because it reflects a great change that has come over Soviet historiography since the
early years. Pavel Nakhimov, commander of Russian forces in the Black
Sea during the Crimean War, has come to be rated by Soviet spokesmen
as the greatest naval genius the Russians ever produced. Though he
served one of the most reactionary of the tsars, he has been placed in the
gallery of heroes. Following the Great Patriotic War, his career was portrayed in glorified form in an extravagant moving-picture film in techni-
color.

Alexander Suvorov was a renowned military commander during the
reign of Catherine the Great. From 1773 to 1775 Emilian Pugachev, an
untutored Cossack rebel, led a revolt in the Volga Valley against the
throne, proclaimed the abolition of serfdom, and defeated Catherine's
armies. Finally, she "was so frightened that she recalled General Suvorov
from the Turkish front and put him on the trail of the Cossack leader.
Pugachev was forced from the Volga Plain into the Ural Mountains where
he was betrayed by one of his followers. He was sent to Moscow and
there executed (1775)." [38] M. N. Pokrovskii, dean of Bolshevik historians in the twenties, gives a somewhat different account of the events:
"The peasant revolt was suppressed with barbarous cruelty, whole villages were 'razed' by punitive detachments. And for a long time thereafter near all the villages of the region of the revolt gallows and racks
stood in all their splendour to frighten 'villains and criminals.' " [39] In the
schools of the first decade after the revolution, Pugachev, and not Suvorov, was the hero of Catherine's time. But with the establishment of
Stalin's authority in the writing of history the man who successfully defended the imperial regime against popular revolt in the 1770s received

tribute without stint. The most highly coveted award of honor in the Soviet Union is probably the Order of Suvorov. And the organ of the Soviet Academy of Pedagogical Sciences, at the time of the founding of the School of Suvorov, praised the great commander as "the creator of a new and original system of military education and training." [40] However there are some signs that Suvorov will follow Stalin into the shadows. Perhaps Pokrovski, friend of Lenin, will return to his old place of honor.

There is one more system of schools which should be described at this point in the account—the schools of the political police and intelligence services. Because of the dictatorial nature of the regime, and the institution of the permanent purge, these schools must occupy a crucial position in the Soviet state. The political police number hundreds of thousands and permeate the entire social structure. For the combating of enemies and the holding of power they are absolutely essential. Without them the regime could not stand. And they must be loyal beyond question to either the dictator or the "collective leadership." In the army, as noted above, they are the guardians of the guardians. The program of selection and training must therefore be surpassingly thorough. That such schools exist is known. But their number and mode of operation remain largely a mystery. They constitute one feature of the Soviet system that is as secret as the deliberations of the Presidium of the Central Committee of the Party. However, there is available an account by two former officers of the MVD of the most important of all these schools—The Institute of the Soviet Ministry of Internal Affairs in Moscow.

The Institute is the highest training school of the Ministry of Internal Affairs (MVD). Its basic task is to train "highly qualified specialists for leading posts in the state-security organs." Graduates are assigned to service in both the Soviet Union and foreign countries, "where they organize and conduct intelligence work." They *may* serve as "diplomatic aids" and "military attachés" in Soviet embassies and consulates all over the world. A candidate for admission must be an officer of the MVD, possess the equivalent of a "secondary and military education," be not more than thirty-two years of age, and succeed in a highly competitive examination. He must be a member of the Party in excellent standing and be cleared by the "heads of the counter-intelligence section." The four-year program of instruction embraces the "complete curriculum" of the Frunze Military Academy and an additional year devoted to the special problems of the several branches of the MVD. Besides technical subjects, heavy emphasis is placed on Marxism-Leninism, foreign languages, and the intelligence services of other countries, particularly the United States and Britain. The regimen is severe, with prescribed activities for every hour of the day and an allotment of seven hours for sleep. Because of the privileges associated with the higher posts of the Ministry of Internal Affairs, the competition for admission to the Institute is unusually rigorous.[41]

V

Finally, a word should be said about the role of the system of people's schools in the political education of the soldier. Lenin said over and over again that political and military training should not be separated. The union of these two forms of education for all male children and youth was consummated during the Great Patriotic War and has continued in somewhat softened form down to the present time. As a consequence, Soviet young men enter the armed forces with a measure of military training and orientation.

On October 24, 1942, the Soviet of People's Commissars of the Soviet Union issued a decree "on the military-physical preparation of pupils in grades one to four, and the preinduction preparation of pupils in grades five to ten." In response to the decree military classes were introduced into all schools in the third quarter of the academic year "in accordance with a firm plan and schedule." The children were found "to love and show great interest in these studies." Very quickly "military laboratories, gymnastic halls, and even shooting ranges" were provided for "practically all schools." Military training, however, was by no means the "sole responsibility of the military instructor." The director, every teacher, and each subject was assigned special and general tasks. Physics, mathematics, geography, chemistry, literature, and history were all required to assist in the acquisition by the pupil of the skills, knowledges, and attitudes necessary to the equipment of the "warrior"; and "all teachers must form a united front for the inculcation of discipline" and the appropriate traits of character. Military games were devised and excursions were directed to the achievement of the common objective.[42]

The demand for the "militarization of the school" was called forth by the revelation of certain weaknesses or defects in the educational program during the war. The school had failed to develop in the pupil "strong will, perseverence, stability, and other moral qualities necessary to the future warrior on the battlefield." It had failed to "arm the pupils with sufficient elementary knowledge of military science" and to "train the younger generation in strict discipline." To overcome these defects, it was proposed to reorganize the curriculum in order to give "knowledge of contemporary weapons, grenades, and chemical warfare," to develop physical endurance through "exercise, weight lifting, long marches, and skiing," and to inculcate the moral qualities of "bravery, heroism, stability, iron military discipline, initiative, promptness, and contempt for death." In all of this "moral qualities are paramount," because "they determine the outcome of a war." These qualities are derived most effectively from the "passionate love of the Soviet people for the socialist Motherland," and such love is "indissolubly linked with irreconcilable hatred of the enemy." As the great Russian writer Nekrasov said: "That heart will not learn to love which has grown tired of hating." Moreover, "hatred is the mother of victory." [43] This theme of hatred of the enemy, whether the enemy of the proletariat, of Communism, of the Party, or of the socialist Motherland runs like a flaming thread through the fabric of Communist ideology. Although it reached its most extreme expression in the life and words of Stalin, it did not originate with him. And it probably will not be interred with his bones.

12

THE EDUCATION

OF THE POLITICAL ELITE

The preceding chapters have presented in broad outline the major features and divisions of the Soviet educational program. This account has included the sources and goals of Soviet education and the most important institutions and processes employed. Particular attention has been devoted to the general, political, and moral education of the younger generation, to the transformation of the intellectual class, to the training of specialists, to the political education of the people, to the reeducation of the offender, and to the political education of the soldier. All of this constitutes a gigantic undertaking—an undertaking without rival in the history of education since ancient times. It is the more impressive because all these institutions and processes have been coordinated and directed toward a common objective through a system of monolithic control. The point should be made, moreover, that limitations of space have made necessary the exclusion from the account of many minor agencies for the molding and the informing of the minds of its citizens and future citizens. But there remains one branch of the total program which cannot be omitted, for it may be the most important of all.

The keystone of the great arch of the Soviet educational program is the system of institutions and processes for the education of the political elite—for the education of the members of the Communist Party. While the number of persons immediately involved has always been small in comparison with the number enrolled in the system of people's schools, its significance in the evolution of Soviet society can scarcely be overemphasized. This was particularly true during the first two decades of Bolshevik rule before the maturing of the first postrevolutionary generation. Yet the Party schools of all grades and types have continued to play a central role in the total social and cultural apparatus down to the

264

present. To be sure, some institutions have been abolished or transformed through the years in response to changing conditions, tasks, and conceptions. The death of Stalin has already been followed by the appearance of new programs and institutions. But the general pattern established in the early years persists to this day.

One part of the total program for the education of the political elite merits special consideration. Because of the nature of Bolshevism, the Party has made provision from the beginning for the training of foreign Communist leaders in revolutionary ideology, strategy, and tactics. The fact must not be forgotten that the Russian Bolsheviks have never abandoned the Marxian tradition and conception of a world-wide "proletarian" revolution. In this respect they differ from most of their predecessors in the history of revolution under the tsars. Lenin certainly regarded the seizure of power in 1917 as only the beginning of the "war of classes" which was destined to overthrow the institution of private capitalism in all countries. He even cherished the thought that the great event was not far away and that he himself would live to see the establishment of the "dictatorship of the proletariat" throughout the earth. In this thought he was proved mistaken, but an institution bearing his name has trained many Communist leaders who have played crucial roles in the development and direction of the world Communist movement. Unfortunately, the Soviet state, particularly during these latter years, has guarded with care the operations of these institutions. Nothing is said about them in the pedagogical literature or in the *Large Soviet Encyclopedia*. Consequently, this part of the account will have to be very brief and partial.

II

The importance of the program for the education of the political elite can be understood only in terms of the role of the Party in Soviet society. The nature of that role has been stressed in every chapter of the present volume. The Party is the architect of the revolution, the "vanguard of the working class," the "inspirer and organizer of all of our victories," and the "guiding and directing force" of all departments of Soviet life. It provides the directives for the resolution of "every important organizational or political question." It is the builder and supervisor of all institutions. It is the creator of the State Planning Commission, the author of all five-year plans, the superintendent of construction, and the ultimate manager of enterprise. It defines the domestic and international goals of Communism and formulates the strategy and tactics necessary for their achievement. In the last analysis, it is responsible for both the successes and the failures of Soviet society, although the leadership at a given time usually finds a scapegoat for the failures in Party "deviationists," domestic "counter-revolutionists," or foreign "capitalists." Of course, because of the hierarchical organization of the Party and the concentration of power at the top, it is the Central Committee that is the moving force in all these things. The role of the ordinary Party member will be considered in a subsequent paragraph.

Of special significance is the role of the Party in the general field of education. As we have seen, the Bolsheviks set themselves the goal, not only of transforming society, but also of transforming people, of even changing human nature itself. This meant first of all the eradication of old outlooks and loyalties and the building of new outlooks and loyalties in the individual—the outlooks of Marxism-Leninism and the loyalties required by the Party and the Soviet regime. In order to achieve these purposes as speedily as possible, it was necessary to prepare a contingent of devoted Party workers to serve as a channel for transmitting the ideas and values of Bolshevism to the broad masses of the people. In the early years of the revolutionary order, before the system of people's schools had been fully developed, the very existence of the revolutionary order was at stake. Moreover, many Party members at the time, though of the desired class origin and background, were practically illiterate in both language and politics. In a word, they were quite unable to discharge effectively some of the most elementary and necessary functions of Party membership.

The role of the Party is greatly enhanced by the fact that it is the bearer, the guardian, and the interpreter of a body of sacred doctrine. Only the theocratic states of history have shown a comparable devotion to the teachings of their leaders and prophets. According to Communist dogma, Marxism-Leninism is a priceless heritage. It guided the Bolsheviks to victory in 1917 and to the establishment of the "dictatorship of the proletariat." It provides the theoretical foundations of Soviet society, reveals the universal laws of social development, illuminates all policies and programs, ensures success at home and abroad, points the way from capitalism to socialism, and guarantees the ultimate triumph of Communism throughout the world. It is the "science of the sciences" and "the truth of the toiling masses" of all lands. It is a mighty and invincible weapon in the hands of those who wield it with courage and understanding. Every member of the Party, therefore, must strive unceasingly to master it. But, since Marxism-Leninism is a highly abstract body of doctrine, full of contradictions, what it means as a guide to practice at any given time may not be altogether clear. Consequently, there must be some authority clothed with the power of infallible interpretation. Such an authority is the Central Committee of the Party, and particularly the collective leadership of the Presidium, or even a single powerful individual, as in the case of Stalin. Lenin, of course, went far beyond the original teachings of Marx and Engels in adapting them to a backward peasant land.

The demands on the Party member under such a system are many and exacting. He must strive without surcease to master Marxism-Leninism in both its past and its present. He must be able to give the orthodox answers to all important questions of theory, even though he may not understand them. Also he must be able to repeat the theoretical arguments for the support of all Party policies, even though he may not believe in them. While a member of the ruling elite of Soviet society, he must regard himself as a soldier in the ranks of a political army which is carrying the Soviet Union and all mankind to the promised land of Communism. On entering the Party he surrenders all rival claims to individuality and binds himself to follow the line laid down by the leadership on all questions. He must even be ready to forsake his dearest convictions, except the basic conviction that the Party is right and is leading to victory. He must put loyalty to the Party above all else, even to his own personal detriment. If he is asked to undertake a distant and hazardous assignment, he must not hesitate or equivocate, even though it means separation from family and friends. In the same spirit, he must accept criticism and even demotion, punishment, and public humiliation. He must confess his errors of thought and action, and do so again and again, while promising with enthusiasm to mend his ways. It is a severe discipline, and certainly beyond the powers of many Party members. For one reason or another, millions have collapsed on the way or been thrust over the precipice. But this is the ideal to which he is committed. Obviously, the education of the Communist is both important and arduous. Yet all the time he may be sustained with the dream of eventually being called to serve with the elite of the elite on the Central Committee of the Party.

The mentality bred in a Party member was clearly revealed at the Twentieth Congress of the Party in February, 1956. The new line in both domestic and foreign affairs was presented to the delegates in a long address by Nikita Khrushchev, First Secretary of the Central Committee. Although he announced changes in the current interpretations of Marxism-Leninism, his positions were received with voluble enthusiasm by all present. During the course of his address, as reported in *Pravda*,[1] he was interrupted twenty-five times by "applause," thirty-five times by "prolonged applause," seven times by "tumultuous applause," eleven times by "tumultuous prolonged applause," and four times by "laughter in the hall." As he concluded, he was greeted with "tumultuous prolonged applause, passing into an ovation. All rise." It may be safely assumed that, if he had taken opposing stands on the questions involved, his remarks would have been accorded the same reception. Particularly significant was his suggestion, later elaborated, that Stalin was to be removed from his pedestal and cast into outer darkness as a megalomaniac. Although most of those present had praised the old dictator without restraint for many years and although the members of the tiny ruling circle in the Central Committee had been raised to their positions of power by Stalin, not one person rose to the defense of the man who had dominated the Party for a quarter of a century and whose body lay beside that of Lenin in the red granite mausoleum on the Red Square. And one may assume, despite scattered reports of shock and resistance on the part of members of the younger generation, that the new line will triumph. It will triumph because every member who does not wish to follow Stalin into disgrace and oblivion will accept the discipline of the Party and proceed to persuade his associates in factory, shop, mine, village, army, school, or institute that the decision was eminently wise and just. Only a division at the top could change this.

As pointed out in an early chapter of this volume, the Soviet system is reminiscent of Plato's *Republic*, though in a corrupted form. The ancient philosopher provided for three distinct classes in his ideal state—the husbandmen and craftsmen, the soldiers, and the philosophers. The last would be endowed with all the powers and responsibilities of rule. While the rank-and-file members of the Party could scarcely be placed in the category of Plato's philosophers, the members of the Central Committee, the foremost masters of Marxism-Leninism, would probably qualify. And every Party member is urged by almost every issue of *Partiinaia Zhizn* (*Party Life*) to increase his ideological stature. A leading Bolshevik has said in the spirit, if not in the words, of Plato that "the Central Committee of the Party and its Politburo are the brain, the heart, and the militant staff of the country." [2] To be sure, if Plato, like Lenin, had actually built his republic, he might not have demanded strict orthodoxy of doctrine throughout his society. But who knows? For he seemed to have the right answers to all the questions raised by his interrogators.

In yet another respect a parallel may be drawn between the Soviet state and the *Republic*—the common emphasis on the great power of education. Each of Plato's classes and each of the corresponding classes in Russia was to receive a very special kind of education—an education suited to its function in society. And the Central Committee, like the philosophers, shapes the programs of instruction for all. Plato recognized the difficulties which might arise from opposition on the part of the husbandmen and craftsmen. He found the answer, however, in the fable of the metals and the power of education. "Citizens," he has the spokesman of the *Republic* say, "you are brothers, yet God has framed you differently. Some of you have the power of command, and in the composition of these he has mingled gold, wherefore also they have the greatest honour; others he has made of silver, to be auxiliaries; others again who are to be husbandmen and craftsmen he has composed of brass and iron; and the species will generally be preserved in the children." In order to reconcile the workers to their lot, the spokesman warns: "For an oracle says that when a man of brass or iron guards the State, it will be destroyed." [3] The reconciliation is to be achieved through the processes of nurture and education. The Bolsheviks would, of course, repudiate the hereditarian principle of Plato, but the consequences are not too serious. In fact, Stalin once uttered a few relevant words which the "collective leadership" of the Party would hardly repudiate today. "We, Communists," he said on the occasion of the death of Lenin, "are people of a special stamp. We are cut from a special material. We are those who compose the army of the great proletarian strategist, the army of Lenin." [4] And the pupils in the Soviet school are taught that the Party is composed of our "best people."

A third resemblance between the members of the Central Committee and the philosophers of the *Republic* should be noted. Socrates and his pupils are discussing the subject of lying. All agree that such a practice should not be encouraged. Yet lying is comparable to medicine and has its value. The use of the latter should be left to the physicians, and of the former to the rulers: "Private individuals have no business with them." The question is elaborated as follows:

> Then if any one at all is to have the privilege of lying, the rulers of the State should be the persons; and they, in their dealings either with enemies or with their own citizens, may be allowed to lie for the public good. But nobody else should meddle with anything of the kind; and although the rulers have this privilege, for a private man to lie to them in return is to be deemed a more heinous fault than for the patient or the pupil of a gymnasium not to speak the truth about his own bodily illnesses to the physician or to the trainer, or for a sailor not to tell the captain what is happening about the ship and the rest of the crew, and how things are going with himself or his fellow sailors. . . . If, then, the ruler catches anybody beside himself lying in the State, . . . he will punish him for introducing a practice which is equally subversive and destructive of ship or State.[5]

Materials presented in preceding chapters demonstrate clearly that the Communist leadership takes the same position. The merest glance at the pages of *Pravda* (which means "Truth"), the textbooks in history, or the *Large Soviet Encyclopedia* gives ample evidence for this judgment. To be sure, when the Bolsheviks falsify, they do so in accordance with the moral precepts of the *Catechism of the Revolutionist*. They do so for the "revolutionary cause," for the "working class," for the "people," for our "socialist Motherland," for "Communism," for the overthrow of "capitalism," or for victory over some "enemy of all progressive mankind." In a free society, of course, there is an abundance of falsification, as anyone who follows the course of a political campaign knows. But there is a crucial difference. In a free society, no party or interest possesses a monopoly on falsification, whereas in a totalitarian society the falsification is monolithic. All agencies for the informing and molding of the mind tell precisely the same falsehood. Also in a free society the voice of truth can be heard and falsehood challenged.

III

The Communist Party, as the Bolsheviks have proudly declared from the first days of its existence, is a "party of a new type." It is the instrument for achieving a distant goal, for the building of Communism in a hostile world. The power and efficiency of the instrument are not to be measured in terms of numbers but rather in terms of quality. At the very birth of Bolshevism in 1903, Lenin deliberately antagonized and forced the withdrawal of certain elements in the Russian Social Democratic Labor Party in order to realize his conception of an organization capable of creating his ideal social order. This meant, in the first place, a rigorous selection and testing of members. Lenin insisted that they come in large measure from the revolutionary social class, that they possess the correct ideological orientation, that they be willing to submit to severe discipline, and that they place the interests of the Party above all else. It meant, in the second place, that the members should pursue a thorough and systematic study of Party ideology, policies, programs, strategy, tactics, and methods of work among the people. In addition, they were expected to devote a large share of their leisure time to Party work and thus achieve an integration of theory and practice. Attention will first be directed to the process of selection.

Because of the nature of the Party as the leading and directing force in the revolution and the building of Communism, membership is carefully guarded. However, according to the "rules" introduced by Lenin at the Second Congress of the Russian Social Democratic Labor Party in 1903, anyone was to be considered a member of the Party "who accepts its program, supports the Party financially, and participates personally in one of the Party organizations."[6] By 1913, at the Sixth Congress, the Bolshevik wing of the Party added several features characteristic of Bolshevism. In addition to accepting the Party program, giving financial assistance, and working in a Party organization, the member was required to "submit to all Party decisions." Also he would be admitted only on the "recommendation of two members of the Party." A third important addition was provision for the "expulsion of a member" and the publication of "notice of expelled members" in the Party organs.[7]

At a conference of the Party in 1922 the method of admission and expulsion was further elaborated and standardized. The individual must first be admitted as a candidate, and the "order of admission" is prescribed in terms of social class. The following three categories were established: "(1) workers and Red Army men of worker and peasant origin; (2) peasants and artisans who do not exploit the labor of others; (3) others (office workers, etc.)." Persons of the first and second categories required "recommendations of three Party members of three years' standing." Persons of the third category required recommendations of "five Party members of five years' standing." If an individual was a former member of some other party, he had to be recommended by "five members of five years' standing." An associated provision was designed to encourage the member to think twice before recommending anyone: "Persons recommending members are responsible for them and are subject to penalty, even to expulsion from the Party." After being accepted as a "candidate," the individual was placed on probation for varying periods, according to social category: "Six months for workers and Red Army men of worker and peasant origin, one year for peasants and artisans, and two years for others." Former members of other parties, regardless of class origin, were placed on probation for two years. The aim of the probation requirement was to enable the candidate to "familiarize himself with the programs and tactics of the Party" and to enable the Party "to check the personal qualities of the candidates." For the purpose of providing the desired political education a "school of political literacy" was established.[8] Although these rules of admission were profoundly changed with respect to social categories at the Eighteenth Congress in 1939, they reveal quite clearly the seriousness with which Party membership is regarded in the Soviet state.

The rules express in unequivocal terms the original Bolshevik attitude toward social class. The individual of proletarian stock and of proletarian occupation was favored above all others. Again and again during the 1920s the Party leaders sought to increase the percentage of industrial workers in the membership. The ideal was at least 50 per cent from this class, with the great majority coming directly "from the bench." And they approached very close to their goal in the early thirties. They not only encouraged industrial workers to enter the Party but also purged the ranks of large numbers of persons of the other categories. Next to the proletariat, the Party looked with favor on the poor peasants and dissatisfied elements in the village. The white-collar workers were regarded with suspicion, even though they might be poorly paid office employees. A member of the intelligentsia, on applying for admission, was invariably subjected to a searching interrogation. Persons from the disfranchised classes, such as priests, merchants, and all private employers of labor, were naturally excluded altogether. Under the "dictatorship of the proletariat," the "vanguard of the proletariat" at least should be composed preponderantly of proletarians, even though most of the leaders actually came from other classes.

As the Party proceeded to build the new order, particularly after the launching of the First Five-Year Plan, it quickly discovered that simple proletarian status left something to be desired. The industrialization of the country placed a premium on persons with technical, scientific, and managerial talents. The mechanization of agriculture and the program for the increase of production on the collective farms had a similar impact on life. At the same time, a new Soviet intelligentsia, reared and trained in Soviet institutions, emerged as a strategic element in society. Because of these developments, if the Party was to supply the leadership required, it would have to open its ranks to nonproletarian elements. And this is precisely what it did in 1939. While the practice of requiring recommendations and a probation period was retained, the rules were revised to read: "Workers, peasants, and intellectuals who are conscious, active, and devoted to the cause of Communism may be admitted to Party membership." [9] By this time, according to the official doctrine, socialism had been established and social classes abolished. The three categories mentioned are merely the broad occupational divisions of a classless society. Consequently, the Party has come to be composed increasingly of members of the intelligentsia and persons with secondary or higher education. Some estimates place the figure at close to 50 per cent.[10]

Another great change has been the tremendous increase in the size of the Party. Beginning in 1917 with approximately 240,000 members, according to some estimates, it has grown to a mammoth organization numbering between seven and eight million persons. This growth has been forced upon the leadership by the extension of its operations. Obviously, if the Party was to be the "leading and directing force" in Soviet society, from the great urban factory to the most distant collective farm, from the state publishing house to the local newspaper, from the gold mines of Kolyma to the coal pits of the Ukraine, from the kindergarten to the university, from the theater to the scientific research institute, from the village soviet to the Supreme Soviet of the Union, and from the army to the political police, it would require millions of members. And this numerical growth has greatly increased the task of Party educational institutions, even though all Soviet citizens are now expected to acquire some understanding of the basic principles of Marxism-Leninism in the course of their formal education.

The purging process, already discussed in the chapter on the education of the offender, plays an important role in the selection and education of the Party member. Without question it is a most powerful instrument of control. According to the original idea, expulsion would be applied primarily to careerists who entered the Party for personal advantage or to individuals who grew weary in discharging the heavy obligations of Party membership. But there was from the beginning the provision that the member, regardless of his prior convictions, would accept without reservation any and every decision of the Party and do everything possible to support it. During Lenin's time, under the doctrine of "democratic centralism," decisions were made presumably through a process of full discussion of issues in the Party units, the election of delegates to the Party congress, and free debate by all those present. Under such conditions the member, though defeated on a particular issue, might feel that he had actually participated in the process of decision making and was therefore willing to abide by the result. But with the rise of Stalin to power the entire process was inverted. Delegates were actually picked by the ruling hierarchy and invariably voted unanimously for proposals presented by the Central Committee or the Politburo. In this respect, the Twentieth Congress, in spite of its repudiation of Stalin, followed faithfully the pattern established by the old dictator.

The reports in the press of student revolts at the University of Tiflis immediately after the great reversal reveal with fateful precision the operation of the purging principle. The leader of the Party in the university was ousted in March, 1956, on the grounds that he had been lax in the political indoctrination of the students. As a matter of fact, their actions might suggest that the indoctrination had been extraordinarily successful. Had they not all been taught from their kindergarten days that Stalin was the "great leader and teacher of the Soviet people," the "greatest man of the ages," and so on, ad infinitum? But from the standpoint of Bolshevik theory, a great mistake had been made. The students had not been prepared to accept such a profound change in the Party line. This incident demonstrates clearly the full meaning of Party discipline. It also demonstrates the necessity of changing human nature in accordance with the teachings of Peter Tkachev.

It is at the times of profound shifts in Party policy and leadership that the basic principles of Bolshevism are put to the test. And it is at such times that the purging process plays its greatest role. The individual member who refuses to conform or who is suspected of refusing to conform is thrown out of the Party. If the sentence passed on him falls short of execution or a term of years in a "corrective-labor camp," he nevertheless sees his career in ruins. The expulsion of a person from the Party is and always has been a most serious matter. The fact is made public, placed in his personal record, and can never be fully erased. A former Party member can only be listed among the most unfortunate citizens of Soviet society, particularly if he is expelled for failing to submit to discipline. Clear recognition of this feature of Party membership constitutes a basic element in the selection and the education of the elite. Even when not mentioned, the purge is ever present as a silent teacher of the fundamentals of Bolshevism.

IV

Schools of different types and grades for the political education of members of the Party have been established. But the account should begin perhaps with a brief reference to the Communist organizations for children and youth—the Society of Young Pioneers and the League of Young Communists. These organizations were launched in the early years of the Soviet regime and placed under the close direction and tutelage of the Party. Composed of carefully selected children and youth, their purpose was originally threefold: to carry the doctrines, outlooks, and loyalties of Bolshevism to the younger generation, to serve as the eyes and ears of the Party in all their relationships, and to prepare persons from childhood for Party membership. As noted in an earlier chapter, the one organization today admits children from nine to fourteen years of age, the other youth from fourteen to twenty-six, overlapping by eight years the age of admission to the Party. Since, from the standpoint of training, the League of Young Communists is the more important, attention will be confined to this organization in the present account.

The particular functions and responsibilities of the League have changed during the years. In terms of numbers, it has grown from 22,000 members in 1918 to 2,000,000 in 1928, and to the enormous figure of over 18,000,000 in 1956. Also it has developed from a small militant organization into a great mass organization enrolling a large proportion of Soviet youth. The original expectation, therefore, that members of the League would be admitted into the Party almost automatically has long since been abandoned. It is now both a training institution for Soviet youth and a proving ground for Party membership. Only the best in terms of ideological orientation, discipline, energy, industry, and loyalty are now admitted to Party membership.

The Communist education of these select youth has had two emphases from the beginning, one theoretical and the other practical. These two emphases were clearly stated at the Party Conference in 1921. The Party instructed the League to "give particular attention to the ideological education of the youth" and "at the same time, to give special attention to Communist work among the village youth who have not experienced the harsh conditions of the old tsarist regime and consequently are easily influenced by anti-Soviet agitators." [11] The Party Conference in 1925 followed a similar line, calling for the "intensification in every possible way of the Leninist education of worker and peasant youth entering the organization." It asked that "special attention be given to the development of the Komsomol press," that the Party "assist the Komsomol to train propagandists out of its own membership," and that "appropriate preparatory courses" be organized to train "two thousand Komsomol workers to strengthen the educational apparatus" in the villages. All of this was to be done in strict accordance with the Party line.[12] The active role of the Komsomol in Soviet society was summarized in these few words by the Eighteenth Congress of the Party: "The All-Union Leninist Communist League of Youth assists the Party in all governmental and economic construction. Komsomol organizations must demonstrate through deeds that they are active conductors of Party directives in all spheres of socialist construction and particularly in places where there are no primary Party organizations."[13] And Khrushchev at the Twentieth Congress spoke in similar vein: "Our glorious Leninist Komsomol occupies an important place in the social life of our country. Uniting in its ranks more than 18 million youth, the Komsomol participates actively in economic and cultural construction and assists the Party in the education of the younger generation in the spirit of Communism."[14] Clearly the League is a vital training and testing institution for Party membership.

For the systematic education of Party members and candidates in the theoretical and practical aspects of Communism, the Party has developed a vast network of institutions under the close supervision of the Central Committee. At the base of this network are schools and courses designed to give a degree of "political literacy" to the rank and file. At the top are Communist universities and academies organized to prepare persons of highest qualification for service in important Party posts. The over-all object is to achieve the greatest possible ideological unity of the total membership and to train persons to perform efficiently the many specialized functions demanded by an organization committed immediately to the building of a Communist society in the Soviet Union and ultimately to the triumph of Communism in all countries. In view of the fact that there have been important changes in the character of the institutions since the 1930s, the account will begin with the situation following the revolution.

The need for special schools for the education of Party members was recognized even before the seizure of power. The reason is obvious. Most of the original members were attracted to the Party by propaganda which appealed to the sentiments and the aspirations of the most underprivileged elements of the population—the industrial workers and the poor peasants. Many of them had not even graduated from the four-year primary school and could neither read nor write. In the critical days of July and August, 1917, the Bolshevik wing of the Russian Social Democratic Labor Party resolved in Congress assembled "to create Party schools where workers could learn to give public speeches without assistance" and "to publish popular-scientific materials from which workers could gather materials for speeches on current events and elements of our program." [15] This was just the beginning of a development which was destined to influence the course of history not only in Russia but throughout the world. The importance of this aspect of the Soviet educational program can scarcely be overrated.

The need was dramatized by the first great purge of Party ranks, which began in 1921, the year marked by the famine in the Volga Valley, the general collapse of the economy, the Kronshtadt rebellion, and the launching of the New Economic Policy. It has been estimated that one-third of the members were expelled. In the words of a decree of the Eleventh Congress of the Party in the spring of 1922, "the purge has revealed the extremely low level, on the whole, of the political preparation of the members of the Party," and hence presents the "problem of raising the level of the political-Marxian education of the mass of Party members." This problem could be resolved only "through a system of Party schools, from schools of political literacy to higher Party schools." [16] That the task assigned to these institutions was difficult is indicated by the following characterization of the students: "The persons attending the contemporary Party schools are young and without sufficient practical experience. They are accustomed to think in images and are unfamiliar with abstractions; they lack a firmly established world outlook and possess practically no general educational knowledge and skills; yet they do have a revolutionary mood, great energy, and a desire to learn." [17]

The general structure of the Party educational institutions was developed in the early twenties. It embraced schools at four levels: the school of political literacy, the lower Soviet Party school, the higher Soviet Party school, and the Communist university. But from the very beginning they all had a common aim—"the preparation of *Party members and active workers* of lower or higher qualification" able to "organize and conduct the work of political enlightenment" [18] at their respective levels of competence. While imparting to the student a "given body of theoretical and practical knowledge," the school "must give a Communist education" and "train a professional revolutionist." It must strive "to eradicate petty bourgeois attitudes and cultivate those qualities and traits which are necessary to a Communist-revolutionist." [19] Being a Party member, the graduate of any of these institutions would be assigned to the post where he was most needed, whether in city, town, or village. But wherever he happened to go, he was always commanded to support Party policies and combat all anti-Communist manifestations. He was to regard himself as a warrior for socialism. By 1927 the number of Party schools of all types, but preponderantly schools of political literacy, reached approximately 17,000.[20]

The school of political literacy was the elementary institution in the system of Party education. It was designed to meet the situation that prevailed during the first decade or so following the revolution—a situation marked by an extremely low cultural level throughout the masses of workers and peasants. Every candidate to Party membership was expected to attend and acquire within a few weeks or months the elements of Communist doctrine and policy. The school assumed many forms. Some were conducted in the evenings, and some by correspondence and self-study. Although a basic program of instruction was common to all, adaptations were made for workers and peasants, for men and women, and for different regions and nationalities. The subject matter changed from time to time in response to shifting Party programs, tasks, and problems. Thus the New Economic Policy of 1921, the First Five-Year Plan of 1928, the collectivization of agriculture in the early thirties, and the continuing struggle against "deviations" were all reflected in the shifting courses of instruction. Literally thousands of these schools were organized in the twenties.

The meaning of political literacy at this level is revealed in the subjects listed in the programs of study. The following are illustrative: industry and agriculture in capitalist countries and the Soviet Union; the union of workers and peasants under the Soviet government; the essential elements of the New Economic Policy; the role of state industry in the socialist economy of the Soviet Union; Party policy toward the various classes of peasants; the role of cooperation in building socialism in the village; the main tasks of the Party in the present period; the Party and the soviets in the village; the Komsomol and its work in the village; the Party, the workers, and the peasants in the struggle against the tsarist autocracy; the Party, the workers, and the peasants in the February and October Revolutions; the Party, the workers, and the peasants at the end of the civil war and in the period of the New Economic Policy; the role of the Soviet Union in the present epoch; and the prospects of world revolution.[21] This program was devised for a rural situation. In the programs for Party members working in the cities, more attention was devoted to the proletariat, the concept of dictatorship, the operation of the Party, and the struggle against "opportunism."

The Soviet Party schools of both grades provided a much more extensive and systematic program of training for ambitious and talented Party members, usually of proletarian or poor peasant origin. The period of study was commonly two years in length and the graduates were expected to occupy the lower posts in the Party apparatus. Particular stress was placed on the preparation of agitators and propagandists able to carry the Party line to other members and the people generally. In a word, they were expected to become "professional revolutionists" thoroughly dedicated to the "cause of Lenin." The lower Soviet Party school prepared workers for the smaller administrative divisions, and the higher school for the larger divisions and urban regions. The director of the former had to be a Party member of not less than three years, and of the latter not less than five years.[22] By 1935 there were in the Soviet Union 279 Soviet Party schools with a total student body of 37,600.[23]

The course of study of the Soviet Party school changed from time to time and varied with region, clientele, and purpose. In the course of the years, however, the program became somewhat standardized, and textbooks were prepared for teaching "political literacy" at the higher level. The second edition of such a textbook was published in 1933 with this opening sentence from the publisher: "The present textbook of political literacy is intended for students of city Party schools and for the self-education of candidates, young Party members, sympathizers, and the non-Party worker activist."[24] The chapter headings provide a rather satisfactory definition of the meaning of political literacy at the time: "Two Worlds," "Our Final Goal—Communism," "The All-Union Communist Party (of Bolsheviks)," "The Party in the Struggle for the Industrialization of the USSR," "The Organizational-Economic Strengthening of Collective Farms and State Farms," "Contemporary Tasks of the Proletarian Dictatorship," "The National Question," "The Communist International—the Party of the World Proletarian Revolution," and "Marx-Engels-Lenin-Stalin." The appended bibliography was composed almost wholly of programs of the Communist International and the works of Lenin and Stalin, with some mention of the writings of Marx, Engels, Kaganovich, and Molotov.

The institutions for training Party members of highest qualification in the twenties and thirties were the Communist universities. The first of these institutions, and the most famous, was founded on the initiative of Lenin in 1918 and was named the Sverdlov Communist University. During the following years many others were organized in the major cities of the Soviet Union, reaching the number of seventy-nine in 1936 with a total enrollment of 42,200.[25] The course of study at the outset emphasized Marxism-Leninism and was designed to prepare persons to serve the Party throughout the cultural apparatus. The subjects taught were economics, history, Marxism, Party work, Soviet law, natural science, mathematics, and language. The Communist university gave special attention to preparing students to work in, guide the development of, and mold the system of people's schools. The importance which the Party attached to this institution is shown by the fact that the president was always appointed by the Central Committee of the Party and was held "responsible for the entire work of the university." In the 1930s many of the universities were converted into higher schools for the training of Party specialists for industry and agriculture. According to the *Large Soviet Encyclopedia,* "the Communist Universities during their existence prepared tens of thousands of highly qualified Party and Soviet workers." [26]

The original program for the training of Party members and the elaboration of Party doctrine provided for the establishment of institutes of research. The highest and most important of these institutes was the Marx-Engels Institute founded in 1920. It survives to this day as the Marx-Engels-Lenin Institute and is the leading center for the investigation of the writings and lives of the founding fathers of Marxism and Bolshevism. According to the *Large Soviet Encyclopedia,* its aim is the "collection and preservation of the documentary material of Marx, Engels, Lenin, and Stalin, the preparation for publication (in various languages) of their works and bibliographies, the study of the lives of Marx, Engels, Lenin, and Stalin, and the collection and study of documents on the history of the Party." It is a "department of the Central Committee of the Party." [27] Unquestionably it is the leading center in the world for the study of the origin and early development of Bolshevism. Through the years the authorities have literally searched the libraries and private collections of the earth for every scrap of written material that came from the pens of these prophets and leaders of the "proletarian revolution." Doubtless the Institute has received instructions since the Twentieth Congress to prepare a radical reappraisal of the life and works of I. V. Stalin.

V

Following the Great Patriotic War, the Central Committee proceeded to the reconstruction and improvement of the whole system of Party schools and agencies of propaganda. At the secret meeting of Communist leaders of European countries in Poland in September, 1947, to launch the Cominform, Georgi Malenkov described the measures being undertaken and the reasons therefor. "The tremendous quantitative growth of Party membership and the changes in its composition," he said, "raised with great force the question of the strengthening of the political education of Communists." A large part of the members who had entered the Party during the period of the war had "not yet received the necessary political education." There was consequently a disparity "between the quantitative growth of the Party and the level of political education of members and candidates." The Party, therefore, had already undertaken measures, "not to force a further growth of its ranks, but to

promote the political education of members and candidates." He then
appealed to one of the most basic principles of Bolshevism, a principle
proclaimed by Lenin in 1903: "In the last analysis quality is more important than quantity." [28]

In resolving the problem confronting the Party, Malenkov referred to
the publication within a period of two years of "90 million copies of the
classics of Marxism-Leninism." But without the stimulation and guidance
of qualified Party members these classics would remain on bookshelves
and be unread by rank-and-file Communists. The answer was to be
found in the "education and the reeducation of Party and Soviet personnel directed toward the task of assisting millions of the masses working in the Party and governmental apparatus to master Marxist-Leninist
science, and to arm them with knowledge of the laws of social development, with knowledge of the economy of the country and the economic
policies of the Soviet government, and also with understanding of questions about the international situation and Soviet foreign policy." This,
he said, is "one of the most important tasks on which the Party is now
working." [29] In these statements and in other paragraphs in the same
address Malenkov was reporting to the delegates the essence of a comprehensive decree on Party education issued by the Central Committee
the preceding year. The specific recommendations of this very important
directive guided the reorganization of the system of Party schools during
the postwar period.

The decree was issued on August 2, 1946, and was entitled "On the
Training and Retraining of Leading Party and Soviet Workers." The
reader should note that the decree was the initial step in a Union-wide
campaign to remove from the minds of the Soviet people the friendly
feelings toward the Western democracies which had developed in the
course of the common struggle against Hitler and the Axis powers. It
was followed twelve days later, on the fourteenth of August, by the first
of the five powerful "decrees on ideology," a decree which, as we have
seen, was directed specifically at two literary journals and two literary
writers. Obviously, the Party schools to be established under the decree
of August 2 were designed to support the "decrees on ideology" and the
postwar aggressive foreign policy adopted as the war was drawing to a
close.

The decree criticized severely the quality of the theoretical and practical training being provided at the time by the system of Party education. Under the reorganization proposed, this system would be composed
of institutions of three levels: the Party School, the Higher Party School,
and the Academy of the Social Sciences. The nature and functions of
each of these training agencies will be briefly reported.

The Party School is designed to train and retrain carefully selected members for the lower posts in the Party and governmental apparatus, in the fields of organization, agitation, propaganda, and journalism. The Central Committee called for the establishment of such schools in fifty leading cities of the Union and in other undesignated centers. The course of study is two years in length and the academic year runs from September 1 to August 1. Admission is open to Party members under forty years of age "who, as a rule, are graduates of the middle school and who work as secretaries, departmental managers, propagandists, and instructors in the Party." Candidates for admission must pass an "examination on the Constitution of the USSR, the Russian language, geography . . . and the history of the Party." The curriculum comprises "history of the Party, history of the USSR, general history, political economy, dialectical and historical materialism, logic, international relations, foreign policy of the USSR, economic and political geography of the USSR and foreign countries, Russian language and literature, foundations of Soviet economy and management of its several branches, Party construction, state law and Soviet construction, and journalism." At the end of the two-year course the student must "take a state examination on the history of the Party, political economy, foundations of Soviet economy, and the subject of his or her specialization." The selection of directors, assistant directors, and teaching personnel is conducted under the close supervision of the Central Committee of the Party. The school also offers six-month courses for the retraining of Party and Soviet workers.[30] In his address in September, 1947, Malenkov reported the organization of 177 Party schools with an enrollment of 30,000 students.

The Higher Party School offers a three-year program and prepares workers for the higher posts in the Party and governmental apparatus. It also organizes nine-month courses for retraining "leading Party workers" and "leading Soviet workers." The admission requirements are similar to those of the Party School, but at a somewhat higher level and marked by more severe selection. The curriculum is likewise approximately the same, except for the addition of foreign-language instruction. Seminars are organized for a more profound study of the basic subjects, and "scientific degrees" may be awarded for the defense of dissertations. During the second year the student devotes one and one-half months to "practical work in Party and Soviet organs."[31] In 1947, according to Malenkov, approximately fifteen hundred students were attending the Higher Party School.

The Academy of the Social Sciences crowns the system of Party schools. It was established under the immediate direction of the Central Committee for the purpose of preparing "theoretical workers for the central Party institutions" and for "leading Party committees in republics, regions, and provinces." Also it prepares instructors in the social

sciences for "higher institutions of learning" and theoretical personnel
for "scientific-research institutions and scientific journals." The following
fields of specialization are recognized: "political economy, economics and
politics of foreign countries, theory of the state and law, international law,
history of the USSR, general history, international relations, history of
the Communist Party, dialectical and historical materialism, history of
Russian and Western philosophy, logic and psychology, theory and history of literature, theory and history of art, and foreign languages." The
period of study for regular students is three years. But "for the purpose
of improving the qualifications of instructors of the social sciences in
higher institutions" the Academy offers nine-month retraining courses.
In terms of methods, discipline, examinations, dissertations, and degrees,
it follows generally the pattern of the Soviet university.[32]

As one might expect, the entrance requirements are far more severe
and selective. Admission is limited to members of the Party of not less
than five years' standing who are under forty years of age, who are graduates of a higher school, who have had experience in Party propagandist,
instructional, or literary work, and who have demonstrated talent in
"scientific activity." A candidate for admission must present a certificate
of professional competence, an autobiographical sketch, a copy of his
diploma of graduation from a higher school, a certificate of health, a
credential from his last place of employment, and two photographs. He
then takes a competitive examination, which embraces the subject of his
chosen specialty, the foundations of Marxism-Leninism, and a foreign
language.[33] The graduates of the Academy are supposed to be the cream
of the cream of the scholars of the "science of the sciences." The repudiation of Stalin and the "cult of personality" is placing on the Academy and
all Party schools a responsibility of the first order of magnitude.

At the Twentieth Congress Khrushchev proposed the creation of a
school which would provide for the systematic education of the elite from
early childhood. He began by referring to the "school of aristocratic education" of prerevolutionary society, which under boarding arrangements
educated privileged children "in accordance with the interests of the prop-
erty-owning classes." He then stated that a "socialist country could and
should deal with the question of the education of children in an immeasurably better and more perfect way." The object should be the molding,
"not of an aristocratic caste, deeply hostile to the people, but the builders
of a new society, persons of noble spirit and lofty ideals, of selfless devotion to their people who march in the vanguard of all progressive mankind." At this point the speaker was interrupted by "prolonged applause."

The practical resolution of this task was obvious to Khrushchev. It is
necessary, he said, "to launch the construction of boarding schools (we
must give some thought to the name), located in the suburbs, in resort

places, in wooded areas conducive to good health." These schools should be equipped with "bright and spacious classrooms, fine bedrooms, well-arranged dining rooms, and thoughtfully appointed centers for every kind of extra-curriculum activity which would create all necessary conditions for the all-round physical and spiritual development of a young citizen of the Soviet land." The children would be taught by "carefully selected teachers," by teachers "imbued with the high calling of engineers of the souls of the younger generation." With some exceptions, tuition fees would be charged. In precisely what manner boys and girls are to be chosen for the enjoyment of the special privileges provided by these schools Khrushchev did not make clear. But it may be confidently predicted that there will be no discrimination against the offspring of members of the Communist Party.[34] It may be predicted also that every pupil who travels successfully the full route from the first to the tenth grade is destined to join the privileged ranks of the political elite. The schools are apparently designed to perform the functions in civil life which the schools of Suvorov and Nakhimov perform in the armed forces. Both are designed to train from early childhood a generation of thoroughly disciplined leaders and commanders for Soviet society. It should be added, however, that there are some intimations in the Soviet pedagogical press that the boarding school is regarded as the ultimate form of general education for all Soviet children.

VI

One of the most profound commitments of Bolshevism is its fanatical devotion to the ultimate triumph of Communism in all lands by means of a proletarian revolution led by the "vanguard of the working class"— the Communist Party. A heritage from the doctrines of international revolutionary socialism formulated by Karl Marx, it runs consistently through Bolshevik thought and action from Lenin to Khrushchev. It should be clearly understood that the latter in his address before the Twentieth Congress gave not the slightest intimation that this basic feature of Bolshevism was to be abandoned. The most that he said was that the tactics employed should be adjusted to changing conditions in the Soviet Union, in the world as a whole, and in the several countries of "capitalism."

In March, 1919, Lenin launched the Third International to conduct the battle beyond the borders of the Soviet Union, always under the direction of the center in Moscow. But it is not so well known that at the same time the Bolsheviks established a number of institutions to train Communist leaders of other countries in the ideology, strategy, and tactics of the revolutionary seizure of power. These institutions are patterned in doctrinal emphasis after the Communist schools and universities of the

Soviet Union, with the program of training adjusted to the conditions prevailing in each country involved. For the most part their operations are shrouded in secrecy. They are never mentioned in Soviet pedagogical literature; nor are they described in either edition of the *Large Soviet Encyclopedia*. The Communist University of Sun Yat-sen is known to have existed from an early day. It has been dedicated to the training of Communist leaders, not only for China, but also for Japan, Korea, Viet Nam, and other oriental countries. Some of the heads of state in Communist-controlled lands in Asia today received their revolutionary training in this institution. Higher schools of similar purpose and program, directed toward the Communist education of leaders of the various national minorities of the Soviet Union, were established shortly after the October Revolution. The most famous are the Communist University of the National Minorities of the West and the Communist University for the Toilers of the East—the one has trained Communist leaders for the non-Russian peoples of Western Russia, and the other has performed the same functions for those of Central Asia, Siberia, and the Far East. That both have enrolled students from outside the Soviet Union is known. But the most important of these institutions for persons of American citizenship is the Lenin School, or Lenin University, located in Moscow.

This institution has served the cause of Communism in the nations of Europe and America as the Communist University of Sun Yat-sen has served it in the lands of Asia. Its purpose, program, and mode of operation are known in some measure from reports by former American Communists who attended the school. The fullest account, to the knowledge of the author, was given in 1953 before a congressional committee by Joseph Zack Kornfeder. Mr. Kornfeder joined the American Communist Party at the time of its founding in 1919. After holding responsible positions in the organization he was sent to Moscow in 1927 for further training. There he attended the Lenin School for the full course of three years. After returning to America in the spring of 1930, he gradually became disillusioned and finally left the Party in the fall of 1934. His statement presented to the committee was based on extensive notes which he made while a student at the school.

The students were composed of the "more able members and officials" from Communist parties in the "more developed countries, like Germany, England, France, the United States, and Italy." The program of training was severe, demanding "about 16 hours a day either in classes or reading assigned material pertaining to the subjects." The length of the school year was ten and one-half months, and the remaining weeks were spent in "various Party-controlled government institutions." The curriculum embraced subjects already familiar to the reader: dialectical and historical materialism, Marxian economics and the class struggle, successful and unsuccessful revolutions, imperialism, colonialism and war, and the decay and overthrow of capitalism. Particular attention was given to the Leninist "concept of the Party as a political army," as the militant "vanguard of the working class," and Lenin's whole philosophy of strategy and tactics for the seizure of power. Detailed instruction was given in such subjects as the formation of Communist-front organizations, the penetration and capture of labor unions and other associations, the best way to make use of liberals, intellectuals, clergymen, and discontented elements of the population. Also much emphasis was placed on the organization and conduct of agitation and propaganda.

The role in the revolutionary struggle of disruptive, aggressive, and violent tactics was stressed. The students were taught how to organize and train "assault groups," how to heckle and break up "enemy meetings and demonstrations," how to "terrorize opponents by assaults," how to stage "street brawls," how to punish " 'bad' cops," how to sabotage government and industry, how to organize "incendiarism," and finally how to infiltrate the armed forces and foster the class struggle between officers and soldiers. Since all this pointed toward an armed struggle for power, the course was crowned with a technical study of the military and quasi-military tasks involved in the conduct of a successful insurrection. And if a student was unfamiliar with the weapons of warfare, he was required to master the necessary skills and knowledges. The instructors "for military subjects were all Red Army staff officers of the high command." [35] Clearly, as reported by Kornfeder, the course provided genuine training in the theory, the morals, and the practices of Bolshevism.

13

IN RETROSPECT
AND PROSPECT

A century ago, in 1848, the *Communist Manifesto* issued a challenge to modern capitalism in its famous opening lines: "A specter is haunting Europe—the specter of Communism. All the powers of old Europe have entered into a holy alliance to exorcise this specter." Yet more than two generations were to pass before the appearance of the first revolutionary state bearing the banners of Karl Marx. This happened on November 7, 1917, when the Russian Bolsheviks under the leadership of Lenin, the greatest of the long line of Russian revolutionists, seized power and in the course of a few years took violent possession of almost the entire empire of the tsars—one-sixth of the land surface of the globe.

Today it is no longer a specter that is haunting Europe. On the contrary, it is a thing of flesh and blood, of bone and muscle. It is a thing of great material power fraudulently carrying the Marxian promises of equality, social justice, and economic abundance to all men. But this thing is no longer haunting "old Europe" alone. It is haunting all lands and continents, and even the islands of the sea. It stands by the side and whispers into the ear of every statesman of the free world who refuses to nurture the pleasing illusion that liberty is destined by the nature of man and the laws of the universe to be victorious in the "struggle between two worlds—we and they." It penetrates the consciousness of all men who love freedom and are familiar with the stern realities of the contemporary epoch. It already holds in thrall one-third of the people of the earth and is pressing forward relentlessly to win the whole of mankind to its standard. Its continued triumphs raise in many a thoughtful mind the question of the viability of the free way of life under the strange conditions of the industrial age—the question of the capacity of free men to summon

286

the moral, intellectual, and spiritual resources necessary to sustain the struggle through both prosperity and adversity.

The thing haunting the world today, however, is not communism in the long historical meaning of the word. Nor is it the thing that Marx and his followers contemplated in the nineteenth century as the social order which would follow the overthrow of capitalism by the universal proletarian revolution. It is in fact a new form of state which, while reminiscent of the despotisms of history, possesses its own peculiar qualities and energies. It is a *totalitarian* state, that is, a state which assumes responsibility not only for shaping economic and political institutions and the outward forms of social life but also for molding the arts and the sciences and the inner life of belief and value to achieve a distant social goal. That Lenin and his associates had prevision of the totalitarian ends to which their doctrines, policies, and programs would lead is highly improbable. To employ the analogy developed in an early chapter, the Bolsheviks have indeed carried the peoples of Russia a long way from the starting point in 1917. But it is clear that they have not reached the utopia of their dreams. Although they talk constantly of the perfect state of Communism which lies immediately ahead, the impartial observer must conclude that from the beginning they have sailed in the wrong direction.

Not a few citizens of the free world, including statesmen and political leaders, have been encouraged, since the death and repudiation of Stalin, by the thought that the "collective leadership," having discovered the Soviet ship of state to be off its course, is proceeding to take new bearings from the fixed stars of Leninism. The weakness of such an inference from the known facts is that these are precisely the stars that have furnished guidance since the death of Lenin in 1924. Stalin loved to regard himself as the "continuer of Lenin's work" and invariably sought support from Lenin's words and deeds for everything he said and did. The clear logic of Bolshevism from its birth in 1903 leads inexorably to totalitarianism. Only when Khrushchev and Bulganin proclaim the unqualified abandonment of that logic, the logic inherent in the rule by a tiny oligarchy of self-appointed "morally and intellectually developed" persons, can men of sober mind afford to hope for a significant change in the character of the Soviet state. Nor can they assume the moderation of the outward thrust of Bolshevism.

During the present period, marked by the "meeting at the summit," the Twentieth Congress, and the peregrinations of Khrushchev and Bulganin, Malenkov and Mikoyan, it would be well to cast the eyes backward through Soviet history and learn to draw a distinction between goals and tactics. In the summer of 1917 Lenin did not hesitate to make promises which he did not intend to keep and which he completely repudiated after the seizure of power. Then, as we come down through the years, we see the great reversals of Bolshevik domestic and foreign policies in 1921, 1928, 1935, 1939, 1941, and 1945–1946. In each of these instances many in the free world interpreted the new face which the Bolsheviks presented to mankind as meaning the genuine abandonment of positions and goals formerly held. And in each instance the gullible were proved mistaken by events. In the autumn of 1948, in the middle of the Berlin blockade and the cold war, the present author, after reviewing the record of these reversals and contemplating another, wrote as follows: "No democratic statesman should be fooled by the political maneuvers of the Kremlin. Soviet policies come and go. Soviet tactics change from moment to moment, but Soviet goals are today the same as yesterday, and doubtless will remain the same tomorrow, and perhaps the day after tomorrow." [1] In their visit to Britain in April, 1956, and at other times and places, Khrushchev and Bulganin have smiled and waved their arms, and assured the world that they were prepared to do anything and everything to promote universal peace, except make concessions of substance. There will be rational grounds for hope only when the Bolshevik leaders liberate some of the states and peoples made captive during the war years.

The student of Soviet affairs knows that Bolshevik tactics change in terms of conditions at home and abroad, in terms of minor and major shifts in the factors of power, in terms of the flow and the ebb of the revolutionary tide in the world. They thus changed in the time of Lenin and in the time of Stalin. And they are changing again now under the "collective leadership" of Khrushchev and Bulganin. The fact that Stalin is dead naturally leads many to conclude that the shift is genuine, even though it follows the pattern set by the great dictator and is no more radical than changes which he engineered. As a matter of fact, Stalin was a master of political strategy and tactics in the struggle against his enemies both at home and abroad. His successors have shown themselves to be apt pupils of their old mentor. Stalin could smile and laugh and tell jokes to Churchill and Roosevelt at Teheran and Yalta, so successfully indeed that some American leaders of the highest rank concluded after the war that he was a "prisoner of the Politburo." Now we are told on the authority of Khrushchev that the "members of the Politburo were prisoners of Stalin." And some of our political leaders believe the new version just as readily as they believed the old. Quite probably Stalin is being sacrificed for the "cause of Communism" as he sacrificed so many others in accordance with the principles of Bolshevik morality. The reader should recall that within the month preceding the public appearance in Moscow of Guy Burgess and Donald Maclean, Khrushchev denied to a foreign inquirer any knowledge of the existence or whereabouts of these two British defectors. Would he be any more candid about Soviet goals and tactics? The chances are that he would be inclined rather to obey the canons of truth set forth in the *Catechism of the Revolutionist* and approved by Lenin. Yet it should be recalled that in the course of several speeches in the autumn of 1955, he is reported to have made the following remarks: "If anyone believes that our smiles involve abandonment of the teachings of Marx, Engels and Lenin he deceives himself badly. Those who wait for that must wait until a crayfish learns to whistle. And you know very well when a crayfish whistles." [2]

The shift in tactics in the present instance may prove more stable than earlier shifts because it rests on the solid foundations of power. In the prewar decades the Bolshevik leaders pursued their policy of extending the sway of Communism beyond Soviet borders by the only weapons they possessed—agitation, propaganda, sabotage, organization, conspiracy, espionage, and assassination. Today the situation is profoundly changed. The Soviet state is one of the two great powers of the earth. It has probably the largest and most effective armed force in the world. The fact, however, that the "collective leadership" will probably do everything possible to avoid a full-scale nuclear war does not mean that they will abandon the policy of aggression. They have other weapons. In the course of three decades they have developed a mighty industry. They can consequently employ economic power for the advancement of their purposes; they can export machinery, capital, and military equipment at a price determined by political considerations. Also they have immense stocks of gold, authoritatively estimated at seven billion dollars.[3] This ranks the Soviet Union second to the United States; and the Soviet internal economy has far less need of gold than the American. One can easily imagine how this hoard of gold can be used *peacefully* to disrupt the economies of the world and to advance the cause of Communism. Then there is the great strength created by the swift expansion of Soviet educational institutions, and particularly in the realm of scientific and technological training. Here is a vast resource, nonexistent in the days of Lenin and in most of the days of Stalin, which is being and will be used in arming the outward thrust of Bolshevism. And in order to divert this resource to the capture of foreign peoples, Khrushchev and Bulganin will not be required to present their proposals to a recalcitrant Congress or to the vagaries of public opinion in a free society. For well over a generation the Soviet people of all ages have been conditioned by a monolithic system of mind control to follow the leadership of the Central Committee of the Party. This constitutes a mighty weapon, not only to advance domestic programs, but also to equip Soviet Communism in its struggle for the world. Indeed, Soviet education has been a crucial factor in the incarnation of that mysterious specter which haunted Europe a century ago. With all these weapons in their arsenal, they are doubtless convinced that within a decade or so of "peaceful coexistence" the scales will be tipped decisively in their favor.

II

It is now appropriate to attempt an appraisal of the total Soviet educational program. As pointed out in the first chapter, this program constitutes the most comprehensive and sustained effort in history to reach distant social goals by employing all the agencies and processes of twentieth-century society for molding and training the minds of all the elements composing a vast population of many nations and peoples. The Bolsheviks have actually sought to do what Peter Tkachev and his associates only contemplated. They have endeavored on a scale without precedent to change a whole people and even to alter human nature itself. They have attempted to condition that people from infancy and early childhood to live in and serve a totalitarian state committed to the triumph of its doctrines, values, and institutions in all countries. The more important features of the program have involved the liquidation of illiteracy and cultural backwardness, the mastery of science and technology, indoctrination in the teachings of Marxism-Leninism, the cultivation of Communist morality, and the transformation of the intellectual class. The achievements in each of these spheres of effort will be briefly reviewed. Thereafter a number of fundamental considerations concerning the success of the program, negative and positive, will be examined.

Regarding the liquidation of illiteracy and cultural backwardness, little need be said. With great energy and resourcefulness the Bolsheviks launched from the earliest years a comprehensive program to overcome for the masses of the people the deficiencies in the heritage from the past. It is not necessary to accept at its face value the official Soviet pronouncement that the task of achieving universal literacy had been accomplished by 1939 to recognize that the achievement was truly impressive. Today the Soviet Union undoubtedly stands among the literate nations of the earth. In the realm of the mastery of the elements of knowledge in language, literature, mathematics, science, and history the record is equally worthy of note, with the reservation that the knowledge acquired in relevant fields has been made to conform with the doctrines of Marxism-Leninism. This perversion has been particularly marked in the teaching of history, literature, and some branches of science. One measure of the achievement is expressed in the development of the middle school. It seems quite probable that by the end of the forties universal attendance through seven years was achieved in all but the most remote and backward regions and that by the end of the Sixth Five-Year Plan in 1960 such attendance in the full ten-year middle school or its equivalent will be approached. And the point should be made that since the early thirties Soviet pupils have been subjected to a severe regime of discipline and study. That the quality of instruction varies from place to place and from school to school in terms of teaching staff and physical equipment is recognized by the Soviet authorities.

The advance in the realm of science and technology, in the training of specialists of lower, middle, and higher qualification, has also been phenomenal. The fact has been stressed over and over again in the American press during the past two or three years that Soviet vocational, technical, and higher schools at the present time are graduating each year two or three times as many specialists of the several grades as the corresponding institutions in the United States. It is necessary at this point, however, to utter a caveat. Comparative data on graduation from schools and colleges may not provide a wholly accurate measure of the achievements of the two countries. In general cultural standards the Russians still lag behind the advanced countries of the West. As a consequence, many Soviet youth have had to learn in schools technical skills and knowledges which a child reared in a modern industrial society acquires in the process of growing up amid machines and in a culture marked by a high general level of technical and scientific knowledge and skill. Certainly many American boys and girls achieve a remarkable degree of mastery of the automobile, the tractor, the radio, or the electric washing machine without the assistance of formal tuition. Such a qualification, however, should not lead to complacency. In this realm the Bolsheviks have advanced with unprecedented rapidity, and the total culture is already teaching Soviet children and youth many things that had to be learned in school two or three decades ago. In the not too distant future they may reach the goal announced in the famous slogan of the First Five-Year Plan of "overtaking and surpassing" the United States of America.

The mastery of science merits a special word in this connection. No society in history has ever committed itself so unreservedly in *words* to the mastery and development of mathematics and the natural sciences. Every youngster who completes the full middle school takes ten years of mathematics, six years of geography, six years of biology, five years of physics, four years of chemistry, and one year of astronomy. This is truly a formidable offering. The emphasis continues in the higher schools in the training of specialists, and the program of research in all branches of science is organized according to a comprehensive plan and is supported with unprecedented generosity. In addition, the scientist occupies a highly privileged position in Soviet society. That thought and research in the sciences may be forced into the molds of political conformity and the sacred doctrines of dialectical materialism is true. This has happened dramatically on a number of occasions, most notably in the field of genetics and biology in 1948. Yet the achievements of Soviet scientists in the realm of nuclear physics leave little ground for those who contend that science can develop only in a free society.

The third, and perhaps the most distinctive, feature of Soviet education is the emphasis on indoctrination in the teachings of Marxism-Leninism, and particularly of Leninism—the materialistic world outlook, the laws of social development, the reactionary nature of capitalism, the class struggle, the proletarian revolution, the building of socialism, the guiding role of the Party, and the ultimate victory of Communism throughout the world. This process of indoctrination is supposed to begin in the nursery school and the kindergarten, and even in the family. It is continued systematically and comprehensively from grade to grade to the final year of study in the university. It is carried on through all the agencies of communication and throughout the entire cultural apparatus. While the child, youth, or adult may witness a play or read a book that is more than propaganda, it is rare indeed that he has the opportunity of encountering a vigorous presentation of opposing and contrary doctrines and outlooks. A partial exception to this generalization may be found in the continued publication and distribution of the great classics of prerevolutionary Russian literature. Another is the existence and the teachings of a limited number of churches and religious sects. And another might be the private conversations of friends and relatives. Certainly the full power of the monolithic state supports the policy of indoctrination as far as its writ runs. How successful this total program has been is a question that cannot be answered today, even though speculation has been rife through the years. In view of the history of the Russian people, the task of liquidating religious belief would appear to be far more difficult than the task of liquidating illiteracy.

The cultivation of Communist morality became a basic and persistent feature of Soviet education in the thirties. The component elements of this morality need not be elaborated here. They include the many ancient middle-class virtues which are set down in the code of "Rules for School Children"—industry, promptness, obedience, truthfulness, respect for elders, and so on. Included also are the virtues of a Communist society—attitudes toward labor, public property, and social class. More important from the standpoint of the stability of the regime are patriotism and love of the Motherland, hatred of enemies, loyalty to the Party and its Central Committee, and proletarian internationalism. With the rise of Stalin to power, patriotism became the most basic ingredient of Communist morality. History would seem to demonstrate that the cultivation of this virtue in the young should not be too difficult. The same may be said of the teaching of hatred of enemies. Here enters perhaps the most distinctive and fateful constituent of Communist morality—unquestioned and unquestioning loyalty to the Party and its Central Committee. In Soviet education this virtue is invariably and tightly linked with love of the Motherland. Since the Party always defends and advances the highest and most abiding interests of the Motherland, the one loyalty naturally embraces the other. At the same time, love of the Motherland is in complete harmony with proletarian internationalism, with devotion to the welfare of the toiling masses of all lands, because the Soviet Union is committed through socialism and communism to the abolition of social classes, to the achievement of equal justice among peoples, and to the elimination of war from the earth. Also, by definition the Soviet Union is the most advanced nation in the world and consequently represents "all progressive mankind." These moral outlooks and loyalties are cultivated throughout the educational system and the entire cultural apparatus as thoroughly as the basic doctrines of Marxism-Leninism or the axioms of mathematics.

The transformation of the intellectual class constitutes a final feature of Soviet education, although according to the official view this belongs now to the past. Throughout the first twenty years of the Soviet regime the creation of a new intellectual class, "flesh of the flesh and blood of the blood of the proletariat," was a major concern of the Party. It was pure Leninism. The founder of Bolshevism, with his unwavering commitment to the class struggle, seemed to believe that the success of the revolution would depend in large measure on the training of industrial workers and poor peasants to become teachers, physicians, engineers, managers, artists, writers, and scientists. Only such people could be trusted to serve without reservation the ideals of socialism and communism, the cause of the toiling masses and the proletarian state. That a heroic effort was made in this direction through diverse agencies and processes cannot be denied. However, most students of the question reject the claim that the Soviet intelligentsia today is derived preponderantly from genuine workers and peasants. Soviet data themselves scarcely support the claim. But this does not mean that the desired transformation did not take place in considerable measure. It appears quite likely that in many cases the "bourgeois" inheritance was weakened and even transformed through the processes of education. This would seem to be sound Marxian, materialistic, and environmentalist doctrine. However, the fact should be noted that the Central Committee has never had sufficient confidence in the new "socialist intelligentsia" to give its members complete freedom in their creative work and their political activities.

III

We enter now the fascinating world of speculation about the future. What will be the impact on the regime itself during the coming years of this tremendous program to educate the people? May not the Party, quite unwittingly, have released forces which in time will destroy the foundations as well as the superstructure of the totalitarian state? Are not literacy and education in their very nature liberating factors in history and society? If an individual is taught to think in accordance with the scientific method in physics or astronomy, may he not transfer the method to the social and political realms? Do not the great masses of the Soviet people already resent the dictatorship and long for political liberty, the free-enterprise system, and the Constitution of the United States? Or can human nature be molded to any pattern according to the wishes of the molder? May not the Communist philosophers be correct in their claim that the experience of the Soviet state has demonstrated already the possibility of transforming the nature of man?

There exists, of course, no calculus by which such questions can be answered. The ordinary American, because of his traditional commitment to a free society, seems inclined to answer all of the above questions in terms of the triumph of liberty. He is so accustomed to regard education as a support of free society that he has difficulty in entertaining the thought that education might serve to sustain a despotism, or at least a certain type of despotism. Indeed, he has difficulty in understanding why the Great Russian people, noted for their revolutionary tendencies, did not overthrow the Bolshevik regime long ago. In judging the effectiveness of the Soviet educational program, not in the sphere of the mastery of prescribed knowledge and technical proficiency, but in the realm of the intangibles of moral and spiritual values and convictions, it would be well for us to divest our minds of stereotypes formed in a free society and consider soberly some of the basic realities in the situation. The analysis will begin with a review of the negative considerations, that is, those considerations which would appear to support the thesis that Soviet education is certain to weaken the foundations of the totalitarian state. Later the positive considerations will be examined.

The arguments on the negative side of the question are many and compelling. First, perhaps one should ask, how monolithic is the so-called monolithic control? Although the Party has taken into its hands all agencies and organized processes for the molding of the mind, and although technology has vastly increased the number, sweep, and power of such agencies and processes, the control can never be absolute. Even under the severest dictatorship, some areas of life and experience will be beyond its reach. In the secret places of the heart and the mind of the individual, unsatisfied longings and subversive thoughts are certain to rise. Also, in spite of known penalties and the watchful eyes of the agents of the political police, men will gather together in intimate groups and, with or without the aid of vodka, express opinions unfavorable to the regime. It is well known, for example, that even in the darkest days of Stalin's rule, anti-Soviet and anti-Stalin jokes circulated in the land. It is known too that in a closely supervised school a child, quite innocently, may ask an embarrassing question and start a train of thought in the minds of others which fosters doubt regarding basic "Soviet truths." Also, while the dictatorship has converted literacy into a powerful weapon of mind control, an individual possessing the ability to read may by chance or design turn the leaves of some proscribed book and encounter strange and corrupting ideas. Perhaps more significant is the probable impact on the regime of the trained mind. Although intellectual power gained in one sphere does not automatically transfer to another, the brilliant mind disciplined by the canons of scientific truth will be tempted to apply those canons in the social and political realms, even though he may do so in silence.

Closely related is the survival of the "vestiges of capitalism in the minds of people." As the reader knows, here is one of the perpetual laments of all Soviet leaders and spokesmen from Lenin to Khrushchev. That it should have been a concern of the former is easily understood, since the people at the time had all been reared under the institutions of "capitalism." That they should be critical of authority, competitive in spirit, interested in material gain, hungry for private property, enamored of the profit system, careless in the treatment of public property, and insensitive to the glory and heroism of hard physical labor—all of this was to be expected. But the fact that these anti-Communist traits persist after the passage of forty years and after the rearing of a new generation educated in the spirit of Communist morality is quite a different matter. The fact might even suggest that the "vestiges" are not "survivals" from prerevolutionary times at all but responses to the harsh and highly competitive conditions of life under Soviet institutions. At the very least it demonstrates that in this realm the system of education has not been wholly effective. To be sure, 100 per cent success has never been achieved in any society in terms of its announced purposes. Deviationism and general sinfulness appear to mark the life of man in all ages and societies.

This brings the analysis to one of the most characteristic features of the Soviet regime—the fact of widespread and continuing popular hostility and resistance. To be sure, since the Kronshtadt rebellion in 1921, the number of organized protests has been small. But the existence of dissatisfaction and opposition is clearly revealed in the policies of the regime. The most persuasive and compelling evidence is found in the system of political police, the network of forced-labor camps, and the use of terror as an instrument of rule. Although the number of agents of the Ministry of Internal Affairs and other security administrations is not given in Soviet statistical reports, the ratio of policemen to teachers is probably much higher than in any non-Communist modern state. The same can be said about the ratio of inmates of penal institutions to pupils in schools and colleges. There is sound reason for believing that the peasants as a class have not yet become reconciled to the system of collective agriculture. All this would seem to indicate that the program of indoctrination in Communist ideas, policies, and loyalties has been far from successful. And this judgment must stand until the Soviet regime abandons or greatly reduces its dependence on force and terror. While there has been some relaxation since the death of Stalin, the gates of the forced-labor camps have been opened only for limited categories, and penal servitude for political dissenters remains an essential feature of the system of control. In fact, the ritual of confession to deeds never committed was applied successfully to Beria, Bagirov, and their associates by the present "collective leadership."

A fourth important consideration is the ever-present contradictions between doctrine and the facts of life. Children and youth are taught in school that the Soviet Union is a classless society. Although this is true in the formal Marxian sense that there is no division of the population into owners of the tools of production and employees, the differences in compensation among the occupational categories are as great as they are in contemporary "capitalist" society. They are taught that "there is no other land where men may breathe so freely." Yet the free expression of political opinions and the free organization of political parties are outlawed. They must also have knowledge of the secret police, penal servitude, internal passports, control of travel, and censorship of press, art, and literature. They are taught that the Soviet Union is a friendly family of free and equal peoples. But many youth belonging to the national minorities must know of the liquidation of the Kalmuks, Crimean Tartars, and others and the steady pressure toward the Russification of the non-Russian peoples. They are taught that the general standard of living of the population of the Soviet Union is rising rapidly and is probably now the highest in the world. In actual fact, the standard has not risen markedly since 1928 and life for the masses of the people is hard. These and many other contradictions between doctrine and the facts of life must occasionally raise doubts in the minds of members of the younger generation.

The contradictions are sharpened by promises deferred. Lenin triumphed in his struggle for power by making promises which he did not and could not keep. And so it has been from decade to decade down to the present time. As pointed out in an earlier chapter, this has been one of the continuing realities in the history of the Soviet regime. At the very beginning the peasants were urged to confiscate the estates and redistribute the land with the expectation that the land would be theirs. Then, under the First Five-Year Plan, they were forced to surrender their holdings, yield their livestock, and enter the collective farms. In the early twenties the workers were assured that they would have a strong voice in the management of industry through their councils and unions. They soon found themselves shorn of power and subjected to rigorous regimentation by the state. They were promised that the principle of equality of compensation would rule, only to be informed later that this was "left deviationism" and that each should be paid strictly according to his work. The Great Stalinist Constitution of 1936 guaranteed to all citizens the civil and political rights of a free society. This was followed immediately by a ruthless strengthening of the dictatorship, the swift expansion of the numbers and the powers of the political police, and the conversion of the entire intelligentsia into militant soldiers of Communism. In the late thirties the Soviet people were assured that if war should come the battleground would be the territory of the enemy. The Nazi armies marched 1,200 miles to Stalingrad and laid waste the land. After Stalin's death Malenkov promised to divert productive energies of the economy from heavy and strategic industry to the making of consumers' goods and the raising of the standard of living. Under Khrushchev the policy was reversed and the age of material abundance postponed. These are but a few of the promises deferred or repudiated. Members of the older generation in particular must grow weary of sacrifice.

The great shifts in Party doctrine and policy announced from time to time by the Central Committee must raise many questions in the minds of persons who can read, think, and remember. Again and again in the history of Bolshevism, what was declared true and right yesterday is pronounced false and wrong today. And this is commonly done so suddenly that the shock to thoughtful people must be tremendous. The abandonment of War Communism and the launching of the New Economic Policy in 1921, as we have noted, led to a great purge of the Party. Men glorified in the twenties as associates of Lenin and devoted leaders of the revolution—Trotsky, Zinoviev, Kamenev, Bukharin, Rykov, and Radek—were declared in the early and middle thirties to have been saboteurs, traitors, enemies of the people, and agents of hostile foreign powers. In 1933 the German Social Democrats were labeled "social Fascists" and consigned to the lowest category of the human race. Two years later they became "dependable fighters against fascism," supporters of the rights of the working people, friends of democracy, and trustworthy allies in the struggle for freedom and socialism. At the same time Hitler was a beast and fascism the "enemy of all progressive mankind." But in 1939 Stalin made his pact with Hitler and fascism was declared a matter of political taste. In the twenties America, France, and particularly Britain were imperialistic powers threatening the peace of the world and the cause of the working class. After the rise of Hitler to power, these same states took on the image of the "great democracies of the West." But in 1939 they again became imperialistic powers, only to be transformed into peace-loving peoples after the German invasion of Russia in June, 1941. Yet, following the war all three, and America in particular, assumed the role of the Fascists as "enemies of all progressive mankind," dominated by "ruling circles" bent on loosing a third "blood-letting world war." Of course, the degradation of Stalin is probably the most disturbing reversal in the whole course of the Soviet state. A man who had been worshiped in words for almost a quarter of a century, who had been called "our great leader and teacher," the "coryphaeus of science" and music, the "greatest scholar of the epoch," the "greatest man of all time," and so on—this man now is denounced as a "tyrant, torturer, murderer, megalomaniac, sexual pervert, and falsifier of history." One may well doubt that the Bolshevik conception of truth as that which serves the cause of Communism can endure the strain of such mighty shifts in doctrine. If Soviet citizens do not entertain serious doubts about the entire regime, then the program of education has been fabulously successful and human nature has indeed been transformed in the spirit of Peter Tkachev.

The link with the Russian past is another consideration which merits brief comment. Following the revolution the Bolsheviks adopted the policy of deploring and breaking with that past, of presenting Russian history in the blackest colors, practically unrelieved except for the struggles of rebels and revolutionists against the autocracy. But this was another policy which in about fifteen years was reversed. The record of the Russian people in nearly every sphere of human endeavor was clothed in garments of grandeur. This rewriting of history was done, of course, for the purpose of strengthening loyalty to the regime. As another powerful and all-pervading link with the past, a link which may have consequences of high significance, the Russian language should not be overlooked. We should recall here the insight of the great Russian educator of the "age of the enlightenment," K. D. Ushinsky: The language of a people is the enduring and indestructible reservoir of the thought, the sentiments, the values, and the aspirations of a people. Language is a powerful anchor which inevitably keeps a people moored, so to speak, to its past and perpetuates through the generations its peculiar genius. The fact should not be forgotten, moreover, that the great Russian writers achieved the heights in the realm of literary expression and ethical idealism. And the Bolsheviks have not disowned them. On the contrary, they have attempted to appropriate them as their legitimate ancestors. Even Dostoevsky has recently been restored to the gallery of the immortals. There emerges the spectacle of a totalitarian state paying homage to and publishing the works of Pushkin, Lermontov, Gogol, Turgenev, Chekhov, and Tolstoy, Hertzen, Belinsky, and Chernishevsky. A people permitted to read the great Russian classics must encounter ideas which challenge the moral and ideological foundations of the Soviet state.

A final factor which may be expected to have some impact on the Soviet program of indoctrination is the world beyond the borders of the Soviet Union. If Russia were completely isolated from that world over a long period of time or if all countries were brought under the monolithic control of the Party, the basic teachings of Marxism-Leninism might prevail. The situation then would be comparable to that of a primitive tribe dwelling in some remote and inaccessible region. Under such conditions, protected from contacts with other peoples and cultures, a human community may evolve a system of institutions and values of almost any conceivable pattern. But this is not possible in the Soviet state. Even though the Bolsheviks have sought with varying rigor to isolate their people from the contaminating influence of bourgeois societies, they have by no means been wholly successful. The guarding of the borders, the limitations on travel abroad, the control of movements of foreign visitors, the jamming of radio broadcasts, and the censorship of the mails do not constitute an impenetrable barrier to communication. Many Soviet citizens do visit other lands. Although they are all, even members of trade missions, carefully selected and thoroughly trained to withstand the lures of capitalism, they can scarcely fail to gain some impressions contrary to the teachings of the Soviet textbooks. Also, many citizens of other countries visit the land of Lenin and, despite the guides and interpreters of the Soviet travel agency, may exchange ideas with Russian people. It is possible that contacts between the West and the East will increase in the post-Stalin era. And every issue of a Soviet newspaper tells its readers about the strange world beyond the borders. The fact that the accounts are deliberately and extravagantly falsified may not diminish the degree of curiosity and the desire to know.

IV

As one contemplates all of the foregoing considerations, one is tempted to accept the judgment of those who contend that the Soviet system of indoctrination is certain to fail and that it will be undermined by its own successes. That this is possible cannot be denied, particularly if the question is considered in its total social and historical perspective. Moreover, the Soviet regime is itself highly dynamic and, like everything else on the planet, will in time pass away or be profoundly changed. Yet there are positive considerations which in some measure counter the negative and may prevail through the proximate future.

One of the most important of such considerations is the fact that the regime has already survived the greatest ordeals. The civil war and the famine of the first years of Soviet power constituted such an ordeal. The economy in its more complicated forms almost ceased to function, and cannibalism was actually practiced in the most severely stricken regions. Then, the early five-year plans placed on all the people the heaviest of burdens. The mighty industrial plant of giant factories, mills, mines, canals, railroads, and power stations was built with all speed out of the sacrifices, out of the blood, sweat, and tears of the people. This must have placed a tremendous strain on the loyalties of young and old. And it was linked with the revolt of the peasants against collectivization, the purging of the Party, the police, and the army, the arrest of millions of dissenters, and the spread of the vast network of forced-labor camps. In 1941 came the Great Patriotic War, which shook the Soviet order to its very foundations, brought fire and destruction to the most fertile and productive regions of the Union, visited death on twenty or more millions of men, women, and children, and for more than four years demanded sacrifices almost to the limit of human endurance. It seems probable that the regime will never again be called upon to pass through ordeals of like depth and sweep. The Soviet leaders may well believe that the worst is over. Their major danger lies in the direction of a third world war. But we may be sure that they will avoid such a war until the free world is so reduced in relative strength that the outcome would not be in doubt and the cost in blood and treasure not excessive. That they will strive to continue their advance until the world is won for Communism should be taken for granted. But, as we have already noted, they are hoping and expecting to achieve victory by other and more subtle means. They are certain that time is on their side.

It is true that the masses of the people have not prospered under the Soviet rule. At the same time, they can take pride in spectacular and "grandiose" achievements. While they have endured heavy sacrifices in terms of standards of living, they know that the position of Russia in the world has been greatly enhanced. They know that within an extraordinarily brief historical period their country has become a powerful industrial state, master of advanced science and technology. They can visit cities with giant steel mills and factories—cities which did not exist in 1917. They can ride over highways and traverse canals built since the revolution. They can even take passage on the famous Moscow subway. Also, while they were forced to endure the terrible hardships of the Great Patriotic War, they displayed heroic qualities and emerged victorious. It is well known, moreover, that many a Russian émigré who had fled the revolution and lived twenty years in the West followed the fortunes of the Red Army with the sentiments of a true patriot. The visible achievements in the realms of education and cultural affairs can be made to appear in an equally glorious garb. As a consequence, the Russian citizen is no longer portrayed as an illiterate and uncouth muzhik. And a smile or a frown on the face of Stalin, or a quip from his lips, became front-page news in the press of the world during his later years. The same may be said of Khrushchev or Bulganin today. Children are told from infancy in most extravagant terms of the glories of their country and the heroic accomplishments of the revolution. Every people, of course, has myths by which it lives. The child growing up in the Soviet Union acquires myths which to outsiders may seem to pass the bounds of credibility, but which nevertheless have some foundation in fact. The power of these myths over the mind should not be minimized. And they are associated invariably with the Communist Party and its Central Committee. The Soviet myth was given clear expression in a decree of the Central Committee published in *Pravda* on July 2, 1956. Devoted to an attack on the "cult of personality," it contained the following sentence reminiscent of Peter Tkachev: "In the course of the first five-year plans, as a result of the strenuous and heroic efforts of the people and the Party, an economically backward country has made a gigantic jump in its economic and cultural development."

Another important asset of the regime is its planned program for the promotion of social mobility and the "circulation of the elite." During the first twenty years of the revolution hundreds of thousands from the lowest ranks of society were raised by special institutions and privileges to positions of honor and prestige. With some reservations, this applied to both sexes and all nationalities. From the mid-thirties, after the establishment of the system of people's schools, elaborate provision has been made to encourage the more gifted, industrious, ambitious, and conforming members of the younger generation to excel in their studies and advance to the upper levels of the system. That the policy was tempered from 1940 to 1956 by the introduction of tuition fees for the last three years of the secondary school is true. But now it appears that the Bolshevik leaders are removing all artificial obstacles to the ascent of the educational ladder and are returning to the earlier policy of generous maintenance stipends in higher and professional institutions. By such methods potential leaders and spokesmen of popular discontent are enlisted on the side of the regime. The result is already expressed in the emergence of a new privileged class of bureaucrats, teachers, managers, engineers, physicians, scientists, writers, and artists—the new Soviet intelligentsia. That this may be contrary to the basic tenets of communism would not appear to constitute a serious threat to the social order. On the contrary, it would seem to add a powerful stabilizing factor, even though it might lead to a weakening of the Bolshevik commitment to the promotion of Communist adventures abroad.

It has been said that coming events have a way of casting their shadows before them. In 1953 Malenkov proposed that the productive energies of the economy be diverted in part from the heavy and strategic industries to the production of consumers' goods and the raising of the standards of living of the people. Although this proposal was largely repudiated by Khrushchev, the time will doubtless come in the not distant future when it will be honored in substance. Speculation regarding the consequences of such a move would therefore seem to be appropriate. It might well bring the greatest challenge to free society since the revolution. Even a modest improvement in living conditions would have a pronounced influence on the attitude of the Soviet people toward the regime. One may be sure that meetings would be organized throughout the Union to celebrate the event. Resolutions without number would be passed thanking the Party for its deep concern over the well-being of the people, for its fatherly care of the least of the citizens. These resolutions would be published in *Pravda* and all other newspapers in the land to demonstrate the superiority of socialism in its historic competition with capitalism. And the message would be carried by Communist propagandists to all countries. At the same time, barriers to foreign travelers would be moderated and delegations would arrive by boat, plane, and locomotive to view the wonders of the "First Workers' Republic in History." The fact that the people had no voice in the making of these decisions would probably arouse discontent in only a small minority. The human record would seem to suggest that men do not love political liberty above all else. Indeed, they have been known time and again to barter freedom for security or even the promise of security.

But let us suppose that the Party will relax its controls over the liberties of the people. This has, in fact, already begun in the announced reforms involving the powers of the political police, the system of forced labor, and the attachment of the worker to his job. Reforms of this character can be introduced without changing the basic features of the regime. Also, until the regime itself, with its monolithic Communist Party, is transformed, any concessions to the people can be reversed without notice to meet some actual or alleged crisis. Yet the smallest relaxation of the rigors and terrors of Bolshevik rule would be heralded at home and abroad in precisely the same manner as improvement of living standards. One is reminded of the well-known Jewish folk tale about the farmer with a large family living in a one-room house. To him life is intolerable. So he goes to the rabbi for counsel. The latter advises him to take his chickens into his house and return for further instructions. Though he reports that the chickens have made conditions much worse, he is told to take the goat and later the cow into the one room. By this time he is utterly distraught. So the rabbi tells him first to turn the cow out to pasture, then the goat, and finally the chickens. After all this is done he returns to his spiritual mentor a happy man. He finds that the little cottage is truly a palace and is unable to understand why in the first instance he was so discontented. The reader should recall the gratitude expressed by Soviet citizens in 1954 to the Party and the government for being permitted to discuss the merits of coeducation—"a question of much importance to them, affecting, as it did, the education of their children." The rise and fall of Stalin may serve the purpose of the chickens, the goat, and the cow in the folk tale.

So the harshness, brutality, and cruelty of the Stalin epoch may stabilize and strengthen the Bolshevik state. By repudiating Stalin and some of his methods, the "collective leadership" will win the gratitude of the people and deepen their loyalties. But the essence of Bolshevism will remain—government by the small minority of "morally and intellectually developed" persons holding tightly in their hands the reins of power and leading a docile people into the future. The reader should be reminded here of one of the basic tenets of historical materialism. The system of human slavery constituted an important advance over the alleged tribal communism of primitive man, because it instilled in the members of the human race the discipline and habits of orderly work and thus raised to a higher level the productive energies of the economy. Stalin doubtless left a heritage of social discipline which may survive for years and decades. Even as Khrushchev proclaims the break with the immediate past, he makes use of and relies on this heritage. Indeed, he himself is its living embodiment, profoundly molded by his long years under the close tutelage of the great dictator. The author is reminded of a conversation with a Soviet educator in 1936, a man who had been reared in the liberal and humanistic tradition of Russia. The subject was Stalin and his role in the history of the revolution. The educator was dismayed by the human misery caused by the First Five-Year Plan. Yet he regarded this as a necessary cost of progress and believed that only a man of Stalin's iron will and ruthlessness could have done the job. "Lenin," he said, "could never have done it. He was too soft." And Khrushchev in his denunciation of Stalin spoke at the same time with great pride of the "grandiose" achievements of the era in the realms of economic, social, and cultural construction. He might have added the conquest of the nations of Eastern Europe.

All of this does not mean that the Bolsheviks have changed human nature in accordance with their extravagant claims; but they have probably given that nature a novel expression and altered the course of Russian history. The rigors of the Stalin regime and the entire program of education may have achieved their basic purpose of carrying the Soviet people into a new epoch and a new human image. Moreover, Edmund Burke observed long ago that despotism is "the simplest form of government" and is therefore "infinitely the most general." A good part of the human race prefers to be told what to do by some authority which it regards as wise and benevolent. Such is the conception of the Party which has been sedulously cultivated in the minds of the members of each succeeding generation in the Soviet Union.

The Soviet system of education, in all its departments and forms, is charged not only with the inculcation of loyalties to country and Party but also to the fixing of belief regarding the nature of the universe and the destiny of man. At this point the Bolsheviks were confronted with the gigantic task of transforming the centuries-old religious traditions of the Russian people. The success of that effort is a subject of controversy. Some students are of the opinion that historical religion is perishing and is being replaced with the world view of dialectical materialism. Others maintain that the people continue to cling with great tenacity to the ancient teachings of the churches. The question in dispute can scarcely be resolved unless and until complete freedom of worship is established. In the meantime, we may draw tentatively on the experience of the past, at least in appraising the forms of the Soviet undertaking. In 1877 Charles Sanders Peirce, long before the birth of Bolshevism, described the well-tried method of authority in the "fixing of belief" in human history, and he did so in words which suggest that he had made a careful study of the Soviet Union. Here is the essence of his prescription:

> Let the will of the state act, then, instead of that of the individual. Let an institution be created which shall have for its object to keep correct doctrines before the attention of the people, to reiterate them perpetually, and to teach them to the young; having at the same time power to prevent contrary doctrines from being taught, advocated, or expressed. Let all possible causes of a change of mind be removed from men's apprehensions. Let them be kept ignorant, lest they should learn of some reason to think otherwise than they do. Let their passions be enlisted, so that they may regard private and unusual opinions with hatred and horror. Then, let all men who reject the established belief be terrified into silence. Let the people turn out and tar-and-feather such men, or let inquisitions be made into the manner of thinking of suspected persons, and when they are found guilty of forbidden beliefs, let them be subjected to some signal punishment. When complete agreement could not otherwise be reached, a general massacre of all who have not thought in a certain way has proved a very effective means of settling opinion in a country. If the power to do this be wanting, let a list of opinions be drawn up, to which no man of the least independence of thought can assent, and let the faithful be required to accept all these propositions, in order to segregate them as radically as possible from the influence of the rest of the world.[4]

Peirce states that "this method has from the earliest times, been one of the chief means of upholding correct theological and political doctrines, and of preserving their universal or catholic character." He then proceeds to support his position with evidence from the historical record. The point should be emphasized, moreover, that the Bolsheviks have been able to employ powerful media of mass communication and weapons of coercion which were quite unknown in earlier ages and which Peirce himself saw only in embryo. One should therefore hesitate to appeal to "human nature" and predict certain failure of the Soviet effort. The Bolsheviks may have succeeded already in considerable measure in substituting a materialistic-atheistic for an idealistic-theistic religion, if the terms themselves are not mutually contradictory.

A final positive consideration which should not be overlooked is the appeal of the apocalyptic vision of the coming of Communism—that perfect state of man toward which the whole of human history has been tending from primitive times. As we have seen, the Bolsheviks have appropriated this vision of international revolutionary socialism and have combined it with Soviet patriotism and love of the Motherland, even in some measure with Great Russian messianism. Members of the younger generation have been and are saturated with the doctrine that their country is destined by the laws of social development to lead all mankind to Communism. It is in terms of this great end that the sacrifices of the people and the hardships of the regime are justified. The appeal has solid foundations in the history of the race and in human society. Even primitive peoples have been known to entertain conceptions of tribal grandeur, superiority, and mission. Practically every political or religious faith during the period of its vitality carries an outward thrust and sends its missionaries to the "benighted" members of the human family. That this vision may have lost some of its appeal to the citizens of the Soviet Union, and particularly to the older generation, is possible. The new tactics announced by Khrushchev at the Twentieth Congress and before have been interpreted at the highest level of statesmanship as marking the "mellowing" of Bolshevik international doctrine. In support of this interpretation, analogies are drawn from the courses of the more dynamic religions of history. The time will doubtless come when the outward thrust of Communism will be moderated, if its triumph is postponed indefinitely; but a careful reading of the speeches of the Soviet leaders provides no sufficient reason for believing that the time has actually arrived. The most that can be said is that they expect to attain the old ends by other and more effective means. We should not forget that the extension of Bolshevik power in the world since 1917 is one of the most extraordinary phenomena of history. To expect Communism to retreat at the very pinnacle of success would scarcely seem to be warranted.

Some evidence on the successes and failures of the Soviet effort to mold the minds of the people comes from the testimony of Soviet defectors.

While they are naturally hostile to the regime and tend to minimize the effectiveness of the program of indoctrination, they speak well of the quality of instruction following the great reforms of the early thirties. Some of them compare Russian students favorably with their American contemporaries in seriousness of purpose and devotion to intellectual interests. Nevertheless, there is some support for the thesis that world outlooks and social conceptions have been considerably influenced by life and education under the Bolshevik regime. George Fischer in his comprehensive study of the ideology of the elements of the "Vlasov Movement," comprising the massive defection of soldiers during the war, comes to this conclusion. He declares that the "Soviet heritage" has left "a large element of authoritarianism in the ideology of the opposition" to the Communist state. These men generally rejected as wrong and mistaken the idea of a government of limited and defined powers and an economy based on the institution of private property in the means of production. Indeed, to them any "political organization other than statism" seemed "well-nigh inconceivable." Fischer concludes his study with the statement that "the ideology of opposition reflects almost completely the values and experiences of Soviet life." [5] The defectors seemed to favor a system much like the Bolshevik but without the terrors and cruelties of the Stalin era. In view of what we know about the whole conditioning process in the life of man, this judgment is in no way surprising.

Yet there exists a bit of testimony to the effectiveness of the Soviet system of indoctrination and propaganda that is surprising indeed. According to *The New York Times* of June 20, 1956, "an Army intelligence expert estimated . . . that one-third of all American prisoners in the Korean war cooperated or collaborated with their Communist captors 'in some degree or other.'" These young men had all been reared under the free institutions of America, and the period of indoctrination was only a few months.

V

In conclusion we may return to the thesis of the opening chapter. Education is one of the most fundamental realities of the Soviet system. The Bolshevik leaders from the first have regarded organized education with utter seriousness, far surpassing in this respect the leaders of any free society on the earth. They give quite as close attention to the method and content of the program for shaping the minds of both young and old as they do to the equipment of their armed forces or the administration of their economy, because they regard education as a "mighty weapon" in the "cause of Communism." Without their vast system of educational agencies the Bolsheviks would not be standing in the position of power which they occupy in the world today. Without it their sensational shift in tactics would not have been contemplated.

Through the years the American people have given little thought to the Soviet program of education. They have supported many studies of the Soviet economy, the Soviet government, the Soviet armed forces, the Soviet ideology, the Soviet literature and art, but they have shown little interest in the means by which the people are being molded in the image set by the dictatorship. This means that they regard Soviet education no more seriously than they regard their own. Education is of course good in some vague way for the individual and for American democracy, but scarcely involves the destiny of the Republic. They have been rudely awakened from their complacency during the past two or three years by the discovery that the Soviet schools are graduating each year more technicians and engineers than the American. The challenge here can easily be understood in terms of our national pride in technical progress and our recognition of the relation between science, technology, and power. Yet the achievements of Soviet technical education would have comparatively little significance for America and the rest of the world if they were not linked with the extraordinary program of general, political, and moral education of every category of the population. And one of the greatest of mistakes would be to minimize Soviet accomplishments in any sphere of educational endeavor and find comfort in the illusion that the Soviet schools are undermining the Bolshevik regime. The present volume will have achieved its primary purpose if it provokes the reader to think more profoundly regarding the nature, the power, and the resources of Soviet and world Communism.

VI

The author originally contemplated the preparation of a concluding section devoted to the task of meeting the challenge of Soviet philosophy and practice to American education. That the challenge is there cannot be doubted. It is present in every chapter. It needs to be answered in terms of an education as appropriate to a free society as the Soviet program is suited to the values and purposes of a totalitarian state. Unfortunately, our American education falls wide of the mark at this critical juncture in history. But to deal with the subject adequately would require another volume. This task must be left for the future.

APPENDIX

In the late spring of 1956 the Government Statistical Publishing House in Moscow published a statistical manual (*Narodnoie Khozyaistvo SSSR*)—the first such volume to appear since 1939 and the best since 1936. Although all Soviet statistics must be viewed with a degree of skepticism, this publication is invaluable to the student of Soviet affairs. Unfortunately, it reached the author's desk after the manuscript had gone to press. Consequently, it was deemed desirable to include in this appendix the more relevant data on Soviet education contained in the manual—data which are probably more reliable than some of the materials presented in the present work. The fact should not be forgotten that in the Soviet Union statistics are expected to serve the "cause of Communism."

Table I

Number of pupils and teachers in thousands in schools of three levels in the specified years

	1914–15	1927–28	1940–41	1950–51	1955–56
Pupils in schools of general education	7,896	11,589	35,528	34,752	30,070
Pupils in schools of middle vocational education including correspondence	36	189	975	1,298	1,961
Pupils in schools of higher and professional education including correspondence	112	169	812	1,247	1,867
Teachers in all schools	231	341	1,237	1,475	1,733

Table II

Total output of specialists of schools of middle and higher qualification in thousands in the specified years

	First Five-Year Plan 1929–32	Second Five-Year Plan 1933–37	Third Five-Year Plan 1938–40	The War Years 1941–45	Fourth Five-Year Plan 1946–50	Fifth Five-Year Plan 1951–55
From higher schools	170	370	328	302	652	1,121
From middle schools	291	623	678	540	1,278	1,560

Table III

Mass libraries and moving-picture establishments

	1913	1940	1950	1955
Mass libraries	13,880	95,400	123,100	147,200
Moving-picture establishments	1,510	28,000	42,032	59,285

Table IV

The press

		1913	1927	1940	1950	1955
BOOKS	Titles	27,000	33,400	45,800	43,100	54,700
	Copies in millions	89	226	462	821	1,015
JOURNALS	Titles	1,472	1,645	1,822	1,408	2,026
	Copies in millions	–	229	245	181	361
NEWSPAPERS	Titles	1,055	1,197[1]	8,806	7,831	7,246
	Copies in millions	3.3	9[1]	38	36	49

[1] For 1928.

NOTES

Chapter 1

1. *Pravda*, Jan. 15, 1956. 2. *The New York Times*, June 3, 1956.
3. *The New York Times*, Nov. 2, 1955.
4. *New York Herald Tribune*, Mar. 15, 1956.
5. Nicholas S. Timasheff, *The Great Retreat* (New York, 1946), pp. 393–394.
6. *Pravda*, Feb. 15, 1956.
7. *Sovietskoie Iskusstvo* (Moscow), Nov. 23, 1946.
8. *Pravda*, Oct. 25, 1955. 9. *Ibid.*, Feb. 4, 1955.
10. *New York World-Telegram and Sun*, Oct. 31, 1955.
11. George S. Counts, *The Soviet Challenge to America* (New York, 1931), p. 2.
12. "Remarks on Education in the Soviet Union." Manuscript in the possession of the author.

Chapter 2

1. The Central Committee of the C.P.S.U., *History of the Communist Party of the Soviet Union* (New York, 1939), p. 115.
2. Friedrich Engels, *The Condition of the Working-class in England in 1844* (London, 1892), pp. 109–110.
3. Karl Marx, *Capital* (New York, 1929), pp. 521–522.
4. Karl Marx and Friedrich Engels, *Sochineniia*, "Instruktsii delegatam Vremennogo Central'nogo Sovieta po otdielnym voprosam" (Moscow, 1936), vol. XIII, pt. 1, p. 199.
5. Quoted in Edward S. Mason, *The Paris Commune* (New York, 1930), p. 270.
6. V. I. Lenin, *Selected Works* (New York, 1937), vol. VI, p. 17.
7. *Ibid.*, vol. VII, pp. 294–295.
8. For the history of education under the tsars see William H. E. Johnson, *Russia's Educational Heritage* (Rutgers, N. J., 1950), *passim*. Also Michael T. Florinsky, *Russia* (New York, 1953), two vols., *passim*.
9. *Sotsialisticheskoie Stroitel'stvo-Statisticheskii Ezhegodnik* (Moscow, 1936), p. 577.
10. *Ibid.*, p. 572. 11. *Ibid.*, p. 587.
12. *20 Liet Sovietskoi Vlasti* (Moscow, 1937), pp. 85–86.
13. Florinsky, *op. cit.*, vol. II, p. 797.
14. For a full account of the effort of the autocracy to control the university see Nucia P. Lodge, "Higher Education in Soviet Russia and the New Student," in I. L. Kandel (ed.), *Educational Yearbook of the International Institute of Teachers College* (New York, 1934), pp. 293–337.
15. Florinsky, *op. cit.*, vol. II, p. 728. 16. *Ibid.*, p. 1112.
17. Quoted in Johnson, *op. cit.*, p. 230. 18. *Ibid.*, pp. 236–249.
19. Olga Kaidanova, *Ocherki po Istorii Narodnogo Obrazovaniia v Rossii i SSSR na Osnove Lichnogo Opyta i Nabludenii* (Berlin, 1938), p. 55.
20. *Ibid.*, pp. 27–28. 21. *Ibid.*, p. 26. 22. *Ibid.*, p. 43.
23. *Ibid.*, p. 16. 24. *Ibid.*, p. 57. 25. *Ibid.*
26. *Ibid.*, p. 28. 27. *Ibid.*, p. 47. 28. *Ibid.*, pp. 71–72.
29. See Thomas G. Masaryk, *The Spirit of Russia* (London and New York, 1919), vol. I, pp. 430–471.
30. *Politicheskiie Protsessy 60-kh g.g., Materialy po Istorii Revolutsionnogo Dvizheniia v Rosii* (Moscow, 1923), vol. I, pp. 259–269.
31. See Max Nomad, *Apostles of Revolution* (Boston, 1939), pp. 228–233.
32. Michael Karpovich, "A Forerunner of Lenin: P. N. Tkachev," in *Review of Politics*, no. 6, 1944, pp. 336–350.

33. S. Mitskevich, "Russkiie Yakobintsy," in *Proletarskaia Revolutsia* (Moscow, 1927), nos. 6–7, p. 11.
34. *Politicheskiie Protsessy 60-kh g.g., op. cit.*, pp. 261, 264.
35. P. N. Tkachev, *Izbrannyie Sochineniia* (Moscow, 1933), vol. III, p. 180.
36. *Ibid.*, p. 243.   37. *Ibid.*, p. 225.
38. Mitskevich, *op. cit.*, p. 15.   39. Tkachev, *op. cit.*, pp. 223–224.
40. *Ibid.*, p. 224.
41. "Iz Proshlykh Let," in *Russkoie Bogatstvo* (St. Petersburg, January, 1913), no. 1, p. 62.
42. V. D. Bonch-Bruievich, "Biblioteka i Arkhiv RSDRP v Zheneve," in *Krasnaia Letopis* (Moscow, 1932), no. 3 (48), p. 113.
43. V. D. Bonch-Bruievich, "Lenin o Khudozhestvennoi Literature," in *Tridtsat Let* (Moscow, 1934), no. 1, p. 18.
44. *Ibid.*
45. Nicholas Valentinoff, *Vstrechi s Leninym* (New York, 1953), p. 117.
46. Peter Lavrov, *Russkoi Sotsial'no Revolutsionnoi Molodiozhi po Povodu Broshury: Zadachi Revolutsionnoi Propagandy v Rossii* (London, 1874), pp. 42–46.

Chapter 3

1. *Sotsialisticheskoie Stroitel'stvo* (Moscow, 1936), p. xxx.
2. *Ibid.*, pp. xx–xxvi.
3. V. I. Lenin, *Sobranie Sochinenii* (Moscow, 1922), vol. XV, p. 218.
4. *Ibid.* (Moscow, 1922), vol. XVI, p. 336.
5. *Ibid.*, (Moscow, 1923), vol. XVII, p. 355.
6. *Ibid.*, pp. 321, 323.   7. *Ibid.*, p. 145.
8. V. I. Lenin, *Selected Works* (New York, 1937), vol. VII, p. 357.
9. D. Nodtocheev, "Leninskii Plan Stroitel'stva Kommunizma v SSSR," in *Kommunist* (Moscow), vol. XXXII, no. 13, September, 1955, pp. 17–18.
10. *Ibid.*, p. 17.
11. *Partiinoie Stroitel'stvo* (Moscow), 1946, no. 9–10, p. 338.
12. I. Stalin, *O Nedostatkakh Partiinoi Raboty i Merakh Likvidatsii Trotskistskikh i Inykh Dvurushnikov* (Moscow, 1937), p. 28.
13. S. P. Melgunov, "*Krasnyi Terror*" *v Rossii, 1918–1923* (Berlin, 1924), 2d ed., p. 72.
14. I. V. Stalin, *Voprosy Leninisma*, 2d ed. (Moscow, 1930), pp. 134–135.
15. *Bol'shevik* (Moscow), vol. XXV, no. 17, Sept. 15, 1948, p. 51.
16. *The New York Times*, June 3, 1955.
17. *Kommunist* (Moscow), vol. XXXII, no. 15, October, 1955, p. 72.
18. V. I. Lenin, *Selected Works* (New York, 1943), vol. XI, p. 658.
19. See William Henry Chamberlin, *Soviet Russia* (Boston, 1930), pp. 306–323.
20. *Kul'tura i Zhizn* (Moscow), no. 24, Aug. 31, 1947.
21. V. I. Lenin, *Sochineniia*, 4th ed. (Moscow, 1950), vol. 31, p. 262.
22. I. V. Stalin, *Voprosy Leninisma*, 10th ed. (Moscow, 1934), p. 445.
23. *Direktivy VKP(b) po Voprosam Prosveshcheniia* (Moscow, 1931), p. 11.
24. I. V. Stalin, *Voprosy Leninisma*, 10th ed. (Moscow, 1934), p. 610.
25. *Literaturnaia Gazeta* (Moscow), Sept. 21, 1946.
26. Nodtocheev, *op. cit.*, p. 23.

Chapter 4

1. A. A. Ershov, *Obshchestvenno-Poleznaia Rabota Sovietskoi Shkoly* (Nizhni-Novgorod, 1929), p. 21.
2. *Direktivy VKP(b) i Postanovleniia Sovietskogo Pravitel'stva o Narodnom Obrazovanii 1917–1947* (Moscow-Leningrad, 1947), pp. 7–9.
3. See S. T. Shatsky, *Gody Iskanii*, 2d ed. (Moscow, 1925).

4. Albert P. Pinkevich, *The New Education in the Soviet Republic* (New York, 1929), p. v.
5. *Ibid.*, p. 310.　　　　6. *Ibid.*, p. vi.　　　　7. *Ibid.*, p. 163.
8. A. Katanskaia and E. Livshits (ed.), *Obshchestvenno-Poleznaia Rabota Shkoly* (Moscow, 1928), p. 32.
9. V. I. Lenin, *Chemu i Kak Uchitsa* (Moscow, 1925), pp. 7–8.
10. *Ibid.*, p. 31.
11. The State Scientific Council, *Novyie Programmy Edinoi Trudovoi Shkoly Pervoi Stupeni* (Moscow, 1924), pp. 52–53.
12. *Ibid.*, p. 58.　　　　13. Pinkevich, *op. cit.*, p. 270.
14. Katanskaia and Livshits, *op. cit.*, p. 34.
15. Quoted in G. D. Ilin and E. M. Tsimkhes, *Ob Antileninskoi Teorii "Otmiraniia Shkoly"* (Moscow-Leningrad, 1931), p. 25.
16. *Ibid.*, p. 30.　　　　17. Pinkevich, *op. cit.*, p. 299.
18. See *Pervyi Vserossiiskii S'ezd po Politekhnicheskomu Obrazovaniu* (Moscow-Leningrad, 1931).
19. Pinkevich, *op. cit.*, p. 213.
20. I. A. Kairov (ed.), *Pedagogika* (Moscow, 1948), p. 375.
21. *Osnovnyie Uzakoneniia i Rasporiazheniia po Narodnomu Prosveshchiniu* (Moscow-Leningrad, 1929), p. 22.
22. *Narodnoie Obrazovaniie, Osnovnyie Postanovleniia, Prikazy i Instruktsii* (Moscow, 1948), pp. 42–45.
23. *Ibid.*, p. 44.
24. *Direktivy VKP(b) i Postanovleniia Sovetskogo Provitel'stva o Narodnom Obrazovanii za 1917–1947* (Moscow-Leningrad, 1947), p. 163.
25. *Narodnoie Obrazovaniie, op. cit.*, p. 47.
26. *Direktivy VKP(b) i Postanovleniia, op. cit.*, pp. 288–289.
27. *Narodnoie Obrazovaniie, op. cit.*, pp. 140–141.
28. *Ibid.*, pp. 70–71.
29. *Direktivy VKP(b) i Postanovleniia, op. cit.*, p. 180.
30. *Ibid.*, p. 218.
31. *Narodnoie Obrazovaniie, op. cit.*, pp. 102–107.
32. *Ibid.*, p. 153.　　　　33. *Ibid.*, pp. 47–48.
34. *Sovietskaia Pedagogika* (Moscow), October, 1943, vol. X, p. 2.
35. I. A. Kairov, *Pedagogika* (Moscow, 1948), pp. 292–296 *passim.* Also P. N. Shimbirev and I. I. Ogorodnikov, *Pedagogika* (Moscow, 1954), pp. 276–277.
36. *Sbornik Dokumentov o Shkolie* (Molotov, 1944), pp. 87, 88.
37. Kairov, *op. cit.*, pp. 366–367.　　　　38. *Ibid.*, p. 371.
39. P. N. Shimbirev and I. T. Ogorodnikov, *Pedagogika* (Moscow, 1955), p. 103.
40. Yesipov and Goncharov, *Pedagogika*, p. 129.
41. Kairov, *op. cit.*, p. 113.
42 *Narodnoie Obrazonvaniie, op. cit.*, pp. 59–66.
43. Kairov, *op. cit.*, p. 414.
44. Yesipov and Goncharov, *op. cit.*, p. 400, and Shimbirev and Ogorodnikov, *op. cit.*, p. 414.
45. *Direktivy VKP (b), op. cit.* (Moscow, 1947), pp. 204–205.
46. For a discussion of the modified conception of polytechnical education see Shimbirev and Ogorodnikov, *op. cit.*, pp. 261–265.

Chapter 5

1. P. P. Blonsky, *Trudovaia Shkola* (Moscow, 1919), pt. II, p. 62.
2. V. I. Lenin, *Sochineniia* (Moscow, 1935), 3d ed. vol. XX, p. 305.
3. *Ibid.* (Moscow, 1929), vol. XXIII, p. 199.
4. Albert P. Pinkevich, *The New Education in the Soviet Republic* (New York, 1929), p. 154.

5. *Ibid.*, p. 152.　　　　6. *Ibid.*, p. 153.

7. A. A. Ershov, *Obshchestvenno-Poleznaia Rabota Sovietskoi Shkoly I-oi Stupeni* (Nizhnii-Novgorod, 1929), p. 29.

8. M. N. Pokrovsky (ed.), *Obshchestvovedeniie v Trudovoi Shkolie* (Moscow, 1927), vol. I, p. 11.

9. *Ibid.*, vol. II, p. 6.

10. I. M. Kataev, *Voprosy Prepodavaniia Obshchestvovedeniia* (Moscow, 1926), p. 17.

11. *Ibid.*, p. 10.

12. S. N. Dzubinskii and B. N. Zhavoronkov (eds.), *Bor'ba za Obshchestvovedeniie* (Moscow, 1925), p. 27.

13. B. N. Zhavoronkov, *Rabota Obshchestvoveda* (Leningrad, 1926), p. 20.

14. P. Rudnev, in Pokrovsky, *op. cit.*, vols. II–III, p. 35.

15. T. D. Korneichik, in *Ibid.*, p. 15.

16. *Direktivy VKP(b) i Postanovleniia Sovietskogo Pravitel'stva o Narodnom Obrazovanii* (Moscow-Leningrad, 1947), p. 169.

17. *Ibid.*, p. 182.

18. I. A. Kairov, *Pedagogika* (Moscow, 1943), pp. 239–240.

19. *Ibid.*, p. 240.　　　　20. *Ibid.*, pp. 93–97 *passim.*

21. *Ibid.*, pp. 104–105.　　　　22. *Ibid.*, pp. 100–106 passim.

23. *Ibid.*, p. 96.　　　24. *Ibid.*, pp. 97–99.　　　25. *Ibid.*, p. 99.

26. A. M. Pankratova (ed.), *Istoria SSSR* (Moscow, 1945), vol. III, pp. 326–327.

27. *Ibid.* (Moscow, 1946), vol. III, p. 381.

28. *Ibid.*, 10th ed. (Moscow, 1951), vol. III, p. 388.

29. *Ibid.*, 14th ed. (Moscow, 1955), vol. III, p. 386.

30. *Ibid.*, p. 374.　　　31. *Ibid.*, p. 381.　　　32. *Ibid.*, p. 397.

33. *Ibid.*, p. 400.　　　34. *Ibid.*, p. 356.　　　35. *Ibid.*, p. 357.

36. *Ibid.*, pp. 358, 360.　　　37. *Ibid.*, p. 386.　　　38. *Ibid.*, p. 402.

39. *Ibid.*, p. 394.　　　40. *Ibid.*, pp. 403–404.　　　41. *Ibid.*, pp. 421–422.

42. *Ibid.*, pp. 404–405.　　　43. *Ibid.*, p. 407.　　　44. *Ibid.*, p. 415.

45. *Ibid.*, p. 417.　　　46. *Ibid.* p. 418.

47. See David J. Dallin, *Soviet Espionage* (New Haven, 1955); E. H. Cookridge, *The Net That Covers the World* (New York, 1955); and Nicola Sinevirsky, *Smersh* (New York, 1950).

48. *Ibid.*, p. 425.　　　　49. *Pravda*, Feb. 22, 1956.

50. *Ustav Vsesouznogo Leninskogo Kommunisticheskogo Souza Molodezhi* (Moscow, 1929), pp. 1–8.

51. *Nakaz Pionerskogo Sleta* (Moscow, 1929), in Appendix.

52. E. N. Medynsky, *Narodnoie Obrazovaniie v SSSR* (Moscow, 1947), p. 88.

53. *Ibid.*, p. 90.

54. *Young Communists in the U.S.S.R.*, translated by Virginia Rhine (Washington, 1950), p. 2.

55. *Fifteen Years of Religion and Anti-religion, 1917–1932.* Translated from the Russian (Paris, 1933), *passim*. Life in Soviet Russia Pamphlet Series nos. 2–3.

56. N. C. Popova, *Uchebnik Arifmetiki dlia Nachal'noi Shkoly*, pt. II (Moscow, 1936), p. 23.

Chapter 6

1. V. I. Lenin, *Chemu i Kak Uchitsa* (Moscow, 1925), p. 17.

2. Friedrich Engels, Preface, *Manifesto of the Communist Party* (New York, undated), p. 6.

3. *Direktivy VKP(b) po Voprosam Prosveshcheniia* (Moscow, 1931), p. 7.

4. A. K. Bushlia, *Vospitanie Kommunisticheskoi Morali v Detei* (Moscow, 1948), p. 9.

5. *Ibid.*, p. 9.　　　　6. Lenin, *op. cit.*, pp. 18–19.

7. Monitoring Section, British Broadcasting System, transcript in author's files.

8. V. I. Lenin, *Selected Works* (New York, 1937), vol. VII, p. 297.

9. *Slovar' Russkogo Iazyka* (Moscow, 1949), p. 455.
10. *Sovietskaia Muzyka* (Moscow), no. 1, January-February, 1948, pp. 9–14.
11. *Sovietskaia Pedagogika* (Moscow), no. 10, October, 1955, p. 17.
12. A. Ia. Zis', *O Kommunisticheskoi Morali* (Moscow, 1948), p. 8.
13. John Dewey, *Problems of Men* (New York, 1946), pp. 151, 184.
14. Zis', *op. cit.*, p. 8.   15. Bushlia, *op. cit.*, p. 3.
16. *Literaturnaia Gazeta* (Moscow), Sept. 21, 1946.
17. *Direktivy VKP(b) i Postanovleniia o Narodnom Obrazovanii za 1917–1947* (Moscow, 1947), p. 191.
18. Paul Blonsky, *Pedagogika* (Moscow, 1924), 7th ed., pp. 90–94.
19. Albert P. Pinkevich, *The New Education in the Soviet Republic* (New York, 1929), pp. 346–348.
20. *Bol'shevik* (Moscow), nos. 23–24, December, 1946, p. 18.
21. B. P. Yesipov and N. K. Goncharov, *"I Want to Be Like Stalin,"* a translation of the sections on moral education in their *Pedagogika* (New York, 1947), p. 36.
22. I. A. Kairov (ed.), *Pedagogika* (Moscow, 1948), p. 209.
23. Zis', *op. cit.*, p. 23.
24. P. N. Shimbirev and I. T. Ogorodnikov, *Pedagogika* (Moscow, 1955), pp. 244 ff.
25. Klaus Mehnert, *Stalin versus Marx* (London, 1951), p. 14.
26. A. M. Pankratova (ed.), *Istoriia SSSR* (Moscow, 1945), vol. I, p. 139.
27. A. V. Shestakov (ed.), *Istoriia SSSR, Kratkii Kurs* (Moscow, 1955), p. 51.
28. *Ibid.*, pp. 4–5.
29. Yesipov and Goncharov, *op. cit.*, pp. 36–37.
30. Kairov, *op. cit.*, p. 266.
31. Yesipov and Goncharov, *op. cit.*, pp. 34–35.
32. *Ibid.*, pp. 62, 70.   33. Kairov, *op. cit.*, p. 250.
34. *Uchitel'skaia Gazeta* (Moscow), Jan. 24, 1953.
35. Yesipov and Goncharov, *op. cit.*, pp. 71–80.
36. *Ibid.*, p. 72.
37. *Uchitel'skaia Gazeta* (Moscow), no. 43, Sept. 14, 1946.
38. Kairov, *op. cit.*, p. 209.
39. I. T. Ogorodnikov and P. N. Shimbirev, *Pedagogika* (Moscow, 1950), p. 266.
40. I. Stalin, *O Velikoi Otechestvennoi Voine Sovietskogo Souza* (Moscow, 1946), p. 173.
41. *Voks Bulletin* (Moscow, 1944), nos. 4–5, pp. 25–29.
42. Ogorodnikov and Shimbirev, *op. cit.*, p. 276.
43. Yesipov and Goncharov, *op. cit.*, pp. 60–61.
44. *Moskovskii Komsomolets* (Moscow), Mar. 6, 1949.
45. *Literaturnaia Gazeta* (Moscow), Jan. 1, 1949.
46. Robert F. Kennedy, *The New York Times Magazine,* Apr. 8, 1956.
47. A. K. Bushlia, *op. cit.*, pp. 26–27.
48. Yesipov and Goncharov, *op. cit.*, pp. 81–84.
49. *Ibid.*, pp. 94–95.   50. Kairov, *op cit.*, p. 211.
51. Yesipov and Goncharov, *op. cit.*, p. 124.
52. Kairov, *op. cit.*, p. 326.
53. *Sbornik Dokumentov o Shkole* (Molotov, 1944), pp. 41–42.
54. Kairov, *op. cit.*, p. 237.
55. Yesipov and Goncharov, *op. cit.*, p. 39.
56. *Uchitel'skaia Gazeta* (Moscow), no. 21, 1947.
57. V. I. Lenin, *Selected Works* (Moscow and New York, undated), vol. II, p. 280.

Chapter 7

1. Lyford P. Edwards, *The Natural History of Revolution* (Chicago, 1927), p. 38.
2. See William Henry Chamberlin, "The Tragedy of the Russian Intelligentsia," in *Soviet Russia* (Boston, 1930), pp. 339–351.

3. *Znamia* (Moscow), October, 1946, no. 10, p. 9.
4. V. I. Lenin, *Sochineniia* (Moscow, 1946), vol. VII, p. 240.
5. *Ibid.*, 3d ed. (Moscow, 1931), vol. XXII, pp. 164–165.
6. Quoted in S. Kaftanov, *Sovietskaia Intelligentsia i eio Zadachi v Novoi Piatiletke* (Moscow, 1947), p. 7.
7. *Bor'ba s Naslediem Kapitalisticheskoi Kul'tury: Sbornik Statei i Rechei V. I. Lenina* (Leningrad, 1926), p. 135.
8. *Ibid.*, p. 139.   9. *Ibid.*, pp. 45–46.
10. *Direktivy VKP(b) po Voprosam Prosveshcheniia* (Moscow, 1931), pp. 43–44.
11. *Ibid.*, p. 81.   12. *Ibid.*, p. 87.
13. *Sobraniie Uzakonenii i Rasporiazhenii Rabochego i Krestianskogo Pravitel'stva* (Moscow), Aug. 7, 1918, no. 57, p. 689.
14. Quoted from *Novyi Mir* in Fredrika M. Tandler, *The Workers' Faculty (Rabfac) System in the USSR*, doctoral dissertation in manuscript, p. 44.
15. *Spravochnik dlia Postupaushchikh v Vysshiie Uchebnyie Zavedeniia* (Moscow, 1929), pp. 75, 82–84.
16. *Direktivy VKP(b) po Voprosam Prosveshcheniia* (Moscow, 1931), p. 144.
17. *Ibid.*, p. 162.
18. Fredrika M. Tandler, *The Workers' Faculty (Rabfac) System in the USSR*, a doctoral dissertation in mansuscript (1955), p. 54. This is an excellent study.
19. *Ibid.*, p. 192 ff.   20. *Ibid.*, p. 212 ff.   21. *Ibid.*, p. 269 ff.
22. *Ibid.*, p. 165 ff.
23. S. Kaftanov, *Vyssheie Obrazovaniie v SSSR* (Moscow, 1950), p. 7.
24. Tandler, *op. cit.*, p. 292.
25. *Sotsialisticheskoie Stroitel'stvo SSSR* (Moscow, 1936), p. 576.
26. E. N. Medynsky, *Narodnoie Obrazovaniie SSSR* (Moscow, 1947), p. 168.
27. J. V. Stalin, *Voprosy Leninisma* (Moscow, 1952), p. 628.
28. M. I. Movshovich, *Osnovnyie Postanovleniia, Prikazy i Instruktsii* (Moscow, 1948), p. 547.
29. S. Kaftanov, *Vyssheie Obrazovaniie v SSSR* (Moscow, 1950), p. 112.
30. M. S. Rozofarov, "Trudovyie Rezervy SSSR" in *Sbornik Ofitsial'nykh Materialov* (Moscow, 1950), p. 3.
31. *Pravda*, Feb. 15, 1956.
32. M. Prots'ko, *Sovietskaia Intelligentsiia v Bor'be za Kommunizm* (Moscow, 1950), pp. 14–15.

Chapter 8

1. *Sotsialisticheskoie Stroitel'stvo SSSR* (Moscow, 1936), p. 572.
2. E. N. Medynsky, *Narodnoie Obrazovaniie* (Moscow, 1947), p. 169.
3. *Partiinoie Stroitel'stvo* (Moscow), July, 1945, nos. 13–14, p. 6.
4. Medynsky, *op. cit.* (Moscow, 1947), pp. 144–152.
5. *Ibid.*, pp. 153–158.   6. *Ibid.*, p. 166.
7. George S. Counts, *The Soviet Challenge to America* (New York, 1931), pp. 96 ff.
8. *Sotsialisticheskoie Stroitel'stvo SSSR* (Moscow, 1936), p. 572.
9. A. M. Ivanova, *Chto Sdelala Sovietskaia Vlast' po Likvidatsii Negramotnosti Sredi Vzroslykh* (Moscow, 1949), p. 82.
10. Counts, *op. cit.*, p. 188. 11. *Ibid.*, pp. 189–204.   12. *Ibid.*, pp. 201, 207.
13. I. A. Kairov, *Pedagogika* (Moscow, 1948), p. 44.
14. *Sotsialisticheskoie Stroitel'stvo* (Moscow, 1936), p. 572.
15. For a comprehensive and scholarly account of this development see Nicholas DeWitt, *Soviet Professional Manpower* (Washington, D.C., 1955), pp. 80, 156.
16. *Ibid.*, p. 168.   17. *Ibid.*, p. 84.   18. *Pravda*, Jan. 15, 1956.
19. In the following pages the author will rely heavily on Nicholas DeWitt, *Soviet Professional Manpower* (Washington, D.C., 1955), and Eric Ashby, *Scientist in Russia* (Harmondsworth, Middlesex, England, 1947).

20. DeWitt, *op. cit.*, pp. 106–108.   21. *Ibid.*, p. 27.
22. *Ibid.*, pp. 140–141.   23. *Ibid.*, pp. 192–196.   24. *Ibid.*, pp. 142–144.
25. See decrees listed in M. I. Movshovich, *Vysshaia Shkola* (Moscow, 1948), pp. 496–547.
26. Merle Fainsod, *How Russia Is Ruled* (Cambridge, 1953), pp. 233–235.
27. *Pravda*, Feb. 10, 1946.   28. DeWitt, *op. cit.*, p. 257.
29. Ashby, *op. cit.*, p. 206.   30. DeWitt, *op. cit.*, pp. 153–154.
31. *Ibid.*, p. 126.   32. *Ibid.*, pp. 150–151.   33. *Ibid.*, pp. 170–171.
34. See S. V. Kaftanov, *O Patrioticheskom Dolgie Sovietskoi Intelligentsii* (Moscow, 1947).
35. P. N. Shimbirev and I. T. Ogorodnikov, *Pedagogika* (Moscow, 1955), p. 105.
36. E. N. Medynsky, *Prosveshcheniie v SSSR* (Moscow, 1955), p. 200.
37. *Ibid.*, p. 201.   38. *Ibid.*, p. 194.
39. *Sovietskaia Pedagogika* (Moscow), no. 4, April, 1956, p. 8.
40. DeWitt, *op. cit.*, p. 114.
41. B. P. Yesipov and N. K. Goncharov, *"I Want to Be Like Stalin"* (New York, 1947), p. 12.
42. M. I. Movshovich, *Vysshaia Shkola—Osnovnyie Postanovleniia, Prikazy i Instruktsii* (Moscow, 1948), p. 100.
43. *Pravda*, Aug. 15, 1946.   44. *Ibid.*, Feb. 15, 1956.
45. B. P. Yesipov and N. K. Goncharov, *Pedagogika*, p. 41.
46. For a brief account see E. N. Medynsky, *Prosveshcheniie v SSSR* (Moscow, 1955), pp. 177–189.   47. *Pravda*, Feb. 15, 1956.

Chapter 9

1. A. M. Ivanova, *Chto Sdelala Sovietskaia Vlast' po Likvidatsii Negramotnosti Sredi Vzroslykh* (Moscow, 1949), p. 19.
2. *Ibid.*, p. 13.   3. *Ibid.*, p. 14.   4. *Ibid.*
5. George S. Counts, *The Soviet Challenge to America* (New York, 1931), pp. 152–153.
6. Ivanova, *op. cit.*, p. 20.   7. *Ibid.*, pp. 23–25.   8. *Ibid.*, p. 20.
9. Counts, *op. cit.*, p. 124.   10. Ivanova, *op. cit.*, p. 44.
11. Olaf Caroe, *Soviet Empire* (New York, 1953), p. 157.
12. Ivanova, *op. cit.*, p. 60.   13. Counts, *op. cit.*, p. 134.
14. *Direktivy VKP(b) po Voprosam Prosveshcheniia* (Moscow, 1931), p. 25.
15. Ivanova, *op. cit.*, p. 17.   16. *Ibid.*, p. 28.
17. Counts, *op. cit.*, pp. 181–182.   18. *Direktivy VKP(b)*, *op. cit.*, pp. 9, 27.
19. *Ibid.*, p. 39.   20. *Ibid.*, pp. 69–71.   21. *Pravda*, May 5, 1946.
22. *Sotsialisticheskoie Stroitel'stvo SSSR* (Moscow, 1936), p. 587.
23. *Bol'shaia Sovietskaia Entsiklopediia* (Moscow, 1955), vol. 32, pp. 635–638.
24. George S. Counts, *American Education through the Soviet Looking Glass* (New York, 1951).
25. *Pravda*, Mar. 26, 1949.
26. *Kul'tura i Zhizn* (Moscow), no. 23, Aug. 20, 1947.
27. *20 Liet Sovietskoi Vlasti* (Moscow, 1937), p. 85.
28. *Osnovnyie Uzakoneniia i Rasporiazheniia po Narodnomu Prosveshcheniiu* (Moscow, 1929), pp. 538–552.
29. *Direktivy VKP(b) op. cit.*, pp. 234–235.
30. *20 Liet Sovietskoi Vlasti* (Moscow, 1937), p. 86.
31. *Direktivy, op. cit.*, p. 25.   32. *Ibid.*, p. 81.   33. *Ibid.*, p. 324.
34. For this whole story see Paul Babitsky and John Rinberg, *The Soviet Film Industry* (New York, 1955), pp. 1–51.
35. See Max Eastman, *Artists in Uniform* (New York, 1934); Juri Jelagin, *Taming of the Arts* (New York, 1951); and Gleb Struve, *25 Years of Soviet Russian Literature* (London, 1944).

36. *Bol'shevik* (Moscow), no. 9, May 15, 1948, pp. 45, 47.
37. A relatively full account of this whole episode is given in George S. Counts and Nucia Lodge, *The Country of the Blind—The Soviet System of Mind Control* (Boston, 1949).
38. *Literaturnaia Gazeta* (Moscow), no. 39, Sept. 21, 1946.
39. Counts and Lodge, *op. cit.*, p. 143.   40. *Ibid.*, pp. 84, 85.
41. *Literaturnaia Gazeta* (Moscow), no. 37, Sept. 7, 1946.
42. *Sovietskaia Muzyka* (Moscow), no. 1, 1948, pp. 65–79.
43. *Literaturnaia Gazeta* (Moscow), no. 37, Sept. 7, 1946.
44. *Pravda*, Aug. 27, 1948.   45. *Ibid.*, Nov. 9, 1948.
46. Ludmilla B. Turkevich, "Soviet Propaganda and the Rebellious Artist," *The Russian Review*, January, 1956, p. 56.
47. *Pravda*, Feb. 15, 1956.
48. *Bol'shevik* (Moscow), no. 11, June 15, 1947, pp. 4–5.
49. Counts, *op. cit.*, pp. 51–52.
50. Manya Gordon, *Workers before and after Lenin* (New York, 1941), p. 115.
51. *Direktivy VKP(b)*, *op. cit.*, p. 30.
52. *Ibid.*, pp. 32–33.   53. *Ibid.*, p. 37.   54. *Pravda*, Oct. 25, 1955.
55. *Professionalnyie Soiuzy* (Moscow), nos. 9–10, September-October, 1946, p. 4.
56. Alex Inkeles, *Public Opinion in Soviet Russia* (Harvard, 1950).

Chapter 10

1. V. I. Lenin, *Kak Organizovat' Sorevnovaniie?* (Moscow, 1929), p. 15.
2. *Bol'shaia Sovietskaia Entsiklopediia*, 1st ed. (Moscow, 1937), vol. 31, pp. 784–794.
3. David Shub, *Lenin* (Garden City, 1948), pp. 33, 36.
4. David J. Dallin and Boris J. Nicolaevsky, *Forced Labor in Soviet Russia* (New Haven, 1947), p. 159.
5. *Bol'shaia Sovietskaia Entsiklopediia*, 1st ed. (Moscow, 1940), vol. 47, p. 39.
6. *Ibid.*, 2d ed. (Moscow, 1953), vol. 20, pp. 383–385.
7. *Ibid.* (Moscow, 1953), vol. 22, p. 499.
8. Dallin and Nicolaevsky, *op. cit.*, pp. 151–152.
9. A. Ya. Vyshinsky (ed.), *Ot Turem k Vospitatel'nym Uchrezhdeniiam* (Moscow, 1934).
10. Dallin and Nicolaevsky, *op. cit.*, p. 160.
11. Vyshinsky, *op. cit.*, p. 10.   12. *Ibid.*, p. 68.   13. *Ibid.*, p. 213.
14. *Bol'shaia Sovietskaia Entsiklopediia*, 2d ed. (Moscow, 1955), vol. 18, p. 603.
15. *Ibid.*, p. 602.   16. Lenin, *op. cit.*, p. 15.
17. *Sobranie Uzakonenii i Rasporiazhenii Rabochego i Krestianskogo Pravitel'stva* Apr. 24, 1919, no. 12, art. 124, pp. 148–149.
18. *Ibid.*, June 3, 1919, no. 20, pp. 257–261.
19. Vyshinksy, *op. cit.*, pp. 65–66.
20. George S. Counts, *The Soviet Challenge to America* (New York, 1931), p. 278.
21. *Ibid.*, pp. 276–277.
22. Dallin and Nicolaevsky, *op. cit.*, p. 207.
23. See William Henry Chamberlin, *Russia's Iron Age* (Boston, 1934), pp. 82–89.
24. Quoted in Dallin and Nicolaevsky, *op. cit.*, p. 258.
25. Quoted in *The Dark Side of the Moon* (New York, 1947), p. 51. Written by a Polish "woman of scrupulous integrity" and with a preface by T. S. Eliot.
26. Dallin and Nicolaevsky, *op. cit.*, p. 86.
27. *Ibid.*, p. 71.   28. *Ibid.*, pp. 108–109.
29. Albert Konrad Herling, *The Soviet Slave Empire* (New York, 1951), pp. 13–14.
30. *The Dark Side of the Moon*, pp. 11–12.
31. Vladimir Petrov, *Soviet Gold* (New York, 1949).
32. Herling, *op. cit.*, pp. 218–224.
33. Transcribed and translated from a phonographic record in the file of the author.

34. Zbigniew K. Brzezinski, *The Permanent Purge* (Cambridge, 1956), p. 175.
35. Boris Souvarine, *Stalin* (New York, 1939), p. 406.
36. *Report of Court Proceedings in the Case of the Anti-Soviet "Bloc of Rights and Trotskyites"* (Moscow, 1938), p. 779.
37. F. Beck and W. Godin, *Russian Purge and the Extraction of Confession* (New York, 1951).
38. *The New York Times,* June 5, 1956.
39. Joseph Scholmer, *Vorkuta* (New York, 1955), pp. 21–22.
40. Stepan Shchipachev, *Pavlik Morozov* (Moscow, 1951).
41. *Osnovnyie Uzakoneniia i Rasporiazheniia po Norodnomu Prosveshcheniiu* (Moscow, 1929), p. 267.
42. Nicholas Voinov, *The Waif* (New York, 1955).

Chapter 11

1. A. V. Yefimov, *Novaia Istoriia* (Moscow, 1950), pp. 254–255.
2. *Pravda*, Feb. 15, 1956.
3. G. M. Stekloff, *History of the First International* (London and New York, 1928), pp. 240–241.
4. Friedrich Engels, "Vvedeniie" to Karl Marx, in *Klassovaia Bor'ba vo Frantsii* (Odessa, 1905), pp. 7, 12, 13, 17, 18, 19.
5. V. I. Lenin, *Selected Works* (New York, 1935), vol. III, p. 313.
6. *Petrograd Pravda,* July 21, 1920.
7. Dmitri Daniel Fedotoff White, *The Growth of the Red Army* (Princeton, 1944), p. 17.
8. L. Trotsky, *Kak Vooruzhalas' Revolutsia* (Moscow, 1925), vol. III, bk. 2, p. 212.
9. *Ibid.,* p. 5.   10. *Ibid.*   11. *Ibid.,* p. 46.
12. White, *op. cit.,* p. 105.   13. *Ibid.,* p. 331.   14. *Ibid.,* p. 234.
15. *Pravda,* Oct. 10, 1952.
16. Zbigniew Brzezinski (ed), *Political Controls in the Soviet Army* (New York, 1954), p. 14.
17. *Direktivy VKP(b) po Voprosam Prosveshcheniia* (Moscow, 1931), p. 26.
18. *Ibid.,* p. 37.   19. Brzezinski (ed), *op. cit.,* p. 8.
20. *Ibid.,* p. 32.   21. *Ibid.,* p. 38.   22. *Ibid.*
23. *Pravda,* Oct. 15, 1952.   24. Brzezinski (ed.), *op. cit.,* pp. 54–57.
25. *Ibid.,* p. 60.   26. *Ibid.,* pp. 61–62.
27. Anonymous, *Politischeskaia Rabota (Politrabota) V Krasnoi Armii.* An unpublished manuscript prepared under the auspices of Research Program on the U.S.S.R. (East European Fund, Inc.), Doc. no. 8, p. 63.
28. See George Fischer, *Soviet Opposition to Stalin* (Cambridge, 1952).
29. White, *op. cit.,* p. 43.   30. *Ibid.,* pp. 56–57.
31. *Bol'shaia Sovietskaia Entsiklopediia* (Moscow, 1951), vol. 8, pp. 469–470.
32. *Upravleniie Morskikh Sil RKKA* (Moscow, 1937), p. 452 ff.
33. *Izvestia,* Aug. 22, 1943.
34. *Bol'shaia Sovietskaia Entsiklopediia,* vol. 29, 1954, pp. 271–272.
35. W. W. Kulski, *The Soviet Regime* (Syracuse, 1954), p. 482.
36. *Krasnaia Zvezda* (Moscow), Dec. 2, 1943, no. 284, p. 3.
37. B. Izmuskii, *Nachalo Puti—Zapiski Ofitsera-Vospitatelia* (Moscow, 1950), p. 55.
38. S. F. Platnov, *History of Russia* (New York, 1925), p. 277.
39. M. N. Pokrovskii, *Russkaia Istoriia* (Moscow, 1933), p. 110.
40. *Sovietskaia Pedagogika* (Moscow), August-September, 1943, nos. 8–9, p. 38.
41. Vyacheslav P. Artemyev and Grigori S. Burlutski, *The "Institute" of the Soviet Ministry of Internal Affairs.* Manuscript to be published, prepared under the auspices of Research Program on the U.S.S.R. (East European Fund, Inc.).
42. *Sovietskaia Pedagogika* (Moscow), May-June, 1943, nos. 5–6, pp. 30–31, 33–37.
43. *Ibid.,* February-March, 1943, nos. 2–3, pp. 10–20.

Chapter 12

1. *Pravda*, Feb. 15, 1956.
2. Em. Iaroslavskii, *Chego Partiia Trebuet ot Kommunista* (Moscow, 1935), p. 40.
3. Benjamin Jowett, Translator, *The Republic of Plato*, 3d ed. (London, 1927), vol. I, p. 415.
4. Iaroslavskii, *op. cit.*, p. 8.   5. Jowett, *op. cit.*, p. 389.
6. *V Pomoshch' Partrabotniku* (Moscow, 1927), p. 328.
7. *Ibid.*, p. 357.   8. *Ibid.*, pp. 400 ff.
9. *Rezoliutsii XVIII S'ezda VKP(b)* (Moscow, 1939), pp. 59–60.
10. For a full discussion of this question see Merle Fainsod, *How Russia Is Ruled* (Cambridge, 1953), pp. 209 ff. See also Institute for the Study of the U.S.S.R. *Bulletin* (Munich), vol. III, May, 1956, no. 5, pp. 30–33.
11. *V Pomoshch' Partrabotniku, op. cit.*, p. 388.
12. *Ibid.*, pp. 446, 447.
13. *Rezoliutsii XVIII S'ezda VKP(b), op. cit.*, p. 73.
14. *Pravda*, Feb. 15, 1956.
15. *Direktivy VKP(b) Po Voprosam Prosveshcheniia* (Moscow, 1931), p. 24.
16. *Ibid.*, p. 41.
17. *Sovpartshkoly i Komvuzy* (Moscow, 1926), p. 6.
18. *Ibid.*, p. 5.   19. *Ibid.*, p. 14.
20. Samuel Northrup Harper, *Civic Training in Soviet Russia* (Chicago, 1929), p. 280.
21. This list was taken almost verbatim from *ibid.*, p. 277.
22. *Osnovnyie Uzakoneniia i Rasporiazheniia po Narodnomu Prosveshcheniiu* (Moscow, 1929), p. 569.
23. *Sotsialisticheskoie Stroitel'stvo SSSR* (Moscow, 1936), p. 572.
24. S. Ingulov, *Politgramota* (Moscow, 1933), p. 3.
25. *Sotsialisticheskoie Stroitel'stvo* (Moscow, 1936), p. 572.
26. For a general account see *Bol'shaia Sovietskaia Entsiklopediia* (Moscow, 1938), vol. 33, pp. 575–577.
27. *Ibid.* (Moscow, 1953), vol. 18, p. 224.
28. G. Malenkov, *Informatsionnyi Doklad o Deiatel'nosti Vsesoiuznoi Kommunisticheskoi Partii* (Moscow, 1947), pp. 26–27.
29. *Ibid.*, pp. 24–25.
30. *KPSS v Resoliutsiakh i Resheniiakh S'ezdov, Konferentsii i Plenumov ZK*, 7th ed. (Moscow, 1954), vol. III, pp. 480–482.
31. *Ibid.*, pp. 476–479.   32. *Ibid.*, pp. 482–484.   33. *Pravda*, Jan. 31, 1952.
34. *Ibid.*, Feb. 15, 1956.
35. *Investigation of Communist Activities in the New York Area—Part 6* (Government Printing Office, Washington, D.C., July 7, 1953), pp. 2036–2042.

Chapter 13

1. George S. Counts and Nucia Lodge, *The Country of the Blind* (Boston, 1949), p. 76.
2. *The New York Times*, Sept. 18, 1955, and *Pravda*, Nov. 26, 1955.
3. *The New York Times*, May 1, 1956.
4. *Collected Papers of Charles Sanders Peirce*, edited by Charles Hartshorne and Paul Weiss (Cambridge, 1934), vol. V, pp. 235–236.
5. George Fischer, *Soviet Opposition to Stalin* (Harvard, 1952), pp. 151–154.

INDEX

ABOUT THE AUTHOR

George S. Counts has had a long and distinguished career in American education. Born in Baldwin City, Kansas, in 1889, he attended a one-room country schoolhouse and local public schools before entering Baker University in 1907. Convinced of the need for vitalizing educational subject matter, Dr. Counts enrolled in the graduate school of the University of Chicago, and after receiving his doctorate began teaching at Delaware College, Newark, Delaware. Successive posts at Yale and the University of Chicago led him, in 1927, to Teachers College, Columbia University, where he remained as professor of education until his retirement in 1955.

Dr. Counts' lifelong interest in Russia was brought to a focus when, as associate director of the International Institute of Teachers College, he made three extended tours of the Soviet Union, including a nine-month, six-thousand mile automobile journey from Leningrad to the Caucasus and from Odessa to Kiev and Nizhni Novgorod. Here he was able to see the Soviet school system in action and note the incipient totalitarianism which was to concern him increasingly in such works as *The Country of the Blind,* "*I Want to Be Like Stalin,*" and *American Education through the Soviet Looking Glass.*

A member of the United States Educational Mission to Japan in 1946, Dr. Counts is widely known for his leadership of the American Federation of Teachers, the American Civil Liberties Union, and other groups. He has received the John Dewey Award of the New York Teachers Guild, the Medal for Distinguished Service at Teachers College, and the B'nai B'rith Annual Educators Award, given to the educator in New York who has contributed most to democratic human relations among students, teachers, and the community. He presently lives in New York and spends his leisure time on a farm near New Hope, Pennsylvania.